Past and Present Publications

Social Relations and Ideas

Past and Present Publications

General Editor: T. H. ASTON, *Corpus Christi College, Oxford*

Past and Present Publications comprise books similar in character to the articles in the journal *Past and Present*. Whether the volumes in the series are collections of essays – some previously published, others new studies – or monographs, they encompass a wide variety of scholarly and original works primarily concerned with social, economic and cultural changes, and their causes and consequences. They will appeal to both specialists and non-specialists and will endeavour to communicate the results of historical and allied research in readable and lively form. This new series continues and expands in its aims the volumes previously published elsewhere.

Volumes published by the Cambridge University Press are:
Family and Inheritance: Rural Society in Western Europe 1200–1800, edited by Jack Goody, Joan Thirsk and E. P. Thompson*
French Society and the Revolution, edited by Douglas Johnson
Peasants, Knights and Heretics: Studies in Medieval English Social History, edited by R. H. Hilton*
Towns in Societies: Essays in Economic History and Historical Sociology, edited by Philip Abrams and E. A. Wrigley*
Desolation of a City: Coventry and the Urban Crisis of the Late Middle Ages, Charles Phythian-Adams
Puritanism and Theatre: Thomas Middleton and Opposition Drama under the Early Stuarts, Margot Heinemann*
Lords and Peasants in a Changing Society: The Estates of the Bishopric of Worcester, 680–1540, Christopher Dyer
Life, Marriage and Death in a Medieval Parish: Economy, Society and Demography in Halesowen 1270–1400, Zvi Razi
Biology, Medicine and Society 1840–1940, edited by Charles Webster
The Invention of Tradition, edited by Eric Hobsbawm and Terence Ranger
*Also issued as a paperback

Volumes previously published with Routledge and Kegan Paul are:
Crisis in Europe 1560–1660, edited by Trevor Aston
Studies in Ancient Society, edited by M. I. Finley
The Intellectual Revolution of the Seventeenth Century, edited by Charles Webster

R. H. Hilton

Photo: Philip Rahtz

Social Relations and Ideas

Essays in Honour of R. H. Hilton

Edited by

T. H. ASTON   P. R. COSS

CHRISTOPHER DYER   JOAN THIRSK

CAMBRIDGE UNIVERSITY PRESS

Cambridge
London   New York   New Rochelle
Melbourne   Sydney

Published by the Press Syndicate of the University of Cambridge
The Pitt Building, Trumpington Street, Cambridge CB2 1RP
32 East 57th Street, New York, NY 10022, USA
296 Beaconsfield Parade, Middle Park, Melbourne 3206, Australia

First published 1983

Printed in Great Britain at the Pitman Press, Bath

Library of Congress catalogue card number: 82-9727

British Library Cataloguing in Publication Data
Social relations and ideas – (Past and Present publications)
1. Hilton, R. H.   2. Europe – Social conditions – Addresses,
essays, lectures   3. Europe – History – 476–1492 – Addresses,
essays, lectures   4. Europe – History – 1492–1648 – Addresses,
essays, lectures
I. Aston, T. H.   II. Series
940   HN373
ISBN 0 521 25132 X

Contents

Preface

This volume in honour of Rodney Hilton is published to mark the occasion of his retirement in the autumn of 1982 from his Chair of Medieval Social History at the University of Birmingham which he held with such distinction from his appointment in 1963. It has a dual origin. In the first place, some of his many pupils, friends and colleagues wished to show their appreciation of his work, his influence and his inspiration. In the second place, the Past and Present Society, while also paying tribute to an outstanding medievalist, wanted more particularly to register its gratitude for his services to *Past and Present* and its associated activities over the years: he was one of the founders of the Journal in 1952, and has been a member of its Editorial Board ever since, being Chairman from 1972. Dr P. R. Coss and Dr Christopher Dyer represent, so to say, the first area of origin among the Editors, while Mr T. H. Aston and Dr Joan Thirsk represent the second.

It can never be easy to make a *Festschrift* a unified whole. Especially is this so with a scholar such as Rodney Hilton with his wide-ranging interests: these include the social structure, the rural economy and the *mentalité* of the middle ages; and on the side of source material not just the customary vocabulary of social history, but for example medieval literature with which he has been much concerned, and medieval archaeology in which he has played an active and pioneering role. Rodney Hilton has combined these various concerns with apparent and enviable ease and made of them a coherent and penetrating historical approach pursued with the greatest success, thereby exercising a very important influence on the way we look at medieval history as a whole. Thus we hope that in this volume, with its intentional diversity and range, we have caught at least something of the spirit which has inspired the scholar in whose honour it has been produced.

T. H. ASTON, P. R. COSS,
CHRISTOPHER DYER and
JOAN THIRSK

July 1982

Acknowledgements

We are most grateful to Mrs Angela Coss for kindly compiling the index to this volume; to Lady Cynthia Postan and Dr John Hatcher for assistance in the article by the late Professor Sir Michael Postan; to Professor Philip Rahtz for providing the frontispiece; and to Mr Charles Philpin, Assistant Editor of *Past and Present*, and Dr Michael Aris, Sub-Editor of *Past and Present*, for their help throughout the preparation of the volume. We are also grateful to the President and Fellows of Corpus Christi College, Oxford, for permission to reproduce the picture on the jacket. We are additionally grateful to our printers, the Pitman Press, and to the staff of the Cambridge University Press for all their assistance and in particular for their meticulous attention to detail. We are finally grateful to all the contributors for agreeing to participate in this expression of regard for an outstanding scholar.

Introduction

EDWARD MILLER

From one point of view no introduction to a collection of essays for presentation to Rodney Hilton is called for: the very fact of their presentation is itself indicative of his standing and reputation among the economic and social historians of his generation, not only in this country but throughout Europe and beyond. The essays, however, will be read in the future as well as in the present, a prospect which makes appropriate a few preliminary words about Hilton and his work. The outline story of his career can be quickly told. Born in 1916, he was educated at Manchester Grammar School and from there went on to Balliol College and later Merton College, Oxford. It was at Oxford that, under the guidance of R. V. Lennard, he was launched into research on the social and economic history of the medieval English countryside. His book on the Leicester and Owston abbey estates during the later middle ages, indeed, was all but completed when in 1940 he was absorbed, like so many of his contemporaries, into the armed services. As an earnest of future intentions, however, he also left behind him a short article on a thirteenth-century poem about disputed villein services. In due course it appeared in the pages of the *English Historical Review*, the first of his many works illuminating the condition of the medieval English peasantry. In the meantime he was continuing his education in very different circumstances to those of pre-war Oxford. As a by-product of service in the Middle East, he was able to observe peasant societies at close range and developed the sympathetic knowledge of 'third world' problems that has persisted as a background to so much of his work.

Hilton returned to civilian life in 1946, taking up an appointment at the University of Birmingham. There he has remained, first as Lecturer, then as Reader and since 1963 as Professor of Medieval Social History. His contribution to the University he has served for thirty-five years could only adequately be evaluated by a colleague; but even an outsider may recognize the fact that the Birmingham School of History has become one of the most active centres of research into medieval social history in this country and appreciate, too, the distinction of many of Hilton's pupils in that School. The outside viewer, however, is no less likely to be impressed by Hilton's own record of publications. He has been and continues to be a prolific author, whose writings possess a certain intrinsic unity. His interests have kept their original focus upon the late medieval English countryside. This countryside is viewed in breadth and in depth, and its denizens include the inhabitants of market towns as well as of villages, rural craftsmen as well as agriculturalists, clerics as well as laymen, landlords as well as tenants. On the other hand Hilton's instincts and sympathies lead him to view this 'fair field' from the angle of the peasant majority. It was logical, therefore, that when he was invited to be Ford's Lecturer at Oxford in 1973 he should have chosen to discourse upon the English peasantry in the later middle ages.

It is appropriate to dwell for a moment on these Ford lectures. They illustrate better than anything else Hilton's approaches to the social history of the middle ages; they sum up a number of the conclusions to which he has been led; and they also face certain of the theoretical questions which a study of the medieval peasantry is likely to raise. Evidently, here and elsewhere, Marxism provides no small part of his own theoretical framework. It is a Marxism the 'classical' doctrines of which have been modified and developed particularly by the work of those sociologists and social anthropologists who have expanded our knowledge of the social structures and transformations in the recent or contemporary 'third world'. This framework of discussion Hilton developed even more fully in his earlier book, *Bond Men Made Free*, where it is seen in its application to a wider European context, and this again is entirely characteristic. Even when his concern is with England, he constantly draws our attention to the larger European background and to comparisons with what was happening in the other western lands. Probably, indeed, he would acknowledge some initial inspiration from Marc Bloch; and since then he has been one of an international group of scholars (they have included E. A. Kosminsky, M. M. Postan, Georges Duby and Emmanuel Le Roy Ladurie) who have formulated the questions we now ask about medieval society. The outcome may not have been total agreement or even consensus, but there are whole areas in which a deeper understanding has been attained. This is no single scholar's achievement, but Hilton has made a distinctive and substantial contribution to it. That, in turn, makes no more than natural the close personal association he has enjoyed with so many leading social historians in so many countries.

The quality of Hilton's contribution to the study of medieval society, however, is also rooted in another of his characteristics: his unwillingness to divorce abstract ideas from the real world of people and places. His points of departure are always the medieval sources, scrutinized with patience and in scrupulous detail. A characteristic example is to be found in the pages of *Bond Men Made Free* dealing with the revolt at St Albans in 1381. Sources that would illumine the social structure of St Albans itself fail him, but he has found in the Public Record Office fourteenth-century tax returns for neighbouring Watford and Barnet which provide pointers to the kind of small-town society which, at St Albans, had to face the great abbey which dominated the town. These returns give a point and precision to his discussion of the revolt at St Albans which would otherwise have been lacking.

This rooting of description and analysis in the sources is characteristic of virtually everything that Hilton has written, and by no means least of his Ford lectures. The evidence out of which these lectures were constructed, he tells us, 'is mainly drawn from the documentation of thirty or forty villages in the counties of Stafford, Worcester, Warwick and Gloucester', that west midland area the sources of which he knows with a unique intimacy. Some of them (the Stoneleigh leger book and minister's accounts from the Clarence estates in Warwickshire) he has himself edited; and he has also encouraged a liberal attitude as to what sources are. He has done much to further medieval archaeological investigation, as well as making effective use of its results. Even in an area as fortunately endowed as the west midlands, written records need supplementation, so that visiting historical monuments is one of the ways in which he adds to them. He also goes beyond those documents which are apt to be the normal fare of the historian. Nearly twenty years ago the poem, *A Good Short Debate between Winner and Waster*, was put under contribution in his paper on capital formation in feudal society; and what could be learned from literature was likewise demonstrated, with all due caution, in the Ford lectures. In his discussion of the social structure of villages recourse is had to fourteenth-century sermons, Gower's *Vox clamantis*, Langland and other writers in his tradition, the Towneley plays and *Mum and the Sothsegger*. Hilton's sense of literature as historical evidence makes his contribution to the perennial debate about the Robin Hood ballads no more than a natural extension of his interests.

His intimate familiarity with the west midland sources in particular has borne two sorts of fruit. One was the book *A Medieval Society* published in 1966: an attempt to take a total view of 'the society of peasants, townsmen, knights, barons and clergy' inhabiting the region in the years around 1300. There is no other regional study for this period that in any way compares with *A Medieval Society*. It remains a model still awaiting imitators. The other fruit of Hilton's mastery of the west midland sources is the readiness of the denizens of his 'fair field' to take on a human face and human attributes. We know much more about the peasant cultivator after encountering John Mashon of Ombersley and learning of the crops he had sown in the fields, his livestock, his poultry, his implements, his firewood, the bacon in his larder. It is almost a disappointment to learn that he owes his immortality to the fact that he was a horse-thief on the run. There is also enlightenment about the costs of war in what Hilton tells us about Painswick in 1442. In that year the widows of the manor cried out against its lord, the earl of Shrewsbury, who had taken sixteen of his tenants with him to the French war and brought only five of them home again. The widows of those who did not return lost not only their husbands but their holdings, although happily their outcry ended in the righting of this last injustice.

In 1940, when Hilton was completing the draft of his study of the Leicester and Owston estates, the fourteenth and fifteenth centuries were something of a neglected age in English rural history, if only because this was the time when the rich vein of earlier seigneurial records was becoming attenuated. This neglect has ceased, and for that much of the credit and responsibility must go to Hilton. He has established outlines of social development that are both credible and of profound significance for the evolution of a later society in England; he has done so without losing sight of the fact that the actors in these historical dramas were individual human beings; and he has stimulated others to pursue parallel or converging lines of enquiry. These are good reasons for offering him this present tribute.

To those of us who have been privileged to enjoy Rodney Hilton's friendship or acquaintanceship the compilation of this volume is also a happy inspiration, a timely remembrance of the man as well as the scholar at the point when he relinquishes many of his more onerous responsibilities. Remembrance of the man will be, no doubt, a reflection of all sorts of personal equations; but few will deny him a splendid capacity for gusto, a mastery of the throw-away line, a down-to-earth common sense, a willingness not to see everything in too serious a light. These are perhaps some of the qualities that have made him so successful as a teacher as well as so acceptable as a friend. It may also not be too fanciful to think that he has dwelt so long with peasants that he has taken on a somewhat rustic appearance, so that a village hostelry appears a perfectly natural setting for him. Not least characteristic of him, however, is his instinctive sympathy with the young, and this as well as his qualities as a scholar has contributed to the influence which this volume demonstrates.

1. The Origins of the Manor in England*

T. H. ASTON

Comparatively little has been written recently on the origins of the manor. The exposition given by Maitland and Vinogradoff and closely followed by Sir Frank Stenton has been modified for certain areas; it has seldom been questioned as a whole.[1] The basis of early society, according to this view, was the free ceorl, owning absolutely one hide of land or its equivalent, and owing only royal dues, such folk-worthy and law-worthy men being associated together in free, lordless and nucleated villages. The gap between these men and medieval villeins, between these free villages and the manor, was bridged in a variety of ways. Grants of royal rights to ecclesiastics and laymen exposed the ceorls to the pressure of great lords who took advantage of economic insecurity, wars, famines, plagues, commendation and similar factors to depress them so that, in the end, in place of their free ownership of a hide, they came to hold normally between a quarter and a whole virgate or less, on most onerous and servile terms. Some place was, indeed, allowed to the creation of tenancies by lords themselves, but this was largely incidental. 'The central course of Old English social development', wrote Sir Frank Stenton, 'may be described as the process by which a peasantry, at first composed essentially of free men, acknowledging no lord below the king, gradually lost economic and personal independence'.[2]

Ultimately the evidence presented for this thesis must be subjected to detailed analysis, but certain of its limitations are

---

* I wish to thank Dr A. L. Poole, Professor D. Whitelock and Mr H. P. R. Finberg for their help. This article is here reprinted from *Trans. Roy. Hist. Soc.*, 5th ser., viii (1958) with the kind permission of the Society.

1 F. W. Maitland, *Domesday Book and Beyond* (Cambridge, 1897); P. Vinogradoff, *The Growth of the Manor*, 2nd edn (London, 1911); F. M. Stenton, *Anglo-Saxon England*, 2nd edn (Oxford, 1947).

2 *Op. cit.*, p. 463. Cf. Vinogradoff, *op. cit.*, p. 235.

obvious: much of it is of late date, and it draws heavily on the legal rather than the economic aspects of peasant history. No one would wish to deny that independent landowning peasants existed at all times, some with a hide of land or more. Yet they are very elusive figures. If the laws do indeed prove their existence, they certainly afford no evidence that such men were characteristic of early society.[3] Centuries later, in Domesday Book and afterwards, the free peasants were to make an impressive tale in some areas, but it is not easy to relate them to the origins of English society; while the 'free' elements in ancient demesne, which so impressed Vinogradoff, are hardly older than the thirteenth century, and insignificant beside the servile aspects of all villein tenure. Again, it is plain enough that some independent peasants were depressed; so too were some thegns. But even were we to grant for a moment that independent landowning freemen were originally ubiquitous, the reasons given for their general economic depression would hardly appear convincing. If the ordinary villager had a hide of land, can he really have been, as Maitland said, 'seldom far removed from insolvency',[4] when later, without substantial improvement in agricultural technique, the great majority of peasants lived on at most a quarter of that? Ceorls with a hide of land are surely nearer to yeomen, even gentlemen, than to crofters; and it is hard to believe that economic fluctuations (severe though they were throughout the middle ages), gelds, devastations, sentences in the courts, partible inheritance or similar causes could have brought about their general economic depression. Indeed, when the detailed history of the ceorl class is written, we shall find many rising, in an under-developed countryside, to noble rank; there would otherwise have been less point to the nostalgia of the eleventh-century writer on status.[5]

---

[3] By contrast, for ceorls with lords, see Northumbrian Priests' Law, comparing caps. 50, 53, 56, 59, 60, F. Liebermann, *Die Gesetze der Angelsachsen*, 3 vols. (Halle, 1903–16) [hereafter cited as Liebermann, *Die Gesetze*], i, pp. 383 f.; cf. *Anglo-Saxon Charters*, ed. A. J. Robertson, 2nd edn (Cambridge, 1956) [hereafter cited as RC.], no. cx. For freemen, see Laws of Ine, cap. 3.2; cf. cap. 70.

[4] *Op. cit.*, p. 326. Cf. Stenton, *op. cit.*, pp. 463 f.

[5] Liebermann, *Die Gesetze*, i, pp. 456 f., 460 f. Cf. *Codex diplomaticus aevi Saxonici*, ed. J. M. Kemble, 6 vols. (London, 1839–48) [hereafter cited as KCD.], no. mcclxxxii; *Select English Historical Documents*, ed. F. E. Harmer (Cambridge, 1914), no. ii.

More important are the chronological difficulties. The precise, even the broad, chronology of the growth of the manor was never systematically worked out, but it was generally agreed that most manorial development came shortly before and shortly after the Conquest. 'The advent of the manorial epoch', according to Vinogradoff, 'is roughly marked by the Norman Conquest' and the history of the generations following the Domesday Survey 'is full of details as to the systematic simplification and elaboration [sic] of the hurried manorial scheme into a comprehensive and national order'.[6] It is clear that this emphasis on the importance of 1066 and the post-Conquest period is no longer satisfactory. Almost all the detailed work on Domesday Book and the early estate surveys has emphasized that the Conquest did not interrupt the general continuity of agrarian and manorial life and that, for all the many changes in individual fortunes, there was no social revolution among the peasantry.[7] Nor can the development of the manor as an economic unit be pushed into the twelfth century for there was then a substantial decline in two of its most important constituents, demesne and labour services;[8] a decline which, indeed, continued later on a great many estates. Thus the legal definition of the manor and its tenurial relationships in the later twelfth and thirteenth centuries came after the manor as a functioning economic unit, a farm, had suffered notable reduction. It could, of course, still be true that the manor grew in the ways envisaged in the traditional view of its history, even if the Normans are seen to have given it little more than its name. But, when forced mainly into the Anglo-Saxon period, the whole picture of its growth becomes less plausible. Is there time between the alleged flourishing of a free peasant society (exemplified in seventh- and ninth-century laws) and the mid-eleventh century, for the gradual rise of landlordship, in which the Danish invasions played a large part, and the emergence of a manorialism, with

---

[6] *Op. cit.*, pp. 291, 302.

[7] E.g. Stenton, *op. cit.*, p. 473; *Feudal Documents from the Abbey of Bury St. Edmunds*, ed. D. C. Douglas (Oxford, 1932), p. cxxxiii. And compare the *Rectitudines singularum personarum* (Liebermann, *Die Gesetze*, i, pp. 444–53) with twelfth-century estate surveys.

[8] M. M. Postan, 'The Chronology of Labour Services', *Trans. Roy. Hist. Soc.*, 4th ser., xx (1937), pp. 169–93.

large demesnes and heavy labour services, already on the point of decline, indeed already declining?[9] It is possible; but is it likely?

*   *   *

Few historians have ever doubted that, in its upper ranks, Anglo-Saxon society was, from the beginning, very aristocratic and organized by lordship.[10] Around the king was a courtly group, military and ecclesiastical, whose members constituted a nobility with important legal privileges; and these lords, in their turn, had followers bound to them as closely as they themselves were to the king. In times of crisis, these bonds of lordship might weaken; does not Alfred emphasize them because they are one of the traditional elements of society which, like the kingship itself, is in danger?[11] But normally they seem much more vital and effective than those ties of kinship by which some historians have set such store.

For many reasons rural society could hardly fail to reflect this. From a variety of motives – the conventions of good lordship and piety; bribery;[12] the social necessity of enabling young men to marry and set up in their own households;[13] the military, economic and perhaps governmental advantages in encouraging colonization – kings and (though we have less evidence) other lords were most prodigal in grants of land. Most conspicuously is this so in grants to the church. But the reluctance with which the landbook seems to have been adapted to purely secular gifts does not argue any absence of unwritten grants to laymen.[14] If, for instance, Vortigern gave land to the leaders and possibly to all the Germanic *foederati* he invited, it is likely enough that similar grants by natives or by the Saxons themselves accompanied the settlement elsewhere. Ine's laws, while showing noblemen unendowed with land, make it clear that what was (or at least became) the normal

---

[9] R. S. Hoyt, 'Farm of the Manor and Community of the Vill in Domesday Book', *Speculum*, xxx (1955), pp. 147–69, gives examples of demesne leasing.

[10] E.g. H. M. Chadwick's powerful remarks in *The Origin of the English Nation* (Cambridge, 1907), ch. 7.

[11] Laws, Introduction cap. 49.7; caps. 1, 4.

[12] E.g. Anglo-Saxon Chronicle, a. 757A–E.

[13] Bede, *Epistola ad Ecgbertum Episcopum*, cap. 11, ed. C. Plummer (Oxford, 1896), i, p. 415; *Historia abbatum*, cap. 1 (*ibid.*, p. 364).

[14] F. M. Stenton, *The Latin Charters of the Anglo-Saxon Period* (Oxford, 1955), pp. 59 ff.

class of *gesið* had substantial estates, and suggest it was this which distinguished them from the 600 shilling *gesiðas*, in much the same way as size of estate was used to classify the subject Welsh.[15] Perhaps the early grants were limited to life or service, though even then hereditary claims may have been in practice strong.[16] But by the late ninth century, the preface to Alfred's version of St Augustine's *Soliloquies* assumes that the follower will hope to dwell for a time only on 'land loaned from his lord', 'until, through his lord's kindness, he may earn bookland and perpetual possession'.[17] By this date too, the word *gesið* was normally restricted to noblemen or companions with land.[18]

Anglo-Saxon landlords, except those whose corporate or official character precluded it, seem usually to have lived in fairly close relation with the lands from which they drew their livelihood, whether by journeying about them or – which we may think was the common case with lesser *gesiðas* at least – as residents on estates.[19] However, such association of lords with villages leaves undetermined their exact relationship to those villages, so that we cannot escape an old and famous question about the grants by which these lords came to hold their estates. This should most properly be asked of the earliest grants, but their apparent informality forces attention on the latter ones made under book. What exactly do they grant? If they are to be taken at their word – and vague though they are on many things, they are hardly ever vague about this – it is usually the land itself, in perpetual ownership, that is being handed over. Since Maitland's classic discussion,[20] however, this has not been the received interpreta-

---

15 Caps. 24, 32, 51, 63–6. A 'functional' criterion appears in cap. 33. Cf. the provisions on changes of rank in Liebermann, *Die Gesetze*, i, pp. 456–61.

16 H. M. Chadwick, *Studies on Anglo-Saxon Institutions* (Cambridge, 1905), Excursus v, pp. 367–77. Cf. *Cartularium Saxonicum*, ed. W. de G. Birch, 3 vols. (London, 1885–93) [hereafter cited as BCS.], no. 600 (cited by Stenton, *Latin Charters of the Anglo-Saxon Period*, p. 61 n. 1).

17 *König Alfreds des Grossen Bearbeitung der Soliloquien des Augustinus*, ed. W. Endter (Bibl. der Angelsächsischen Prosa, xi, Hamburg, 1922), p. 2.

18 H. R. Loyn, 'Gesiths and Thegns in Anglo-Saxon England', *Eng. Hist. Rev.*, lxx (1955), pp. 533–40.

19 Bede, *Epist. ad Ecgb. Episc.*, cap. 11 (ed. Plummer, i, p. 415); *Hist. Eccles.*, iii. cap. 14 (*ibid.*, p. 156, ll. 2 ff.); *Beowulf*, ll. 837–40, 1125 ff.; Laws of Ine, caps. 63, 68. Note also the practice of burying noblemen in ordinary village cemeteries, as shown by finds of swords, etc.

20 *Op. cit.*, pp. 230–42.

tion of their solemn words which have, instead, been taken as normally transferring what Maitland called a 'superiority' over the land, an immunity. But persuasive as his argument is, it is not free from internal weaknesses, and his apologetic language may suggest he had not altogether satisfied himself. For instance, to maintain that charters convey actual land is hardly to say that the land itself is either waste or cultivated only by slaves and *coloni* of the donor.[21] Again, as Maitland admitted, 'the charters of this early period seldom suggest any such confusion between political power and ownership as that which we postulate'.[22] Indeed, the reverse is true somewhat later when, with developed diplomatic, landbooks became more precise in explaining intentions and effects. There will be charters which expressly do no more than alienate certain royal rights;[23] most seem to grant land as well as immunity, but sometimes with the revealing difference that the areas over which the two sorts of rights are granted do not coincide.[24] We may plausibly think that many of these so-called grants are really confirmations, or in effect merely the creation of an immunity for the existing landlord.[25] But in any case the grantee will have landlord rights. That charters could confuse political power and ownership is true enough, but those who used and devised them generally and not unnaturally took pains to avoid this. Further, there are common-sense points to be urged, especially since Maitland's interpretation of the landbooks must apply equally to grants by will. For whatever the nature of any public rights conveyed – be the royal *feorm* as heavy as can be imagined – these rights over, in many cases, not extensive areas could alone hardly have provided that adequate support for the beneficiaries which donors obviously intended. The royal rights over, say, twenty hides will support no noble household, no

---

[21] It is, of course, a very long time before documents of transfer will distinguish between land in hand (demesne) and tenanted land. I use 'land' to cover both.

[22] *Op. cit.*, p. 234.

[23] E.g. grants of dues on ships. Or BCS., no. 416.

[24] E.g. *Early Yorkshire Charters*, ed. W. Farrer, 3 vols. (Edinburgh, 1914–16), i, no. 8. Cf. BCS., no. 1112, and RC., nos. liv. lxxxiv.

[25] E.g. BCS., nos. 1077–8, and RC., no. xxxiii; J. M. Davidson, 'On Some Anglo-Saxon Charters at Exeter', *Jl. Brit. Archaeol. Assoc.*, xxxix (1883), pp. 285–9; BCS., no. 967, if genuine, is probably a confirmation, see *Anglo-Saxon Wills*, ed. D. Whitelock (Cambridge, 1930) [hereafter cited as W.], pp. 106 f.

private monastery; that warriors and communities were supported by grants of this magnitude – nobles often by much less – is a fact not lightly to be undermined.

Thus, even without the chronological and other difficulties in that scheme of manorial origins for which Maitland's interpretation of the landbook was an indispensable basis, that interpretation itself could hardly be sustained. The books must be taken at their face value. Whether as original grant or confirmation, they normally speak of actual land, usually at least partly colonized. Over it the grantee has landlord rights, generally fortified by an immunity over a similar or identical area. Maitland's own words on the significance of such an interpretation are worth quoting: 'If we hold by the letter of the charters, if we say that the king really does confer landownership upon the churches, there will be small room left for any landowners in England save the kings, the churches and perhaps a few great nobles'.[26]

*   *   *

What, then, was the structure of these estates? It is possible that some grantees cultivated all the available land directly with their own slaves. But in Wessex at least, by the late seventh century, most, if not all, lay lords had a proportion settled with tenants. Chapters 63–66 of Ine's laws deal with the *gesiðcund mon* who wishes to leave his holding: if he has twenty hides, he is to show twelve hides of *gesett land*, if ten then six, and if three then one and a half. Easy as they are to place broadly in the context of an expanding kingdom, these laws are difficult to interpret and they have not received the emphasis they demand. What is *gesett land*? Many historians, including Liebermann, Sir Frank Stenton and Professor Whitelock, have taken it to mean 'sown land'.[27] Maitland favoured 'cultivated land', but he went on to elaborate this, with reference to the *seten* of Ine cap. 68, in a way which suggests that he intended land which had been let out to husbandmen.[28] Despite the weight of authority in support of 'sown land', the

---

[26] *Op. cit.*, p. 232.

[27] Liebermann, *Die Gesetze*, i, p. 119, ii (2), p. 297c; Stenton, *Anglo-Saxon England*, p. 309; *English Historical Documents, c. 500–1042*, ed. D. Whitelock (London, 1955), p. 371.

[28] *Op. cit.*, p. 238 n. 1; cf. *The Laws of the Earliest English Kings*, ed. F. L. Attenborough (Cambridge, 1922), pp. 56–9, 192.

meaning 'land settled by tenants', which was adopted by Vinogra-doff and earlier by Seebohm, seems to me clearly the right one.[29] Mere words may easily deceive, but the vocabulary of later estates drew not infrequently on *gesettan* and allied words, and drew on them in a consistent sense. In East Anglia, some estates will have *landsetti*, men holding *landsettagia*, or tenements *in landsettagio*;[30] on the other side of England, there are *gesettan landmen* in the *Dunsǣte*;[31] everywhere, though the spelling will vary, there are *kotsetlan*, *cotsetti* and the like; we have the word 'settlers' still. To come nearer Ine's laws, the survey of Tidenham (Gloucestershire) draws its firm contrast between *gesett land* (or *gafolland*), the land let out to peasants, and *inland*, which, as the Domesday Book entry shows, here certainly meant manorial demesne.[32] This is precisely the contrast implied in Ine's laws though there we are left to deduce the *inland* by subtracting the *gesett land* from the total assessment.

The exact purpose of these laws will tell us more. At a later date, *inland*[33] often also meant land exempt from many, if not all, public burdens. After the Conquest, only the *warland* or *utland* of a tenant-in-chief's demesne manors will pay geld; only, as the Northamptonshire Geld Roll puts it in at least one entry, the land that is *sett 7 gewered*.[34] From this to Ine's laws is a short step if, as I believe we should,[35] we postulate tax exemption for the non-*gesett land* in his reign. The king seems to have a limited object in mind; to prevent a *gesið* taking large numbers of his tenants with him when he leaves an estate, since this would reduce its taxes. But, though strictly applicable only to the moment of a lord's depar-ture, these regulations would, of course, have been useless had they not been closely related to the usual structure of estates. Thus, in effect, Ine came very near to stating a normal minimum

[29] Vinogradoff, *The Growth of the Manor*, p. 128; *English Society in the Eleventh Century* (Oxford, 1908), pp. 193, 195; F. Seebohm, *The English Village Community*, 4th edn (London, 1905), pp. 128, 136 f.

[30] D. C. Douglas, *The Social Structure of Medieval East Anglia* (Oxford, 1927), pp. 34, 48 f., 188 n. 1, 194. The one use of these terms outside East Anglia referred to on.p. 48 n. 8 is an obvious misplacement in the Ramsey Cartulary, and belongs to the following survey of Brancaster (Norfolk).

[31] Cap. 6, Liebermann, *Die Gesetze*, i, p. 376.

[32] RC., no. cix. Domesday Book [hereafter cited as DB.], i, 164ai.

[33] The other meanings of this 'overworked term' (Stenton, *Anglo-Saxon England*, p. 477 n. 1) need not concern us.

[34] RC., App. I, no. iii (p. 234).   [35] See Stenton, *loc. cit.*

for the tenant land and a corresponding maximum for the demesne or exempt land. For obvious reasons, however, he had no wish to discourage nobles having *more* tenant or *less* demesne land.

Despite their fiscal context, these laws must be the starting-point for any enquiry into the structure of early estates in England. Their language assumes that dichotomy between demesne and peasant land which is central to manorial history; and it does so at an early date and in circumstances of rapid expansion of settlement which must have been altogether similar to those of one or two centuries before. At the same time, their purpose suggests that, while a *gesið* will not normally have more than 40 or 50 per cent of his land in demesne, he may have less, even (we might conjecture) none at all.[36]

No other early English king or landlord, so far as we know, had occasion to elaborate on these distinctions, and few Old English documents mention them at all. The Tidenham survey, which divides the 30-hide estate there into 9 hides of *inland* and 21 hides of *gesett land*, is not certainly earlier than the mid-eleventh century,[37] while the description of the 16 hides of arable land at Bury as 6 hides in demesne (*into pæra byrig*) and 10 hides held by the peasants (*.x. hida manna earningaland*) does not antedate the Confessor's reign and may be post-Conquest.[38] Perhaps Brihtric and Ælfswith, when they left Harrietsham (Kent) to two brothers, the *inland* to Wulfheah and the *utland* to Ælfheah, were implying that the two parts were approximately equal, but we cannot be sure.[39] The statements in the Old English section of Offa's grant of Bexhill (Sussex) in 772, that there were 8 hides of *in land* and 20 hides of *gauolland pas ut landes*, cannot be contemporary and are, in any case, very difficult to interpret.[40] It may be worth recording

---

36 The frequency with which the *inland* is around 40 or 50 per cent of the total assessment of a Hundred in the Northants. Geld Roll makes an interesting comparison with Ine's laws.

37 RC., no. cix. Although it has often been connected with King Eadwig's grant of Tidenham in 956 (BCS., no. 927) or with the lease of the manor to Archbishop Stigand, datable to 1061–5 (RC., no. cxvii), there is no convincing reason for associating it with either; they do, however, provide limiting dates, since the abbey of Bath did not regain possession after the lease.

38 RC., no. civ (p. 194); but cf. *byrigland* in *ibid.*, App. I, no. iii (p. 234).

39 W., no. xi. But cf. J. E. A. Jolliffe's remark, *Eng. Hist. Rev.*, xlvi (1931), p. 319; and his *Pre-Feudal England: The Jutes* (Oxford, 1933), ch. 1.

40 BCS., no. 208, probably otherwise genuine; but cf. Jolliffe, *op. cit.*, p. 75. Cf. RC., no. lxxxi.

the difficulty of finding an indisputable case in Old English sources of an estate which had no demesne, but this becomes less impressive when it is remembered how little reason contemporaries had for noting these matters in writing.[41] There is a certain cumulative weight in these facts, few and scattered though they are; but no more. They certainly cannot be safely used as evidence that demesnes normally approached the maximum proportions implied in Ine's laws, even in the south of England.[42] Indeed it is hard to see how the history of demesnes can be carried beyond Domesday Book except in isolated cases; and that record is eloquent in forbidding generalization from these. The antiquity of many of the later eleventh-century variations in the importance of manorial demesnes, between different regions, landlords and (less plausibly) races, has often been asserted. It would be optimistic to suppose it can ever be substantiated in detail.

Because of this, and because demesne and peasantry normally developed in sympathy, our understanding of the other constituent of the estate, the tenantry, must remain unsure. Its variable terminology – it appears, for instance, as *gesett land, gafolland, utland, warland*[43] – reveals a dual nature which did much to determine its history and to confuse our understanding of it. The tenants of the lord (the settlers) are also taxpayers (*gafolgeldan*) of the king.[44] Not only therefore are their obligations of a twofold kind, but the lord's interests in letting out his land are correspondingly mixed. From some of his tenants he may require no more than an oath of loyalty in addition to the taxes incumbent on the

---

[41] I cannot agree with Sir Frank Stenton's interpretation of KCD., no. dccclxxi, in his *Types of Manorial Structure in the Northern Danelaw* (Oxford, 1910), pp. 37 ff. Even allowing that the oddities of this charter do not put it out of consideration for eleventh-century conditions, the grant of 'terram nostram de Hikelinge et terram de Kinildetune cum firma et seruitio, sicut habetur in dominio nostro' hardly indicates absence of demesne. The transaction is of a common enough type; a donor wishes to continue in occupation and becomes in effect a lessee for life. No direct light is cast on the structure of the estates, except (in my view) to hint that there was land in demesne.

[42] E.g. even allowing for the effects of a hard winter, BCS., nos. 618–19, suggest a proportionately small demesne.

[43] For these terms, see e.g. Laws of Ine, caps. 64–6; RC., no. cix; W., no. xi; BCS., no. 208 (above, p. 9); 'The Burton Abbey Twelfth Century Surveys', ed. C. G. O. Bridgeman, *Collections for a History of Staffordshire* (William Salt Archaeol. Soc. for 1916, London, 1918), *passim*. Cf. *geneatland* in II Edgar, cap. 1.1.

[44] See especially RC., no. cix, where *gesett land* and *gafolland* coincide.

land; from most he will also exact miscellaneous rents and services. The confusion of private and public obligations, which has impressed all historians, is thus fundamental to the structure of the estate from its beginning. It is heightened, not created, when the king alienates some or all of his public rights to the landlord. At the same time, *gafolland, warland* and *utland*, being terms of public not private bearing, are not confined to the taxable part of lordly estates; they can be applied equally well to any taxable land. It is with this in mind that we may probably best understand that controversial phrase in Alfred and Guthrum's treaty, 'the ceorls who dwell on *gafolland*',[45] or the *gafolland* occupied by *geburas* at Chinnock (Somerset) and by *geneatas* and *geburas* at Tidenham.[46] Such statements merely record that the land in question is taxable; those who hold it may or may not be tenants of a lord.

Equally fundamental is the intermixture of free and slave elements which makes it impossible to assess accurately the relative importance of persons of different ancestry among the Old English peasantry. Certainly the dominance of servitude in the later manor, and the evident numerical importance of slaves and freedmen in Anglo-Saxon England, argue the influence of slavery in the evolution of the tenantry.[47] And now and again manumitted slaves can be seen entering the peasantry;[48] for instance those who, in the late Old English period at least, were granted service holdings: ploughmen, shepherds and the like.[49] But it is truly seldom that they preserve any cohesion in the manorial population; there are, after all, fewer than nine hundred persons called *coliberti* in Domesday Book, though many more slaves had been

---

[45] Cap. 2. See Vinogradoff, *The Growth of the Manor*, pp. 132, 240 f.; R. H. C. Davis, 'East Anglia and the Danelaw', *Trans. Roy. Hist. Soc.*, 5th ser., v (1955), pp. 33 f. Compare, for example, Stenton, *Anglo-Saxon England*, p. 259 n. 1. If the phrase implies other ceorls who did not dwell on *gafolland*, these would presumably include those without any land or dwelling only on the *inland* of an estate.

[46] W., no. iii; RC., no. cix. Compare the gavelkinders in Kent.

[47] Slaves seem normally to have been landless in England. For exceptions, see, e.g., H. P. R. Finberg, *Tavistock Abbey* (Cambridge, 1951), p. 60; W., no. xxxiv (p. 88, ll. 22 f.); *Liber Niger Mon. S. Petri de Burgo*, ed. T. Stapleton (Camden Soc., xlvii, London, 1849), p. 163 (Castor, Northants.). Landed slaves may have been more numerous earlier.

[48] Cf. Alfred's use of *ceorl* to translate *libertinus*, *King Alfred's Orosius*, ed. H. Sweet (Early Eng. Text Soc., lxxix, London, 1883), p. 162.

[49] M. M. Postan, *The Famulus: The Estate Labourer in the Twelfth and Thirteenth Centuries* (Econ. Hist. Rev., Suppl. no. 2, London, 1954), pp. 5–14.

freed well within memory.[50] This is partly because, now as later, men are described by their tenures and the tenements they hold, less frequently by their present status, and hardly at all by reference to their ancestry. Yet such assimilation of freed with free would not have been possible but for the curious fact that outside Kent (at least in the seventh century) with its three groups of *lætas*, and the early Danelaw, there was, so far as is known, no legal class of freedmen with a distinct position in the hierarchy of wergilds and *mund* values.[51] The legal depression of the ordinary manorial tenantry, much of which only occurred in the post-Conquest period, has one of its origins in this easy and widespread absorption of freedmen, in which those of free birth were so obviously liable to suffer.

This assimilation, casually assumed perhaps in Ine's use of the unparticular *mon* in cap. 67 of his laws, is accurately reflected in the normal term for peasant. *Ceorl* is a general, a legal word which, of itself, denoted no particular economic or social position.[52] True, we may piece together a fair amount of information from the laws,[53] but the prevailing impression is that the jingle *eorl and ceorl* persisted because one of its terms at least was beautifully vague. There is a gulf between the reeve Abba and the ceorls at Hurstbourne (Hampshire) which, making full allowance for differences of time and place, no precise social or economic terminology could possibly have overlooked.[54] The confidence, therefore, with which historians have often written about the history of the ceorl has not only gone beyond the evidence; it has also gone against the ambiguity of the name itself. When kings or surveyors wished to

---

[50] H. Ellis, *A General Introduction to Domesday Book*, 2 vols. (London, 1833), ii, p. 511, gives 858 *coliberti* and 62 *buri*. There is none recorded in Essex despite the large manumissions there between 1066 and 1086.

[51] Laws of Æthelberht, cap. 26. Alfred and Guthrum's Treaty, cap. 2. Is this why the obviously important class of Danish *liesengas* (ON. *leysingjar*) virtually disappears (but see W., no. xxxvi)?

[52] See Chadwick, *Studies on Anglo-Saxon Institutions*, pp. 85 ff.; H. P. R. Finberg, *Roman and Saxon Withington. A Study in Continuity* (Univ. of Leicester, Dept of Eng. Local Hist., Occasional Papers, no. 8, Leicester, 1955), p. 36 n. 4.

[53] E.g. Laws of Ine, cap. 42 (cf. place-names such as Charlton), which, however, warrants no deductions as to their tenurial independence, etc. See also Laws of Æthelberht, cap. 27, Alfred, cap. 40.

[54] *Select Eng. Hist. Docs.*, ed. Harmer, no. ii (though Abba may not have been a ceorl, for 'min wærgeld two ðusenda' is very obscure); RC., no. cx.

refer to something less than the whole group between noble and slave they normally eschewed *ceol* in favour of more particular terms, such as *geneat, cotsetla* and *gebur*; all were ceorls, that is, they shared a uniform legal worth and recognition in the public courts.

The tenancies of the *geburas* have been described in detail often enough elsewhere. What demands attention is the fact that their tenements, if taken with their later equivalents, bear all the marks of lordly policy. They are, in the first place, regular in size; not, indeed, as regular as used to be thought, but sufficiently so to make it impossible to see them as mere fragments of once larger holdings, and to argue strongly for some ordered creation and control of the tenements by a superior.[55] And this is what the evidence shows. In a famous chapter of his laws, which has generally been associated with the *geburas*, Ine refers to holdings of a yard of land or more, held at rent or at works and rent, which have been created by the landlord, a point underlined in the *Rectitudines singularum personarum* by the lord providing the tenant with his first requisites.[56] Since these two sources, however, deal only in generalities, we are fortunate in being able to cite particular cases of such settlement of tenants. The most revealing is on the Somerset estate of Chinnock in the tenth century.[57] Wynflæd, or an ancestor, had apparently leased it from the nuns of Shaftesbury, to whom it was to revert on her death. But she owned the stock and the men, and so, in addition to disposing of the slaves and stock, she grants 'the *geburas* who dwell on the *gafolland*'. Though they were in fact given to Shaftesbury, the whole transaction, and especially the careful distinction between land and men, is most readily comprehensible on the assumption that she (or an ancestor) had settled the tenants there. That they remained liable to eviction is obvious, and there is a hint of this also at Ebbesborne Wake (Wiltshire) fifty or so years before.[58] But the frequency with which estates were transferred, as in the

---

[55] Cf. RC., no. cix, in which the *gesett land* is described in yards. For regularity of village plan, see Sutton Courtenay (Berks.) and Sir Frank Stenton's remarks, *Anglo-Saxon England*, p. 283 n. 3.

[56] Cap. 67; Liebermann, *Die Gesetze*, pp. 446 ff.

[57] W., no. iii (? *c.* 950). And see n. 59.

[58] *Select Eng. Hist. Docs.*, ed. Harmer, no. xvii.

event was Chinnock,[59] with stock and men suggests that, in practice, the *gebur*, like the later villein, enjoyed substantial security of tenure. There is similar variation in the degree to which the *gebur* was fixed to his holding. Ine cap. 67 implies a measure of free bargaining between lord and tenant, but its assumption seems to be – though it is no very clear matter – that, within the limits the king is prescribing, the tenant is tied to his yard of land. Other sources show the same. Two persons at Bedwyn (Wiltshire), not later than about the year 1000, were released from the *geburland*, with licence to go where they wished, for 300 pence – for slightly less a slave could buy his freedom;[60] and the meticulous care with which the genealogies and marriages of the *geburas* at Hatfield (Hertfordshire) were recorded can reasonably be interpreted as a sign that they were tied to the land no less than to the lord.[61] In the tenth and eleventh centuries, therefore, the *gebur* seems in many respects very similar to the *colonus* with whom glossators and translators could identify him.[62] But too much – the decline of slavery, the rise of private jurisdiction, and so on – stands between him and his ancestors in the seventh century to permit much confidence about his earlier position, or about the precise way in which his economic subservience was grafted into a law which admitted his free status.

The cottagers and lesser peasantry were an altogether more miscellaneous group, as the unusual wealth of Domesday Book terminology suggests. Their poverty and variety of condition hint, for instance, at the operation of demographic factors and considerable recruitment into the poorer peasantry from the full or half yardlanders.[63] But many had clearly been settled by lords in the humble tenements in which we find them; for example, most of the *coliberti* of Domesday Book,[64] or the many slaves who, in

---

[59] And see Laws of Ine, caps. 63–6, 68. By contrast, see the cases of Bupton (Derbys.) and Longdon (Staffs.) in Wulfric Spot's will, W., no. xvii; and the freedmen at Charlton (Dorset), W., no. iii.

[60] M. Förster, *Der Flussname Themse und seine Sippe* (Munich, 1941), App. I, no. 3, pp. 794 f. It is possible, if unlikely, that these two persons were still slaves, though holding *geburland*.

[61] *A Hand-Book to the Land Charters and Other Saxonic Documents*, ed. J. Earle (Oxford, 1888), pp. 275 ff. Cf. restrictions on the service of a manumitted slave in W., no. iii, p. 10, ll. 28 f. On the other hand, see Laws of Wihtred, cap. 8.

[62] Cf. *Leis Willelme*, cap. 29 (Liebermann, *Die Gesetze,* i, p. 512).

[63] E.g. in Essex between 1066 and 1086, as DB. shows.

Essex at least, were absorbed among the bordars between 1066 and 1086.[65] No doubt these tenants shared in the same servitude as the *geburas*; one of the few personal notes in the history of freedmen in England shows a certain Kynemerus (Cynemær) son of Ulmer (Wulfmær), *colibertus*, 'oppressed by the work and the name', giving the Abbey of Gloucester a fishery for his freedom in the course of the eighth century.[66]

More fortunate were the closer personal dependents of lords, those who, in subordinate capacities, ministered to them in their halls, on their journeys, on the chase, or in their primitive administration. Like many medieval servants, these *geneatas*, reeves and the like, could be elevated by their service, and though they are found towards the end of the Old English period among the upper ranks of the peasantry and shade easily into the thegnly class, there is no necessity to believe that they all descended from freeborn servants rather than slaves. Here too, therefore, assimilation of heterogeneous elements was of importance. The stages, however, by which these men entered the tenantry must remain obscure and cannot, in any case, be sharply distinguished from those by which more substantial followers were also obtaining land. But that they most normally received grants from their masters by way of reward or from future service is not to be doubted.

This is, indeed, the crucial point. The groups we have been considering – and they comprise a large proportion of the known Old English tenantry – show no sign of having ever been, as a whole, unattached landowning peasants. Their tenements and tenure, their customs and even their status, have evolved from the beginning to meet the complex needs, private and public, of great lords from the king downwards. The evidence is admittedly fragmentary; its geographical and chronological limitations are

---

[64] At Wallop (Hants) (i. 38bii) and perhaps at Cosham (Hants) (i. 38aii), DB. equates *coliberti* and *buri*, but this cannot be applied generally. Normally the DB. *colibertus* is clearly a very small holder, sometimes perhaps a 'service *famulus*'.

[65] Cf. *cotseti* and the like settled on former demesne land on some manors of Burton Abbey in the early twelfth century ('The Burton Abbey Twelfth Century Surveys', ed. Bridgeman, e.g. p. 235A).

[66] *Hist. et Cart. Mon. S. Petri Gloucestriae*, ed. W. H. Hart, 3 vols. (Rolls Series, London, 1863–7), i, pp. 77, 124; iii, p. 274. Mr Finberg kindly drew my attention to this.

obvious; and it leaves uncertain many vital matters in the history of tenant right. But that a source as early as Ine's laws should show estates, demesnes and tenantry in the forefront of social institutions, and should show them in a way readily intelligible in the light of later records from the south and west of England, are challenging facts. Even if estate history could be pushed no earlier and no further afield, some large readjustment in our ideas of Old English social history would seem to be necessary, since, on any view, much of England must have been settled in this way.

The vocabulary of settlement, indeed, often shows it to have been so. But this vocabulary does much more. For the association of individuals with particular settlements is widely and impressively stamped on the nomenclature of the countryside, in all areas and at all dates. As early as 1911, Sir Frank Stenton stated clearly the social implications of this: 'When at last English place-names as a whole have undergone detailed investigation, the most notable result of the work will be the recognition of the seignorial idea as a primitive force in the organization of rural society'.[67] The commonest types of such individual association, a genitival composition with personal, family or 'class' name, or the use of -ing with genitival force with such elements, leave, it is true, a great deal unexplained, and, in view of the varied relationships which could be indicated by the genitive, should not uniformly be taken as signifying a proprietary connection.[68] Nor, of course, does the mere association of an individual with a settlement necessarily imply an estate rather than a peasant holding; a -cot normally had humble beginnings whatever its prefix. But not infrequently we plainly have to do with a person of some eminence, as with certain 'class' names, for instance cyning, ealdormann: or with known individuals of substance.[69] Again, the element with which the personal name is compounded may indicate a sizeable estate, as in most uses of -ham and probably many -tun and -ingtun names. Such name formations do much to extend the area and, in some

[67] The Place-Names of Berkshire. An Essay (University College, Reading, Studies in Local History, Reading, 1911), p. 25. Cf. his Types of Manorial Structure in the Northern Danelaw, pp. 90 f.

[68] See especially E. Tengstrand, A Contribution to the Study of Genitival Composition in Old English Place-Names (Uppsala, 1940).

[69] Cf. BCS., no. 449. A considerable number of the landowners of 1066 gave their names to villages. Cf. the use of monothematic (probably upper-class) personal names in early place-name formation.

cases (e.g. *-ham*), the chronological limits, within which private estates can be shown to have existed. But they hardly penetrate at all into the social composition of those estates. Hence the vital importance of the *-ingas* names. Admittedly their etymology is still a matter of some uncertainty, and probably must remain so; but, according to a recent authority, the early type, formed from personal names, is properly to be interpreted as 'the dependents and followers of a certain individual'.[70] No doubt such names could cover many relationships, from (it may be) the most military[71] to the most agricultural, but it is surely hard not to see in them signs of that estate structure already traced in written evidence as early as Ine's reign. The importance of such a conclusion is obvious, for these *-ingas* names have been generally recognized as marking lines of primary Anglo-Saxon penetration.[72] That this settlement was organized very often in the same general way as the later kingdom of Wessex, by estates and under lordly direction – this seems to be the meaning of our early *-ingas* names.

*   *   *

In many places, *-ingas* settlements must originally have been unitary, estate and village, manor and vill, being one. Along the Sussex coastlands, for instance, or up the western Rother, their density often leaves little room for more extensive groupings. And on general grounds, it is probable that unitary settlements were much commoner in early Anglo-Saxon times than can now be proved. For, overlaying them, 'discrete' estates (estate units covering more than one significant settlement) would be formed as an early and inevitable consequence of the expansion of population and settlement.[73] It is, therefore, unlikely to be coincidence that many such estates later give the appearance of antiquity, or that early charters frequently convey land which was already or soon came to be composed of more than one settlement. The topography of discrete estates, however, varied very considerably, particularly according to the disposition of the wastes, woods and

---

[70] A. H. Smith, *English Place-Name Elements*, 2 vols. (Eng. Place-Name Soc., xxv–xxvi, Cambridge, 1956), i, p. 300.

[71] See E. Ekwall, *English Place-Names in -ing* (Lund, 1923), pp. 125 f.

[72] *Ibid.*, pp. 106–26; Smith, *op. cit.*, *s.v. -ingas*; A. H. Smith, 'Place-Names and the Anglo-Saxon Settlement', *Proc. Brit. Acad.*, xlii (1956), pp. 73–88.

[73] See, e.g., Smith, *English Place-Name Elements*, *s.v. prop.*

pastures on which secondary units appeared. Thus, the detached pasture and other rights of a group of east Sussex villages gave rise to distant appurtenant holdings, with arable and tenants, which, in 1086, still bore in their names unmistakable signs of their original parentage.[74] The degree of integration of the discrete estate differed accordingly. Where the whole was contiguous or reasonably compact, there was likely to be a fairly uniform structure, though not necessarily one where demesne and peasant land were evenly distributed. At Tidenham, for example, the 9 hides of demesne land and 21 hides of tenant land were divided unequally between the five or so adjacent places which composed the estate.[75] Elsewhere the outliers or berewicks may have had little or no demesne, being occupied mainly or entirely by a subject peasantry owing dues and services to the parent village, in ways reminiscent of some late Roman estates with their groups of *coloni*. This could, perhaps, explain the equation in one of the two versions of a forged Abingdon charter of the phrase *gebura tun* with the Latin *appendicium*.[76] Again, the very distance of the Sussex outliers just mentioned seems often to have dissuaded lords from developing any arable demesnes and so ensured a large measure of what one might call tenemental autonomy. Structural variations of this kind (those instanced are but a sample) in the cells of discrete estates, even in the different cells of one estate, are of the utmost importance in manorial history. Not only did they give a complexity to estate structure from very early days: they opened the way to even greater variety in the future when any parts became separate manors.

But discrete estates were not only formed, so to speak, naturally. Many were, in one way or another, artificial groupings following on the acquisition by a lord of nearby estates or rights. Such artificial or centripetal groupings proceeded from a variety of motives, more or less agricultural, more or less administrative, and did not therefore necessarily affect significantly the working of the parts. Many of those for the render of private food farms, as

---

[74] *V.C.H. Sussex* (1905–), i, pp. 357 f.

[75] RC., no. cix.

[76] BCS., no. 366. Cf. the topography of Welford (Berks.) at a later date, see DB., i, 58bii; D. C. Douglas, 'Some Early Surveys from the Abbey of Abingdon', *Eng. Hist. Rev.*, xliv (1929), p. 625; *Chron. Mon. de Abingdon*, ed. J. Stevenson, 2 vols (Rolls Series, London, 1858), ii, pp. 301–6, 310.

on the Bury estates,[77] can have had only the most superficial effects on the individual settlements. On the other hand, groupings might arise from causes which imply integration with the head unit. A lease by Bishop Oswald of two hides less sixty acres at Wolverton (Worcestershire) mentions that this land had been attached by him to his manor of Kempsey as wheat-growing land.[78]

The difficulty, often the impossibility, of distinguishing in practice these artificial groupings from the natural, centrifugal ones may easily hide the fact that they belong, as their impermanence and untidiness sometimes indicate, to a different aspect of estate history. Despite their frequent unificatory effects, they should be seen as part of the disintegration of the primitive estate. Expansion of settlement, sales and mortgages, leases and rewards, inheritance and family arrangements, forfeiture, piety, illegality:[79] these and other factors gave to estate and village history a vitality and movement which could not fail to complicate the relative simplicity of the early estate, and to obscure and ultimately destroy that unity of lordship and settlement on which it was based. They might for long leave a manor untouched. They might subdivide a discrete manor, causing merely a different arrangement of settlements – though even then any variety of structure in the cells of the old estate could lead to considerable abnormalities in the new. But in other cases, and everywhere if the process continued long enough, they led to the subdivision of villages themselves.[80] Such changes have a central importance for the study of the manor. For, whether or not we work explicitly back from Domesday Book, any theory of the origins of the manor in early Anglo-Saxon history must rest not only on the hazardous phrases of the laws and charters, but also on its ability to explain the first sure and general facts we have, those of 1066 and 1086. The contrasts between the complex agrarian structure they reveal, even in the old kingdom of Wessex, and the relative simplicity we

---

[77] RC., no. civ.

[78] RC., no. lv. Cf. Ashford (Kent) in W., no. xxxii. For an early Kentish example, BCS., nos. 97, 98, on which see G. Ward, 'The Wilmington Charter of A.D. 700', *Archaeol. Cantiana*, xlviii (1936), pp. 11–28.

[79] E.g. RC., no. liv.

[80] As these remarks indicate, it may be difficult to know the precise effects of a particular transaction. But the conclusions are unaffected by this slight uncertainty over some of the examples.

have alleged for the original manorial settlements, are deep and striking, and, viewed in isolation, might cast doubt on the earlier half of the picture. The evidence of intervening changes not only justifies those contrasts. It demands them.

At the same time, by isolating change from origin, we shall be in danger of oversimplifying and implying too neat and rigid a time sequence. For manors were being created and being altered not only at the same time but by the same steps. Consider, for instance, the contrary effects of the demands of good lordship and the good household on social and estate structure. We have seen how important in the creation of peasant holdings were grants to *geneatas* and freedmen. But the former, as suggested by Domesday Book's vacillating treatment of larger sub-tenancies (now put among the ordinary peasantry, now described as sub-manors), are not easily distinguished from grants to thegns which, by their size, must be reckoned as assisting the fragmentation of the parent manor and the emergence of additional and smaller estate units. And then consider that good lordship does not only tear manors apart. It can, and much has been made of this, attract landowners to commend themselves to a dominant lord and so reassert the lost unity of a village, or even create it for the first time. The impossibility of clearly describing these contrary tendencies as a whole must not prevent us thinking of them as one in the final analysis; only thus can we explain the complexity of manorial topography and structure in 1066. Nonetheless, we must manage now on a few selected themes.

Certainly one of the chief solvents of the early estate unit was family arrangements, in particular the existence of co-heirs, or co-heiresses.[81] Each of the heirs might be given one or more complete manors,[82] but on smaller lordships partition of manors and villages was extremely common, and Domesday Book provides countless examples both of the ubiquity of partible inheritance among the upper classes and of its consequences. The heirs could, of course, keep the manor together, merely dividing the profits. But frequently, perhaps usually in the end, a physical division would be made, as with the five hides at Whaddon

---

[81] Since, however, partible inheritance is the only cause of division which can be readily detected outside the wills, its importance may appear comparatively greater than it was.

[82] E.g. W., no. x.

(Gloucestershire) which, in 1066, were held by five brothers 'pro .v. maneriis . . . 7 pares erant'.[83] Wives often had to be provided for in addition to their morning gift, and this could not invariably be done with whole manors. Ælfhelm, in his will made between 975 and 1016, left half his estate at Conington (Cambridgeshire), already shorn of four and a half hides granted by him to others, to his wife and daughter 'to divide between them'.[84] Many other relatives might make calls on a man's generosity, sometimes causing subdivision. The same Ælfhelm left his property at Troston (Suffolk), less a part already given away, 'to be divided among my three brothers'.[85]

Relatives and followers were never mutually exclusive categories, as several of Bishop Oswald's leases show,[86] and similar conventions of good lordship embraced both. Followers and servants could be lavishly rewarded, though even then not necessarily with whole manors,[87] but the characteristic gifts were comparatively modest. Æthelflæd, daughter of Ealdorman Ælfgar and second wife of King Edmund, granted at Donyland (Essex) two hides each to her *cniht* Brihtwold, two of her priests and her kinsman Ælfgeat.[88] More common still were grants of up to about half a hide or the division of an estate between a body of followers. Leofgifu, in her will between 1035 and 1044, thus rewarded, among others, three stewards, a reeve and various priests in several of her manors, and Lawford (Essex) went to 'Æthelric my household chaplain and Ælfic [and] my *cnihtas* who will serve me best'.[89] Outside the wills and charters it is not easy to trace such rewards – some of our Knightons must surely reflect them[90] – and

83 DB., i, 168bii. The effects would be heightened if the brothers then commended themselves to different lords, e.g. DB., i, 144ai (Stone, Bucks.), 152bi (Datchet, Bucks.). For division between co-heiresses, see, e.g., DB., i, 32ai (Weybridge, Surrey), or between mixed heirs, e.g. W., no. xxi (Butcombe, Somerset). A partial division only might be made, e.g. DB., i, 45ai (Wickham, Hants). Cf. the duplicate entries for Chardford (Hants) in DB., i, 44bii, 46ai, for the difficulty of knowing if a physical division was made.
84 W., no. xiii; and, e.g., no. xxiv (Roydon, Norfolk).
85 W., no. xiii.
86 E.g. RC., no. xlvi, and p. 343 for other references.
87 E.g. W., no. xx (Chalton, Hants).
88 W., no. xiv.
89 W., no. xxix, in which the size of reward, when stated, is small. See also no. xxxix (Limber, Lincs.). A follower might, of course, receive more than one small reward.
90 Possibly those in DB., i, 39bi, 54ai, 63bi.

one has to speak with caution on their importance. But, plainly, they could violently alter the structure of a manor, sometimes in a way which can be misleading to historians. For instance, they explain some of the unattached or merely commended freemen of Domesday Book. At Dullingham (Cambridgeshire) in 1066 three sokemen held 2 hides 10 acres, 'and they could not withdraw', according to the *Inquisitio commitatus Cantabrigiensis* one of them was named Wichinz (Vikingr) and was a man of Earl Harold. It is only by chance that we know that this man was no archaic survival from some distant past, free Danish or free Anglo-Saxon, weighed down by commendation, but recently a *cniht* of Thurstan, who had rewarded him with this very holding.[91]

Without at all challenging the conventions of good lordship – no lord would wish to do this consistently – many greater lords were obviously aware from an early date of the serious effects of such grants to their kinsmen and their household. Hence the arrangements for a temporary division only, with remainder of the entire holding to a survivor or a third party.[92] Hence, more important, the lease.[93] But the lease, by facilitating rewards and the creation of a following by land grants, may even have increased the volume of lordly grants without significantly reducing their disintegrating effects on manorial structure. During the term of a lease, its results were not distinguishable from those of permanent grant, except that the attachment to the parent manor was usually preserved by rents, services or commendation.[94] At its end, if the claims of heirs were defeated, the estate would revert, and in theory it could be fully reabsorbed. In practice, however, by the later Old English period at least, loan land could not easily or often be restored to demesne.[95] Thegn-land and associated

[91] W., no. xxxi and pp. 194 f., for the other references. For another possible case, see W., no. xxxi, and DB., ii, 31a (half a hide at Ongar, Essex). Partible inheritance may similarly mislead; cf. DB., i, 206aii (Gidding, Hunts.), where we are only incidentally told that the six sokemen were brothers.

[92] E.g. W., no. xviii (Dumbleton, Glos., and Tew, Oxon.).

[93] To relatives as well as other followers; e.g. above, n. 86; Bishop Esne's leases at Taunton, A. G. C. Turner, 'Some Old English Passages Relating to the Episcopal Manor of Taunton', *Proc. Somerset Archaeol. and Nat. Hist. Soc.*, xcviii (1953), p. 119.

[94] See B. Dodwell, 'East Anglian Commendation', *Eng. Hist. Rev.*, lxiii (1948), pp. 289–306, especially pp. 303–6. For an exception, see, e.g., DB., i, 72aii (Highway, Wilts.).

[95] Exceptions are not, however, uncommon in DB.; see, e.g., *V.C.H. Wiltshire* (1953–), ii, pp. 82 f.

tenures, such as dreng-land and reeve-land, were thus major factors in the long- no less than in the short-term fragmentation of manors. For though leases could be made of complete manors, individual holdings were frequently divided or, which is quite as important, brought together in strange, new combinations.[96]

On lay lordships piety contributed greatly to the division of manors.[97] Certainly, monastic and episcopal churches would often receive whole manors, but an estate did not always allow this. Queen Ælfgifu Emma granted five hides at Hayling Island to the Old Minster, Winchester, and the same amount there to Wulfweard the White, and although she intended the latter half to pass to Winchester on Wulfweard's death, her wishes did not take effect.[98] Much more often, manors lost part of their land through grants to village and private churches; these could be very small[99] and seldom exceeded half a hide. For instance, Thurstan left to Merewine, his wife and their children, his estate at Dunmow (Essex), less half a hide for the church; in Domesday Book, the manor duly appears as four and a half hides, the church's half hide apparently being omitted from the survey.[100]

Division could also arise in less straightforward ways, as when the earl had a third of all forfeitures and the king or a royal grantee the remainder. The Domesday Book disputes in the west riding of Lincolnshire record that: 'The shire bears witness that Gonnewate's land, one manor, having one carucate in demesne, was forfeited, two parts to St Mary of Stow, and the third part to the earl's use . . . Likewise also with respect to Stangrim's land, 18 bovates of land'.[101]

In the late Old English period, if not before, another development altogether began to influence manorial history. The disintegration of manorial demesnes due to leasing to large groups of men, often all the villeins of the manor, is now a familiar enough

[96] For dispersed thegn-lands, see, e.g., RC., nos. xliii, xlvi, lxv, lxvii; BCS., nos. 1204–5. Thegn-lands often occupy only part of a settlement in DB., e.g. in Wiltshire; similarly among Bishop Oswald's leases, e.g. RC., nos. lvi, lviii.

[97] Cf. divisions resulting from payment of soulscot in land, e.g. W., no. xix (Tardebigge, Worcs.).

[98] RC., no. cxiv and p. 462. See also, e.g., RC., no. xxix; W., no. xxxi.

[99] E.g. W., nos. xxxiii, xxxiv.

[100] W., no. xxxi; DB., ii, 69a.

[101] DB., i, 376aii. This division of forfeitures is said to apply to all the wapentake of Well.

feature of the twelfth century.[102] But, as Domesday Book shows, it had begun before the Conquest, at least on ecclesiastical estates in the south of England.[103] For example, in 1066 and 1086 the villeins held the five hides at Millbrook (Hampshire); no demesne is mentioned, and the statement 'non est ibi aula' seems to underline the effects of the leasing.[104] The incidental way in which such matters could be mentioned, and the fact that the final version of the Domesday survey could omit them even when available at an earlier stage of the inquiry,[105] make it certain that these leasings were more common than Domesday Book records. How much more common it is impossible to say, but some at least of the manors without demesne are likely to conceal such a history.

It would, however, be quite wrong to give the impression that Anglo-Saxon estate history was entirely one of fragmentation, of large families clamouring to divide their inheritances, and of demesnes disappearing. Family settlements were not always permanent; nine carucates and five bovates at Wymeswold (Leicestershire) were once held by two brothers as two manors, but, before 1066, one bought out the other and 'fecit unum manerium de duobus'.[106] A lease will revert: peasant land can be brought into demesne.[107] Things done may be undone, or partly so. More than that, some landlords, especially (it may be) ecclesiastical lords, make new manors.[108] Purchase of land or mortgages, pious gift, brute force and local influence could soon assemble a property. Commendation had a similar if obscure role, often, it is true, merely preserving existing tenurial relationships, but sometimes, at least in the late Old English period and in some localities, creating new ones.[109] It would, in fact, be hard to cite any period

[102] Postan, 'The Chronology of Labour Services', *passim*.

[103] Hoyt, 'Farm of the Manor and Community of the Vill', *passim*.

[104] DB., i, 41bii.   [105] Hoyt, *op. cit.*, pp. 152 ff.

[106] DB., i, 233aii. Cf. i, 159bi (Orgar's holdings in Berrick Salome and Gangsdown Hill, Oxon.). Above, n. 92.

[107] E.g. DB., i, 159ai (Nuneham Courtenay, Oxon.). Professor R. R. Darlington's interpretation of such entries (*V.C.H. Wiltshire*, ii, p. 83) cannot be sustained. They carry no implication of 'wrongful encroachments' on 'the villeins' own land'. Their purpose was to prevent lords obtaining tax exemption for additions to demesnes.

[108] See, e.g., *Liber Eliensis*, ed. D. J. Stewart (London, 1848), i, *passim*; RC., no. xl.

[109] Dodwell, 'East Anglian Commendation', *passim*.

in which the determined Anglo-Saxon lord could not make manors and amass an estate; the very impermanence of many such accumulations made them the easier to come by. But making manors, no less than making great estates, was not normally very neat work. It was, therefore, not only the disruptive tendencies in society which caused the complexity and untidiness of manorial (and estate) topography in 1066; it was also, perhaps equally, men's efforts to reverse them.

The facts of Anglo-Saxon manorial history can never be easy to manage. Their intractability goes deeper than mere difficulties in the evidence, of terminology, authenticity and date – great though these are. Like King William's surveyors, we must struggle to discipline them, but if, in the end, they seem a tangle still, we have not necessarily failed to understand and see them as they were; this much almost any will or folio of Domesday Book can show. When, however, the chronicle of estates in the later Old English period is told in detail – and from Domesday Book, the wills and charters this may yet be done – we shall surely be led back, by many and devious routes, primarily to that organization of settlement and agriculture which, so our place-names seem to tell us, was already old when Ine described it in his laws.

A Postscript*

Any article written about a quarter of a century ago (and first sketched out five years before that) is liable to have something of a 'period', almost antique look about it. Mine, reprinted above, perhaps conforms to this general pattern. For although at the time of its composition Dr Austin Lane Poole warned me that 'you cannot in some 5,000 words obliterate the classic volumes of famous historians'[1] – he was thinking principally of Maitland, Vinogradoff and Stenton – in fact, despite the odd criticism here and there,[2] the general thesis seems to have passed more or less into current orthodoxy so that it might almost seem one could wonder what all the trouble and argument was about. Certainly this will be true unless one looks at the background against which it was written where the entrenched idea of the manor originating in the steady suppression and depression of a once free peasantry was the overriding theme. From this it followed that, from the point of view of the evolution of types of rural organization, the manor, even the lordly estate of whatever structure, was deemed a late development, far from dominant – in some respects only just emerging – even in southern England in the mid-eleventh century

---

* I am much indebted to Dr T. M. Charles-Edwards, Dr P. R. Coss, Dr Christopher Dyer, Mr T. A. R. Evans, Dr Rosamond Faith and Dr Joan Thirsk for having read and commented on various drafts of this Postscript. I take this opportunity of paying tribute to the work of the late Professor H. P. R. Finberg who not only laid many groundworks in his study of charters and the like, but showed an originality and an understanding in all he touched in so many inevitably obscure aspects of Old English history. Thus his brief remarks on 'Forms of Settlement' in *The Agrarian History of England and Wales*, vol. i, pt 2, *A.D. 43–1042,* ed. H. P. R. Finberg (Cambridge, 1972), at pp. 423–7, substantially repeated in H. P. R. Finberg, *The Formation of England, 550–1042* (The Paladin History of England, ed. Robert Blake, London, 1974), at pp. 83–5, seem to me to show insights into many of the aspects with which this Postscript is concerned which few if any other scholars have achieved. While, to take a more particular example, his redating of the survey of Hurstbourne Priors, in 'The Churls of Hurstbourne', in his *Lucerna. Studies of Some Problems in the Early History of England* (London, 1964), pp. 131–43, lends significant and concrete support to the thesis advanced in my original article reprinted above.

[1] Private letter to the author.

[2] For example, H. R. Loyn, *Anglo-Saxon England and the Norman Conquest* (London, 1962) – a challenge to my interpretation of the words *gesett land* in Ine caps. 64–6 which seems to me to have no force in it whatever; and Eric John, *Orbis Britanniae* (Leicester, 1966), pp. 101 ff., restating against me a longstanding difference of opinion regarding the nature of the rights transferred in royal grants by book.

when Domesday Book shows it as the norm in 1086 and, of course, also in 1066.

For this unavoidable 'period' quality I make no apology. But there are other 'period' aspects which are, I think, of more interest. My article was concerned primarily with the origins of the earliest manors; in other words with the question, when did manors first appear on the scene? It was not focused much on the question of the evolution of the manor in the Old English period. It does, however, contain in its concluding sections a few suggestions drawing attention to the changing character of estate organization, to in effect the dynamic quality of manorial history. Of these dynamic elements, two in particular should demand our attention: inheritance customs and trends in population and thus in settlement. Tempting as it is to try to discuss both of these here, I shall only touch briefly on the first and concentrate on the second.

*   *   *

Few factors can be so important in the social development of pre-industrial societies as inheritance patterns – whether they be obligatory (strictly legal, or more properly speaking customary) or individually determined. So far as concerns the upper classes, Domesday Book is ample testimony to the universality of the rule of partible inheritance outside the case of bookland. As to this latter it is clear that the freedom to determine descent both *inter vivos* and on death was a most highly valued privilege from which we may conclude that the rule of partible inheritance was by no means always welcomed. It is frequently, indeed I think normally, assumed that the freedom of alienation granted by the book was prized precisely because it allowed unfettered granting away; and the extant wills, showing what one might regard as a reckless exercise of this right, would seem to bear this out. But these wills are a very skewed sample, being almost without exception preserved via ecclesiastical beneficiaries.[3] And I would suggest that there may well have been a quite contrary tendency, more widely practised even though no documentary proof (supposing it ever existed) survives. For the book's freedom of alienation not only

---

[3] For the sources of the wills, see Dorothy Whitelock, *Anglo-Saxon Wills* (Cambridge, 1930) in the annotations to each of the wills.

allowed alienation of the kind evidenced by the surviving wills. It also allowed one to keep one's inheritance together, to a greater or lesser extent, by leaving it or the major part to a single heir against the otherwise obligatory descent by partibility.

As for the economically and legally free peasantry, the later sokemen and so on, the existence of partible inheritance not only among the gavelkinders of Kent but also, as is now well known, in certain parts of the so-called Scandinavianized regions of England, is quite clear.[4] Moreover, if for instance the field-name evidence can be trusted,[5] it held good over a far further area, one might even guess universally so. Yet, when dealing with so long a period as that of Anglo-Saxon England, we must not lightly assume that even so basic a concept remained unchanged or that custom necessarily inhibited *ad hoc* arrangements of a different kind – as commonly happened much later. And in fact I am greatly disposed to think that the quite different social development of southern and central England as opposed to more easterly and northerly areas may well have had its origin, in large part, in a *de facto* or *de jure* avoidance of partible inheritance – a kind of peasant equivalent of bookland. To take but one factor making for this. Since rise to thegnly status by the later Old English period if not before was dependent on the possession of a minimum of five hides – and in the *Norðleoda Laga* hereditary *gesið* or noble status required such tenure for three generations[6] – there would have been a powerful incentive to hold a tenement together, even for example by providing for the non-inheriting members of the family to continue in residence as, in some form or other, tenants of the principal beneficiary.

---

[4] Referred to by F. Pollock and F. W. Maitland, *The History of English Law*, 2nd edn, 2 vols. (Cambridge, 1923), ii, p. 270, and H. L. Gray, *English Field Systems* (Cambridge, Mass., 1915), p. 337, but first systematically discussed by G. C. Homans, *English Villagers of the Thirteenth Century* (Cambridge, Mass., 1942), ch. 8, and then by H. E. Hallam, *Settlement and Society. A Study of the Early Agrarian Landscape of South Lincolnshire* (Cambridge, 1965), ch. 10, and 'Some Thirteenth-Century Censuses', *Econ. Hist. Rev.*, 2nd ser., x (1957–8), pp. 340–61.

[5] See, for instance, T. A. M. Bishop, 'Assarting and the Growth of the Open Fields', *Econ. Hist. Rev.*, vi (1935–6), pp. 13–29, esp. pp. 22–4; and more generally, Joan Thirsk, 'The Common Fields', *Past and Present*, no. 29 (Dec. 1964), pp. 3–25. See also below, pp. 41–2.

[6] F. Liebermann, *Die Gesetze der Angelsachsen*, 3 vols. (Halle, 1903–16), i, pp. 458–61; trans. in *English Historical Documents*, vol. i, ed. Dorothy Whitelock (London, 1955), pp. 432–3.

Finally, the position regarding the tenants on manorial estates must remain to a considerable extent highly obscure. Again the field-names point towards partible inheritance at least for some of the period. In addition it is not too difficult to postulate circumstances in which the virgate, supposing it to have been a 'primeval' tenement (and it is after all evidenced as a typical tenement in Ine's laws),[7] was often eroded by subdivision so that the tenemental structure became such as is revealed by our earliest estate surveys in the twelfth century. And yet there seem some very considerable differences from those free areas where partible inheritance persisted. Twelfth-century manors, after all, were in the typical case made up of groups of more or less uniform tenements – virgates, half-virgates, cotlands (quarter-virgates, so to say), and lastly a certain number of miscellaneous smallholdings.[8] In free areas of partible inheritance the tenemental structure is, of course, altogether different and altogether more variegated. So it would almost seem as if lords, as on occasion later, normally pursued a positive policy of not allowing fragmentation (by partible inheritance or otherwise) to proceed beyond a certain point.

*   *   *

Turning to the second dynamic element with which we are concerned, population and settlement trends, medieval historians are fairly familiar now – and the knowledge has been building up for at least a generation – with the main directions of population changes from the twelfth to the fifteenth centuries, and later historians have developed demography into something of a major industry, not to say an arcane science with its own methodology and vocabulary. And with this knowledge has come a deepening awareness of the effects of population changes on social and estate structure, on the fortunes of both the upper and lower ranks, on

---

[7] Ine cap. 67: Liebermann, *Die Gesetze*, i, pp. 118–19; *The Laws of the Earliest English Kings*, ed. and trans. by F. L. Attenborough (Cambridge, 1922), pp. 56–9.

[8] See, for instance, the earliest of such surveys, those of Burton Abbey: 'The Burton Abbey Twelfth Century Surveys', ed. C. G. O. Bridgeman, *Collections for a History of Staffordshire* (William Salt Archaeol. Soc., for 1916, London, 1918), pp. 208–300; or the mid-twelfth-century surveys of manors of the Abbey of Ramsey in *Cartularium Monasterii de Rameseia*, ed. W. H. Hart, 3 vols. (Rolls Ser., 1884–93), iii, *passim*.

not only the pattern but the nature of settlement and so on. By contrast, Old English historians, lacking anything corresponding to the direct evidence of those engaged on later periods, have generally had little if anything to say on this fundamental of historical development. Not surprisingly and as with so many other aspects of the social history of the period, Seebohm – much discredited for far too long – with his acute eye for the ground, saw how important increase of population and expansion of settlement were and, for example, drew attention to the reference in the preface to Alfred's translation of St Augustine's *Soliloquies* to the creation of new properties in the wastes and woodlands of an old.[9] That population increase and consequent expansion of settlement took place between, say, the mid-fifth and the mid-eleventh centuries has, I dare say, seldom been doubted.[10] But its implications for the history of settlement, of estates and of social structure have often been completely ignored. Thus Professor Loyn, though I think well aware of such expansion, has no reference to it in his discussion of what he calls the 'Major Social Changes' in the Old English period.[11] This obviously makes for a certain degree of simplicity in that social changes can be treated as if they took place within a more or less static overall framework. But it is a simplification which, in my view, makes it quite impossible to determine the real course of social history. To do

[9] F. Seebohm, *The English Village Community*, 4th edn (London, 1890), pp. 169 ff.

[10] I take this as a convenient opportunity of saying that I cannot in the least agree with Professor P. H. Sawyer's statement that 'The period between the English and Norman conquests was therefore not marked by a great movement of colonization', though I readily concede that factors such as natural disasters and climatic change must be taken into account, or that 'from the earliest period after the English conquest the resources of the landscape were fully exploited in most parts of England' (whence, then, twelfth- and thirteenth-century colonization?). In fact it is not altogether clear to me that he really believes this himself, for he goes on to note 'the progressive abandonment of single farms and the formation of larger nucleations', something difficult to envisage without assarting and the like. See P. H. Sawyer, 'Medieval English Settlement: New Interpretations', in P. H. Sawyer (ed.), *English Medieval Settlement* (London, 1979), p. 8 and *passim*. Contrast on all this H. P. R. Finberg's views on increasing population and settlement stated, though unfortunately not really discussed, in *The Agrarian History of England and Wales*, vol. i, pt 2, *A.D. 43–1042*, ed. H. P. R. Finberg (Cambridge, 1972), *passim*.

[11] Loyn, *Anglo-Saxon England and the Norman Conquest*, ch. 7. For a very brief and tentative outline of Anglo-Saxon population history, see David M. Wilson, *The Archaeology of Anglo-Saxon England* (London, 1976), pp. 43–4.

this we must put expansion of settlement – and at least the possibility of contraction (far more difficult though it is to discern)[12] – very much in the forefront of our thinking, even if in so doing we are introducing a factor of whose chronology and details we are singularly ill-informed.

Ill-informed but by no means totally in the dark. With over fifty volumes of the English Place-Name Society behind us, Ekwall's overall Dictionary[13] and various general and local studies such as Stenton's pioneering work on Berkshire,[14] we have indelible imprints of our Old English past; there is an increasing body of archaeological evidence; while twelfth- and thirteenth-century history may furnish us with comparative insights. Of course much in place-name study remains obscure, even impenetrable: for instance, the dating of most of our place-names is, at least as yet, inscrutable so far as concerns the detail we would really like to know. And, as is clear, place-names could and on occasion did change, thus obviously confusing our understanding of things, while the actual meaning of many place-names is by no means as clear now as it seemed to be some time ago.[15] But if we ask the right kind of questions they have an immense amount to tell us, as have field-names too. Similarly with the archaeological evidence. And what in fact we are seeking to determine is the differing effects of increase of population and expansion of settlement. Here I shall attempt merely to suggest some of the variety in these effects.

Much expansion of settlement no doubt took place in the Old

---

12 One naturally thinks first of the very early period, but disasters of one kind and another (to humans, crops or stock) are evidenced at various dates over the whole of the Old English period. See, for example, Wilfrid Bonser (with an Appendix by Sir William Macarthur), 'Epidemics during the Anglo-Saxon Period', *Jl. Brit. Archaeol. Assoc.*, 3rd ser., ix (1944), pp. 48–71. The effects of plague and of high and varying mortality and fertility in contrast to other influences on settlement patterns cannot, I think, now be determined (unless archaeology should come more to our aid), but they should certainly not be forgotten in any study of overall influences.

13 E. Ekwall, *The Concise Oxford Dictionary of English Place-Names*, 4th edn (Oxford, 1960).

14 F. M. Stenton, *The Place-Names of Berkshire. An Essay* (University College, Reading, Studies in Local History; Reading, 1911). For discussions of more general questions, see for example Margaret Gelling, *Signposts to the Past. Place-Names and the History of England* (London, 1978).

15 For changes in place-names, see below, n. 32. For problems concerning the meaning of place-names, see for example Gelling, *Signposts to the Past*, ch. 7.

English period as later on the fringes of existing group settlements. In some cases this need not have brought about any very significant changes in social organization. For instance, if the parent settlement were under a lord, if we are dealing with a manor of one kind or another, then there would be a strong chance that the new areas of settlement would, at least in the end, come under his lordship – though this could be without noticeable changes in tenemental pattern. If, on the other hand, the parent settlement were a group of economically and legally free peasants one might expect any extension of settlement more or less simply to increase the size of the group. But in many cases casual or fringe extension of settlement would or could make for change. What for instance of the very large numbers of bordars, cottagers and the like found in the last half of the eleventh century and evidenced in the *Rectitudines singularum personarum* for a slightly earlier period?[16] If later, at least on some manors, the availability of land nearby encouraged the formation of tiny holdings to a more marked extent than on more stable manors,[17] is there not at least a chance that something of the same thing happened earlier in some cases? Or, to take an example from an area of pronounced peasant freedom, it has been observed, especially by Professor Hallam,[18] that later local population increase could be closely related to partible inheritance customs; and that an expectation among all the sons and daughters of some share in the inheritance not only encouraged early marriage but also discouraged migration and thus made for high population densities and smaller average holdings. How far such factors operated in the Old English period we cannot in any way be sure. But there are certainly some areas where in Domesday Book peasant freedom (probably with partible inheritance and free alienation) and dense population are found together in a striking way. Professor Davis has observed that 'the "free" districts of East Anglia were those in which the

---

[16] Liebermann, *Die Gesetze*, i, pp. 444–53; trans. in *English Historical Documents*, vol. ii, ed. D. C. Douglas and G. W. Greenaway (London, 1953), pp. 813 ff.

[17] For example, see J. Z. Titow, 'Some Differences between Manors and their Effects on the Condition of the Peasantry in the Thirteenth Century', *Agric. Hist. Rev.*, x (1962), pp. 1–13.

[18] Hallam, *Settlement and Society*, ch. 10, and 'Some Thirteenth-Century Censuses'.

recorded population per square mile was highest';[19] and something of the same conjunction is found in parts of Lincolnshire also.[20] Assarting and reclamation on the edges of existing group settlements, whether by inhabitants or incomers, were thus, we cannot doubt, powerful factors making for social and estate change.

But it must be reckoned as virtually certain that the more catalytic types of expansion were those which took place outside the confines of established settlements or at least at some distance from their centre – far out on the waste or common lands it may be. In regard to such assarting we may keep in mind two broad points. First, that in size such new settlements could in origin be anything from an individual and isolated farmstead or lesser holding (a *cot* or the like) up to group settlements of various kinds. And secondly, that they would vary in their degree of independence from simple and complete dependence on a parent manorial settlement to more or less complete independence (manorialized or not as the case may be) from any parent at all. Difficult as it is to distinguish between different origins of this nature – for a secondary settlement of whatever kind was itself a dynamic unit subject to all manner of changes that could utterly obscure, for us, its actual origins – we can at least discern a few general points.

That some new settlements were group settlements is not, as already indicated, to be doubted. For instance, we might see them behind such place-names as Lazenby (*by* of the freed man or freed men) in Yorkshire, of which there are two cases in Domesday Book, and perhaps some of our Charltons (settlements of ceorls)[21] and the like. Moreover, some place-name elements such as *-tun* come to have the meaning of estate or village[22] so that if the name is original we seem again to be concerned with a group settlement. Nor is it to be doubted that the earliest Anglo-Saxon settlements were often nucleated or something very similar. A marauding lord

---

[19] R. H. C. Davis, 'East Anglia and the Danelaw', *Trans. Roy. Hist. Soc.*, 5th ser., v (1955), pp. 23–39.

[20] Hallam, *Settlement and Society*, p. 201.

[21] H. P. R. Finberg, 'Charltons and Carltons', in his *Lucerna. Studies in Some Problems in the Early History of England* (London, 1964), pp. 144–60; see esp. pp. 159–60 for the economic and legal status of the ceorls on such settlements.

[22] A. H. Smith, *English Place-Name Elements*, 2 vols. (Eng. Place-Name Soc., xxv, xxvi, Cambridge, 1956), *s.v.*, *-tun*. For examples of other place-name elements cited below, see *ibid*.

would surely have had no difficulty, and every incentive, in taking over a Roman or pre-Roman settlement more or less intact: thus, for instance, with the case of Withington (Gloucestershire) as Finberg, to my mind, conclusively demonstrated.[23] Or again our *-ingas* names may be taken to imply the existence of group settlements, albeit now recognized as dating from an immediately secondary phase of settlement after the initial conquests.[24] Or yet again, the seventh-century westward expansion of Wessex gave plentiful opportunities for the removal of whole groups of persons, maybe under their lord, to the newly conquered areas.[25] Archaeology will also provide its quota of larger settlements – for example, Chalton (Hampshire) or perhaps Catholme (Staffordshire)[26] – though it may be noted in passing that it will tend to give the impression of more such settlements than was actually on average the case, because of the difficulty of knowing how many of the excavated houses were in use initially or at any one time in the history of the settlement. Thus we have the case of West Stow (Suffolk) which at first sight appears as quite a sizeable settlement but is more usually regarded as a hamlet.[27] And there is also the consideration that lesser settlements and particularly individual farmsteads may so easily escape discovery by archaeologists.

But, taking the evidence as a whole, it may confidently be said that far too much attention has been, until comparatively recently, centred on the nucleated village and large settlement as if these were the normal starting-points.[28] Rather do we need, as the

[23] H. P. R. Finberg, *Roman and Saxon Withington. A Study in Continuity* (Univ. of Leicester, Dept. of Eng. Local Hist., Occasional Papers, no. 8, Leicester, 1955).

[24] See J. M. Dodgson, 'The Significance of the Distribution of the English Place-Name in *-ingas, -inga-* in South-East England', *Medieval Archaeology*, x (1966), pp. 1–29; and also Gelling, *Signposts to the Past*.

[25] Ine's laws, caps. 63–6, on which see below, p. 38 and n. 39.

[26] For Chalton, see Barry Cunliffe, 'Saxon and Medieval Settlement-Pattern in the Region of Chalton, Hampshire', *Medieval Archaeology*, xvi (1972), pp. 1–12; P. V. Addyman and D. Leigh, 'The Anglo-Saxon Village of Chalton, Hampshire: Second Interim Report', *ibid.*, xvii (1973), pp. 1–25. For Catholme, see Stuart Losco Bradley, 'Catholme', *Current Archaeology*, no. 59 (1977), pp. 358–63.

[27] S. E. West, 'The Anglo-Saxon Village of West Stow: An Interim Report of the Excavations, 1965–8', *Medieval Archaeology*, xiii (1969), pp. 1–20.

[28] As long ago as 1921, Maitland remarked, in the context of the evidence of Domesday Book and topography, that 'The error into which we are most likely to fall will be that of making our vills too populous' (F. W. Maitland, *Domesday Book and Beyond* [Cambridge, 1921], p. 17), a point taken up by Finberg: 'We

place-name and the growing body of archaeological evidence shows, to see the social and agrarian landscape as much more variegated, ranging from such villages (more or less nucleated) down through hamlets and very small groups to mere isolated farmsteads: in other words, not all that dissimilar from that of later medieval England. Indeed, many – and one might guess the majority – of the settlements which began in the Old English period had altogether modest origins. We are familiar enough now with isolated farmsteads created out of the waste in the course of the twelfth- and thirteenth-century colonization on the uplands of Dartmoor,[29] or of north-west Sussex,[30] for instance. We have also to become familiar with much the same phenomenon in the centuries before. Very occasionally the archaeological evidence bears out the point, as at New Wintles (Oxfordshire),[31] but we should not (at least yet) expect much help from this direction in view of the fact, already noted, that nothing is so likely to escape detection now on the ground as a single homestead, or, of course, to become lost as part of an expanded habitation site. The place-name evidence, on the other hand, is altogether fuller and more compelling. For instance, Old English *-cot* or *-boðl* names, very frequently with a personal name as their first element.[32] And the

---

may easily fall into the error of making the early village too populous' (H. P. R. Finberg, *The Formation of England, 550–1042* [The Paladin History of England, ed. Robert Blake, London, 1974], p. 83) and 'The midland settlement which on nineteenth-century maps appears as a large village may well have started life as a nucleus of one or two hardy pioneers, indistinguishable in point of numbers from the population of a south-western hamlet' (*The Agrarian History of England and Wales, A.D. 43–1042*, ed. Finberg, p. 423).

[29] For individual farmsteads and hamlets in Devonshire from the Old English period onwards, see W. G. Hoskins, 'The Making of the Agrarian Landscape', in W. G. Hoskins and H. P. R. Finberg, *Devonshire Studies* (London, 1952), pp. 289–333, at pp. 310–15.

[30] For example, in the parish of Woolbeding, Easebourne Hundred.

[31] M. Gray, 'The Saxon Settlement at New Wintles, Eynsham, Oxon.', in Trevor Rowley (ed.), *Anglo-Saxon Settlement and Landscape: Papers Presented to a Symposium, Oxford 1973* (Brit. Archaeol. Repts., Brit. ser., no. 6, Oxford, 1974), pp. 51–5.

[32] We should not, I am sure, rule out the possibility that such place-name elements and others similar as, for example, *worð* and *worðig* both signifying 'enclosure' and thus perhaps an isolated farmstead, may have originally been applied in many cases where we cannot now trace them by virtue of a change later to some other element as the settlement manifestly acquired larger proportions. In much the same way, some elements altered or enlarged their meaning such as *-ham* (house, village, manor, estate) or *-tun* (enclosure, farmstead, hamlet, village,

Domesday Book evidence for parts of north-east Sussex, for example, shows us something of this kind of settlement pattern, probably reflecting late colonization: in the Hundred of Hawkesborough the survey lists some twenty-six separate holdings, only four of which had, even in 1086, any semblance of a manorial structure, and no less than fifteen of which had only one or two recorded inhabitants.

Here and there these isolated farmsteads and the like retained their original character for centuries, even to the present day, as with some examples of Bartons in Devonshire that Finberg discussed.[33] But over most of England, of course, the typical development in the wake of expanding population was towards the evolution of larger settlements. Thus we have, for example, the changing meaning of the place-name element *-tun* from enclosure or farmstead to hamlet or village to estate or manor and beyond that and later, of course, to town; or, in the Danelaw, the element *-by*. Such important semantic shifts merely reflect a general tendency towards expansion of the original settlement. Thus Domesday Book can furnish countless examples where the descriptive element is altogether humble and yet where, by 1086 if not 1066, we have a collective settlement of some kind or other.

We can detect at least four main ways in which the development of new and expanding group settlements affected the organization and structure of the countryside.

First, in many cases the new settlement must have been in effect

manor, estate) to accord with different social and economic realities. So too in regard to place-names embodying a personal name. For two interesting cases, see Gelling, *Signposts to the Past*, p. 124. For cases in Domesday Book where the personal name corresponds with the 1066 holder, see O. von Feilitzen, *The Pre-Conquest Personal Names of Domesday Book* (Uppsala, 1937), pp. 32–3. Obviously some of these examples may represent new settlements under the person so recorded. But others probably arose through changes of name in the wake of changes in tenure. Similarly, in my childhood in north-west Sussex, most farms were known locally not by their proper name at all but as X's farm, X being the current owner or tenant, a situation that, in an age when comparatively few settlement names were committed to writing, would surely have led to name changes. In other words many Old English place-names were not simple in their history but continuingly descriptive: they were therefore necessarily fluid. That tenacity we associate with the majority of our place-names begins for a certainty only with their encapsulation in the written record, Domesday Book in so many cases, where what we see may indicate not the start but rather the end (maybe not quite even that) of a long and complex evolution.

[33] H. P. R. Finberg, 'Some Old Devon Bartons', in Hoskins and Finberg, *Devonshire Studies*, pp. 139–53.

an offshoot from an older one and have retained a close connection with its parent. One naturally thinks of the countless Nortons, Westons, Suttons and Astons.[34] And where that older settlement was a manor, then we can see that the extension of settlement is making either for new and separate settlements under lordship, or for the formation of a discrete estate, that is an estate with two or more constituent elements, in place of a unitary one, or for a more discrete estate than previously. Thus in parts of Sussex, for instance, where the original estate unit frequently covered a wide area and included distant woods, pastures and so on, subordinate settlements easily and almost inevitably sprang up in the appurtenances and so evolved or further developed a discrete lordship.[35] Or likewise in some areas of Devonshire. On the other hand it should also be observed that, though colonization thus created or extended discrete manors, there were almost certainly factors working to break them up as time went on. For discrete estates must surely have been particularly liable to fragmentation by partible inheritance or by will, leading to their development into a multiplicity of separate estates under a variety of lords.[36]

Secondly, and so closely related to this first type of change as to

---

[34] For the possibility that Charltons fall into this category, see Finberg, 'Charltons and Carltons', p. 159.

[35] Mr Glanville Jones, in his important article on 'Settlement Patterns in Anglo-Saxon England', *Antiquity*, xxxv (1961), at p. 226, criticizes my statement above, p. 17, that '-*ingas* settlements must originally have been unitary, estate and village, manor and vill, being one'. But he omits the important opening words of the sentence which are 'In many places'. I do not think that this can be doubted, but I am very ready to concede now that I underestimated the importance of discrete estates of pre-Anglo-Saxon date. For instance, I am disposed to think that I did not allow adequately for the possibility that at least some of the discrete estates in Sussex to which I referred as 'often' unitary in origin may have been more frequently discrete. It nonetheless remains the case that many originally unitary Old English estates *did* become discrete in the ways suggested and that therefore, as stated *loc. cit.*, 'it is probable that unitary settlements were much commoner in early Anglo-Saxon times than can now be proved' and underlay many later discrete estates. Apart from these considerations, my acceptance in 1958 of the then altogether orthodox view that -*ingas* names marked 'lines of primary Anglo-Saxon penetration' can no longer be sustained: see Dodgson, 'Significance of the Distribution of the English Place-Name in -*ingas*, -*inga*-'; and also Gelling, *Signposts to the Past*, ch. 5. But these names are still recognized as very early indeed, so that the substance of my observations at this point remains largely unaffected.

[36] 'In general, however, fission appears to have prevailed over fusion' writes Mr Glanville Jones in his study of 'Multiple Estates and Early Settlement' in Sawyer (ed.), *English Medieval Settlement*, p. 32.

be now virtually indistinguishable from it, were the new settlements independent and manorial from their origin. Many of these we may infer from the later use of such place-name elements as *-tun* and *-ham*. Unfortunately there appears to be no means of differentiating usage of this kind from earlier occurrences of the elements signifying simply farmstead or the like, or from other uses denoting groups not manorialized in origin. But be that as it may – and it will certainly not argue away all our manor names of this type – we can with some measure of confidence move back to a much earlier date. In the first place, if (as surely he is) Mr Dodgson is right in his reinterpretation of our *-ingas* and *-inga-* names,[37] we have group settlements – often subsequently discrete – under, it would seem clear to me, some kind of lordship,[38] dating from the period immediately after the Anglo-Saxon conquest and constituting perhaps the earliest expansion of settlement of this type. Then in late seventh-century Wessex, chapters 63 to 66 of Ine's laws[39] seem most intelligible against the background of a conquering society in which some lords are being tempted by the attractions of the west into removing all or many of their tenantry with them to establish in Devonshire or elsewhere the kind of estate structure with which they were familiar in the old Wessex from which they were emigrating.

Thirdly, it is clear from a combination of the place-name and the Domesday Book evidence that over much of southern and midland England, where individual farmsteads or very small settlements had grown to any significant size, these expanded settlements had evolved into estates with a manorial structure indistinguishable from that of manors of quite different origins. How this came about we can, and always will, be able only to guess, though the thriving of ceorls to the position of holding five

---

[37] Dodgson, 'Significance of the Distribution of the English Place-Name in *-ingas*, *-inga-*'; and see also Gelling, *Signposts to the Past*.

[38] See, for instance, the overwhelming prevalence of personal names as the first element in such place-names. Thus, of the forty-four *-ingas* names in Sussex listed by Mr Dodgson ('Significance of the Distribution of the English Place-Name in *-ingas*, *-inga-*', p. 23) all but one fall into this category; and of the fourteen in Kent (*ibid.*, p. 21) every single one.

[39] Liebermann, *Die Gesetze*, i, pp. 118–19; edited and trans. in *The Laws of the Earliest English Kings*, ed. and trans. Attenborough, pp. 56–9. See in general W. G. Hoskins, *The Westward Expansion of Wessex* (Univ. of Leicester, Dept of Eng. Local Hist., Occasional Papers, no. 13, Leicester, 1960).

hides is most clearly attested for the early eleventh century.[40] Certainly there is room here for something approaching the traditional view of the origins of the manor in some cases. For doubtless in Anglo-Saxon England as in its successor state there were oppressive lords forcing peasants into economic and ultimately legal subjection. Doubtless too there were groups of free peasant settlers who, faced by conditions of insecurity most obviously in frontier areas or of poverty,[41] thought it expedient to seek the protection of nearby lords who then or gradually became their landlords. And so on. But, and not least because of the contrast with other areas of England where precisely similar settlement origins and development evolved into free settlements, I would not think such more or less sudden or cataclysmic changes the norm. Rather am I inclined to believe that, probably because of inheritance customs above all else, the expanding settlement of the eponymous settler[42] assumed a manorial structure in the simple course of its evolution.

These three developments – what might be called the outgrowth of a sprawling or discrete manor, the establishment of new and independent manors and the manorialization of an erstwhile individual farmstead in the course of expansion – or close variants of them constitute that elusive 'growth of the manor' in the Old English period for which the great scholars to whom Poole referred (in the quotation at the beginning of this Postscript) were searching, a growth having its origins and driving forces in expansion of population and consequent expansion of settlement. True, as already stated, we need not altogether rule out the kind of developments which they saw as fundamental. But we should see them by contrast as incidental, superficial and intrusive rather than structural. This structural growth shows the three aspects just outlined as (to adopt a philosophical term) the essential ones, so that the manors that first come widely and indisputably into view in the mid-eleventh century either dated (as argued in my article) from the earliest days of Old English society or were a 'natural' feature of that society's development and the institutionalization

---

[40] See above, n. 6.
[41] See, for example, Davis, 'East Anglia and the Danelaw', pp. 35–6.
[42] For some cautionary, important and persuasive remarks on 'eponymous' type place-names, that is names that have been interpreted to contain or do contain a personal name as their first element, see Gelling, *Signposts to the Past*, ch. 7.

of its expansion. In brief, the growth of the manor was the growth of society itself.

But the converse is by no means true. For expansion certainly did not always lead in the direction of manorialism. It could, and in much of England did, promote the growth of freedom, by which I mean not simply legal freedom – which, as opposed to slaves, even *geburas* enjoyed – but economic freedom, independence of any manorial routine and so on. That assarting and reclamation in the twelfth and thirteenth centuries increased the importance of the free elements in rural society in many areas is now almost a commonplace. For instance, as Professor Hilton has shown, there were large parts of Warwickshire with a relatively 'free' society which seems to reflect post-Conquest colonization.[43] Or again, the taking in of land from the Fenlands enabled an already free society to expand and maintain its economic standing.[44] We must clearly reckon with similar developments in earlier centuries.

Peasant freedom then is a familiar enough feature – and, I suspect, has been a familiar enough puzzle for many historians – in much of the Scandinavianized area of England. Whether the 'racialist' explanation most closely associated with Stenton's name[45] will stand up to really close investigation[46] is a question that must be mentioned even though it cannot be discussed here. But at least in some areas, it is reasonably certain that what we are dealing with are new settlements made in the last century and a half or so of the Old English period. This would seem to be the case in the Broadland in East Anglia where there is one of the main concentrations of free peasants and Scandinavian-type place-names.[47] In the Wreak valley in Leicestershire much the same is true, as in some areas in the Lincolnshire Wolds and central Kesteven where the proportion of sokemen among the recorded population in Domesday Book rises to the unusually

---

[43] R. H. Hilton, *Social Structure of Rural Warwickshire in the Middle Ages* (Dugdale Soc., Occasional Papers, no. 9, Warwick, 1950), repr. in his *The English Peasantry in the Later Middle Ages* (Oxford, 1975).

[44] Hallam, *Settlement and Society*, ch. 10.

[45] See esp. F. M. Stenton, 'The Danes in England', *Proc. Brit. Acad.*, xiii (1927), pp. 203–46, and 'The Free Peasantry of the Northern Danelaw', *Årsberättelse Kungliga Humanistiska Vetenskapssamfundet i Lund*, 1925–6 (1926), pp. 73–185.

[46] See, for example, Davis, 'East Anglia and the Danelaw'.

[47] *Ibid.*, pp. 30 ff.

high figure of 80 per cent as against an average of about 50 per cent for the whole shire.[48]

One is inevitably reminded in these 'Scandinavian' examples of a problem that puzzled Stenton as long ago as 1910. In the final paragraph of his study of *Types of Manorial Structure in the Northern Danelaw*, he emphasized:

> one grave problem . . . which arises in connexion with the local nomenclature. In 1066 [he went on] the vills of the Danelaw were free, to an extent perhaps without parallel elsewhere in England; they were unmanorialized . . . The presumption is naturally strong that the liberty which they possessed in 1066 belonged to them from the beginning of their history; that the bys and thorpes of the Danelaw resulted from the settlement of groups of free-men; that the lord was in all cases an unoriginal element in the life of these communities . . . This conception agrees well with the evidence supplied by Domesday . . .; but the place-names of the Trent basin raise a silent protest which has hitherto been too little regarded. Brooksby, Thorganby, Gamston, Skegby, are names which will not permit us to deny a primitive superiority, of whatever origin or extent, to Broc, Thorgrim, Gamel and Skegg. We may minimize the significance of the eponymous lord; we may refuse him the ownership of the village lands; we may believe that a village of free settlers coexisted from the beginning beside his dominant homestead; but we cannot explain him away . . .[49]

I wonder if, after all, we cannot explain him away. The problem of nomenclature to which Stenton drew attention comes up in other contexts too. It arises for instance, though on an admittedly smaller scale, with many of the field-names of Yorkshire (and indeed other) villages. Mr Bishop has pointed to the large number of Yorkshire cases in which cultures in the open fields have names embodying a personal name. And he has suggested, and surely rightly, that, though in the later middle ages such cultures were divided into strips and between many cultivators, they originated

[48] H. C. Darby and I. B. Terrett (eds.), *The Domesday Geography of Midland England* (Cambridge, 1954), pp. 332–3; H. C. Darby, *The Domesday Geography of Eastern England* (Cambridge, 1952), pp. 50–1.

[49] F. M. Stenton, *Types of Manorial Structure in the Northern Danelaw* (Oxford Studies in Social and Legal Hist., ed. Paul Vinogradoff, ii, Oxford, 1910), pp. 90–1.

as single units of ownership; and that the subdivision we find later arose through the fragmentation of once unitary plots by partible inheritance, land transactions and the like.[50] More recently Dr Thirsk has, so to say, generalized such thinking into a whole and wholly convincing thesis on the origin of the common fields.[51] May not something of the same be true for the place-names that so worried Stenton? May not their groups of freemen and the like be not original but the result of population increase, immigration and suchlike into a settlement which never had a lord in any meaningful sense whatever? Then Broc, Thorgrim, Gamel and Skegg will not be eponymous lords at all; but humble, land-hungry peasants first creating, out of the superabundant wastes and marshlands, new smallholdings for themselves which grew gradually into the settlements we later find.

*   *   *

The conclusion of this necessarily brief Postscript is thus that there was a growth of freedom no less than a growth of the manor (though not significantly as classically envisaged) in the Old English period. Neither development should surprise us. For, as pointed out at the start of this discussion, we are dealing with, at least over most of the time, an expanding society, a society of wide open spaces, of rich woodlands and no less rich marshlands. It would have been remarkable had the social outcome been uniform. Inheritance customs, to go no further afield, will immensely affect the consequence of population growth, assarting and the like. But when we have come to terms with all such factors, we will not only have reached a truer perspective of things. We may even have the better understood those difficult but not originally numerous Danes.[52]

The fragility and extremely tenuous character of the evidence for all I have discussed needs no emphasis and will always leave the Old English period as something of a dark age in social and economic history. But we can and should also draw on the data and parallels of a later and better documented age much as

[50] Bishop, 'Assarting and the Growth of the Open Fields'.
[51] Thirsk, 'Common Fields'.
[52] For the numbers of the invading and settling Danes, see esp. P. H. Sawyer, 'The Density of Danish Settlement in England', *Univ. of Birmingham Hist. Jl.*, vi (1957), pp. 1–17; and Davis, 'East Anglia and the Danelaw'.

Maitland taught us to do to gain a further measure of insight. Thus we can begin to approach some at least of the basic questions we would like to ask and suggest answers however tentative. Having in my original article concentrated, as already pointed out, for the most part on the origins of our earliest manors, I have tried here to give some impressions of what seems to have happened over the succeeding centuries. I have urged the need to talk more about expansion of settlement and the inheritance patterns that, along with other factors, did so much to shape its social outcome. And I believe I have thereby been able to identify the outlines of a few of the major changes both in the growth of the manor and in the growth of freedom. But no one who has worked in this period can be under any illusions that many of his conclusions are but hopeful hypotheses which may well turn out to be, in the end, at best what Professor Hugh Trevor-Roper once felicitously described as 'fertile error'.[53] Who, a generation or less ago, would have guessed our hallowed *-ingas* names would, so to say, fall almost by the way? For, as Maitland himself remarked, 'the evidence is too small in quantity and too poor in quality'.[54] Since he wrote that, of course, much has changed for the better understanding of Anglo-Saxon society – for instance in place-name and topographical study, in archaeology, in work on the charters, the wills, the laws and so on. Nonetheless it still remains true, as he said, that 'Many an investigator will leave his bones to bleach in that desert before it is accurately mapped'.

---

[53] H. R. Trevor-Roper, *History Professional and Lay. An Inaugural Lecture . . . 1957* (Oxford, 1957), p. 22.

[54] This and the following quotation are from F. W. Maitland's essay on 'William Stubbs, Bishop of Oxford', *Eng. Hist. Rev.*, xvi (1901), pp. 417–26, at p. 423; repr. in *The Collected Papers of Frederic William Maitland*, ed. H. A. L. Fisher, 3 vols. (Cambridge, 1911), at vol. iii, p. 506.

2. The Extent and Profitability of Demesne Agriculture in England in the Later Eleventh Century

SALLY P. J. HARVEY

Current orthodoxy has it that the exploitation of great estates swung, significantly if not predominantly, towards farming out demesnes in the twelfth century and towards demesne farming in the thirteenth. The general use of the terms 'farming the demesne' and 'demesne farming' in contrast and opposition to each other illustrates the difficulty in discussing these trends with clarity; it shows too the differing associations which the term 'farm' has developed over the centuries, from a short-term lease of any type of revenue for a fixed return to its present meaning of an agricultural unit. The similarity, indeed possible identity of origin, of the Latin *firma*, a fixed return, with the Old English *feorm*, food or provisions, which many manors in the eleventh century supplied as part of their rent, compounds the complication.[1] English historians' use of the term 'demesne' for two different entities, for a whole manor not sublet as well as for the home farm (that is, the non-rent-paying sector) of a manor makes for further confusion, whereas some French historians use *le domaine* for the former and *la réserve* for the latter. The employment of these terms today attempts to reflect their use in medieval documents, but their use there was relative, not absolute (much as the twentieth-century use of the multi-purpose 'secretary', which, as an office, is definable only in context). Thus, secular trends in agriculture are being defined and used as evidence for secular economic trends, while real confusions derive from the terms employed.

The trends in twelfth-century agriculture argued for England still offer subject for debate. Professor Postan maintained that the

[1] *Sub* 'feorm' the *Oxford English Dictionary* has 'it would be admissible to regard the word as late Latin *firma* and so ultimately identical with "farm"': *The Oxford English Dictionary*, iv (Oxford, 1970), p. 76. See also R. S. Hoyt, *The Royal Demesne in English Constitutional History, 1066–1272* (Ithaca, N.Y., 1950), p. 46; R. Lennard, *Rural England, 1086–1135* (Oxford, 1959), p. 128.

repercussions of political instability and market forces meant an 'underlying economic pressure' in the twelfth century (exemplified in the records of Glastonbury Abbey and elsewhere), making 'the employment of farmers necessary', and leading to a 'slowly contracting demesne', and a concomitant exchange of labour services for money rent.[2] This relationship between the Glastonbury evidence and the secular trends suggested by Postan has been questioned. Lennard queried the application of Glastonbury demesne livestock levels as evidence for underlying economic trends.[3] Dr Bridbury has seen no lessening of economic activity reflected in the leasing of manors to farmers: many farmers were efficient.[4] While Dr Miller has emphasized the continuity of expansionary trends in agriculture from the twelfth to the thirteenth centuries.[5] From this a second debate has arisen, to focus on the motives or determinants in the swing to demesne agriculture at the end of the twelfth century.[6] Participants in these debates seem not, however, to contest the eleventh-century base-line from which their trends are measured. Yet passing references to the relative strengths of direct management, the farming-out of manors, and demesne agriculture, at the time of Domesday Book show that even historians who broadly agree on the twelfth-century trends start from different or obscure assumptions about the eleventh century.

Lennard's work on *Rural England, 1086–1135* provides a full and careful discussion of all types of farms, leases, leasehold conditions and payments, but his general statements do not

[2] M. M. Postan, 'Glastonbury Estates in the Twelfth Century', in his *Essays on Medieval Agriculture and General Problems of the Medieval Economy* (Cambridge, 1973), pp. 249–77, esp. pp. 261, 251, 277.

[3] R. Lennard, 'The Demesnes of Glastonbury Abbey in the Eleventh and Twelfth Centuries', *Econ. Hist. Rev.*, 2nd ser., viii (1955–6), pp. 355–63; R. Lennard, 'The Glastonbury Estates: A Rejoinder', *Econ. Hist. Rev.*, 2nd ser., xxviii (1975), pp. 517–23.

[4] A. R. Bridbury, 'The Farming Out of Manors', *Econ. Hist. Rev.*, 2nd ser., xxxi (1978), p. 518.

[5] E. Miller, 'England in the Twelfth and Thirteenth Centuries: An Economic Contrast?', *Econ. Hist. Rev.*, 2nd ser., xxiv (1971), pp. 1–14.

[6] C. G. Reed and T. L. Anderson, 'An Economic Explanation of English Agricultural Organization in the Twelfth and Thirteenth centuries', *Econ. Hist. Rev.*, 2nd ser., xxvi (1973), pp. 134–7; E. Miller, 'Farming of Manors and Direct Management', *Econ. Hist. Rev.*, 2nd ser., xxvi (1973), pp. 138–40; P. D. A. Harvey, 'The Pipe Rolls and Demesne Farming in England', *Econ. Hist. Rev.*, 2nd ser., xxvii (1974), pp. 345–59.

resolve apparent contradictions. Lennard concluded that 'many manors definitely described in Domesday Book as held in demesne were let out to a farmer on lease'. Yet, he wondered where the evidence was for the employment of more direct forms of seigneurial administration as it would be 'unwarrantable to assume' that the greater landlords 'played no active part in agrarian life'.[7] Postan has distinguished the first phase of the development of the manorial economy as 'covering the greater part of the twelfth century, when the movement away from the demesne proceeded fast', thus assuming a significant demesne economy to move away from. In all, the 'farming [that is, leasing] of monastic demesnes had apparently been less general before 1125 . . .'. At other points, however, Postan seems to adopt a different position. 'Manors, especially monastic ones, which appeared to be directly managed by local agents, were in fact required to deliver fixed amounts of food and money, and were thus, to all intents and purposes, "farmed"', and 'farms' (i.e. leases) 'must have always existed on royal estates'.[8] Similarly Miller, who, on the one hand recognized 'a contraction of demesnes' in the twelfth century, and helpfully separated that and a concomitant decline of labour services from a second process, 'the demise of manors to lessees for fixed returns'.[9] On the other hand, declining to attribute these features to a stagnant or unpropitious economic climate, he described the farming (leasing) of manors as 'a traditional method of land management', 'when subsistence was the end in view' whose 'survival into the twelfth century owed something to inertia'.[10] In the ensuing debate Miller reinforced this position by questioning direct management as the general pattern at any previous period. Finally, his synopsis on *Rural Society and Economic Change* stressed the similarity in the eleventh century, if not the identity, of a demesne vill, a manor in demesne farm, and a farm or lease for a fixed rent, the last being an arrangement that was 'ubiquitous' in Norman England.[11] One

---

[7] Lennard, *Rural England, 1086–1135*, pp. 106, 207.

[8] M. M. Postan, *The Medieval Economy and Society* (Cambridge, 1972), pp. 96, 98–9, 97–8.

[9] Miller, 'England in the Twelfth and Thirteenth Centuries: An Economic Contrast?', p. 4.

[10] *Ibid.*, p. 13.

[11] E. Miller and J. Hatcher, *Medieval England: Rural Society and Economic Change* (London, 1978), p. 204.

wonders, then, whether the concept of a swing towards leasing in the twelfth century is not a chimera if farming out and leasing were 'traditional' and already 'ubiquitous'.

The problems may be made more clear-cut by dividing them. The battleground of debate wages over the question of 'farming' (or leasing) versus 'direct management' of whole manors as well as over the size of manorial demesne that the holder of a manor, perhaps lord, perhaps lessee, thought it worthwhile to maintain. 'Demesne agriculture' will be used here for enterprises with large manorial demesnes, whoever held them, as distinct from complete manors 'directly managed' by the lord. Distinctions on these lines have already been made in the course of debate by Dr Miller and Dr Bridbury.[12] As Bridbury emphasized, farming out a manor did not necessarily mean the end of the demesne sector, which just answered to a different master. It is true that direct management of several manors by a large landholder might enable individual manors to specialize or to supply distant and more profitable markets. On the other hand, if, on leased out manors, large demesnes were still maintained profitably, this too argues effective and sufficient marketing of their produce. To use agricultural conditions as a key to the character of the economy we need to differentiate when and where it paid a farmer or subtenant to continue the demesne economy from where the peasant inhabitants could offer the largest return by taking on the farm of the manor or by renting pieces of the demesne, which will also give important clues as to what opportunities were available to small producers and how much they had to pay for them.

Can the country-wide survey of Domesday Book not contribute further to our thoughts on how extensive and how viable demesne agriculture was in the eleventh century, and hence supply some yardstick for measuring twelfth-century trends? As Domesday Book does not supply evidence consistently on the sitting tenants of manors and even less on the character of their tenure this study can contribute little more to the question of the extent of the leasing of manors. We shall just make two general points here which, in other ways, reinforce two of Lennard's *dicta*: that 'we have no means of knowing whether farming out was the predomi-

---

[12] Miller, 'England in the Twelfth and Thirteenth Centuries: An Economic Contrast?', pp. 4, 13; Miller, 'Farming of Manors and Direct Management'; Bridbury, 'Farming Out of Manors', pp. 518–19.

nant form of estate management' in Norman England, and that distinctions were not drawn sharply at the time: 'one type of estate management shades into another'.[13]

The first point is that Domesday Book and its contemporaries often use the term 'farm' in senses other than to denote the farming out of a manor for a fixed sum. One sense is that of an annual or perhaps two- or three-yearly arrangement, which *is* a farming out of resources but does not carry the same economic implications as longer-term arrangements. In the eleventh century when manors were put out to farm (*ad firmam*) the sum could be arranged annually, and this seems to have applied in the late Anglo-Saxon period too. Land of St Guthlac's 'demesne farm' had then been put 'at farm' to Hereward by the abbot at a return to 'be agreed between them each year', and the land had been resumed because Hereward had not kept the agreement.[14] When the primary sense was that of the Anglo-Saxon *feorm*, or 'provisions', the basics were fixed, but not entirely so. In the Canterbury Cathedral Priory list of 'farms' originating in the late eleventh century the amounts were revised from time to time. The 'farm' of four weeks there laid down consisted primarily of a wide range of provisions but included a cash sum for the kitchen as well. A fine (*garsumma*) here was a frequent addition to the farm and varied from place to place.[15] If it was an entry fine paid by a farmer as Lennard argued, then it was one paid frequently from most manors:[16] it seems rather to be a variable cash requirement on top of the food-farm (though these two interpretations are not exclusive). The large manors of Domesday Book said to be 'in demesne' or 'for the food of the monks' were thus not likely to be farmed out for a fixed sum for an extended period. A third variant of the word 'farm' is, of course, for the sum representing the dues paid by the men of the county and hundred which were often attached to a hundredal manor. These are very changeable at this time and among the most swollen. So effectively had freemen been attached to manors over the period of the Norman Conquest

---

13 Lennard, *Rural England, 1086–1135*, pp. 207, 111.
14 *Domesday Book, seu liber censualis Willelmi primi regis Angliae*, ed. A. Farley, 2 vols., and *Libri censualis, vocati Domesday Book*, ed. H. Ellis, 2 vols. (Rec. Comm., London, 1783–1816; hereafter *D.B.*), i, fo. 337b–c.
15 Canterbury MS., Register K., fos. 69ᵛ–70; cf. Canterbury Lit. MS. D.4.; Canterbury MS., Register P.
16 Lennard, *Rural England, 1086–1135*, p. 181.

that Domesday Book was puzzled by the few who were not and once gave them separate tenurial status as 'the freemen of the king who do not belong to any farm'.[17]

The 'renders' recorded in Domesday Book as well as the 'farms' on the royal estates have often been taken as verbal symptoms of the farming out of manors. The argument here is that though some of these royal manors were undoubtedly at farm, a 'render' does not have a single specific association with a farm of fixed returns. It appears in the royal returns for two Gloucestershire manors whose reeves 'used to render what they wished' to their two Anglo-Saxon lords before 1066: the reverse of any fixed agreement.[18] Rather, these 'renders' usually stem from particular assets exploited in addition to the demesne and its attached peasantry. Manors heading hundreds are chief and most notable of those Domesday curiosities with a render higher than their value. 'Render' rather than 'value' is often used when freemen and sokemen paid extra dues over and above the value of the manorial unit. Such dues were, of course, usually organized by some royal agent and often, therefore, 'farmed'. Other sources of revenue were also expressed in 'renders', especially those of extensive pasture and woodland rights. One Hampshire manor had a value of £20; nevertheless its holder 'rendered' £52. 6s. 1d. 'with those assets which lie in the Forest'.[19] We know that the rights over woodland, pannage and pasture in a hundred could be attached to a manor, so the dues from these assets may often be comparable with those paid by freemen and sokemen.[20]

Thus, in Domesday Book the words 'farm' and 'render' were not used specifically; each had several meanings, some parallel. Such usage was parallel too to similar terms in the twelfth-century pipe rolls examined by Professor P. D. A. Harvey with precisely the question of farming out manors in mind.[21] In the pipe rolls, he concluded, 'farm' (*firma*) was used in several contexts, from, most tellingly, 'the farm of the manors which were not at farm this year'

---

[17] *D.B.*, ii, fo. 109a.   [18] *Ibid.*, i, fo. 164a.

[19] *Ibid.*, fo. 38d; Pershore, fo. 175b; also, for example, ii, Witham, fo. 126a; and n. 70 below.

[20] For example, *ibid.*, i, Droitwich, fo. 172c; Wallop, fo. 38c; Molland, fo. 101a.

[21] Harvey, 'Pipe Rolls and Demesne Farming in England', pp. 347–9. Vinogradoff also made it clear that in Domesday Book the term 'farm' had several different meanings: P. Vinogradoff, *English Society in the Eleventh Century* (Oxford, 1908), pp. 376–8.

to the wide use where it included all sorts of additional cash rents. The same was true of the phrase *redditus assisae*. If then 'farm' (*firma*) and part of the verb 'to pay' (*reddo*) can be used by Domesday Book and other documents in several ways – as short-hand for 'food-farm', for a payment by an entrepreneur for a manor at farm, for a fee-farm, or for a group of rents and dues, the terms ought not to be quoted out of context to supply automatic evidence of the 'farming out' of manors at a static rate.

A second point follows on from the short-term character of many agreements: types of estate management shade into one another from the general view of rent levels because, however lands were exploited, high returns were demanded in the second half of the eleventh century. The king led in the way he 'sold his land on very hard terms, as hard as he could', as the Anglo-Saxon Chronicler said, and the repercussions were widespread.[22] Later on, in Henry I's reign, royal lands were at farm for fairly nominal sums, leaving large margins for the 'farmer' or sheriff. In William I's reign the clearest statements of the payments by royal sheriffs and others for land in the king's hand show not a similar but a very different picture.[23] On one occasion the sum asked by the king from the official was the total of the Domesday values of the manors administered, with only an allowance for coin weight as difference.[24] From the huge royal manor and administrative unit of Milton, worth £200 in all, the sheriff had only £12, and £3 from another Kentish manor producing £31.[25] 'Farms' were kept at an economic rate, or even above, by changes in payment from kind to cash, or vice-versa, by change of reeve, or shire-reeve, by increments, and underlying all, by competition between Englishmen anxious to keep land and Normans anxious to gain it. Professor DuBoulay, agreeing with Lennard that in 1086 the 'demesne manors' of Domesday Book were in fact let at farm, quotes the example of Charing (Kent), a manor of the archbishop of Canterbury which stayed in the same lay family for much of the twelfth century for a farm of £32. Yet, as he points out, the manor had to

---

[22] *The Anglo-Saxon Chronicle*, ed. D. Whitelock (London, 1961), p. 163.
[23] Cf. R. W. Southern, 'The Place of Henry I in English History', *Proc. Brit. Acad.*, xlviii (1962), pp. 164–6, for a different argument.
[24] *D.B.*, iv, fo. 97b; cf. i, fos. 100d–101b.
[25] *Ibid.*, i, fo. 2c–d. Also, in the detailed but confused case of Bergholt, it is at least made clear that the king expected the varying sums due: *ibid.*, ii, fo. 287.

pay £60 in 1086[26]. So, though the sum became fixed and nominal in the twelfth century, it was neither fixed nor nominal in the eleventh. The corollary to the Lennard thesis that many values of manors in Domesday were actual payments 'at farm' is that the changes in many values on large manors witnessed between 1066, 1070 or so, and 1086 show that if payments for leases they were, they were not fixed; in the late eleventh century little scope was left for considerable margins from agriculture to be diverted from the landholder as some longer-term leases and fee-farms may have allowed later. Many 'farmers' may have been closer in character to 'custodians'.[27]

Though it is not possible to estimate the prevalence of the practice of farming out manors from the abbreviated record of Domesday Book, it is possible to examine the extent of demesne agriculture at a manorial level. In addition, by comparing the values of manors of comparable size but different structure we can gain some guide as to the profitability of demesne agriculture. Moreover, a number of manors on the same estate with considerable demesne sectors bespeaks landlordly interest even if in the past or at second hand, as leases were often of stock as well as of land. As Kosminsky's comparative work with the Hundred Rolls indicated, the data of Domesday Book is suited to an examination of the structure of manors in recording the plough-teams in demesne and the plough-teams belonging to the peasantry of the manor as two of its most consistent items.[28] The objections to this approach are twofold: one is that a demesne may have a strong interest in livestock which would not show up in the number of plough-teams on the demesne, a valid point except that for eight counties, four from the east of England and four from the west, figures for demesne livestock survive, so we cannot go completely astray.[29] Elsewhere, high values of manors not accounted for by

[26] F. R. H. DuBoulay, *The Lordship of Canterbury* (London, 1966), pp. 198–201; *D.B.*, i, fo. 3d.

[27] The word 'custodit' does occasionally appear in Domesday Book used in a specific sense, though not, apparently, invariably: Lennard, *Rural England, 1086–1135*, pp. 146–7.

[28] E. A. Kosminsky, *Studies in the Agrarian History of England in the Thirteenth Century*, ed. R. H. Hilton, trans. R. Kisch (Oxford, 1956).

[29] Cf. the criticism of Kosminsky's work on these lines by M. M. Postan, 'The Manor in the Hundred Rolls', *Econ. Hist. Rev.*, 2nd ser., iii (1950–1), p. 123; also, Lennard illustrates one difficulty of the use of plough-team figures with the

the plough-teams or other assets can alert us to the possibility of considerable livestock.[30] The other objection is that the demesne arable might be larger than its own plough-teams indicate, by reason of the services of the plough-teams of the peasantry. Yet the services mentioned in Domesday Book are usually only an acre per tenant plough or less, and the early custumals do not specify a significant amount of ploughing with non-demesne oxen.[31] Both points are hazards, but insufficient to justify bypassing a regular and considerable class of data.

The first consideration of this article, therefore, is the structure of manors. The mean average of ratio in Domesday Book of plough-teams belonging to the demesne to plough-teams of the peasantry, county by county, often approximates 1 : 2, proportions described by Lennard and others as those of the 'ideal manor'. However, this mean is not at all representative: 1 : 2 would certainly not constitute the mode of ratios. In Domesday Buckinghamshire, for instance, the average ratio of demesne ploughs to tenants' ploughs in the county as a whole is almost exactly 1 : 2, that is $689\frac{1}{4}$: $1,367\frac{1}{2}$. Yet on closer look we see how unrepresentative the 1 : 2 ratio is. Out of 348 manorial units in the county only 24 had a 1 : 2 ratio of plough-teams. There were more, 34 manors, where the plough-teams were exactly equal, and at least 12 units had a 2 : 1 ratio of plough-teams; but, for the majority, the ratio was much more commonly 1 : 4 or so. As Kosminsky has already shown for the thirteenth century, the numerous small units of landholding tended to be balanced in their proportions or nearly so, whereas the larger the manor the greater the proportional difference between demesne arable and that of the peasantry, even if the demesne had a significant and indeed dominant role. Kosminsky also pointed out that Domesday Book shows that this pattern was already laid down by the eleventh century.[32] As the larger manors were much fewer in number, the two types together often produce an average ratio of about 1 : 2,

---

example of Cheshire but, as he says, Cheshire was 'far from being a highly manorialized county' and it does not appear as such in Domesday Book: Lennard, *Rural England, 1086–1135*, p. 218.

[30] For example, the high values of upland manors in Berkshire: P. H. Sawyer, review in *Econ. Hist. Rev.*, 2nd ser., xvi (1963–4), pp. 155–7.

[31] For example, *D.B.*, i, fo. 180; ii, fo. 2a.

[32] Kosminsky, *Studies in the Agrarian History of England in the Thirteenth Century*, esp. pp. 94–6, 273, 278–82.

so that even markedly different county averages tell little on their own. A high ratio of demesne could either be the result of a number of large manors with a strong demesne interest, as in Gloucestershire, or of a county composed of small manors in which demesne and tenants' land tended to be balanced, as in Hertfordshire. As Professor Duby has pointed out, it is remarkable that almost all the tenurial units in Domesday Book have some manorial demesne.[33] On the other hand it is also remarkable, given the impressions left by the secondary literature with the exception of Kosminsky's work, how many large manors do not have demesnes of substantial size (say more than 3 plough-teams), and how restricted in type and geographical distribution are those that do, with their predominance in the west midlands and south-west.[34] But on a few outstanding estates a decisive pattern recurring in several counties suggests particular interest in large-scale demesne agriculture and definite landed policies at work.

One pattern which emerges is an expected one, given all the practical advantages of locally accessible foodstuffs: that of manors with a very large demesne sector at or near to the main seat of the magnate or institution. It seems axiomatic that such manors would be directly managed even if there is nothing beyond 'in demesne' to say so. Of smaller institutions Wenlock Abbey, a monastery created out of a pre-conquest minster, is probably the clearest example. At Wenlock were $9\frac{1}{2}$ demesne : 17 tenants' teams, whereas only two of the abbey's eleven other manors in Shropshire had as many as 2 teams in demesne.[35] Examples of major abbeys with demesne-orientated manors included Abingdon with the manor of Cumnor having 9 : 26 teams, Peterborough itself with 5 : 2 teams, Wilton with Broad Chalke 10 : 50 teams.[36] The resiting of the seats of many bishoprics in the

[33] G. Duby, *Rural Economy and Country Life in the Medieval West* (London, 1968), p. 200. The second contention there that 'this demesne always occupied a considerable proportion of the arable land' is, however, supported by the examples of Burton Abbey and the bishopric of Winchester. The Burton manors were small: the number (not ratio) of plough-teams often amounted to only 1 : 1 or 1 : 2; and Winchester was extraordinary (see pp. 58–60 below).

[34] A more detailed consideration of the manorial structures and characteristics of different landholding institutions in Domesday Book will appear in *The Agrarian History of England*, ii, ed. J. Thirsk (forthcoming).

[35] *D.B.*, i, fo. 252c–d.   [36] *Ibid.*, fos. 58c, 221b, 68a.

thirty-five years previous to the Domesday Inquiry is reflected clearly in the structure of their manors, and they vindicate the method. The resiting from Crediton to Exeter in 1051 still shows up in 1086 in the character of Crediton, a huge multiple manor with 13 demesne teams.[37] The Wiltshire/Dorset see's movements are betrayed by the structure of Ramsbury with 8 : 29 teams, and Sherborne 5 : 11 teams.[38] Lichfield had a huge demesne with 10 : 21 ploughs, even though the bishopric was now sited in Chester.[39] The important demesne sectors of the newly sited Lincoln see, once Dorchester, were still in Oxfordshire.[40] Though these old ecclesiastical centres continued to sustain small groups of canons or priests, the examples show that the organization of a demesne sector seems to have been strong enough to survive decades beyond the loss of the original purpose.[41]

Yet few large demesnes were rapidly created on the sites of the major castle bases of the Norman lords. To this there are three outstanding exceptions. Adjacent to Henry de Ferrers's castle at Tutbury were 4 : 0 demesne teams and Rolleston with 4 : 14 teams. Here indeed it looks as though the strength of the pre-conquest demesne may have been a determinant of the castle site as there were 12 demesne teams in 1066 before the castle works were started.[42] Earl Roger of Montgomery's castle base near Montgomery, too, had 4 demesne teams alone attached to it and Roger had two remarkably large demesnes in the vicinity of his castle of Arundel: Singleton with 7 : 33 teams and Harting with 10 : 51.[43] Richard fitz Gilbert had 7 : 34 teams at his castle site at Clare (12 : 36 teams in 1066), and demesnes nearly as large at nearby Hundon and, to the north, Desning. All three of Richard's manors had been held by the same Anglo-Saxon family and all three had had remarkably large demesnes in King Edward's reign.[44] So, large demesnes seem to have attracted castle sites in two places and not only did their new lords find the organization worth retaining, but the same lords became outstanding for the maintenance of large demesnes on their manors elsewhere (see below).

---

[37] *Ibid.*, fo. 101d.   [38] *Ibid.*, fos. 66a, 77a.

[39] *Ibid.*, fo. 247a.   [40] *Ibid.*, fo. 155c–d.

[41] F. Barlow, *The English Church, 1000–1066* (London, 1963), pp. 219, 221.

[42] *D.B.*, i, fo. 248c.   [43] *Ibid.*, fos. 253c, 23a–b.

[44] *Ibid.*, ii, fos. 389b–390a.

Most of the great estates with a large demesne near the home base reveal one of two policies in the structure of the remainder of their manors. The sees of East Anglia and Rochester exemplify one in which, a single strong demesne apart (Rochester had 5 : 11 teams at adjacent Frindsbury), their manors were characterized by small demesnes displaying markedly increased returns.[45] Together with 'renders' from manors considerably in advance of their values, the structure of manors points to the general conclusion that in these two bishoprics there was little interest in demesne agriculture beyond the home base, yet there was considerable and dramatically successful pressure to raise rents and dues to the extent of almost doubling landed revenues in twenty years on both bishoprics. An almost positive movement away from demesne agriculture is featured in the bishopric of London. The very small number of ploughs in demesne tallies with the fragmentary Domesday record of the practice of farming out the demesne to a group of villeins: one of the four explicit Domesday descriptions of the practice is on St Paul's estates which include several other manors consisting of villein land only (a state of affairs possibly influenced by the opportunities of the urban market).[46] Small demesnes were characteristic of Middlesex generally, yet the trend at St Paul's may amount to a policy on these lines.

A second pattern outstanding is of estates whose manors show a consistent maintenance of large demesnes. It is important that one or two of the greatest estates which betray signs of such a policy were lay estates, in view of our shortage of knowledge about lay administration. The lay magnates already mentioned provide the clearest traces of internal policies on their manors: on the Montgomery estate in respect of labour and on the Clare estate in respect of livestock. The consistent presence of a force of slaves amounted to an almost regimental rule on Montgomery lands from Sussex to Shropshire. The large Sussex demesnes had larger complements of slaves, but on many Montgomery manors, 22 in Shropshire alone, there were 2 slaves per demesne plough, usually 6 teams, 12 slaves, and a riding-man. It was a demesne policy which did not, however, seem to be at the expense of the dependent peasantry generally, who had a large number of

---

[45] *Ibid.*, i, fo. 5c–d.
[46] *Ibid.*, fos. 127d–128d, 133c; R. S. Hoyt, 'The Farm of the Manor and the Community of the Vill', *Speculum*, xxx (1955), pp. 154–6.

ploughs and included relatively few smallholders. A policy as regards livestock is visible on Richard fitz Gilbert's bases in Suffolk. Both Clare and Hundon had had their demesne teams halved sometime between 1066 and 1086 but they had been built up again. The sheep flocks had however been given even more attention: Clare's flock had been built up from 60 to 480 sheep and Hundon's from 80 to 480 sheep. Desning's flock had been increased to 960, just double the other two, thus suggesting that on Richard's estates there was a carefully calculated and uniform ratio of sheep to shepherd and coherent stocking policies at work here following a demesne interest continued from the Anglo-Saxon family.[47] The other member of the new Norman ruling group whose manors stand out for their high proportion of demesne, averaging as much as 1 : 1.5, was Ernulf de Hesding. His interest in agriculture was chronicled by William of Malmesbury, and the consistent increases in value of his lands have been already pointed out by Lennard.[48] Interest in demesne agriculture may occasionally have been contagious. The only subtenant of Odo of Bayeux's many to have a substantial demesne was William de Arcis with 14 : 45 teams attached to Folkestone; among his several subtenants, his son Hugo had the only large demesne, which we are told had been carved out of former villein land.[49]

One or two Anglo-Saxon lay lords left demesne-structured manors still evident in 1086. All the eight manors with more than four teams in demesne on the extensive lands of Gilbert de Gand had once belonged to Ulf Fenisc, one of the most powerful landholders of King Edward's day. Of forty manors and their berewicks held by Count Alan of Brittany in 1086, those with the most teams in demesne had invariably been held by Ralf the Staller.[50] Similarly, manors of the Staller (whose son Ralf forfeited his lands in rebellion in 1075) which were still in the king's hands in 1086 stand out there in the higher proportion of their demesnes. A considerable number of manors with substantial demesnes once belonged to Earl Harold and his mother, Gytha. As well as revealing an interest in demesne agriculture by a handful of powerful laymen in Anglo-Saxon England, policies on such geo-

---

[47] *D.B.*, ii, fos. 389b–390a.
[48] Lennard, *Rural England, 1086–1135*, pp. 210–12.
[49] *D.B.*, i, fo. 9c.
[50] For example, *ibid.*, fos. 354c–355d, 347a–348d.

graphically widespread manors suggest the use of powerful estate officials.

On ecclesiastical estates the outstanding institutions of demesne agriculture were largely of the south-west: the bishoprics of Exeter, Salisbury, Wells and Winchester, and Glastonbury Abbey. Glastonbury Abbey, the wealthiest of the abbeys in 1086, was amongst the very highest investors in demesne teams. The ratio of demesne in the Somerset manors was high (as it was in Somerset generally), namely 1 : 1.7. But on manors the size of Glastonbury's these ratios are outstanding; on one or two of the largest manors the demesne teams equalled those of the peasantry with 5 : 5 at Glastonbury and 10 : 10 at Pilton. Pilton carried substantial demesne livestock, including a flock of 500 sheep, yet East Brent with 8 : 16 teams and Wrington with 6 : 20 teams and with demesne flocks of only 82 and 278 sheep were both worth more than Pilton,[51] thus illustrating the point borne out consistently elsewhere that manors with substantial demesne teams and livestock did not give as high returns as manors with a large peasantry well-endowed with plough-teams.

This brings us to the second major consideration of this article: the profitability of large-scale demesne agriculture. Even on large manors with substantial demesnes, the really profitable assets emerge as neither the demesne arable nor the arable of the dependent tenantry, but the additional rights attached to the lordship of the unit. At the manor of Wells the bishop's demesne was worth £30, a holding of the canons was worth £12, another holding of the bishop's men was worth £13. Yet each holding had 6 teams in demesne and comparable livestock.[52] What distinguished the bishop's demesne was the 300 acres of meadow as well as leagues of pasture, woodland and moorland attached. This was true on lands of the abbey of Glastonbury generally: in Dorset, Somerset and Wiltshire, knights and subtenants of the abbey possessed nearly 40 per cent of the demesne teams and over 50 per cent of the peasants' teams, yet they held only $\frac{1}{5}$ to $\frac{1}{4}$ in value of the abbey's lands. The bishopric of Winchester's demesne lands too display very high values in distinction to those of their subtenants.

But the revenues from pasture and woodland were not usually derived from their use for demesne livestock. There were some

[51] *Ibid.*, fo. 90; iv, fos. 166–72.   [52] *Ibid.*, iv, fo. 157b; i, fo. 89b–c.

great demesne sheep flocks, but the absence of much livestock is a remarkable feature on many great demesnes. Even the demesne interest of the bishop of Winchester's great manor of Taunton seems confined to arable. Despite its 13 plough-teams, the demesne, worth £154, had less stock, apart from 8 small horses, than two of its subtenants with holdings worth £10 and £12. The three mills, the market and borough, and the extensive jurisdiction over both lay and ecclesiastical dues probably provided the bulk of the revenues. (It is true that the arable of the Vale of Taunton was particularly fertile and may already have been exploited intensively in the middle ages – in 1607 Norden described it as the 'Paradise of England' – thus explaining in part both the large number of slaves and smallholders there in the eleventh century and the high entry fines in the fourteenth.)[53] Taunton's dependent peasantry has a very large smallholding and servile element: 80 villeins and 82 smallholders with 60 teams as well as 70 slaves. The bishop of Exeter's great manor of Crediton with 13 teams, like Taunton, was in 1086 worth less than half of Taunton's value, with a much more substantial demesne livestock and almost treble the teams belonging to the peasantry.[54] Exeter's lands were indeed notable for their substantial demesne teams and flocks; it was not, moreover, a demesne policy at the expense of their peasantry, who were also outstanding for the high number of their plough-teams. Despite this, Exeter's lands were not valuable for their size. Thus, neither demesne agriculture, nor even dependent peasant arable was very profitable for landlords.

One landlord, Winchester, combined both active landlordly policies – a participation in demesne agriculture together with a pressure for higher rents and dues. Many of the bishopric's manors in Hampshire, though large, tended towards a nearly equal number of demesne ploughs to tenants' ploughs (at Alresford 10 : 13 teams). In seven of its Hampshire manors the demesne sector was stronger than the peasants' in ploughs. Many of its Hampshire manors were heads of their hundred, and five manors

[53] Quoted in J. Thirsk, 'The Farming Regions of England', in *The Agrarian History of England and Wales*, iv, ed. J. Thirsk (Cambridge, 1967), pp. 75, 179, 180, form John Norden, *The Surveyors Dialogue* (London, 1607, S.T.C. 18639), p. 230. I owe this reference to Dr Thirsk.

[54] *D.B.*, i, fos. 87c, 101d; iv, fos. 173b–174, 117.

were paying 'renders' significantly higher than their annual 'values' – for three of them, allegedly higher than they could bear.[55] In other counties Winchester manors regularly featured both a high proportion of demesne ploughs and also a substantial slave element to accompany them. On the bishop's manors in Cambridgeshire, Buckinghamshire and Oxfordshire there were usually two slaves to each demesne plough. In Hampshire, Wiltshire and Berkshire numbers of slaves were quite often higher. The high value of the Winchester estates reflects both an extraordinarily heavy and a wide-flung commitment to arable farming on the demesne as well as considerable pressure to raise rents and customary dues as early as the eleventh century. Hence we should reflect before taking the documented pressure on the bishopric's peasantry in general and Taunton peasantry in particular as symptomatic of the degree of general peasant poverty in the thirteenth to fourteenth centuries.[56]

The demands of demesne agriculture in terms of labour are exemplified in the cases of Winchester and Montgomery. Elsewhere, too, the economics of slavery and demesne agriculture seem closely allied, in general and in particular. Small manors, with their relatively high proportion of land in demesne, consistently maintained slaves. At Sporle, where Godric the reeve stepped up the demesne teams from one to four, the slaves also were increased from two to six in number.[57] In Wiltshire, the royal manors with their high numbers of demesne ploughs kept the highest level of servile labour who constituted 25 per cent of the recorded population. In Somerset similarly, slaves and freedmen formed about 18 per cent of the work-force on royal manors, but both Bath Abbey and the bishopric of Winchester relied on slaves even more. Yet numbers of slaves were already declining between 1066 and 1086, sometimes to reappear as freedmen, particularly on royal estates. In Somerset four-fifths of the freedmen were on

---

[55] *Ibid.*, i, fos. 40a–41d.

[56] The evidence supplied by M. M. Postan and J. Z. Titow on the poor opportunities and high entry fines on Winchester manors and particularly at Taunton have been frequently cited as typical even though J. Z. Titow, 'Some Differences between Manors and their Effects on the Condition of the Peasant in the Thirteenth Century', *Agric. Hist. Rev.*, x (1962), pp. 1–13, shows how, even on the Winchester estates, manors in Berkshire and Oxfordshire provided very different opportunities from the costly and limited ones at Taunton.

[57] *D.B.*, ii, fo. 119b.

royal manors and they formed almost a fifth of the Domesday total.[58] This association with slavery raises in turn more basic questions of the viability of large-scale demesne agriculture at this period. Perhaps the decline of slavery during the second half of the eleventh century gave large-scale demesne agriculture a set-back, from which it only recovered when labour was again available at little cost; though the political conditions following the Norman Conquest may for a time have made available for hire a number of Englishmen who formerly worked on or supervised their own holdings. Alternatively, perhaps the rapid permission of the decline of slavery is a further pointer that only a few Norman lords were interested in demesne agriculture.

The necessity of permanent demesne personnel, both non-servile and servile, for large-scale demesne enterprise is demonstrated vividly by three of the largest Domesday units, royal manors, at the one extreme of the demesne ladder. In 1066 Leominster and its dispersed member units maintained as many as 30 plough-teams in demesne and 82 male and female slaves. To oversee their activities were 8 reeves, 8 bailiffs and 8 riding-knights, possibly 8 working teams of three officials each. In addition, the services of 238 villeins and 65 smallholders were attached to the manor with as many as 230 ploughs of their own, so the large demesne here did not seem to be run at the expense of the prosperity of the peasantry. The labour force at Berkeley and Tewkesbury too was substantial. As well as peasantry, Berkeley had 11 demesne teams with 9 slaves and 10 riding-knights, and villages belonging to it totalled $49\frac{1}{2}$ demesne ploughs with 127 slaves, 45 female slaves and 22 freedmen. Tewkesbury with 12 demesne ploughs, maintained 50 slaves, men and women, with 9 riding-knights who had a further 26 teams which performed ploughing and harrowing work on the demesne.[59] It may be that the Domesday returns from royal lands, which were assembled separately, recorded more detail or that less was dropped in abbreviation. Nevertheless these enterprises in the west reinforce the point already made in the eleventh-century treatise on customary services (*Rectitudines singularum personarum*) that on large

[58] H. C. Darby, *The Domesday Geography of South-West England* (Cambridge, 1967), pp. 27, 163–5.
[59] *D.B.*, i, fos. 180a–b, 163a–b.

demesnes both supervisory and fully committed specialist occupations, often servile, were essential.[60]

The supervisory groups on the great demesne manors, apart from the riding-knights of the west midlands, are less evident than the servile. But groups of subtenants were characteristically attached to the largest demesne-orientated manors of the eleventh century, and their position and the structure of their lands call for some attention: they perhaps supply the missing class of officials necessary for demesne agriculture. First, the number of their plough-teams in demesne tended to equal those of their peasantry and not infrequently were more. The two Taunton subtenants who owned as much livestock as the main manor were one Geoffrey with 4 : 3 teams and one Robert with 4 : 4 teams. Manors of the bishopric of Selsey/Chichester had groups of subtenants holding a hide or two apiece, and these groups had up to 6 teams in demesne. All had professional connections with the bishop; they were canons, knights, clerks, priests and even an old-fashioned housecarl. Sub-tenures of canons, priests and knights of Hereford outshone the bishopric's demesnes in number of demesne ploughs. The largest of its manors, Bromyard, had 5 : 39 ploughs, while some of the bishop's knights, priests, a chaplain, a reeve and a riding-man there had 11 : 20 plough-teams. Similar groups held 10 : 8 teams at Ledbury and 7 : 10½ at Burton, and they were balanced between the military, the administrative and the clerical: at Burton four knights and four clerics, at Bromyard three knights, two priests, a chaplain, a reeve and a riding-man.[61] The absentee rule of Bishop Aldred from 1056 to 1060, followed by two incumbents from the Continent, may have strengthened the formation of these tenures for administrative purposes.[62] Such groups were widespread on great demesne manors, from those on the archbishopric of York's estates at Sherburn-in-Elmet and Southwell, to those on the bishopric of Chester's lands at Lichfield, the bishop of Lincoln's Oxfordshire manors, and at Ramsbury, Sherborne and Peterborough. The number of riding-men in similar tenurial positions reinforce the possibility of these ministerial

[60] 'Rights and Ranks of People' (*Rectitudines singularum personarum*), in *English Historical Documents*, ii, ed. D. C. Douglas and G. W. Greenaway (London, 1968), pp. 813–16.

[61] *D.B.*, i, fos. 16c–17a, 182c, 181c.

[62] Barlow, *English Church, 1000–1066*, p. 218.

tenures having a supervisory role in estate management. Three riding-men held from Tewkesbury 10 : 1 teams in demesne with 9 slaves, worth £10 in 1066. At the former royal manor of Deerhurst the riding-knights of 1066 held lands on which 11 : 7 teams worked in 1086. Very high proportions of slaves and smallholders feature on these tenures, yet despite the number of teams in demesne the lands were worth less than the average. The riding-men at Powick in 1066 had 10 : 7 teams together with 'many smallholders and slaves' on land worth £5 in 1086.[63] The tenures of these various knights and ecclesiastical office-holders with their high proportion of land in demesne, not insubstantial returns, yet modest in relation to their demesne effort, take the argument a little further. Demesne agriculture was worthwhile when the holder was frequently in residence and could supervise it himself – especially if the abilities required were also part of his official expertise, as in the case of the reeves and riding-men. When there were no extensive rents of woodlands, meadows, pastures and fisheries to collect, it was worthwhile for the holder of limited land to maximize the demesne sector, especially with a labour force composed largely of slaves. This interpretation also provides an economic rationale for the many small manors of Domesday Book with approximately half the manor in demesne and a small but consistent presence of slaves.

Now, we turn from the characteristics of the demesne-orientated manors to those of large manors with small demesnes. Whereas extensive demesnes were characteristic of royal lands largely in the west and south-west, in the north, east and south-east, royal lands provide good examples of manors which were largely due-paying centres. On many traditionally royal manors the number of demesne plough-teams did not rise above three or four, and one or two were usual. Given the size of royal manors the demesne teams thus covered a very small proportion of the whole: the four royal manors in Kent exemplify this end of the spectrum with teams of 2 : 53, 3 : 15, 3 : 167 and 2 : 24.[64] It is interesting that even in Hampshire and Wiltshire, the manors of Edward the Confessor which used to provide the traditional food-farm for the royal household did not have large demesnes.

[63] *D.B.*, i, fos. 163b, 166b, 174d.
[64] *Ibid.*, fo. 2c–d.

The royal land in the category 'pertaining to the kingdom' all have a small demesne sector – none over three ploughs – in contrast to the large demesnes on manors which formerly belonged to the house of Godwin, particularly land once Earl Harold's, his mother Gytha's, his sister Queen Edith's (Leominster was once Edith's), and his brother Earl Tostig's.[65]

Lennard, analysing Oxfordshire Domesday, did note the low complement of plough-teams and men on royal lands in comparison with other major estates in the country.[66] In fact the royal manors of Oxfordshire had a higher complement of plough-teams in demesne than the royal manors in any other county, and thus indeed averaged 1 : 2, the proportion Lennard suggested for the 'normal' manor, whereas the structure for royal lands was normally about 1 : 5 or 1 : 6. Some counties had royal estates with lower ratios, Norfolk with 1 : 2.5 (this not counting the ploughs of sokemen or freemen attached to the manor), Cambridgeshire 1 : 3, Sussex 1 : 3.1, Dorset 1 : 3.2, Huntingdonshire 1 : 3.5, Wiltshire 1 : 3.6 and Hampshire 1 : 3.9. But in eleven counties the ratios are in the categories 1 : 5 or 1 : 6, and some counties very much higher, with Kent standing out above all with 1 : 26.

The livestock levels on royal estates demonstrate how unwarranted are suspicions that we are underestimating demesne activity by looking only at plough-teams. Domesday Book II, in East Anglia and Essex, and Exeter Domesday for the south-west show that where demesne plough-teams are few, other livestock is at a low level. One of the largest of Suffolk royal manors, Thorney, had only one demesne plough-team in 1066 and none in 1086; without other livestock in 1086, it warrants the conclusion that by 1086 there was no demesne agriculture, further pointed by the disappearance of the manor's slaves. Other large Suffolk royal manors with demesne plough-teams of a half, one, and two teams, maintained very low stock levels, while their peasantry held 18, 18 and 21 plough-teams respectively. One of these demesnes had

[65] *Ibid.*, iv, fo. 83; cf. fo. 93. Cf., for example, F. W. Maitland, *Domesday Book and Beyond* (London, 1960 edn), pp. 207–8; Hoyt, *Royal Demesne in English Constitutional History*, pp. 15–18; neither of whom raise the possibility that the due-paying estate is the more traditional structure of royal lands. This simple, but unobserved, feature of the manorial structure of royal lands may play a part in the later utilization of concepts of ancient demesne by peasants: a possibility which cannot be considered properly here.

[66] Lennard, *Rural England, 1086–1135*, p. 41.

merely 12 pigs and 21 sheep.[67] There is, however, some suggestion of a policy of inter-manorial specialization on royal manors in sheep flocks, when some flocks are said to consist solely of wethers on lowland manors in Somerset.[68]

The royal estates in the three eastern counties supply the best record for assessing trends in agriculture between 1066 and 1086. in general, William I's rule saw a slight run-down of demesne agriculture on royal lands, though it was not nearly as marked as the decrease in the plough-teams of the peasantry thereon. In Norfolk, the demesne policy of Ralf the Staller's former manors was allowed to continue only very slightly diminished with ratios of 1 : 1.6 in 1086 compared to 1 : 1.3 in 1066. Other Norfolk estates in the king's hand had a ratio 1 : 4.3 compared with 1 : 3.6 in 1066. But these ratios were sustained only by dint of a decline in both demesne and peasants' teams of more than 30 ploughs in each sector.[69] In Essex the demesne plough-teams on royal lands were better maintained, and reduced by only four teams all told, whereas on the same manors the peasantry had lost 87 teams in 20 years. The same story was told at Leominster in Herefordshire. Whether the depletions were directly caused by livestock disease or by military demands (there is some evidence of both), or whether higher levels of rent and dues (of which there is plentiful evidence) forced the sale or payment of beasts to the demesne, it is difficult not to conclude that in the eastern counties, and possibly in the south-east too, the higher returns of 1086 compared with 1066 and the maintenance of what small demesne sector there was on royal lands were both secured at the expense of the peasantry.

The revenues of the royal manors in the east and south-east, as with many other great manors, came not from their demesne production but from the rents of rights in meadow, pasture and woodland, the profits of jurisdiction in the hundreds attached, and the appropriation of the more independent freemen and sokemen into holders at rent within the manor. Royal manors in Oxfordshire record the substantial sums obtainable from their non-arable assets, the revenues 'from meadows and pasture, and fisheries, and woodlands, and other customary dues' (or various consti-

---

[67] *D.B.*, ii, fos. 281b–282.
[68] *Ibid.*, iv, fo. 87; R. Trow-Smith, *A History of British Livestock Husbandry to 1700* (London, 1957), p. 78.
[69] *D.B.*, ii, fos. 119b–135b.

tuents of these): at Headington £4 for meadow and £5. 2s. 1d. for other customary dues, £8 at Kirtlington, £18. 15s. 5d. at Benson with its Thames water-meadows.[70] Hundredal dues could double the revenues raised by a manor. At Stow Bedon (Norfolk) £7 was paid for the manor and £7 for the dues of the sokemen. Aluric the reeve who worked under Roger Bigod was responsible for raised rents on three royal manors in Suffolk, at Ringsfield, for instance, arranging that twelve freemen who had paid nothing in King Edward's day rendered £15 in 1086.[71] As with the great ecclesiastical manors, royal manors with such revenues attached were infinitely more valuable than manors with simply a strong demesne interest. One last example must suffice: in Devon, the manors of South Tawton and Holsworthy both had substantial demesne ploughs, 8 each, and comparable assets of demesne stock and attached peasantry. Tawton, however, had considerably more pasture and woodland than Holsworthy and was also head of a hundred; the former was worth over £48 and the latter only £12.[72]

Of course, it was the agriculture (and possibly the crafts) of the peasants and small freeholders that supplied such rents and customary dues, and this prompts a look at the other side of the coin, at the margins of small producers, to see if there are other, more consistent indications of the success of small producers rather than large demesnes at this time. One difficulty may be that, freemen and sokemen of East Anglia apart, if Domesday Book was deficient in its record of population, it was probably in the occasional omission of rent-payers who were not closely tied to the manor. The Burton Abbey surveys of the early twelfth century show a rent-paying element without parallel in Domesday Book,[73] although Domesday Book for Staffordshire is a somewhat inferior production anyway. There are, however, occasional hints that this may have been the case elsewhere. At Newport Pagnell there are passing references to 'the other men who work outside the 5 hides' and a payment of 4s. from 'men who live in the wood'.[74] An important and neglected indicator of a successful livestock-

[70] *Ibid.*, i, fo. 154c–d.

[71] *Ibid.*, ii, fos. 126a, 126a–127b.

[72] *Ibid.*, iv, fos. 93a–b.

[73] J. F. R. Walmsley, 'The *Censarii* of Burton Abbey and the Domesday Population', *N. Staffs. Jl. Field Studies*, viii (1968), pp. 73–80.

[74] *D.B.*, i, fo. 148d.

producing population, whether additional to or part of the peasantry and freemen of Domesday Book, are the rents in pannage
recorded for the manors of the south-east. It was commonly the
custom to pay one pig in seven as pannage dues, though both
higher and lower rates were not unknown.[75] In addition, a number
of manors received payments for pannage in cash, or declared that
pannage was not charged. From the pigs paid the totals of
non-demesne pigs could be estimated as follows:

*Payments in Pigs for Pannage or Pasture and Herd Sizes Projected
Therefrom*

	Pigs paid	Projected herd totals: 1 in 7	Projected herd totals: 1 in 10 to allow for cash payments
Kent	5,350½	37,453½	53,505
Surrey	4,023	28,161	40,230
Sussex	3,566	24,962	35,660
Hampshire	3,734	26,138	37,340
Berkshire	2,691	18,837	26,910
	19,364½	135,551½	193,645

More than 80 manors bordering the Weald received payments of
over 75 pigs a year. With payments in pigs on this scale it is easy to
see why demesnes themselves, especially on great manors, were
little concerned with pig production, and few pigs were kept on
demesnes in East Anglia and fewer still in the south-west. It seems
that in the eleventh century there was extensive non-demesne
pig-rearing on the rough pastures and woodland, in contrast to the
substantial flocks of sheep and the large numbers of cattle and
even goats on demesnes in the south-west.[76] The pig had advantages for the smaller producer. While it required more care than
the sheep, the mature pig was worth considerably more and
though the early medieval pig, like the early medieval sheep, took
some time to mature, probably to its third year, it reproduced at a

---

[75] *Ibid.*, fos. 16c, 35a, 36c; cf. fos. 34d, 180d.
[76] See table in H. C. Darby, *Domesday England* (Cambridge, 1977), p. 164.

greater rate, with two or even more litters a year hoped for.[77]
Payments by swineherds on large manors in the south-west
confirm the importance of specialist pig-producers as well as of
their considerable stock. At North Petherton (Somerset) 20
swineherds paid £5, yet no pigs were kept on the demesne itself,
only cattle and sheep. At Bampton (Devon) the demesne kept
only 6 pigs, but 15 swineherds were attached to the manor, and 13
places in Devon supported groups of between 10 and 30 swineherds.[78] The considerable payments in pigs in the south-east must
represent similar groups, who perhaps, like the unspecified 'men
of the Weald' in a Canterbury schedule, built a 'sumerhus' to take
advantage of the pasturage, and some may have escaped representation in Domesday Book.[79]

We may now draw some conclusions concerning large-scale
demesne agriculture in the late eleventh century. Three or four of
the great lay landlords and a rather larger number of ecclesiastical
landlords maintained large demesnes on one or two manors near
to their home base. In addition to the foregoing, while some
landlords maintained a high proportion of demesne on many of
their manors, others (including some great ecclesiastical institutions) simply followed a policy of maximizing rents and dues. It is
instructive that the bishopric of Rochester, whose cathedral and
monastic house was being built from 1077, when there were only
five canons, appears in 1086 as a landlord interested in expanding
rents, whereas in the twelfth century, with a large house, which by
1108 had established more than sixty monks, the bishopric moved
over to a system of food-farms.[80] One factor in Winchester's
exacting landlord policies may have been its huge building
achievements which, between the early tenth and late eleventh
century, included three of the largest structures north of the Alps.

---

[77] Trow-Smith, *History of British Livestock Husbandry to 1700*, p. 126; *Walter of Henley and Other Treatises on Estate Management and Accounting*, ed. D. Oschinsky (Oxford, 1971), pp. 335, 425, 427.

[78] *D.B.*, iv, fos. 88b, 345b.

[79] Lambeth MS. 1212, fo. 335. A number of swineherds recorded in the Exeter Domesday were omitted from the abbreviated Exchequer Domesday, as also were a number of fishermen and lesser knights: Darby, *Domesday Geography of South-West England*, pp. 417–18.

[80] A. W. Clapham, *English Romanesque Architecture after the Conquest* (Oxford, 1934), p. 24; D. Knowles, *The Monastic Order in England* (Cambridge, 1950), pp. 126, 177; Lennard, *Rural England, 1086–1135*, pp. 138–9.

Proximity to the royal treasury had also given the bishopric experience of the raising of revenues.[81] Demesne agriculture in the later eleventh century was not usually the best proposition for non-resident lords or for building ecclesiastics, yet continued to be generally worthwhile for holders of small manors, where demesne and peasant land was roughly equal. Of course, whether or not to practise demesne agriculture was often decided simply by the traditional structure of a unit or by considerations other than a desire to maximize returns. There was the benefit of local and reliable around-the-year support for the household. A steady cash return, arguably provided best in the eleventh century by smaller units, was to little purpose for many landlords in times of harvest failure, when prices could soar and transport difficulties might prevent the purchase of goods cheaply from a distance. Yet even substantial royal or ecclesiastical manors which raised a food-farm as their form of return did not necessarily have a high proportion of their land in demesne (no doubt because rents in grain, pigs and so forth could easily be assembled to constitute the food-farm owed).

Whether small or large demesne, the great manors of the eleventh century, with the range of rights and jurisdictions associated with full manorial organization, seldom approached the arable structure of 1 : 2 demesne to peasants' land. Those that did were outstandingly the estates of Glastonbury Abbey and the bishopric of Winchester. Hence the evidence of these two estates is not wisely taken as representative of trends in estate management. The trend away from demesne agriculture was already well confirmed on many lay and royal estates in the latter half of the eleventh century. The picture of demesne organization and large staffing portrayed in the *Rectitudines* – the treatise on manorial ranks and services – seems to be a highly idealized one, realizable only on a few great manors, largely in the west and south-west, by the second half of the eleventh century. Large demesnes required much permanent and supervisory labour; proportionally large demesnes, whether on great manors or small, clung tenaciously to slave labour, and profits from demesne enterprise were small. (The very fact that demesne lessees tended

81 F. Barlow, M. Biddle, O. von Feilitzen and D. J. Keene, *Winchester in the Early Middle Ages* (Winchester Studies, ed. M. Biddle, i, Oxford, 1976), pp. 306–13.

to run down livestock in the twelfth century suggests that it was not demesne agriculture which was the profitable sector of the manor.) This seems to be true both of agriculture on the demesne itself and of the arable of the peasantry attached to the demesne. It may help to explain why Norman lords both tolerated the decline of villeins to the status of mere smallholders, and permitted the manumission of slaves. In addition, many factors from the ravages of campaigns to the diversion of men and animals to castle construction probably discouraged the continuity of demesne arable and that of its appendant peasantry.

The political take-over of landholding by a group of foreign lords whose aspirations were often directed elsewhere and who used their English lands simply to fund Continental adventures undoubtedly brought about a situation where the effort of demesne agriculture had to justify itself in cash terms. The customary services of freemen and sokemen and their socio-political support were of little value to a largely absentee magnate class, except when translated into cash. On the other hand, the political and social divisions wrought by the conquest between small free holders and large landholders made the raising of rents and dues from native freeholders easy. (Herein lies an explanation for the occasional record of complaints from the English about the manor which 'renders' more than its worth.) Holders of large manors with extensive assets of grazing, woodland, moorland and, best of all, jurisdiction of a hundred attached, successfully exploited numerous possibilities of exacting a wide range of rents and dues from a large number of people. On royal lands and the large manors of the great ecclesiastics, it was often not a question of a 'farmer' taking on substantial assets of demesne on terms of speculative management, so much as the speculative management of rent- and due-collecting centres or rather of freemen, sokemen and villeins: a very different enterprise.

These policies were made possible by the existence in the eleventh century of many small producers who, partly by extensive livestock-raising, seem to have been able to produce high margins. The evidence of considerably raised returns from manors in the south and east, along with the continual levy of heavy national taxation (in contrast to the partial exemption of many demesnes), suggest the tapping of very considerable surpluses from small producers in the eleventh century. This prompts the argument that the unit of the small producer was more suited than demesne agriculture to the mid and later eleventh-century economy and more successful at maximizing returns. The argument is borne out by the values of manors in Domesday Book. The royal manors of Kent, with the smallest demesne sectors of any, produced the highest returns per man and per plough-team. Kent as a whole, with generally small demesnes and a traditionally free peasantry, produced the highest total returns of any county, and only in Oxfordshire were values per man higher.[82]

From the basis of a study of the structure of manors in Domesday Book it is possible to suggest that it was as a positive rather than a negative response to the political and economic climate that some established demesnes contracted in the twelfth century, and land was given over to rent-payers, as the smaller unit was more readily the more productive. (It seems debatable, as well as unknowable, that contraction of demesne acreage was indeed the *general* trend in the twelfth century, given the development of the huge demesne enterprises of the Cistercians, sometimes at the expense of small rent-payers, and the growth of small tenures into manors with their own demesne, both of which might counterbalance the evidence of the leasing of established demesnes to rent-payers.) Such sparse evidence as Domesday Book provides on assarting in the later eleventh century shows rents from newly ploughed land to be high, providing little stimulus to the commitment in livestock and labour of demesne cultivation.[83] Only small landholders who lived on and supervised their manors themselves found it worthwhile to maintain a large proportion of their land in demesne, and this probably remained true in the twelfth century, if only because it maximized their resources. There is the well-known example of the knight, whose tenure Abbot Samson of Bury St Edmunds refused to renew on the old terms in the 1180s, who offered the abbot £20 – the manor's full worth – suggesting that the knight had

---

[82] Tables in Maitland, *Domesday Book and Beyond*, pp. 464–7.

[83] Assarts from woodland for one plough paid 11s. 9d. at Weobley and 4s. 6d. at Fernhill in sparsely populated Herefordshire. Nearly one hundred years later it was reckoned that an extra plough-team would normally add only £1 in value to the demesne, as would an extra hundred sheep. Yet both demanded considerable animal foodstuffs and labour. *D.B.*, i, fo. 184d; *Rotuli de dominabus et pueris et puellis de xii comitatibus (1185)*, ed. J. H. Round (Pipe Roll Soc., xxxv, London, 1913), pp. 2, 53, 58, 63.

already realized his land's potential.[84] The interest of the great thirteenth-century landholders in demesne agriculture, sharpened by the effects of inflation, is perhaps partly explained by the lack of the easier alternatives which had been available in the preceding periods: in the second half of the eleventh century, raising dues from fairly prosperous small producers, and, into the twelfth century, raising these dues further by allowing conversion of the rough pasture to arable. By the thirteenth century, however, it had become difficult to continue to raise rents on the scale of the early Norman period, not only because the political situation had changed, but also because, with less rough pasture available, many of those who were called on to supply the expected dues had fewer resources.

---

[84] *The Chronicle of Jocelin of Brakelond*, ed. H. E. Butler (London, 1949), p. 33.

3. *Feudalism and its Decline: A Semantic Exercise**

M. M. POSTAN

I

To anticipate the conclusion of this essay: the decline of feudalism, its causes and its dating, poses what is to some extent a non-problem. To use the mathematician's language, it is indeterminate, that is an equation capable of a whole range of answers. If it has, nevertheless, become a fashionable subject of sociological and historical debate, this is undoubtedly due to its Marxist connection. The view of history inherent in Marxist doctrine is that of a linked sequence of economic systems – slavery, feudalism, early capitalism, mature capitalism. To Marx and his followers the rise and fall of economic systems, with the underlying assumption of historical necessity, has provided not only an insight into the past but also a foresight of the future, and thereby inspired their entire eschatology. The main reason why Marxists appear to be interested in feudalism is that its historical record helps them to explain how and why capitalism rose, and to foretell how and why it was bound to fall.

Not unnaturally, the Marxist inspiration behind the present-day debate on feudalism has produced a reaction; but the reaction has merely reinforced the congenital aversion of some historians to what they sometimes call and dismiss as 'system-mongering'. All historians, whom in the absence of another term I must describe, without wishing to denigrate, as antiquarian, as a rule treat the historical past as a repository of bygone facts, and concern themselves with facts only in so far as they happen to be bygone.

* Professor Sir Michael Postan was in the final stages of preparing this paper for publication when he died on Saturday, 12 December 1981. Subsequently it was found necessary to add only a few touches to complete the text, and this was done by John Hatcher. Unfortunately, scarcely any details of the footnotes which Sir Michael Postan proposed to include have been found, which accounts for the rudimentary nature of the citations.

73

Historians so minded have always been reluctant to assemble individual historical phenomena into aggregates – 'universals' – like feudalism, mercantilism or capitalism: a reluctance to some extent justified by the cavalier use of facts by system-mongering historians.

The latter will be found at the opposite pole of historical study. To them the past is a source of evidence for the study of society's problems. If they seek to establish facts, they do so in the hope of being able to use them as tools of social enquiry.

The differences between historians of antiquarian bent and historians operating with systems, whether Marxist or not, are too deeply rooted in personal motivations to be resolved by mere argument. What makes the resolution doubly difficult, however, are the purely conceptual uncertainties in both the antiquarian and the system-mongering historiography. I might therefore be forgiven if, at the cost of some truisms, I try and reduce the debate on feudalism and its decline to a largely semantic discussion of relevant concepts and terminology.

Most easily observed and disposed of are the conceptual and semantic notions implied in the antiquarian refusal to operate with systems. The refusal derives from a belief shared by many historians that the true and only concern of history is with individual, unique, unrepeatable, and *ergo* ungroupable, events. This belief is unfortunately difficult to square with the normal requirements of historical thought, or indeed of any thought. It should be obvious to the point of triviality that in historical writing and in historical thought, as in all writing and in all thought, it is impossible to escape the use of 'universals' or 'group' concepts like war, peace, nation, state, class, conflict, agreement and so forth. In common usage each of these concepts and corresponding terms covers an open-ended collection of individual occurrences. Indeed, it has and can be argued that all nouns, other than personal names, are collective denominations of groups of individual phenomena. In other words, all historians, be they ever so antiquarian, in fact operate with generalized concepts, whether consciously or unconsciously.

The pitfalls of 'model-using' historiography are less obvious but no less real. In my personal view, the attitude of the problem-oriented historians deliberately relying on general concepts is more appropriate to the real purposes of historical study and is therefore more commendable than the unconscious, almost som-nambulic, employment of generalities by historians pretending to avoid them. But commendable as that attitude may appear to some of us, it has not so far proved very productive or, considering the intellectual activity it has promoted, very cost-effective. Its relative ineffectiveness may to some extent be blamed on the excessive hopes invested in it. Problem-oriented historians as a rule operate in the belief that by posing problems and trying to solve them they will add to our understanding of the science of society. Unfortunately, the science of society has proved a most elusive objective; and at least one of the reasons why it has so far eluded sociologically-minded historians is that many of the general concepts employed in the pursuit of social science have proved to be inadequate as intellectual vehicles.

The inadequacy has been mainly that of precision and consis-tency. And yet consistency and precision in formulating general notions are more essential to generalizing historians than to historians of any other kind. As a rule, such general terms as antiquarian historians happen to employ form part of everyday vocabulary and can be used in the ready-made sense, vague and uncertain yet familiar, imparted to them by current usage. On the other hand, concepts and terms, such as 'economic system', are intellectual artefacts. Historians and sociologists who have tried to lay bare the nature of their enquiries as a rule designate the notion of system and other generalized notions of this kind (as I propose to designate them here) as 'models' or 'ideal types'. What distinguishes 'ideal types' and 'models' from the general terms in everyday usage is their artificiality. They are intellectual contrivances fashioned to fit the purposes of enquiries. They must, therefore, satisfy the essential criteria of fitness: they must serve the common purposes of all intellectual enquiry and they must also fit the special purposes of the enquiry in which the enquirer happens to be engaged.

To my knowledge the purposes to which historians should put their models and the manner whereby enquiries are served by models, have never been properly identified. They are neverthe-less clearly exhibited in the use which historians operating with models or ideal types have actually made of them. The main use of a model, as of that of all generalized concepts, is to group individual phenomena for the purposes of recognition. To include a phenomenon in a group makes it possible to recognize it, that is to render it familiar by associating it with phenomena already familiar. Recognition of this kind is the true object of classification; but, whether classificatory or not, recognition is inherent in the very process of explanation. We explain by relating what we wish to understand to what we assume has already been understood. If most explanations are 'causal', it is because the action of causes invoked in explanations is supposed to be known and understood.

The grouping of phenomena in a model of feudalism must, therefore, be so constructed as to serve the common requirements of all models, those of recognition and explanation. In addition, its connotation, that is to say, its selection of feudalism's attributes, must be directly relevant to feudalism's main conundrum, above all to the how and the why of its rise and decline.

The question which this essay must therefore pose is whether and to what extent the current models of feudalism satisfy the general and special requirements of a model.

Unfortunately, the recipe for a perfect and universally acceptable model of feudalism is something that nobody has so far been able to prescribe. Yet it should not be impossible to lay down a few, perhaps no more than two, qualities which an 'ideal type' of feudalism should possess. The qualities are sufficient generality and adequate coherence.

For sufficient generality a model of feudalism must be general enough to fit more than one, that is a group of situations assumed to be 'feudal'. Yet it must not be loaded with characteristics so numerous as not to be found in combination anywhere except in one or very few instances. An example of such an overloaded model is that of peasantry which some recent writers have taken over from Professor Redfield.[1] The latter's definition of a typical peasant postulates at least eight characteristics (or even twelve or fifteen if properly analysed). No wonder historians employing this model have found it very easy to discover that no rural society and certainly no English rural society ever conformed to it. This has enabled them to conclude that peasants never existed.

At the other extreme are models confined to only one characteristic, a single attribute. Concepts of so restricted a connotation

[1] R. Redfield, *Peasant Society and Culture* (Chicago, 1960).

are, as a rule, too wide and too indiscriminate in their range to be of any use for grouping or classification. Thus, to define feudalism as a situation of social and economic inequality, or one of domination and exploitation of many by few, extends the concept of feudalism to a range of situations so wide as to cover all but the entire historical experience of humanity.

An example of a model which is neither so wide as to be unduly exclusive nor so restricted as to be unduly comprehensive is Sir Raymond Firth's definition of peasantry.[2] Another example of a model of sufficient generality is Marx's own image of the typical capitalist active in the age of capitalist development at its height. The image – that of owner/manager – has not only served Marx well in his analysis of the mid-nineteenth-century economy but has also enabled economists and sociologists (indeed Marx himself) to identify the later deviations from the type and thereby to account for some of the most significant developments in the history of modern economy.

Adequate coherence is another requirement which current models do not always satisfy. The collection of attributes assembled in a model must not be accidental. The individual attributes must be interrelated, and their interrelation must be either organic, that is to say rooted in their origins, or functional, that is to say linked in operation, or both. An example of a model which is not thus coherent, which I propose to discuss later, is one in which feudalism is defined as a system depending on conditions of natural economy. But the coherence can also be so excessive as to be supererogatory. A model which defines feudalism as a system of inequality and supplements the definition by various symptoms of an unequal and resulting oppression, is perhaps too omnipresent and coherent to the point of tautology. The tautology and omnipresence of inequality and exploitation may be less apparent in somewhat more restricted models, such as Robert Brenner's, embracing one or two symptoms of exploitation.[3] In Brenner's model the symptom so singled out is the lord's unlimited ability to increase his tenants' payments for land. This ability, however, medieval landlords share with all powerful groups of owners and

---

[2] R. Firth, *Elements of Social Organization*, 2nd edn (London, 1971), pp. 87–9.
[3] R. Brenner, 'Agrarian Class Structure and Economic Development in Pre-Industrial Europe', *Past and Present*, no. 70 (Feb. 1976), pp. 30–75.

rulers who happen to be capable of enjoying a monopoly over natural resources, commodities or markets, and who are to be found in many parts of the world, in many ages, including our own.

II

Thus judged by their generality and coherence, nearly all the models of feudalism at present current are more or less imperfect. Considered as a collection they fall into two parts; one stressing the political or military features of the feudal order, the other relating the feudal order to its economy.

The most familiar and the oldest of the political models is the military one. In its classical version, represented mainly by German medievalists, above all Waitz, and their English followers – Round, Vinogradoff, Stenton and, to a somewhat lesser extent, Maitland – the essence of feudalism is to be found in the fief: the knightly estate charged with the obligation of military service and thereby serving the state's and society's military needs. In this model all other features of the feudal system – the concentration of landed property in the hands of feudal landlords, the political, administrative and judicial authority vested in the landed estate, and consequently the subjugation of the humbler ranks of society and the hierarchy of subordination and superordination in the higher ranks – can all be derived from the functioning of military fiefs.

Another model which is more purely political is that defining feudalism as a system wherein the administrative and judicial functions of government are fragmented and, as a rule, vested in the feudal lordship. In Maitland's definition, feudal order is the one in which 'the estate is the state'. Feudal societies so fragmented are accordingly assumed to have risen on the ruins of national states and empires, and owed their existence to the inability of the state to fulfil its functions.[4]

Other definitions are more economic than political. The one

---

[4] 'As yet the central force embodied in the kingship was too feeble to deal directly with every one of its subjects, to govern and protect them. The intermediation of the lords was necessary; the state could not but be pyramidal': F. W. Maitland, *Domesday Book and Beyond: Three Essays in the Early History of England* (London, 1960 edn), p. 211.

with which Marx and most Marxists have commonly operated defines the feudal system as a political and social order appropriate to natural economy. In conditions of natural economy land is the main source and the only embodiment of wealth, and goods are not 'commodities' in the Marxist sense of the term, that is they are not disposed of or acquired by commercial exchanges but passed on or acquired by direct delivery such as barter, gifts or booty. In societies and economies thus 'natural', the services and allegiances of men in the upper ranks are secured by grants of land, and labour is provided not by wage contracts but by compulsory services. Hence the view of feudal villeinage and servility as by-products of natural economy.

Closely related to this model of feudalism is that defining it as manorial order. On this definition a typical feudal system is one in which the large estate functions not only as a unit of ownership and power, but also as one of production. The needs of the estate as a unit of production account for its regime of dependent cultivation – enforced labour, adscription of tenants to the soil and other features of rural serfdom.

A closer analysis of historical literature would probably reveal the existence of several other models. It appears to me, however, that most of them are mere variants of the four models I have so far discussed. Like these four models they appear to be more or less inadequate.

One of the main inadequacies of the models I have listed is that they are four in number, which is three too many to be of use in any attempt to group the different feudal systems for recognition and explanation. Their redeeming feature is that they all have one common denominator, in that they all postulate a condition of economic and social inequality. But, as I have already stressed, inequality not backed or qualified by other criteria is too general and too comprehensive an attribute to help us to compare different variants of feudal order and to distinguish feudal order from other social and economic orders characterized by great inequalities, such as tribal, capitalist or Marxist-Leninist. In fact, all the current models combine the common denominator of inequality with other attributes, and it is by these other or secondary attributes that the different models are to be distinguished.

Most of these secondary attributes also appear to fit the ideal

type of feudalism badly or not at all. It is not that they are wrong
or irrelevant. Most of them have been formulated by scholars of
great repute and achievement who knew and understood their
evidence. What makes their fit imperfect is not their historical
veracity but the range of their relevance. The range is, as a rule,
restricted either geographically or chronologically, to the extent
that it excludes whole areas of the world in which conditions
commonly recognized and usually regarded as feudal prevailed, or
else that it fails to apply to long stretches of time in the history of
societies similarly and rightly regarded as feudal.

The chronological restriction in the range of relevance is exhibited most clearly by the military school. A model which restricts
the definition of feudalism to societies which meet their military
needs solely or mainly by knightly service and derive all other
features of social and feudal order from the fief, would apply to a
period of time far too short to cover the entire stretch of the feudal
age anywhere in Europe. If we are to believe Stenton, the role of
the fief as the unit of military service, though presaged in response
to Danish invasions in the later Anglo-Saxon era, was defined and
imposed upon the country as a whole as the basic unit of military
and political organization by William the Conqueror. By the end
of the twelfth century, however, its vitality and its impetus had
long since begun to peter out with the development of scutage and
the increasing use of hired soldiery.[5]

Yet the subsequent two or three centuries are commonly and
rightly regarded as feudal, since most other features of the feudal
system will be found in them. In most of them the essential
military needs of the state or even those of the warring feudal
magnates were, in the main, met not by the military services of
knights but from other sources: the rudiments of folk hosts or by
companies of indentured or hired soldiers. In England the short-
lived revival during the baronial conflicts of the fifteenth century
of military allegiances resembling those of feudal contracts were
neither in their substance nor in their consequences feudal, and
Macfarlane was right in describing their feudal affinities as 'bas-
tard'. In a few regions, perhaps in the greater part of France,
knightly service continued to provide the backbone of the royal
and princely hosts until the Hundred Years War of the fourteenth

[5] F. M. Stenton, *The First Century of English Feudalism, 1066–1166* (Oxford,
1932), esp. pp. 123–36.

century. But by that time, even in France, the feudal estate was no longer invested with local power, which it should have possessed according to the strict theory of military feudalism. In Capetian France that power to an increasing extent issued from the state. In Normandy, Blois and Champagne, and perhaps also Flanders, the local powers of administration and jurisdiction similarly derived from the authority of the regional princes. The life-span of military fiefs was even shorter in northern and central Italy.

Almost equally restricted both geographically and chronologically is the range of relevance of the other political model, that which defined feudalism as an order in which the estate replaced the state and which accounts for the rise and existence of the feudal system by the break-up of royal or imperial power, and for the decline of feudalism by the re-emergence of national states. In Europe as a whole, feudalism so defined will be found in, and probably confined to, the century or two following the dissolution of the Carolingian empire. It will not, however, be found in most parts of Europe in the subsequent centuries. In some of them feudal institutions arose and developed not in competition with, or in replacement of, the state but in its service. They were, so to speak, *octroyés*: imposed by royal and princely rulers to serve the purposes of their power and administration. Reconstructing the English polity on the morrow of the Conquest, William the Conqueror established a grid of feudal estates and a hierarchy of feudal powers as a means of dominating and administering the realm. In this he followed the prototype of both Normandy and Sicily where the feudal order was the chosen instrument of Norman rule. It is possible that in the most orderly of the great feudal principalities of northern Europe, those of Flanders, or Champagne and Blois, feudal organization was integrated with princely government and made to serve it.

The classical example of feudalism, established, growing and expanding, not in the replacement of princely power but in its service, is, of course, eastern Europe in the fifteenth and sixteenth centuries. As I shall show presently, some of the factors behind the rise and development of feudal estates in trans-Elbian Germany were economic, but some were unmistakably political. Feudal estates were fostered and favoured by princes so as to serve as agents of state power, and provided the mainstay of princely administration.

Even more interdependent were state and estate in the Romanovs' Russia. In that country the new monarchy established itself by suppressing the ancient aristocracy. It accordingly found itself wholly unprovided with followers and adherents capable of acting as its local agents. A new feudal nobility had to be, and was, conjured up by land grants, fiscal favours and eventually by the subjugation of the peasantry. Feudal order reached its highest point of development in the reign of Catherine the Great, which was also the high-water mark in the rise and establishment of absolute monarchy.

Even more restricted in range and duration is the definition of feudalism as a system of ownership and power derived from 'natural' economy. To assume that natural economy was the essential condition and the prime characteristic of the feudal order is to exclude from that order numerous societies and situations possessing most of the attributes of feudalism and commonly and rightly described as feudal. In eastern Europe the late middle ages saw the emergence and development of a system which was feudal in almost every respect, since it was characterized by unequal distribution of land, by concentration of both wealth and power in the large estate, and by subjugation of the bulk of the working population. Yet one of the driving forces behind the rising feudalism of the fifteenth and sixteenth centuries was the expanding grain market which stimulated the landlord's appetite for land and labour services.

The connection between natural economy and feudalism may at some time and in some places have been closer in western Europe, yet even there the connection was neither universal nor enduring. In England during the greater part of, and perhaps even throughout, the history of landed property, land was granted or taken by would-be feudatories not because other forms of wealth were unavailable but because, in the prevailing scale of social, political and psychological values, land happened to be the most desirable form of possession. Nor was the acquisition and valuation of land wholly uncommercial. Long before the official birth of feudalism in the eighth or ninth centuries land could be sold and bought for money, as it also was throughout the twelfth, thirteenth and fourteenth centuries when the feudal regime is still supposed to have been functioning in full vigour.

Similarly, the agricultural outputs both of the large estate and of the peasant units were never wholly in the nature of 'goods' rather than that of marketable 'commodities'. In some parts of England the main product and the main source of income of many large estates was animal produce, mainly wool; as typical a 'commodity' in the Marxist sense of the word as there ever was. But even in areas of arable or mixed farming, large estates produced partly, sometimes largely, for the market throughout the thirteenth, fourteenth and fifteenth centuries. On their part, the poorer sections of the peasantry depended for their existence on the food they bought, while the wealthier villagers produced and commercially disposed of their surplus outputs. Money, some money, always formed part of tenants' payments for their land. Historians of medieval rural society are now in general agreement that money payments played a large and increasing part in peasants' rents in the twelfth and thirteenth centuries. It is, indeed, possible that at that time payments were almost wholly made in money, and that most villein land was held *ad censum*.[6]

The European region which is frequently cited by historians as 'a land without feudalism' is the Low Countries. It is commonly argued that in the Low Countries the feudal order dissolved very early because of the country's precocious industrial and commercial development and the prevalence in it of money economy. As this view of the Low Countries has been held by some of the most prestigious and best-informed historians writing at the present time, it must be taken seriously. Yet to me it appears doubtful whether even in the Low Countries the link between money economy and the weakness of feudalism is as close as it may at first appear. Manorial serfdom was all but absent, but most of the other political and social features of feudalism were probably as highly developed in the Low Countries as anywhere else in Europe.

Where the region as a whole differed from other feudalized parts of Europe is in the personal freedom of its rural population. In this respect, however, the contrast between the free peasantry of Flanders and the unfree peasants of medieval England is no longer thought to be as great as historians once represented it. In the twelfth and thirteenth centuries, and of course in the fourteenth and fifteenth, manorial servitude, including compulsory

6 J. Hatcher, 'English Serfdom and Villeinage: Towards a Reassessment', *Past and Present*, no. 90 (Feb. 1981), pp. 6–14.

labour services, weighed more lightly on the mass of English villagers than Seebohm and his successors imagined. Some recent writers have argued that in thirteenth-century England, as in western Germany and France, most villagers held for rent, and the numbers of the 'free' or 'semi-free' were larger than those Kosminsky found in the Hundred Rolls.

In so far as the Flemish peasants enjoyed greater freedom than the average English or French villagers (Flemish law under which they lived was commonly regarded as a paradigm of rural freedom) their condition can be put down not so much to commercial development, as to the manner in which the land of Flanders was settled. The continuous process of reclamation and colonization, construction of dykes and polders, required and promoted free enterprise of peasant households: an enterprise for which personal freedom was the essential pre-condition and of which it was an inevitable consequence. In other regions similarly reclaimed and settled by peasant enterprise, freedom and mobility also prevailed. They certainly did so in the recently colonized regions in England, Italy, Alpine Bavaria and the Tyrol. The classical example of Flemish law and Flemish freedom transplanted to new lands is of course trans-Elbian Germany, where colonization was accompanied by the promise and conferment of Flemish law.

Historians may also question the chronological links between exchange economy and the decline of feudalism. The argument behind the exchange economy model derives much of its plausibility from the common assumption that the decline of the feudal order and the commercialization of Europe's economies synchronized in the close of the middle ages. This view is so generally held that any objection to it is bound to meet with stubborn resistance. It has, in fact, met this resistance when the present writer suggested on at least one occasion that in the manorialized areas of England, as in other manorialized areas of Europe, the decline of serfdom at the end of the middle ages should have reduced rather than increased the extent to which transactions between men were commercialized. The argument is that at the height of the manorial development transactions for money were induced by the very functioning of the manorial estate. Villagers had to sell some of their produce in order to meet the landlords' prior claims for money payments: rents, fines, entry fines. In the later middle ages this compulsion got weaker – in some places it disappeared altogether – with the result that the compulsion to sell and to grow for sale should have weakened. It is also probable that the marketable surpluses of manorial estates also declined as manorial demesnes contracted or were altogether liquidated. Certain features of the fifteenth-century economy which some historians, like the present one, have emphasized, that is, economic stagnation accompanied by higher standards of life of the peasantry, may therefore be regarded as the benign accompaniment of a contracting not of an expanding commerce.[7] This argument may still appear to be too disputable to be pressed, but it must be borne in mind in considering the links between declining feudalism and expanding exchanges.

The fourth of the models, the manorial, also suffers from a restricted range of relevance. Its territorial restriction is too obvious to be elaborated. Manorial estates, seigneuries or *Gutsherrschaften*, were never 'universal' and became less so as the middle ages advanced. In England the enormous estates of the Templars were primarily sources of rent income as early as the end of the twelfth century. In western Germany the *Gutsherrschaften*, feudal estates functioning as a unit of production, became an exception by the thirteenth century. The prevailing type of landed estate was *Grundherrschaft*, a mere complex of rents. In France the seigneurie provided with a functioning demesne was, by the end of the twelfth century, confined to a few monastic estates. Yet French lawyers and political writers of the eighteenth century still referred to the French system of landownership and to French society as a whole as feudal. Abolition of feudalism accordingly became one of the avowed objects of the French Revolution in 1789. In fact, the only European region in which the feudal landlords operated as large-scale producers was eastern Europe of the fifteenth, sixteenth and seventeenth centuries. But, as I have already emphasized, the commercialization of east German, Polish and Russian agriculture promoted rather than impeded the development of institutions which were in every other respect feudal.

---

[7] For an early statement of the author's views see 'The Fifteenth Century', *Econ. Hist. Rev.*, 1st ser., ix (1939), repr. in M. M. Postan, *Essays on Medieval Agriculture and General Problems of the Medieval Economy* (Cambridge, 1973), pp. 41–8.

III

This survey of the current models of feudalism and the catalogue of their inadequacies should be sufficient to explain why historians have found it so difficult to agree about the decline of feudalism. They have failed to agree because so disparate is the range of chronological and territorial relevance of the different models that an historian's verdict on the decline of feudalism is bound to differ with the model with which he happens to operate. Historians operating with the military model should date the end of feudalism by the end of the twelfth century and account for it by the growing use of hired soldiery. Historians defining feudalism as an alternative and substitute for the national state may not be able to date the decline of feudalism at all, since states declined, established themselves, were debilitated by feudal institutions or served by them, at different times in different places. Similarly, historians relating the feudal system to natural economy may find that in historical times feudalism never existed, because feudal economies were seldom wholly, or even mostly, natural. Historians identifying feudalism with manorialism are perhaps in a happier condition since manors, seigneuries and *Gutsherrschaften* could be shown to have declined and eventually disappeared all over Europe. Yet the timing of their disappearance was different – the twelfth or the early thirteenth centuries in France and western Germany, the fourteenth and fifteenth centuries in England. Moreover, the manorial model of western feudalism cannot be of any use in dating and accounting for the fortunes of feudalism in eastern Europe. In short, the solution of the problem posed by this essay must remain, as I have warned it would, indeterminate. The possible answers are many: thus leaving historians to choose, *chacun à son goût*, which is perhaps what most of them would prefer.

What may console some historians is that in our indeterminate equation not all the answers are equal. Some, such as that which sees feudalism as the replacement of the state by the estate and that which links it to natural economy, may carry very little weight indeed, because in both cases the links postulated in the models are weak in the extreme. On the other hand, the two models in commonest use, that of the fief and that of the manor, may be more relevant to actual historical situations. Their greater relevance may explain why in historical literature the decline of feudalism is usually accounted for either by the decline of knightly service or by the decline of the manor. It is, however, unfortunate that these two declines happen to be separated by several centuries of medieval history. So, even if the historian's choice is thus restricted to two answers, the equation will still remain indeterminate.

4. *The Matron and the Mis-Married Woman: Perceptions of Marriage in Northern France* circa *1100*

GEORGES DUBY

In northern France the conflict between the two conceptions of marriage held by the laity and by the leaders of the church passed through an acute phase in the half-century around 1100. By then, the episcopate had finished the task of self-reformation. It was purged; and its intellectual framework strengthened with the support of the diligent work of the canonists. The bishops set out to remodel social life, working through that major mechanism, the institution of marriage. They forbade ecclesiastics to marry since sexual abstinence seemed to them the guarantee of a superiority which ought to place clerics at the summit of the hierarchy of earthly conditions. Conversely, the bishops prescribed marriage for the laity: to control them better, to give them a framework, to curb their excesses. But they enjoined them to form pairs according to rules and principles which the evolution of ritual and of religious thought was progressively sanctifying. They affirmed the indissolubility of the conjugal bond; they imposed exogamy in the name of an unlimited concept of incest; they repeated that procreation was the sole justification for copulation; and they had dreams of removing all pleasure from this act. In fact, the order that the prelates were determinedly seeking to impose was not a response to disorder. It came up against a different order, another morality, other practices, that were just as strictly regulated but in no way designed to save souls, tending rather to facilitate the reproduction of social relationships within existing structures. Secular morality and matrimonial practices had themselves become more rigid at the end of the eleventh century, at least among the aristocracy, the only section of secular society whose behaviour can be glimpsed given the effect of changes in the distribution of power. Faced with the bishops' admonitions, the nobles and knights jibbed. It was not only that they wanted to enjoy life. If they were heads of families, responsible for the fate of a lineage, they claimed the right to repudiate their wives at will if they did not give them male heirs, to marry their cousins if the union would be in the interest of the inheritance. If they were bachelors, they claimed the right to practise at will the erotic rituals appropriate to 'youth'. In the prosecution of the Gregorian reform, the confrontation between the two ethical systems sharpened. The struggle was fiercely conducted by a few leaders among the holders of religious power: the pope from afar; his legates closer at hand; and a few fundamentalists, such as Yvo of Chartres, who were on the spot. They conducted it on several levels. They forced the great, who set the example, and first and foremost the king, to follow their instructions, and there were spectacular incidents such as the thrice renewed excommunication of the Capetian Philip I. They propagated a model of conjugality on all sides, developing a pastoral teaching of good marriage. Among the most effective instruments of this propaganda, at least of those most easily accessible to the historian, figure the edifying narratives, the biographies of a few heroes whose conduct the faithful were urged to imitate and who were, for that purpose, ranked among the saints.

At first glance, the lives of the saints seem unattractive. This is because of the stiffness of the literary genre, the weight of formal tradition. But if these writings are taken for what they were, that is to say weapons – and among the most sophisticated weapons – in an ideological battle, they prove very instructive. They reveal how the memory of an actual experience was manipulated for the needs of the cause, dismembered and reassembled, in order to produce a work of indoctrination. I have chosen two of these texts, one written at the beginning (1084), the other at the end (1130–6), of this decisive period in the history of marriage in our culture. Both originate from the same region: the western borders of the Flemish principality, between Boulogne and Bruges. They both emanated from the same type of workshop, the *scriptoria* of Benedictine monasteries. Each of them presents a woman for the veneration of the faithful. Both, therefore, depict a model image of the female condition. Both enjoin that marriage be lived in the way the ecclesiastical authorities wished the laity to live it. They thus reveal the two opposing positions by what they say and what they omit; by the way they adapt the concrete facts of the lives and embellish them or blacken them.

*   *   *

It is best to begin with the later text; it is less rich and, paradoxically, more traditional. It relates the virtues of Ida, countess of Boulogne. This biography was composed some twenty years after the death (1113) of its heroine in the monastery of Vasconviliers, which she had reformed and filled with good Cluniac monks.[1] Here, where her body had been buried after fierce disputes, a cult grew up around her tomb amid the funeral liturgies. In conformity with the rules, the narrative begins with the 'childhood', with all the signs portending an exceptional life and notably with those virtues which are transmitted by blood to those of good birth. It then passes on to adult life, and to the miracles that marked it. It moves forward to death and ends with the miracles performed *post mortem*. All this forms a sort of dossier, well furnished with proofs (including the odour of sanctity emitted from the tomb when it was opened at an uncertain date) intended to justify making a cult official, for the ecclesiastical hierarchy was proving ever more meticulous in canonization procedures.

Born around 1040, Ida was a very great lady. Eldest daughter of the duke of Lothier (Lower Lotharingia), a prince of the highest order, and of a 'no less eminent' mother, she was favoured by birth with power (*potestas*) and wealth (*divitiae*), the two attributes of nobility. Everything predisposed her to magnanimity. The *vita* shows perfect respect for the established order in presupposing that, providentially, the nobles and the rich are good, and assuming a natural correlation between the hierarchy of temporal values and that of spiritual values. In the Cluniac spirit it carefully avoids suggesting that Ida would have dreamt of humbling herself below her leading position, or that she would ever have wished to suffer physically, or that she would have mortified her own flesh. This saint was neither martyr, ascetic, nor one of those fanatics who want to be poor at any price. She was a completely happy wife. The moral preached here is the fulfilment of feminity in marriage.

The moment when, at the appropriate age, Ida, virgin as she was, became a wife (1057) forms, therefore, the major stage in this

[1] *Acta sanctorum . . . Ioannes Bollandus et altera*, x, *Aprilis* ii (Antwerp, 1675), pp. 141–5.

biography. The author took pains to show that the transition was effected in the correct manner according to the social and moral conventions. The man who deflowered Ida was, necessarily, of her rank – a 'hero', 'of very noble birth', 'of the blood of Charlemagne', 'of very extraordinary renown'. The emphasis was placed both on the need for marriage between equals and on the role of reputation which made it possible for 'people of valour to marry'. Indeed, it was the girl's reputation, what was reported of her morals, her beauty, but above all of 'the dignity of her birth', which attracted Eustace II, count of Boulogne.[2] He had been left a widower by the death of a sister of Edward the Confessor. He had no legitimate male child, so it was essential for him to have a wife. He got one, but decently. There was no abduction nor seduction. He sent messengers to her father, who was responsible for her marriage and who took advice. Ida was 'surrendered' by her parents. Then, escorted by members of the two households, she was taken to Boulogne where the bridegroom awaited her. It was there that the wedding took place, solemnly; 'according to the practice of the Catholic church' (*pro more ecclesiae catholicae*), says the text. Is this, perhaps, an allusion to the nuptial blessing? By 1130 this ritual had taken root in the region, though there is nothing to indicate that it had been introduced there as early as 1057.

Thenceforth Ida is seen as a spouse (*conjux*) deploying her moral excellence in marriage (*virtus in conjugio*), consequently appearing as the paragon of good wives. First, she is submissive to her husband, who supports her, guides her, directs her towards the best. She is devout, but 'in harmony with her man and by his wish'. Can it be supposed that a woman might attain saintliness in despite of her husband? She was dutiful, therefore, but also discreet (that is, with the Cluniac *discretio*) in the management of her household and in the way she treated guests; she was on intimate terms with the nobles, yet still 'chaste'. Chastity, in fact, made the good marriage. Thus, 'in accord with the apostolic precept', it was by 'using the man, but as though not having one' that Ida gave birth. Her principal virtue was to be a mother. She brought three sons into the world. (The text says nothing about daughters.) The

---

[2] He was in actual fact a descendant of the Carolingians through his mother, the granddaughter of Charles of Lorraine. Almost nothing is known of his father, who was probably an *homme nouveau*.

second of these was Godfrey de Bouillon, and the last, Baldwin, king of Jerusalem. Ida undoubtedly owed the attentions paid her in her sixties and the odour of sanctity which spread about her tomb to the fate of these two children; to the fact that the first two rulers of the Holy Land had emerged from her womb. The holiness of the conjugal union was indeed measured by the glory of the males who were its fruit. Ida had been made aware of that glory in adolescence. One night, 'as she surrendered to sleep', she had seen the sun descend in the sky and stay for a moment in her breast. Hagiography delights in omens, it gladly evokes dreams. This one, in truth, is dangerously coloured with pre-pubescent eroticism. The monastic writer was well aware of this. He took care. Ida was sleeping, he says, but with her spirit turned 'towards things on high'. The dream, therefore, did not draw her downwards, towards pleasure. It proclaimed that the virgin would be a mother, that the fruit of her womb would be blessed. It proclaimed a holy motherhood. The whole *vita* is organized into a celebration of childbirth.

Genus, gignere, generositas: these words punctuate the first part of the narrative. Note their carnal connotation; they emphasize blood, good blood, noble birth. Ida's functon – like the function of all girls introduced by the rites of matrimony into noble houses – was to form 'by the grace of God' a link in a genealogy.[3] She gave birth, she nourished males. She is not praised for having nourished her sons spiritually, nor for having instructed them, nor for having prepared them by education for the exploits that brought them fame. It is for having breast-fed them, forbidden them to be given milk from another breast so that they should not be 'contaminated by bad morals'.

It is said that Ida continued the function of procreation in another form after she became a widow (*circa* 1070), and was 'deprived of the consolation of a man'. She was 'cheered nevertheless by the nobility of her sons', and 'enriched by the love from above'. Under the authority of her eldest boy, Eustace III, who

---

[3] This is how she appears in the genealogies of the counts of Boulogne, excellently edited by L. Genicot: *Études sur les principautés lotharingiennes* (Louvain, 1975), ch. 10, 'Princes territoriaux et sang carolingien. La *Genealogia comitum Buloniensium*'. The earliest of these dates from 1082–7, when her second son, Godfrey, was not yet heir to anything but the name and the ambitions of his grandfather and maternal uncle. Ida is the only contemporary female in this genealogy to merit an individual eulogy.

had succeeded his father as head of the house, her virtues were perpetuated. As always this was by reproduction, but no longer from her body. Henceforth Ida gave birth via her wealth; more precisely, via her money. After the deaths of her husband and his father, she reached an understanding with his relations to sell off his allods. She used this money, again emanating from the paternal clan (*genus*), to breed new sons, this time spiritual ones: monks. She did not act alone, obviously, but always in harmony with the male into whose power she had slipped. With the 'advice' and 'help' of her son, she 'fertilized' the Boulogne region, reconstructing, reforming and founding three monasteries in succession. They were monasteries of men; carnal or not, only male offspring counted. She did not become a nun herself. 'Her mortal husband having disappeared, she moved on', of course, 'to be united with the immortal bridegroom by a life of chastity and celibacy'. She gradually removed herself from the protection of her son and attached herself to another, spiritual, family. Hugh of Cluny adopted her 'as a daughter'. But she was to live there, as was proper, in a state of subordination, still submissive to men. And when she came to take up residence near the last monastery she had built, la Capelle Sainte Marie, at the door and surrounded by her followers, it was under the authority of the father abbot. Psalm-chanting but 'in moderation', she was foster-mother above all: feeding the poor; feeding the monastic community; 'serving' men, as it is good that a woman should never cease to do.

That the major virtue (*virtus*) of this saint was motherhood emerges again from the specific character of two of the miracles attributed to her. She performed the first during her lifetime in the monastery of la Capelle. Among the people who lived off her bounty was a little deaf and dumb girl. One feast-day, at the morning service, the child's mother brought her to church in the retinue of the countess. It was cold and the little one was shivering. She snuggled under Ida's cloak. It was as though the odour of the clothing gave her new life; she began to hear, and to speak. What were her first words? 'Mater, mater!' Provided by the abbot with a prebend, the subject of the miracle none the less sinned. She herself conceived and gave birth, losing not only virginity but pension and health as well. However, Ida not once but twice extricated her from the weakness into which she had twice relapsed, purifying the sinful motherhood which the girl had been guilty of; finally becoming again, not once but twice, a foster-mother, since at each rebirth the prebend was restored. The other miracle took place at her tomb, probably shortly before the *vita* was written. Again a woman benefited from it. This was the daughter of Eustace III, Ida's own granddaughter, Matilda. Stricken with a bad fever, 'confident and assuming the saintliness of the blessed', she had gone to Ida's tomb as the first pilgrim. She was cured, her grandmother preferring to project her thaumaturgical powers on to her own line, a sort of tree of Jesse springing from her bountiful womb.

The evidence shows nothing exceptional about the life of this princess. It was normal at the end of the eleventh century for girls of her social rank to marry valiant warriors, give birth to others and, when widowed, give of their bounty to monasteries with the agreement of their eldest sons; and to be associated finally with monastic liturgies. There is nothing exceptional in this except to have brought Godfrey de Bouillon into the world.[4] If two of Ida's sons had not been so illustrious, would her remains have been the subject of dispute in 1113? Would her tomb have been opened later? Would she have been declared a saint around 1130? The instigator of this official recognition was probably that same Matilda who was cured by her grandmother from beyond the tomb. Heiress of the county of Boulogne, she had married Stephen of Blois. Her other grandmother was Margaret of Scotland, already regarded as a saint and shown by her earliest biography (1093–5) to have agreed to marry for the sole purpose of becoming a mother. The cult of St Margaret had just been developed, at the same time as that of Edward the Confessor, by Edith Matilda, wife of King Henry I and therefore aunt of Stephen of Blois, but also the maternal aunt of Matilda of Boulogne.[5] When there was some thought of transferring the seat of the bishop from Morinie to Boulogne, when her husband was seeing his hope of succeeding the king of England growing, in all

---

4 We know the legends which blossomed round the person of the first 'advocate' of the Holy Sepulchre. The fable of the swan from which their original seed is said to have issued was told about him and his brother as early as 1184: William of Tyre, *Historia rerum in partibus transmarinis*, 1 vol. in 2 (Recueil des histoires des croisades. Historiens occidentaux, i, Paris, 1844), pp. 571–2.

5 D. Baker, '"A Nursery of Saints": St. Margaret of Scotland Reconsidered', in D. Baker (ed.), *Studies in Church History*, subsidia 1, *Medieval Women* (Oxford, 1978), pp. 119–41.

probability she followed her maternal aunt's example and commissioned a eulogy of Ida from the monks of Vasconviliers.

It seems to me that the monks were a little embarrassed and ill at ease at finding only a talent for procreation as the principal argument for saintliness in the dossier. It can be sensed in the prologue which sets out to justify the course to be taken. The world, says the author, is moving towards its end. Attacks by Satan are multiplying. What is there to call on except the prayers or virtues of the saints? Happily, Providence has distributed saintliness through all 'degrees' of the social order. Even women were to be found among the saints; even married women, on condition, obviously, that they were mothers. It could then happen that they were 'inscribed in the book of life because of their virtues and *those of their sons*'. None the less, to overcome lingering reservations, the biographer judged it necessary to show what was good about the married state. To justify marriage he quoted Paul: 'It is better to marry than to burn' (*melius est nubere quam uri*); marriage was a remedy for lust. He recalled that, 'according to the law', it was prolific fertility which exalted it. Finally, he asserted that it must be lived in chastity, 'without which there is nothing good'; 'of course, virginity is good but it is proved that chastity after childbirth is great'. Once these principles had been set out as a guide, it was permissible for a Benedictine to establish that a wife could be a saint. This he does in relation to the Cluniac lady, discreetly, without causing any offence, and with a sharp sense of social expedience. He suggests a picture of good marriage completely in conformity with the teachings of the Scriptures and of St Augustine. Nevertheless, since the biographer was serving the interests of a house of the highest nobility, he was careful to avoid too great a disharmony between the example proposed and the code of values to which the high aristocracy subscribed. The two systems of morality, that of the church and that of the dynasties, are reconciled here. I am not talking only about the celebration of power and wealth that each of the heroine's exploits illustrates. The two patterns of behaviour are made to coincide mainly at two levels. First, it is asserted that the woman's condition is to be dominated: by her father who gives her to whom he pleases; by her husband who controls and watches over her; then by her eldest son; and finally, when this latter has pushed the mother with whom he is burdened out of the house, by the monks of the family monastery, one of whose roles is precisely to open its doors to the women of the lineage who have become marginal, when they have ceased to be useful. Secondly, there is also agreement on the principle that the wife is destined to co-operate in the glory of the line by providing it with children, with boys who would be valiant. To proclaim the image of femininity and conjugality held by all the heads of noble houses at the beginning of the twelfth century as in accordance with the divine plan was surely the best way of making them acknowledge, discreetly, *en passant*, without overemphasis, that the conjugal pact should be concluded according 'to the practices of the Catholic church' and that it was desirable that the married couple show at least the appearance of chastity.

*   *   *

Some fifty years earlier a picture had been presented by another, or rather by two other texts, since two successive versions of the same *vita* dating from the eleventh century have been preserved. This picture is different because the system of images to which it wished to correspond was not, I think, aristocratic but popular. True, the heroine, Godelive, is well born, 'of famous parents'. She bears a Teutonic name; the second biographer even feels the need to supply a translation: 'dear to God' (*cara Deo*). This name is eminently suited to a saint, so eminently that one might well ask whether the name, if not the person herself, is mythical. Rest assured. Godelive really did exist. The facts given about her descent are indisputably precise. Her father, Heinfridus of Londe-fort in the Boulonnais, is named in contemporary charters. He was a knight of Eustace of Boulogne, Ida's husband, though of humbler birth than Eustace and his family. However, they still stood well above ordinary folk – above the strict line that the seigneurial mode of production drew between dominant and dominated. If I have used the word 'popular' it is because the biography I am analysing was not written at the request of an illustrious family by the monks of an *Eigenkloster*. The devotion inspired by Godelive sprang up in Ghistelle, ten kilometres from Bruges, the village on the Flanders coast where she was buried. The earliest biographer says this happened 'under pressure from numerous of the faithful'. He did not lie. What he tells us about the forms of piety which took place at the tomb, and of the miracles of which he was shown the evidence, shows that the cult actually did spring from the peasantry. He saw the earth adjacent to the tomb miraculously transformed into white stones. He saw these stones, which people had taken home with them 'out of devotion', turn into jewels. He saw people sick with fever, invalids, coming to drink the water of the pool into which Godelive had been plunged. The church leaders had their hands forced by this fervour; they yielded. On 30 July 1084, at Ghistelle, the bishop of Noyon-Tournai, Radebod II, instituted the elevation of the relics of a woman who had died there, perhaps fourteen years earlier. He did this at the very time that he entrusted the church of Oudenbourg to St Arnulf of Soissons in order to establish Benedictines from St-Bertin there, and with the same intentions – of strengthening the ecclesiastical structure on the borders of his diocese. Nevertheless, the prelate wanted the legend adapted to serve the attempt to raise the moral standards of a population which was still very primitive. The manipulation is obvious. Yet there are still traces of the original narrative. They are very clear in the version of the *vita* which the Bollandists published from a manuscript originating in the abbey of Oudenbourg, and therefore later (though only slightly, it would appear) than the canonization.[6] They are even clearer in the text which this adaptation perfected – in the report which Drogo, monk of Bergues-St-Winock, wrote immediately before the intervention by the bishop of Noyon and in order to prepare the way for it.[7]

How far was the process of reordering or officialization taken? Was not the flow of religiosity which the elevation of the relics aimed to stem really very heterodox from the outset? This hypothesis was cautiously formulated by Jacques Le Goff, when I was commenting on this document in one of my seminars. There was no question of sorceresses, or very little, in the eleventh-century texts, he pointed out. Did the church at that time annex such women to herself (those at least whose memory was still alive among the humble) because they had perished tragically, killed by the *ministeriales*, the repressive agents of civil power? Were they

---

[6] *Acta sanctorum . . . Ioannes Bollandus et altera*, xxvii, *Julii* ii (Antwerp, 1721), pp. 403 ff.

[7] Edited by Fr Coens from a St-Omer manuscript emanating from the abbey of Clairmarais: *La vie ancienne de sainte Godelive de Ghistelles par Drogon de Bergues*, ed. M. Coens (Analecta Bollandiana, xliv, Brussels, 1926), pp. 102–37.

systematically exorcized by the 'conversion' of their reputation and transformed into saints? I am not sure that it is necessary to follow this conjecture too far, but the fact remains that if Godelive was canonized, perhaps it was really to remove whatever was controversial from the veneration that was paid her. Two of the four miracles recalled by the first biographer are of a type to support this supposition. Godelive was a healer; she cured paralyses. She came to the aid of a man and a woman whom Heaven had punished for working at a time prohibited by the ecclesiastical authorities. The man was harvesting on a Saturday evening. His hand stayed stuck to the ears of corn. The woman, on a feast day, after mass, was stirring a cauldron of dye with a stick. It stuck to her hand. That Godelive should have freed these two labouring hands, cancelling the effects of divine wrath, puts her on the side of the people. She had overcome the fulminations of the priests. Would she not have been extolled as the champion of resistance to clerical oppression? There is an incentive here to detect snatches of a different, popular, discourse beneath the edifying, soothing phrases of the *vita*. None the less it was remodelled with one main purpose. Like the biography of St Ida, but perhaps in another social field, it was to help propagate the ecclesiastical morality of marriage.

In a typology of sanctity, the daughter of Heinfridus, knight of Boulogne, would take her place among the martyrs. But would she also be counted among the virgins? The Bollandists said so. Her virginity, they wrote, could not be doubted; at Ghistelle she had always been regarded as a virgin. Their reassurance is certainly necessary. In fact the two eleventh-century texts contain nothing which could support this assertion. These manuscripts do not say anything about virginity. For their authors – remarkably enough – this is not the important feature. They emphasize the martyrdom. It is the martyrdom, however, of a wife. Godelive was the victim of a bad marriage. The hagiographies proclaim this loud and clear, with the intention *inter alia* of bringing out, in the negative, what constitutes a good marriage.

The word *virgo* is applied to Godelive only once, to describe her condition before her parents gave her to a husband. Her fate, like that of all girls, was to be married at the end of her childhood (*pueritia*). Unlike Ida's case, however, corrupt procedures were employed from the beginning, from the betrothal (*desponsatio*) and conclusion of the agreement. She was modest and devout, as are all saints in childhood. She was sought, however, by a host of suitors who were on fire with 'love', say the two texts. Faithful to the original texts they were rewriting, they do actually give a place to physical desire, to the attraction of the female body. Both versions of the *vita* stress the young girl's charms. Her only fault was that she was dark, with black hair and eyebrows. But Drogo at once puts this right. Her skin looked all the whiter as a result, 'which is agreeable, pleasing in women, and which holds a place of honour with many'. One of the young men (*juvenes*), Bertolf, was 'powerful', of 'distinguished birth by direct descent', an officer of the count of Flanders in the district of Bruges.[8] It was he who won her. Not that Godelive would have chosen him herself, for she had no say. The gallant, moreover, did not speak to her but to her parents, as those who had the power to give her to him. The agreement was wrongful on two counts. First, Bertolf had acted of his own 'will'. His mother later took him to task for not consulting either herself or his father, and this criticism was valid, for good marriage was not an individual but a family affair. Unless he was an orphan, as was Eustace II of Boulogne, the boy too must leave it to his parents. The second fault was that Godelive's father and mother 'preferred Bertolf for his dower (*dos*)' – he was the richest. A marriage for money is a bad marriage. Popular wisdom is expressed here.

Badly matched, the union was further corrupted in its second conclusive phase. Bertolf took Godelive home; that is, to his mother. She lived apart from her husband, perhaps repudiated by him, and either accommodating her youngest son or else accommodated by him. Whichever was the case he was able to take a wife; the marriage bed in the house was vacant. But his mother was also living there, which did not help matters. Here, another classic theme arises – the complaints of the badly married. The journey from the Boulonnais to the outskirts of Bruges was quite a

---

[8] He was probably the son (a cadet and consequently seeking to establish himself by marriage) of a comital officer settled at Bruges. In 1012 the castellan of Bruges was called Bertolf. In 1067 Erembaud, the father of a different Bertolf, held the same office. The hero of this story, therefore, probably belonged to the famous clan whose members assassinated Charles the Good in 1127, and not to the family of Conon, lord of Oudenbourg and nephew of Bishop Radebod. For the latter suggestion, see N. Huyghebaert, 'Un moine hagiographe: Drogon de Bergues-Saint-Winoc', *Sacris Erudiri*, xx (1971), p. 222.

long one, probably necessitating a night spent *en route*. During the journey the Evil One suddenly struck the spirit of the newly-wed man and he conceived 'a hatred' for his wife. The case of Philip Augustus and Ingeborg naturally comes to mind; not by any means the fiasco (the queen of France in fact vehemently rejected this), but the immediate repulsion. Bertolf was strengthened in this attitude by the long talk his mother gave him when he arrived. 'All mothers-in-law', writes Drogo, 'hate their daughters-in-law'. (Again the people are speaking through his mouth, and in sayings as is their custom.) 'They are afire to see a son married, but immediately become jealous of him and his wife'. This woman not only upbraided her son for not consulting her, but also poked fun at him for his choice. The girl he had brought home was not only a stranger, she was also swarthy: 'so there were not enough crows here, that you go and take one out of a nest in another country (*in alia patria*)'. Bertolf then withdrew, refusing to take part in the marriage ceremonies (*ordo nuptiarum*). He stayed away during the three ritual feast-days on the pretext of business or justice. Appearances were kept up, joy was feigned. The rites, however, were inverted. A woman, his mother, took the husband's role. It was a transgression of the moral order, of the sexual order; an improbable turn of events such as forms the plot of miracle stories.

The corruption of the union was completed in the period following the nuptial ceremonies. Scarcely had he returned than Bertolf was off again, this time to stay with his father. His wife remained at the conjugal hearth, abandoned. She filled her role as best she could; she kept house, she managed the servants. She was, none the less, *desolata*. Solitude was more oppressive at night. Then, she prayed. In the daytime she spun and wove. She spent her time in the fashion of nuns and *béguines*, anxious to conquer idleness, the enemy of the soul, by work and prayer. The author of the second version (a Benedictine) emphasizes these words: 'with this shield, she repulsed the darts of those day-dreams which customarily overwhelm adolescence'. Striving to make the first *vita* more convincing, the hagiographer is really concerned to give assurance that, left alone, this girl did not become unchaste, and asserts that no gossip about her was ever spread abroad. This was a necessary precaution. Did not general opinion aver that women, particularly young women, were natu-rally depraved and succumbed to sin, that is to say lust, as soon as one took one's eye off them? And it was precisely because of this that the husband had to stay close to his wife. The text here extends an exhortation to husbands. They must be there, in adversity as in prosperity, to bear their burdens for them, bound as they are *de jure* to support their companion, to live with her patiently (*patienter*) till death, since they are two in one flesh; since, rather, they form a single body by *copulatio conjugii*.

However perverted, the bond was still not untied. Bertolf now consulted both his parents. He wanted to be rid of his wife. It is indeed remarkable that the simple idea of repudiating her did not cross the minds of these evil people – according to these edifying narratives. Had it already become unseemly at this social level to drive one's wife from one's house, *motu proprio*? In fact all that was planned was to drive away (*deturpare*) the young bride; more precisely, in Bertolf's words, 'to take her colour away'. She was put on bread and water, while the servants gorged. Godelive did not waste away over much. Sympathetic neighbours and female relatives secretly supplied her with food. (There was no miracle, no intervention from Heaven but, as in popular narratives, action by wholly terrestrial persons.) None the less, she grew tired of so many insults and took flight. This was what they were waiting for. Leaving the home was a transgression, and this transgression was her downfall. The monk Drogo does not realize this. But his colleague, who improved the first version, thought it right to acknowledge that Godelive was thus transgressing the 'evangelic precept', the prohibition on separating those whom God had joined together. How can this be admitted on the part of a woman whom one is putting forward as a saint? Then comes the excuse: the physical terror (*trepidatio carnis*) which stirred many martyrs. This sort of addition to the manuscript suggests that Godelive's reputation with scholars was not so secure at the outset as to make support from argument unnecessary. It was this that led to the rewriting, and amplification, of the biography. Starving, barefoot, Godelive journeyed towards her native country. She did not go alone, but with a companion, because women who were not profligate did not travel the roads unescorted. She demanded justice, but through her father. It was not appropriate for the woman, always a minor, to defend her rights herself. She delegated them to a man; if not her husband or son, then a male of her line. Heinfridus welcomed her and decided to appeal to the wicked husband's lord, the count of Flanders, whose *ministerialis* Bertolf was.

At this point the two hagiographic narratives change tack, cease preaching morality and talk about law – the new law which the church was working to get secular society to acknowledge at the end of the eleventh century. Both versions, the second more vehemently, proclaim the exclusive competence of episcopal justice in questions of marriage. I do not find this claim expressed so explicitly in the north of France before this double manifesto grafted on to a story of a dishonoured wife. The monk Drogo skilfully puts into the mouth of a former count a speech addressed to the current count, Robert the Frisian. He hoped in this way to prompt the latter to conduct himself properly and curtail his prerogatives, as his predecessor is thought to have done. The good prince is therefore heard proclaiming that he renounces the right to judgement, and that it falls to the bishop of the diocese to understand matters of that sort, because, he says, they are 'of Christianity'.[9] The prelate must get those who 'deviate from the holy order' back on the straight path – they are to be restrained by the *discretio ecclesiastica*, by the anathema (and specifically the later version), indicating more clearly that these cases must be settled only (*solummodo*) before judges of the church. 'I am only the auxiliary (*adjutor*)', acknowledges the count – the second version says punisher (*vindex*), the term applied to the king of France when striking with the temporal sword those whom God, via his church, has condemned. Authority (*auctoritas*) was on one side, power (*potestas*) on the other. (The monk of Oudenbourg, who was an expert, balanced the two terms one against the other.) This perfectly Gregorian division asserts the superiority of the spiritual over the temporal and locates the jurisdictional power of the bishops in the extension of the provisions of the peace of God which had been established in that region in the preceding generation.

The bishop of Tournai ruled that Bertolf should take his wife back as there had been no adultery, and there was no hint of the husband's impotence nor doubt about the consummation of the

---

[9] The expression *justitia christianitatis* appears at the same period in a charter from the Mâconnais in connection with a division of jurisdiction between a count and a bishop: *Cartulaire de Saint-Vincent de Mâcon*, ed. C. Ragut (Mâcon, 1864), no. 589.

marriage. In accordance with the norms set out in the canonical collections, a divorce could not be pronounced. The best solution in this case was to reconcile the couple and bring them back together. Bertolf submitted, but reluctantly. According to the rewritten version this was primarily out of fear of secular sanctions. In his hatred, his disgust, he saw only one way out: crime. Here, the passion of Godelive begins – her passion, patience and slow spiritual development. The wife is no longer persecuted physically. Bertolf has promised to maltreat her no more. But she remains abandoned, even by her father. She is deprived of man, which seems scandalous. The 'friends', the husband's parents, are shocked. They criticize him, but Godelive, as a worthy partner in the *societas conjugalis*, 'forbids anyone to speak ill of her husband'. They pity her, in particular, for being deprived 'of the pleasures of the body', but she replies: 'I care not at all for what delights the body'. It is joyful constancy, and little by little the exemplary wife shows a tendency to despise all worldly things. The traits and the attitudes she assumes are those which are attributed to the Virgin. The words of the Magnificat make their way into the conversations she holds, notably with the monks of St-Winock who come to visit her and whom she edifies, giving them – herself but a feeble woman – an example of continence and obedience. Resounding with echoes of the Marian liturgies and the text of the Gospels, the narrative leads up to the martyrdom.

Bertolf has prepared his coup. He has got together with two of his serfs, seeking the advice of these low-born persons – another corruption. One evening, before sunset, Godelive sees him coming back towards her. She is dumbfounded. He is smiling. He takes her in his arms, kisses her, makes her sit by his side on the same cushion (in the posture that fourteenth-century Parisian image-makers give to courtly lovers in ivory on the covers of mirrors and perfume boxes). The man draws his wife to him. Fearful, she nevertheless yields to him, obedient and disposed to fulfil all the duties of conjugality when the master requires. Very close to her now, Bertolf coaxes her: 'You are not used to my presence nor to being charmed by soft words and the shared delights of the flesh'. (Words then pleasure; these are really the two successive phases of love-making, of the game of love as it should be played ritually.) He does not know how his spirit has come apart; it is due, he thinks, to the Evil One. But 'I am going to put a real end to the divorce of the spirit, treat you as a dear wife and, gradually, leave hate behind and bring our minds and bodies back to unity . . . I have found a woman who undertakes to unite us by steadfast love, to make us love one another without cease and more than a married couple have ever cherished one other on this earth'. The two serfs will lead her to this sorceress. Then says Godelive: 'I am the servant of the Lord. I entrust myself to Him. If this can be done without crime, I accept'. And the hagiographer exclaims: what virtue! She first puts herself in God's hands, fearing to be separated from Him by magic. It is for this very reason that 'she chooses marriage so as not to be separated from the Lord who unites couples'.

If Fr Coens, editor of the older version, is to be believed, this scene took place on 30 July 1070. On 17 July Count Baldwin died and his subjects were split: the people of the Flanders coast (Bertolf's part of the world) sided with Robert the Frisian; those of the Boulonnais (Godelive's) with the widow. There is great confusion. The moment is perfect for action. Exit Bertolf. Night falls – the time of disaster, the time of evil. The two servants come to take the lady. They escort her in a parody of the nuptial procession, bent towards evil – in the silence, in the depths of the night, at the moment when the creator of popular stories sets the blackest crimes. It leads backwards from the bed to the door, not towards a husband but towards a woman who was worse than her mother-in-law and truly a sorceress. Godelive is strangled and plunged as if newly baptized into water, hallowing the water so that it is able to perform miracles. Finally, she is carried back to her bed and dressed again. In the morning her people find her apparently intact. Immediately, however, the first doubts arise: a suspicion; only whispered, because it is born among the poorest. Immediately too, a miracle occurs: the multiplication of bread for the funeral repast, again in favour of the poor. And lastly, the cult: the water which cures – always the poor – and the stones which turn into jewels.

It was a cult which flouted the two powers: that of the bishop, in that the strange power of the martyred woman made the prohibitions he decreed and the punishments he imposed ineffectual; that of the count, for is not the deceiver in this story – the torturer, with his sergeants, his henchmen – an officer of the count, responsible for levying his dues? Without following Jacques Le Goff all the way in his hypothesis, it is impossible not to perceive in the primitive forms of such a worship, in the original structures of such a legend, a protest in favour of the oppressed, of all innocent victims. The heroine certainly belonged to the class which profited from the seigneurial system. The cruelties inflicted on her reduced her honour, the regard due to her rank. She was, however, a woman and therefore a dominated being, and her husband starved her as he starved the subjects of the seigneurie in his official position. This cult and this narrative probably originated wih the people, in the social, conflictive meaning of that word. They should be considered as one of the forms taken by the class struggle among the free and stubborn peasants of the Flanders coast at a time of upheaval in seigneurial society. Some time later, when the Fleming, Arnulf, was arranging a reconciliation among the great men of Flanders,[10] the count (then leading the inquiry into the murders committed in the land of Bruges) and the bishop (founding the abbey of Oudenbourg) reached an agreement to neutralize this cult and to utilize it to prop the established order. Thus it was that a life of a saint was substituted for the moving story of a victim of a bad marriage.[11]

*   *   *

The established order did not only require deviant cults to be brought back to orthodoxy. It also demanded that the prescribed rules for forming pairs should be observed. The two powers had agreed to impose these norms. The account of the misfortunes of Godelive, therefore, was to reinforce an admonition to marry as the rules dictated. Its exhortation foreshadowed the one which the *vita* of Countess Ida was to convey some fifty years later. The conjugal bond, tied by God himself, could not be untied. It fell to the parents, not to the young people, to conclude the pact, and they had to consider morals more than wealth and avoid *invidia*, the jealousy which destroys alliances. There is scarcely any need, for it is so obvious, to show the wife as obedient, as Mary had

---

[10] *Vita Arnulfi*, ii. 16 (Patrologiae cursus completus, ed. J.-P. Migne, Series latina, clxxiv, Paris, 1854, col. 1413).

[11] In connection with the two texts of the life of Godelive which I have been using, some valuable comments were made at a symposium held in 1970, notably by H. Platelle and E. Warlop. The proceedings were published in *Sacris Erudiri*, xx (1971).

been. The advice is added, though in an undertone, to despise the flesh, in pursuit of the ideal of a devout life based, like the ideal of the heretics in the past and the ideal of the *béguines* in the near future, on the work of the hands, on abstinence, and on fear of pleasure. On the other hand, it is very strongly asserted – was the collusion between the two powers as close on this latter point? – that the right of sitting in judgement on a marriage belonged to the clergy. Such is the basis of the doctrine that the monks are instructed to set forth, with moderation, in this region in this half-century.

Against this background, these two works, whose meaning and intention I have tried to analyse, bring out some further specific points. First, both deal with women. Taking female figures to voice the ecclesiastical ideology offered a double advantage. It rallied that half of its worshippers about whom the church in the past had not been sufficiently concerned and whose importance was now being assessed. On the other hand, it focused attention on naturally passive people through whose example the principles of a submission that was expected from all the laity could be strongly and deeply impressed. Nevertheless the tone of the two works differs, and I attribute this difference to the fact that one leans towards the dominant class, the other towards the domi-nated. In the *vita* of the happy wife, Countess Ida, as in almost all those which have been preserved, the exhortation, because it is addressed to those who command, to the powerful lineages and to the heads of these houses, emphasizes chiefly the genetic function of the female body. The legend of Godelive on the other hand is perhaps told to the people. In any case, it comes from them. That is why it puts the accent on love. It is notable that the terms derived from the word *amor* in the *vita* of Godelive are as plentiful as derivatives of the word *genus* in Ida's. Of course this love respects the relationship of necessary subordination that Pro-vidence has instituted between the two sexes. The love of a husband for his wife is called affection, that of the woman for her husband is called reverence. It is repeated, however, that the man and the woman must be united in their flesh as in their spirit. They make this love themselves; there is no mention of chastity (*casti-tas*). It is as much a love of body as of heart, which leads to an appreciation of the charms of the female body. In addition, recourse to sorcery is authorized should it be necessary in order to establish this love in its fullest form. When the bishop of Noyon-Tournai, swept along by what had sprung from popular feeling, elevated the relics of that brunette with the clear and appealing complexion, he was inadvertently venturing much further than most of his colleagues were to go for a long time to come.

5. Literature and Social Terminology: The Vavasour in England*

P. R. COSS

Social terminology is of immense importance to the historian. Though no past society can be properly understood by reference to its own system, or systems, of social classification alone, the way people view and are taught to view their relations with one another has a direct and obvious bearing on how they behave. On a purely practical level the historian is liable to find his interpretation of his sources resting on the meaning he thinks contemporaries attached to their own social terms. Especially where evidence is sparse, the result may be distortion. A further cause of difficulty is that whilst broad systems may endure, the meaning attached to individual terms is liable to change. For the literary scholar, too, the correct understanding of contemporary terminology is of crucial importance. It is disturbing, therefore, to discover a divergence in the way English historians and Chaucer critics have interpreted a significant social term and in the evidence they have brought to bear in those interpretations. I refer to the vavasour.[1]

In a well-known and influential essay Professor G. H. Gerould argued, persuasively and against current orthodoxy, that Chaucer's Franklin was an established landowner and by no means a 'parvenu' anxious to find his way into the gentry as had hitherto been supposed. 'Franklins', he insisted, 'were gentlefolk'.[2] He based his interpretation, primarily, on an enquiry into the meaning of the words franklin and vavasour. This approach seemed amply justified given that Chaucer concluded the portrait of his

---

* In addition to my co-editors I would like to thank Professor Derek Pearsall and Dr Elspeth Kennedy for their valuable comments on a draft of this essay.

1 For the sake of consistency I have used this form throughout, except of course in quotations. Since it is the form generally employed by historians I have used it in preference to the, slightly later, *vavasseur* or to the Latin *vavassor* (in Italy *valvassor* or, less commonly, *varvassor*).

2 G. H. Gerould, 'The Social Status of Chaucer's Franklin', *Pubns. Mod. Language Assoc. America*, xli (1926), pp. 262–79.

Franklin, it will be recalled, with the summary statement: 'Was nowher swich a worthy vavasour'. In search of evidence Gerould ranged impressively over the centuries, from the late twelfth to the mid-fifteenth, though with scant regard, it must be said, for the possibility that social terms may be anything less than static in their meaning. For the vavasour his most pertinent evidence came from the thirteenth-century treatise on the laws and customs of England, until recently attributed to Henry de Bracton, and from the chronicle of Pierre de Langtoft, written for the most part in the reign of Edward I.[3] 'Bracton' called the vavasours 'men of great dignity' (*viri magnae dignitatis*) and placed them in his classification of men in an intermediate position between barons and knights, a position they occupy equally in Langtoft. For Gerould the words vavasour and franklin were interchangeable, and he concluded that 'Chaucer's Franklin was a member of that class of landed gentry which was already old in the fourteenth century and which has never felt the lack of any higher title than gentleman'.

For the historian there is in this one immediately puzzling feature. Though his evidence certainly does suggest that a vavasour was a substantial landowner, at least in the thirteenth century, it also tells us plainly that he was above a knight. Now, whatever else the franklin of Chaucer's day may or may not have been, he was certainly not the social superior of a knight. That hardly needs to be demonstrated. As disturbing, however, is the fact that this evidence is at variance with how historians have interpreted the word in its, to them, equally famous occurrence, in clause 17 of the Provisions of Oxford of 1258: 'Sheriffs shall be appointed who are loyal men and sound land-holders, so that in each county there shall be as sheriff a vavasour of that same county, who will deal well, loyally, and uprightly with the people of the county'.[4]

All agree that the vavasour here is synonymous with the county knight. For R. F. Treharne 'the provision that sheriffs must be local vavassours secured for the office men with local knowledge and local sympathies . . . men of the class which formed the

---

[3] For references, see nn. 56, 60, 69 below.

[4] 'Les uescuntes seient purueus, leus genz et prodes homes et tere tenanz; issi ke en chescun cunte seit un uauasur del cunte memes uescunte, ke ben et leuement trete la gent del cunte et dreitement': *Documents of the Baronial Movement of Reform and Rebellion, 1258–1267*, ed. R. F. Treharne and I. J. Sanders (Oxford, 1973), pp. 108–9.

characteristic element of the shire court'. 'Of all the other classes', he tells us, 'the county knights or vavassours were the class with which the baronage was in closest touch and had the greatest natural affinity'.[5] On the same clause Sir Maurice Powicke writes that 'Henceforth a sheriff should be a "vavassor" of the shire – that is to say, in general a local man of the knightly class, holding land of some barony or baronies',[6] while E. F. Jacob speaks of the 'radical point of the new proposal – to make mesne tenants, the smaller country gentry, responsible for the work of local government'.[7] Finally, Helen Cam neatly summarizes for us this agreed line of interpretation, in writing of 'the country gentry, the "Bachelery of England" – the vavasours of the shire'.[8]

'In England the word is rare'. The view is Maitland's, and it is shared by an impressive array of scholars.[9] Perhaps this has influenced historians of thirteenth-century politics, for one suspects that they feel themselves to be dealing with an occasional borrowing from Continental terminology, a suspicion deepened by E. F. Jacob when he attempts to elucidate clause 17 by reference to northern France:

> Whatever precise meaning we are to attach to 'vavasur', the word must connote mediacy, the notion of a grade below the tenant-in-chief and above the lower *liberi tenentes*. If he is anything like the 'vavasour' of the *Établissements* of St Louis, he is a manorial lord with a court of his own.[10]

The vavasour in England clearly warrants detailed investigation,

---

[5] R. F. Treharne, *The Baronial Plan of Reform* (Manchester, 1932; repr. 1971), pp. 88, 184. This interpretation runs, in fact, throughout the work.

[6] F. M. Powicke, *The Thirteenth Century* (Oxford, 1962), p. 144.

[7] E. F. Jacob, *Studies in the Period of Baronial Reform and Rebellion, 1258–1267* (Oxford Studies in Social and Legal Hist., ed. Sir P. Vinogradoff, viii, Oxford, 1925), p. 93.

[8] H. M. Cam, 'Pedigrees of Villeins and Freemen in the Thirteenth Century', in her *Liberties and Communities in Medieval England* (London, 1963), p. 128; repr. from *Genealogists Mag.* (Sept. 1933). For the bachelry of England, see n. 77 below.

[9] F. Pollock and F. W. Maitland, *The History of English Law*, 2 vols. (Cambridge, 1895; repr. 1968), i, p. 546; J. H. Round, 'The Origin of the House of Lords', repr. in *Peerage and Pedigree*, 2 vols. (London, 1910), i, p. 345; James Tait, *Medieval Manchester and the Beginnings of Lancashire* (Manchester, 1904), p. 75; H. G. Richardson and G. O. Sayles, *The Governance of Medieval England* (Edinburgh, 1963), p. 129.

[10] Jacob, *Studies in the Period of Baronial Reform*, p. 93.

in the interests both of the historian and of the Chaucer critic, the more so as the only extensive treatment, by Sir Frank Stenton, is confined to the period from 1086 to *circa* 1170. How rare was the term, particularly after those dates? Was it an occasional borrowing or, perhaps, survival, which can be interpreted according to Continental analogy? Or are we dealing with a word of actual parlance, rarely used by central government perhaps, but surfacing in the sources from time to time? Are we to look for a single definition against which the Provisions of Oxford, Chaucer's Franklin, or any other instance can be interpreted? Or did the word evolve? And, if so, in what circumstances?

In order to answer these questions as surely as possible I have divided the following study into three sections. Since the term was clearly imported, the first section begins with a consideration of its meaning on the Continent and continues with its early history in England, building upon the work of Stenton. The central section will then explore its use in England from the late twelfth to the early fourteenth century. The final section will examine its possible meaning for Chaucer and his contemporaries.

I

For the history of vavasour on the Continent the key work is the pioneering study on the origins of the French nobility by Paul Guilhiermoz.[11] Guilhiermoz regarded vavasour as having applied initially only to those elevated personages, often *châtelains*, who were descended from the royal vassals of the Carolingian epoch, the *vassi dominici*. The term alluded to their new position as mediatized vassals of the counts and thus sub-vassals, or *arrière-vassaux*, of the crown. He based his view on the way the term continued to be used in the March of Spain and neighbouring territories, its use in Lombardy in the eleventh century, and on a few miscellaneous sources, including 'Bracton' which he regarded as preserving the memory of the old usage. By the twelfth century, however, it was being used to describe lesser vassals and in contradistinction to *barons* and *châtelains*.[12] Marc Bloch, by

---

[11] P. Guilhiermoz, *Essai sur l'origine de la noblesse en France au Moyen Age* (Paris, 1902).

[12] *Ibid.*, Ch. II (vi), 'Barons et chevaliers', esp. pp. 150–1, 165–9. Not the least of the value of this formidable work lies in the considerable body of evidence which

contrast, paying attention to the etymology of the word,[13] seems to have seen the opposite process at work:

> At the lower end of the scale we have first of all the vavasour, the vassal of vassals (*vassus vassorum*), who was not himself the lord of any other warrior – not, at least, when the term vavasour, which was common to all the Romance languages, was understood in its strict sense.[14]

Other scholars have referred to the imprecision of the term.[15]

Whatever its earliest application may have been, and notwithstanding either its elevated sense in certain regions or its peculiarly restricted meaning in Normandy, the word 'vavasour' was used in France by the twelfth century, if not before, in the general sense of *arrière-vassal*, separated by one or more rungs from the crown, or from a duke or count. The vavasour's social position in northern

Guilhiermoz gathered in support of his text. I have also profited from the following: Du Cange, *Glossarium mediae et infimae latinitatis*, 7 vols. (Paris, 1830–50), vi, pp. 747–9; J. F. Niermeyer, *Mediae latinitatis lexicon minus* (Leiden, 1954–76), fasc. 12, pp. 1065–7; F. Godefroy, *Dictionnaire de l'ancienne langue française*, 10 vols. (Paris, 1881–1902), viii, p. 154.

There can be no doubt of the broad accuracy of what Guilhiermoz perceived in Lombardy and in Spain. In the former, from the early eleventh century, we hear of *valvassores* or *valvassores majores* occupying the social rank immediately below the marquises and counts, the *capitanei*, and holding fiefs of them. A long process of subinfeudation was already under way which was to result in *valvassores minores* and *valvassores minimi*. The situation is revealed clearly in the *Consuetudines feudorum* of the mid-twelfth century; for references, see nn. 85, 86 below.

The elevated position of the vavasour in the March of Spain is shown equally clearly in the mid-twelfth-century *Usatges* of Barcelona. His position in the feudal hierarchy was between the *vicomte* and *comtor* on the one hand and the knight on the other. The compensation for killing a vavasour with five knights, for example, was reckoned at 60 ounces of pure gold; if he had more knights the compensation would grow in proportion to their number: see the extracts given in R. Boutruche, *Seigneurie et féodalité: l'apogée (xie–xiiie siècles)* (Paris, 1970), pp. 441–5. Guilhiermoz believed that the *comtors* had themselves emerged from the ranks of the *châtelains* or *vavassores*: Guilhiermoz, *Essai sur l'origine de la noblesse*, p. 162.

13 Though there have been doubters (notably Pollock and Maitland, *History of English Law*, i, p. 546), the etymological dictionaries are agreed that in origin vavasour means vassal of a vassal or vassals, and is derived from the low Latin *vassus vassorum*: Paul Robert, *Dictionnaire de la langue française*, 6 vols. (Paris, 1953–64), vi, p. 943; A. Dauzat, J. Dubois and H. Mitterand, *Nouveau dictionnaire étymologique et historique* (Paris, 1964), p. 784; *Grand Larousse de la langue française*, 7 vols. (Paris, 1971–8), vii, p. 6390. See also n. 21 below.

14 Marc Bloch, *Feudal Society*, trans. L. A. Manyon (London, 1961), p. 332.

15 Among them Ganshof and Boutruche: F. L. Ganshof, *Feudalism*, 3rd English edn (London, 1964), p. 120; Boutruche, *Seigneurie et féodalité: l'apogée*, p. 271.

France can be seen most clearly by combining the evidence of the *Établissements* of St Louis with evidence drawn from vernacular literature. The *Établissements*, despite its name, is a private work, based largely on the *Coutume de Touraine-Anjou* and on the lost *Usage d'Orlenois*.[16] Both the *Établissements* in general and the *Coutume d'Anjou* in particular were immensely influential and penetrated into numerous provinces where customary law was similar. The vavasour is revealed as the possessor of low justice (*voirie* or *basse justice*).[17] He holds a court for his men, with cognizance over civil and relatively minor penal matters.[18] He organized local weights and measures and enjoyed monopolies (*banalités*). Within certain limitations he could claim the court from a baron whenever one of his men was involved. He was, however, excluded from matters of high justice (*haute justice*), and his judicial authority was restricted by that of the lord of the castlery. He could lose his justice if he overstepped his power.[19] There can be no doubt that the *Établissements* and the *Coutume d'Anjou* reveal in a more systematized way what had generally been true for some considerable time, though of course subject to local variations. Broadly speaking, the exercise of judicial authority flowed from the vavasour's social position, not the other way round. What the feudal lawyers of the thirteenth century were doing was to draw the practical distinctions between baron and vavasour more clearly. As a result a slightly later work, *L'ancien coutumier d'Artois* could define a vavasour as 'one who does not have high justice' (*celui qui n'a pas la haute justice*).[20]

---

[16] Paul Viollet, *Les Établissements de St. Louis*, 4 vols. (Paris, 1881–6). The sources and influence of the work are discussed in vol. i, bks. 1, 3.

[17] Low justice here comprised what was already becoming divided into middle justice (*moyenne justice*) and the low justice of the mere landlord (*basse justice foncière*), or into great and simple *voirie*: *ibid.*, iii, pp. 301, 309.

[18] He may, for example, seize a thief, he may execute him, but only after the lord of the castlery has pronounced judgement on him. He may preside over ordeals by battle in all cases except the most serious (*grands méfaits*): *ibid.*, ii, bk. 1, ch. xlii.

[19] See, in particular, *ibid.*, bk 1, chs. xxxiv, xlii–xliv, cxiii–cxiv, and bk 2, chs. xxxi–xxxiii. He may lose his justice, for example, if he banishes a man from the castlery or if he releases a thief without the assent of his chief lord. Much useful material on the position of the vavasour, drawn from various custumals and the works of jurists, may be found in E. Glasson, *Histoire du droit et des institutions de la France,* 7 vols. (Paris, 1887–96), iv, pp. 746–52. In conflating the vavasour of northern France generally and the vavasour of Normandy, however, he tends to depress the social position of the former.

[20] *Ibid.*, p. 746.

The term is found in French literature from the middle of the twelfth century. In the *Roman de Thèbes* and the *Roman de Troie* it signifies the social grade immediately below the *barons* or *châtelains* (here called *demaines*) and clearly has tenurial connotations.[21] The *romanciers*, however, and principally Chrétien de Troyes, developed a definite literary vavasour (*vavasseur littéraire*). He is predominantly a courteous and hospitable knight who, though not himself active (he rarely participates in tournaments), is nevertheless generally supportive of chivalric life, chiefly by acting as host to the knight-errant. Since his life was generally confined to his estates he was particularly useful to the *romancier* for he could be placed anywhere according to the needs of the plot. Sometimes the vavasour is rich but most often he is described as poor, though wealth, of course, is relative and the heroes of the romances are of high rank. Generally, though not invariably, he is mature in years. Given their sedentary life and their generally modest fortune it is hardly surprising that the vavasours should sometimes be treated with disdain, and Professor Woledge identifies for us alongside the notion of 'the good vavasseur' what he aptly calls 'a pejorative value'. In short, 'The vavasseurs of the romances are the vavasseurs of medieval France, but idealized'.[22]

In Normandy, however, as has long been recognized, the word vavasour has a narrower and distinctive meaning. Guilhiermoz himself pointed to the *vavassories nobles* as a species of the fief of restricted equipment whose tenants served with plain arms only (lance, shield and sword) as opposed to the fief of full arms (*fief de haubert*).[23] Sir Frank Stenton, concerned to show the technical

---

21 *Le roman de Thèbes*, ed. Guy Raynaud de Lage, 2 vols. (Les Classiques Français du Moyen Âge, xciv, xcvi, Paris, 1968), i, ll. 2481–2, ii, ll. 1069–70; *Le roman de Troie*, ed. L. Constans, 6 vols. (Société des Anciens Textes Français, Paris, 1904–12), ii, ll. 1199–1200, iii, ll. 16325–6. See also *Le roman de Brut de Wace*, ed. I. Arnold, 2 vols. (S.A.T.F., Paris, 1938–40), ii, ll. 10169–70.

On this point and for what follows, see in particular B. Woledge, 'Bons vavasseurs et mauvais sénéchaux', in F. Dethier (ed.), *Mélanges offerts à Rita Lejeune* (Gembloux, 1969), pp. 1263–77. I am grateful to members of the University of Newcastle Medievalists' Seminar for first bringing this essay to my attention. See also Charles Foulon, 'Les vavasseurs dans les romans de Chrétien de Troyes', in K. Varty (ed.), *An Arthurian Tapestry: Essays in Memory of Lewis Thorpe* (Glasgow, 1981).

22 Woledge, 'Bons vavasseurs et mauvais sénéchaux', p. 1271.

23 Guilhiermoz, *Essai sur l'origine de la noblesse*, ch. 7, 'Équipement complet ou restreint', pp. 183–8. Guilhiermoz considered, however, that the term was first

precision of Norman feudalism, emphasized the distinction between the *miles* who held a full knight's fee and the *vavassor* whose military duties were rather less and varied, to an extent at least, according to the size of his holding.[24] It can be misleading, however, to lay too much emphasis on the military obligations of the vavasour, and the more recent researches of le Commandant Henri Navel allow us to see him more clearly and in a wider perspective.[25]

The vavasours, or tenants of vavassories, occupied an intermediate position between the *chevaliers* and the *vilains*. They owed, in addition to homage and relief, a few light services and money rent, though never renders in kind or servile labour. Sometimes they served as domanial officers. The *vavassories* themselves varied in size from a few acres to over four hundred. Most were common vavassories (*vavassories roturières*), though some, and not necessarily the most extensive, were noble. Of these last, a few were reckoned as fractions of knights' fees, while the twenty vavassories of Bretteville-sur-Odon and Verson together owed the service of a whole knight with full arms. Some others owed restricted military service and the remainder (those

used here, too, to distinguish the simple knight from the baron. Stenton pointed out, with justice, that the evidence for this was almost all from England and that, in fact, English influence was probably responsible for the appearance of the more general meaning of the word in later writers, such as Wace: F. M. Stenton, *The First Century of English Feudalism*, 2nd edn (Oxford, 1961), pp. 18–19. Ganshof speaks of *vavassores* 'in parts of Western France' serving with incomplete equipment, though he cites no evidence: Ganshof, *Feudalism*, p. 87.

24 Stenton, *First Century of English Feudalism*, pp. 16–19. Stenton's account contains an error which has passed into the second edition. The service with plain arms (*cum planis armis*) was with lance, shield and sword *not* hauberk, shield and sword, the hauberk being the hallmark of service with full arms (*cum plenis armis*), that is the service due from the *fief de haubert*. Both Guilhiermoz and Stenton were, of course, well aware of the existence of *vavasseurs roturiers* who did not owe such service.

25 For what follows, see H. Navel, 'L'enquête de 1133 sur les fiefs de l'évêché de Bayeux', *Bulletin de la Société des Antiquaires de Normandie*, xlii (1934), pp. 5–80, esp. pp. 50–4; H. Navel, 'Les vavassories du Mont-Saint-Michel à Bretteville-sur-Odon et Verson (Calvados)', *ibid.*, xlv (1938), pp. 137–65; and H. Navel, 'Recherches sur les institutions féodales en Normandie (Région de Caen)', ch. v, 'Recherches sur les vavassories', *ibid.*, li (1951), pp. 77–120. See also R. Carabie, *La propriété foncière dans le très ancien droit normand (xie–xiiie siècles)*, i, *La propriété domaniale* (Caen, 1943), pp. 64–70, 137–40. The evidence comes largely from the *Bayeux Inquest* of 1133, the *Inquisitiones Militum* of 1172 and the 1247 *censier* of Bretteville and Verson.

with less than 50 acres) owed perhaps only castleguard, as did some of the better endowed of the non-noble (*vavasseurs roturiers*). All, however, owed escort and carrying service (*service de cheval*), which constituted the characteristic burden on their tenure.

At Bretteville-sur-Odon and Verson, Navel shows that half the vavassories belonging to the abbey of Mont-Saint-Michel were held by lords of some rank in 1172. They were the successors of ducal officers of the tenth century when these parishes had formed a fisc. He argues, persuasively, that the majority of the Norman vavassories were in origin Carolingian manses. The word *vavassor* was being used of their tenants by the eleventh century and the name *vavassorie* (*vavassoria*) had appeared in consequence by the twelfth.

The word is first encountered in England in a manner somewhat akin to the Norman usage. Domesday Book reveals two Buckinghamshire *vavassores* who render 32s. 6d. to their lord, a *vavassor* with two cows in the Isle of Wight, and in Suffolk a substantial number of free men holding directly of the crown whose modest estates are listed under the heading *Terra Vavassorum*.[26] The fact that these three counties belong to different Domesday circuits indicates that the term may possibly have been in more general use in Norman England than the number of instances would suggest. As Stenton himself noted, the situation of these men seems to correspond to that of the lesser Norman vavasours.[27] Interestingly, this correspondence was apparent as late as the second quarter of the twelfth century when a Norman lord could still refer to the purchase of a *vavassor* in Warwickshire with all his land.[28] It is almost certain, however, that it was the basic social position of these men, rather than any specific service due from them which prompted their being so styled.[29]

---

[26] *Domesday Book*, ed. A. Farley, 2 vols. (Rec. Comm., London, 1783), i, fos. 53, 146; ii, fos. 446–7.

[27] Stenton, *First Century of English Feudalism*, p. 19.

[28] Between 1129 and 1146 Roger Abbadon gave various properties in Warwickshire and Leicestershire to the abbey of St Peter, Préaux. His son, receiving six marks for his consent, used it to purchase a *vavassor* from Hugh son of Richard in the vill of Snitterfield, Warwickshire: *Calendar of Documents Preserved in France, 918–1206*, ed. J. H. Round (London, 1899), no. 334.

[29] There is, in fact, no evidence at all of any military burdens imposed on the *vavossores*; nor, surprisingly, is there any evidence of the existence of fiefs of

It is clear enough, however, that by the beginning of the twelfth century this usage had largely been superseded by the broader one common to northern France.[30] Henry I uses the term in this sense as early as 1108, in the ordinance on the holding of shire and hundred courts which was later to find its way into the private compilation known as the *Leges Henrici Primi*. Among those who are expected to be present in the county court are the earls, barons, *vavasores* and 'all other lords of lands' (*ceteri terrarum domini*).[31] The *Leges* tells us further that vavasours have judicial rights:

> Vavassors who hold free lands shall have the pleas where the punishment is payment of the *wite* or of the wergeld in respect of their own men and on their own land, and in respect of the men of other lords if they are seized in the act of committing the offence and are charged with it.[32]

This should be compared with an earlier clause which tells us that archbishops, bishops, earls and others of high rank (*potestates*) have private jurisdictional powers, including the right to hang a thief caught red-handed in their own lands (*infongenþeaf*).[33] Maitland comments:

restricted equipment in Norman England. Several scholars have wondered, however, whether all the knights of Domesday Book really did serve with full arms, especially given the existence of the small or Mortain fees which were subsequently acknowledged as such by the central government: Sir Paul Vinogradoff, *English Society in the Eleventh Century* (Oxford, 1908), p. 78; Richardson and Sayles, *Governance of Medieval England*, pp. 129–30. The authoritative study on the Anglo-Norman knight is now Sally Harvey, 'The Knight and the Knight's Fee in England', *Past and Present*, no. 49 (Nov. 1970), pp. 3–43. The use Dr Harvey makes of the terms *vavassor* and *vavassor knight* is, however, questionable. The evidence does not suggest that vavasour was used in England exclusively for the lesser-endowed knights (those whom contemporaries sometimes referred to as common or rustic knights), nor that it was used of those who could no longer be called knights. The evidence cited in support of this last point refers not to England, in fact, but to Normandy: *ibid.*, p. 37.

30 For what follows see, in particular, Stenton, *First Century of English Feudalism*, pp. 20–3. Stenton felt that this supersession arose from the fact that 'barons and knights from many French provinces had settled in England'. It may well be, of course, that the word vavasour was only at this very time acquiring its general application.

31 *Leges Henrici Primi*, ed. L. J. Downer (Oxford, 1972), c. 7, 2.

32 *Ibid.*, c. 27, 1. The *curia vavasoris* is referred to again in c. 26, 3. The translation is the editor's. The date of this work is between 1108 and 1118; its recent editor suggests 1116–18: *ibid.*, pp. 34–7.

33 *Ibid.*, c. 20, 2.

On the whole, our law seems for the time to be taking the shape that French law took. If we leave out of sight the definitely granted franchisal powers, then we may say that a baron or the holder of a grand fief has 'high justice' or, if that term be too technical, a higher justice, while the vavassor has 'low justice' or a lower justice . . . we observe that the justice of an archbishop, bishop or earl, probably the justice of a baron also, extends as high as *infangenethef*, while that of a vavassor goes no higher than such offences as are emendable.[34]

In a writ of 1109–11 the king pronounces that in any plea arising over land, if it is between his barons then it should be decided in his own court. If, however, it is between vavasours of any of his barons then it should be dealt with in that lord's court. If it is between vavasours of two lords, then it should be dealt with in the county court.[35] From another private work, the *Leis Willelme*, we learn that a vavasour should be quit of relief to his liege lord by his father's horse, and by his hauberk, helmet, shield, lance and sword.[36] The vavasour emerges as a figure not dissimilar from his counterpart of the *Établissements*. He is the holder of a *fief de haubert*, he is an *arrière-vassal* with a court of his own dispensing something akin to the French low justice (*basse justice*).

There is, moreover, evidence to suggest that, up to the third quarter of the twelfth century at least, the use of the word was quite widespread. A number of royal writs are addressed to barons

---

[34] F. W. Maitland, *Domesday Book and Beyond* (Cambridge, 1897), pp. 81–2. He makes the further observation: 'But in this province, as in other provinces, of English law personal rank becomes of less and less importance. The rules which would determine it and its consequences are never allowed to become definite, and in the end a great generalisation surmounts all difficulties: – every lord has a certain civil justice over all his tenants; whatsoever powers go beyond this, are franchises'.

[35] *Die Gesetze der Angelsachsen*, ed. F. Liebermann, 3 vols. in 4 (Halle, 1903–16), i, p. 524.

[36] *Ibid.*, pp. 506–7. The compiler is equating the heriots due from the various ranks of the Old English nobility with the reliefs due from classes of contemporary society. The vavasour is equated with the thegn, the baron with the king's thegn. See Pollock and Maitland, *History of English Law*, i, p. 102, and Stenton, *First Century of English Feudalism*, pp. 22–3. The contention of Richardson and Sayles that the work belongs not to the reign of Henry I but to that of Henry II does not materially affect the issue: H. G. Richardson and G. O. Sayles, *Law and Legislation from Aethelberht to Magna Carta* (Edinburgh, 1966), pp. 121–4.

and vavasours,[37] while the Pipe Roll of 31 Henry I refers both to the *vavassores* of the archbishop of York and to the *vavassores* of Robert Fossard.[38] Between 1143 and 1147 Queen Matilda returned land at Mashbury in Essex to the church of St Martin le Grand with all the customs and liberties which the barons and vavasours of the honour of Boulogne hold, a grant which her son Eustace later confirmed in a writ addressed to all his barons, vavasours and tenants of Essex.[39] Sometime before the summer of 1141 Earl Ranulf II of Chester sent to Richard de Veim and his other vavasours of Bisley in Gloucestershire ordering them to do their service to Miles the Constable, as willingly as they had ever done it.[40] The geographical spread of these instances is worthy of note. As important, however, is the fact that the term was used by men further down the social scale. At a date before April 1169 a Lincolnshire knight, William de Ashby, addressed a charter to all the barons and vavasours of Lincolnshire and to his friends and neighbours, French and English. When in the 1120s Hugh de Flamville was claiming land in Yorkshire, it was provided that he should establish his claim by swearing an oath twelve-handed, half of the oath-helpers to be drengs and the other half vavasours as he is.[41] Stenton's comment that vavasour had become a word of

37 Stenton cites writs of Henry I and Henry II to the barons and vavasours who owe castleguard at Rockingham, and a writ of Henry I which speaks of the barons and vavasours who hold by military service of the church of Ely. To these should be added a writ of Henry I commanding the barons, vavasours, and all other lords who hold land within Well wapentake to come to the wapentake court of the bishop of Lincoln, and its confirmation by Henry II, and Henry I's charter of 1103–6 confirming the lands of Ramsey Abbey and ordering that Abbot Bernard may assess the services of his vavasours to the profit of his church, just as the vavasours of other abbeys of the realm have been assessed: Stenton, *First Century of English Feudalism*, pp. 20, 284; *Cartae Antiquae*, ed. L. Landon (Pipe Roll Soc., new ser., xvii, London 1939), nos. 50, 51; *Registrum Antiquissimum of the Cathedral Church of Lincoln*, ed. C. W. Foster, i, nos. 60, 155 (Lincoln Record Soc., xxvii, 1931); *Cartularium Monasterii de Rameseia*, ed. W. Hart and P. Lyons (Rolls Ser., London 1884–93), i, p. 239.
38 *Pipe Roll 31 Henry I*, ed. Joseph Hunter (Rec. Comm., London, 1833), pp. 30–1.
39 *Regesta Regum Anglo-Normannorum*, 4 vols. (Oxford, 1913–69), iii, ed. H. A. Cronne and R. H. C. Davis (Oxford, 1968), nos. 550, 551.
40 This document is discussed at length by Stenton, *First Century of English Feudalism*, pp. 21–2, 258, and by W. Farrer, *Honors and Knights Fees*, 3 vols. (London, 1923–5), ii, pp. 51–2.
41 Stenton, *First Century of English Feudalism*, p. 21; *Records of the Templars*, ed. B. R. Lees (Brit. Acad., Records of Social and Economic History, London 1935), pp. 250–1; *Early Yorkshire Charters*, ed. W. Farrer, 3 vols. (Edinburgh, 1914–16), i, no. 637.

general application in Yorkshire can be extended with some degree of assurance to much of the country.

II

For Stenton, however, the word vavasour had only a limited life in England:

It is an indefinite term, vaguely denoting a man's social position. Before the end of the twelfth century the outlines of English society had hardened. Knighthood itself had acquired a new social significance. The *vavassores* of the Anglo-Norman time represent the preceding phase of transition. The term is vague because the structure of society was still indefinite.[42]

But is it the case that the term ceased to be current in England after the third quarter of the twelfth century? One possible avenue of approach is through Anglo-Norman literature. Here we find that the word is not at all uncommon, especially during the literature's most flourishing period, from the late twelfth to the mid-thirteenth century.[43] Literary evidence, however, must be

[42] Stenton, *First Century of English Feudalism*, p. 23.

[43] I have confined myself to works which are known to have been written in England (or in one case Ireland) by the middle of the thirteenth century, and in Anglo-Norman. Thus the Jérseyman Wace, for instance, writing most probably on the Continent and in Norman, has been purposely excluded. What follows is based on a study of the more accessible works available in print. It makes no claim to be exhaustive. It could hardly have been written at all without those two works of guidance by Mary Dominica Legge: *Anglo-Norman in the Cloisters* (Edinburgh, 1950), and *Anglo-Norman Literature and its Background* (Oxford, 1963). Vavasours are to be found in the following works: *The Romance of Horn by Thomas*, ed. M. K. Pope (Anglo-Norman Text Soc., ix–x, Oxford, 1955); *Ipomedon*, ed. E. Kölbing and E. Koschwitz (Breslau, 1889); *Protheselaus*, ed. F. Kluckow (Göttingen, 1924); and *The Anglo-Norman Alexander (Le roman de toute chevalerie) by Thomas of Kent*, ed. Brian Foster (Anglo-Norman Text Soc., xxix–xxxiii, London 1976–7), all late twelfth-century romances; in *Der Anglo-normannische Boeve de Haumtone*, ed. A. Stimming (Bibliotheca Normannica, vii, Halle, 1899); and *Gui de Warewic: roman du xiii^esiècle*, ed. Alfred Ewert, 2 vols. (Les Classiques Français du Moyen Âge, lxxiv–lxxv, Paris 1933), thirteenth-century romances; in *La vie de Saint Gile*, ed. G. Paris and A. Bos (Société des Anciens Textes Français, Paris 1881); *St. Modwenna*, ed. A. T. Baker and A. Bell (Anglo-Norman Text Soc., vii, Oxford, 1947); *La vie Seint Edmund le Rey by Denis Pyramus* (Memorials of St. Edmund's Abbey, ii, ed. T. Arnold, Rolls Ser., London, 1892), among saints' lives; in the legend of the Seven Sleepers of Ephesus, *La vie des set dormanz by Chardri*, ed. B. S. Merrilees (Anglo-Norman Text Soc., xxxv, London, 1977); in *Jordan Fantosme's Chronicle*, ed. R. C. Johnston (Oxford, 1981); in *L'histoire de Guillaume le Maréchal*, ed. Paul Meyer, 3 vols. (Paris, 1891–1901); and in *The Song of Dermot and the Earl*, ed. G. H. Orpen (Oxford, 1892), a product of the Anglo-Norman community in Ireland.

used with caution. One immediate objection, perhaps, is that the vavasour may have been a borrowing from the Continental literature which was undoubtedly circulating in England during this period. The court of Henry II was, after all, peripatetic and the aristocracy (not to mention some of the Anglo-Norman writers themselves) had Continental interests and associations. It is an important caveat. However, many works were written in the provinces and have little or no connection with the royal court. One thinks of the romances of the Norman-Welsh clerk Hue de Rotelande, for instance, who wrote *Ipomedon*, probably, and *Protheselaus*, certainly, under the patronage of the lord of Monmouth, and of the romance of *Gui de Warewic* which was written for Thomas, earl of Warwick, by a canon of Oseney.[44] Moreover, Anglo-Norman literature is by no means derivative; indeed, in terms of both taste and technique it tended to be in the van. It has, furthermore, a serious and didactic bias which, to an extent, sets it apart from the literature produced in France.[45] A second possible objection is that literature may have a preservative effect on otherwise obsolete terms especially where one suspects that they may be there to serve the rhyme scheme or to amplify the list of estates. On the other hand the preservative effect is less likely to be present where a definite value can be discerned. Nevertheless, this objection, too, must be borne in mind.

Given, then, that vavasour occurs in the literature, what does it signify? In one case we are hardly given enough to make a judgement. In *Boeve de Haumtone* a messenger is in Germany in search of the emperor:

> e il ad encountre ileoc un vavasur
> si lui demaunde ou est le emperur.
>
> (there he meets a vavasour
> and asks him for the emperor.)[46]

We may have here a variant on the French practice of employing vavasours according to the needs of the plot. Significantly, though, the vavasour as the hospitable host, so prominent in the works of

---

[44] Legge, *Anglo-Norman Literature and its Background*, pp. 85–6, 162.
[45] *Ibid.*, pp. 3–6, and the concluding chapter; see also the introductory chapter to Legge, *Anglo-Norman in the Cloisters*.
[46] *Boeve de Haumtone*, ed. Stimming, ll. 73–4.

Chrétien and featuring in the Vulgate Cycle, seems not to figure in Anglo-Norman literature. Instead we find figures like the vavasour Gudmod in *King Horn*. Gudmod (the hero under an assumed name) tells the king of Ireland's sons of his social origins:

> De Suddene sui niez, un regne mut vaillent;
> Fitz sui un vavasur de povre tenement;
> Dous escuz od le soen aveit en tensement
> Quant alout od seignur a nul turneiëment.
> D'itiel gent sui venu: povre sunt mi parent.

> (Of South Devon I am born, a land of high worth;
> I am the son of a vavasour of poor tenement;
> In feudal dues he owed the service of two
>   armed men beside himself
> When he went with the lord to any tournament.
> From such stock I am come: poor are my parents.)

Wealth, as we have said before, is relative and it has already been made clear to us that Gudmod is a knight, nobly armed and with a fine war horse. Later, he refuses the hand of the king's daughter, explaining that he is engaged to the daughter of a worthy man with whom he once stayed in Brittany:

> Fille est de vavasur e tiel sunt mi parent:
> Bien sumes parigal e d'un ordeinement.

> (She is the daughter of a vavasour and such are my parents:
> We are well-matched and of the same rank.)[47]

A similar situation occurs in *Gui de Warewic* when the hero is offered the hand of the emperor's daughter if he will remain in his service. Gui refuses, for the Greeks would say:

> Que le fiz d'un povre vavasur
> Fait avreient lur empereur

> (That they had made the son of a poor vavasour their emperor.)

Again, later in the story, the barons of Adelstan [=Athelstan]

---

[47] *Romance of Horn*, ed. Pope, ll. 2256–60, 2229–30, 3667–8. See also *ibid.*, ll. 2341, 2444.

complain that he wrongs them in bestowing so much honour on Heralt d'Arderne:

> Qui fiz fu d'un povre vavassur.

> (Who was the son of a poor vavasour.)[48]

A vavasour, then, is gentle and is acceptable to gentle company, but may be treated with scorn if he attempts to step beyond his rank. A more startling example of the *valeur péjorative* is found in the biography of William the Marshal. The young marshal is in the service of his cousin, William de Tancarville, chamberlain of Normandy. Wishing to visit England, he seeks the chamberlain's permission to do so. The chamberlain grants his request but begs William to return as soon as he can:

> Qu'il n'i aveit nul bon sejor
> Se ce n'esteit a vavasor
> Ou a gent qui d'esrer n'ont cure.

> (For there can be no good stay
> Except to a vavasour
> Or to a man with no desire for adventure.)[49]

The biography was written by a man from the Cotentin working from information supplied by the marshal's own squire.[50] Given

---

[48] *Gui de Warewic*, ed. Ewert, ll. 4471–2, 9115.

[49] *L'histoire de Guillaume le Maréchal*, ed. Meyer, ll. 1537–9. Guilhiermoz thought that vavasour was being used here in the restricted Norman sense, even though this would be out of keeping with the way the term is used elsewhere in the biography: Guilhiermoz, *Essai sur l'origine de la noblesse*, p. 184. This interpretation hardly seems justified. See also Sidney Painter, *William Marshal* (Baltimore, 1933), p. 25. If there is a candidate for the restricted meaning in Anglo-Norman it is rather *Vie de Saint Gile*, ed. Paris and Bos, ll. 19–21, where the saint is described as follows:

> Ne fud pas nez de basse main,
> De vavassur ne de vilain:
> Nez fud de princes e de reis.

> (He was not of inferior extraction,
> From vavasour or vilain:
> But from princes and kings.)

It may be noted that Wace uses vavasour in contradistinction to both vilain and baron, though the latter predominates: *Le roman de Rou de Wace*, ed. A. J. Holden, 3 vols. (Société des Anciens Textes Français, Paris 1970–3), for example ii, ll. 810, 3843, and iii, ll. 913–14; ii, ll. 223, and iii, ll. 722, 775, 3813, 5348, 6349.

[50] Legge, *Anglo-Norman Literature and its Background*, p. 306.

also the time he spent abroad, one might expect it to betray more Continental usage than many other Anglo-Norman works. This contempt for the supposed sedentary life of the vavasour stands alone in the biography, however, and does not seem to be paralleled elsewhere in Anglo-Norman literature. To set against it we have Allidès *le vavasour bon* who plays a prominent part in Hue de Rotelande's *Protheselaus*. Ironically, his career mirrors that of the great William Marshal himself. Born in Spain, Allidès spent much time in the service of the king of Apulia. He is described as a vavasour and neither duke, baron nor count. He has little land but can spend well because of his great gains in tournaments. He is gentle and keeps gentle company. For his prowess and good service he is finally rewarded with rich fiefs and made seneschal.[51] We have in Allidès, successful in tournaments and formidable in battle, a figure who rather contravenes the French *vavasseur littéraire*.

Not all of the vavasours in Anglo-Norman literature, however, are described as poor. In the biography of William the Marshal two rich vavasours are captured in the civil war of 1217, whilst *St. Modwenna* tells of Swein Child, 'a wealthy vavasour' (*un tres riche vavasur*) in the time of William the Conqueror. Well-endowed in England, Swein led a large company of bold and cruel men.[52] The vavasours of Anglo-Norman literature seem less idealized and closer to reality than their French counterparts.

The vavasour is found most commonly in Anglo-Norman, however, either within a series, most often a hierarchy, of social grades or in contradistinction to baron. A few examples must stand for many. In the prologue to *La vie Seint Edmund le Rey*, Denis Pyramus declares:

> Li rey, li prince, e li courtur,
> Cunt, barun, e vavasur,
> Ayment cuntes, chanceuns, et fables

> (Kings, princes and courtiers,
> Earls, barons, and vavasours,
> Love tales, songs, and fables)

---

[51] *Protheselaus*, ed. Kluckow, ll. 11705–20, 11764–7, 12407–13.
[52] *Histoire de Guillaume le Maréchal*, ed. Meyer, ll. 15824–6; *St. Modwenna*, ed. Baker and Bell, ll. 7913–21.

And again:

> Rei, duc, prince, e emperur,
> Cunt, barun, e vavasur,
> Deivent bien a ceste oeure entendre.

> (Kings, dukes, princes and emperors,
> Earls, barons, and vavasours,
> Should listen well to this work.)[53]

In *Protheselaus* Jason brought to the battle:

> . . . de chevalers armez
> Mil que barons que vavasors

> (a thousand armed knights,
> both barons and vavasours)[54]

Finally, we must note two occurrences which lend some support to 'Bracton' and Langtoft in distinguishing vavasour from knight. In *Ipomedon* Hue de Rotelande writes how there died in battle:

> . . . barun e vavasur
> Chevalers, citeeins [e] burgeis

> (barons and vavasours,
> Knights, citizens and burgesses.)

While Denis Pyramus describes King Edmund calling a council:

> Ses ercevesques ad mandez,
> Ses evesques e ses abbez,
> Cuntes, baruns, e ses princiers,

---

[53] *Vie Seint Edmund le Rey*, ed. Arnold, ll. 49–52, 84–6. See also *Vie des set dormanz*, ed. Merrilees, ll. 691–3; *Romance of Horn*, ed. Pope, ll. 480–2; *Histoire de Guillaume le Maréchal*, ed. Meyer, ll. 1915–19, 5098–9, 5765–8; *Anglo-Norman Alexander*, ed. Foster, ll. 537–8, 3409–11, 5210–12.

[54] *Protheselaus*, ed. Kluckow, ll. 7805–6. In *The Song of Dermot and the Earl*, ll. 3160–1, we hear how Hugh de Lacy:

> Donat teres e honurs
> Veant baruns e vassaurs.

> (Gave lands and honours
> In the presence of barons and vavasours.)

How far any of these instances was dictated by the needs of the rhyme scheme is, of course, impossible to say. The same applies to some of the instances in Middle English (see section III below).

E vavasours e chivaliers;
Cunseile les ad demande.

(He summoned his archbishops,
His bishops and his abbots,
His earls, barons and princes,
His vavasours and knights;
He asked them for advice.)[55]

A study of the Anglo-Norman literature suggests, then, that the word vavasour was in continuous use in England through to the time of 'Bracton',[56] and that it was used, for the most part, in a way which was consistent with its mid-twelfth-century usage. A vavasour was a man of modest fortune, very likely an *arrière-vassal*.[57] Before looking in detail at 'Bracton's' classification of men it is worth noting that the term 'vavassory' also appears in his treatise. When discussing how a wife's dower should be assigned he says that the rule excepting the *caput* or head of a barony does not apply in the case of a vavassory or of other fees less than a barony.[58] The same contrasting usage of vavassory is found in the records of the central courts in the early thirteenth century.[59] Now let us turn to the section of the treatise which concerns us most. It is necessary to quote it in full:

[55] *Ipomedon*, ed. Kölbing and Koschwitz, ll. 7502–3; *Vie Seint Edmund le Rey*, ed. Arnold, ll. 993–7.

[56] *Bracton de legibus et consuetudinibus Angliae: Bracton on the Laws and Customs of England*, ed. George E. Woodbine, trans. (with revisions and notes) Samuel E. Thorne, 4 vols. published (Oxford, 1968–77). For convention's sake the author of the treatise will almost certainly continue to be known as 'Bracton', even though it seems that the role of the royal judge Henry de Bracton must now be relegated to that of reviser of the text which came into his hands in the mid-1230s. The composition of the work belongs to the 1220s and 1230s, a generation earlier than had been supposed: *ibid*., iii, pp. v–vi, xiii–lii.

[57] On one occasion in the biography William Marshal refers to his own vassals as his good vavasours: *Histoire de Guillaume le Maréchal*, ed. Meyer, l. 14340.

[58] *Bracton on the Laws and Customs of England*, ed. Woodbine, trans. Thorne, ii, p. 269.

[59] *Curia Regis Rolls*, vi, 1210–12, pp. 397–99, and xii, 1225–26, p. 62. At Trinity term 1212 Thomas de Ardern argued that Evinger de Bohun had held two honours, one in Normandy, held *in baronia*; the other in England, held *in vavasseria*. At Hilary term 1225 Odo Danmartin argued that the charters he had granted to John de St John and others were sealed under duress, and that the lands in question were held in barony of the king and were taken from him after the king's prohibition. John and the others replied that on the contrary Odo held *per vavasseriam*. See also: *Rotuli litterarum clausarum in Turri Londiniensi asservati*, ed. T. D. Hardy, 2 vols. (Rec. Comm., London, 1833–44), i, p. 432b.

But with men, in truth, there is a difference between persons, for there are some of great eminence [who] are placed above others and rule over them . . . in temporal matters which pertain to the kingdom, emperors, kings and princes, and under them dukes, earls and barons, magnates or vavasours and knights, also freemen and bondsmen (*duces, comites et barones, magnates sive vavasores, et milites, et etiam liberi et villani*).

After a discussion of the earls and the etymology of their name, he continues:

What the sword signifies.

[for] the sword signifies the defence of the realm and the country. There are other powerful persons under the king who are called barons, that is 'belli robur', the strength of war. Others are called vavasours, men of great dignity. (*Sunt etiam alii qui dicuntur vavasores, viri magnae dignitatis.*) A vavasour cannot be better defined than a vessel selected for strength, that is 'vas sortitum ad valitudinem'. Also under the king are knights, that is, persons chosen for the exercising of military duties, that they may fight with the king and those mentioned above and defend the country and the people of God. [And finally] there are free men and bondsmen under the king, subject to his power.[60]

According to this classification English society must have comprised six basic status groups: earls, barons, vavasours or magnates, knights, freemen and bondsmen. But where did 'Bracton' get this particular schema from? It occurs in the first part of his treatise for which his chief source was the *Summa* of the *Institutes* of Justinian by Azo of Bologna. The paragraph in question, however, is not from Azo at all. Coming to two titles of the *Institutes* which did not interest him, Maitland tells us, 'Bracton' discarded both them and Azo and put in their place 'a discourse on the divers kinds of free men that is all his own'.[61] If this is so, he

---

[60] *Bracton on the Laws and Customs of England*, ed. Woodbine, trans. Thorne, ii, pp. 32–3. The translations and the square brackets are those of the editor, the round brackets are mine.

[61] F. W. Maitland, *Bracton and Azo* (Selden Soc., viii, London, 1895), p. 63. The passage seems to owe something, however, (though not its vavasour) to the *Ordo Judiciarius* of Tancred, archdeacon of Bologna: H. G. Richardson, *Bracton: The Problem of His Text* (Selden Soc. Supp. Ser., ii, London, 1965), pp. 94–5. In the treatise known as *Fleta* (composed *circa* 1290) 'Bracton's' classification appears in rather altered form, having lost its proper descending

seems hardly likely to have inserted vavasour or magnate between baron and knight unless this had some contemporary significance.

But where, precisely, did the distinction between knight and vavasour lie? We may well suspect that it rested primarily on the extent and value of their estates. It could, on the other hand, be urged that the vavasours (*vavassores*) here signify the lesser landowners, the county knights as such, and the knights (*milites*) the household retainers and younger sons, landless or near-landless knights.[62] Are we to believe, though, that 'Bracton' would have described lesser county knights as magnates or men of great dignity (*viri magnae dignitatis*)? The question must be left open for the moment.

So far, it may be objected, we have seen vavasour only as it figures in various forms of literature. Is it to be found in more practical sources? An example of its traditional meaning of *arrière-vassal* is in the chirograph confirming the agreement between the chancellor, William Longchamps, and John Count of Mortain in July 1191. Bishops and abbots, earls and barons, *vavassores* and free tenants are no longer to be disseised at the will of judges and ministers but should be dealt with by judgement of

order: 'the emperor, under whom are princes and kings, and under kings earls and barons, dukes, knights, magnates, vavasours (*vauasores*) and other subjects, free and unfree (*serui*) . . .': *Fleta*, ii, ed. H. G. Richardson and G. O. Sayles (Selden Soc., lxxii, London, 1955), p. 15. 'Bracton's' strange etymology for vavasour seems to have been the cause of Maitland's doubting its derivation from *vassus vassorum*: Maitland, *Bracton and Azo*, p. 65.

62 Richardson and Sayles, for example, argue for the existence of a 'large class of landless knights' in thirteenth-century England: Richardson and Sayles, *Governance of Medieval England*, pp. 131–2. Professor G. H. Gerould offers a third interpretation, by which 'barons and vavasors represented social grades, while knights were functionaries in the business of war . . . Knighthood was in a different category': Gerould, 'Social Status of Chaucer's Franklin', p. 276. Gerould seems to be aware, at this point, of the difficulty into which 'Bracton' is leading him in his interpretation of the social position of the Franklin, but he makes no attempt to explain why the vavasour should appear to occupy the same intermediate position in Langtoft. Taking 'Bracton's' classification as a whole, this interpretation has little justification. The most obvious interpretation, of successive social grades based upon estates, is favoured by the *Third Report of the Lords' Committees on the Dignity of a Peer* (H.M.S.O., London 1822), p. 84. A fourth interpretation, that the vavasour represents the later banneret or knight leading a troop is not really an alternative to the more straightforward one, for they tended to be drawn from among the wealthier knights: N. Denholm-Young, *History and Heraldry* (Oxford, 1965), pp. 22–4. This interesting possibility was suggested to me by Mr Simon Lloyd of the University of Newcastle.

the king's court.[63] The next example takes us closer to 'Bracton':

> King to the sheriff of Lincoln, greeting. Because we were firm in
> our intent to board ship on the morrow of the Nativity of the
> Blessed Mary in order to return to the realm of England, the
> Lord conducting us, we order you to make known to all our
> faithful of your bailliwick, both bishops, abbots and priors, and
> earls, barons and good vavassors (*et bonis vavassoribus*), that
> those who do not hasten to meet us at our mooring should at
> least hasten to us at London on hearing of our arrival there, so
> that it is manifestly evident that they are glad and joyous at our
> prosperous return; moreover, you should cause to come thither
> at our meeting the mayor and four of the better and more
> discreet men of every city and borough to see us and applaud
> our return. [18 September 1243][64]

It would be rash to offer a precise interpretation of what is
meant by 'good vavasours' here. Did the king intend all the county
knights to rush to meet him or just the more substantial among
them? We are on firmer ground with another writ twelve years
later:

> It is ordered to every single sheriff of England that with all haste
> they should cause to be proclaimed publicly throughout their
> bailliwick that all those who hold from the king in chief and owe
> him service should come to the king without delay with horses
> and arms and all their power to set out with him for Scotland, as
> they love the king and his honour, and indeed the lands and
> tenements which they hold from him; and the other vavasours
> and knights who do not hold in chief from the king (*et alios
> vavassores et milites qui de rege non tenent in capite*), should
> similarly come with horses and arms, as they love the king and
> his honour and wish to deserve his grace and favour for ever.
> [16 August 1255].[65]

Here, at last, we have clear confirmation of a distinction
between vavasour and knight. By implication both are landowners, and it seems even less likely now that 'Bracton' was seeking
to contrast the vavasour primarily with the landless knight. 'Other

---

[63] *Chronica Magistri Rogeri de Hovedene*, ed. W. Stubbs, 4 vols. (Rolls Ser.,
London, 1868–71), iii, pp. 135–7.

[64] *Cal. Close Rolls*, 1242–1247, pp. 129–30.

[65] *Ibid.*, 1254–1256, p. 218; (P.R.O., C.54 no. 69 m 7d). I owe this evidence to M.
R. Powicke, *Military Obligation in Medieval England* (Oxford, 1962), p. 81.

vavasours' (*alios vavassores*), moreover, suggests that some vava-sours may have been tenants of the crown, a point to which we shall have to return.

Our last example takes us forward to the time of Pierre de Langtoft. On 14 May 1301 Thomas Grelley granted a charter to the burgesses of Manchester. Like that for nearby Stockport it is modelled on the Salford charter of *circa* 1230. There are, however, significant divergencies, one of them occurring in clause 7: 'That if anyone is impleaded in the borough on any plea he need not make answer to the charge, whether it is brought by a burgess or a villein or even a *vavasor*, save in his borough court, pleas of the crown and theft excepted'.[66]

The *vavasor* occurs in neither the Salford nor the Stockport charter. A further difference is that whereas in those towns thieves were tried in the borough court, in Manchester such cases were reserved for Grelley's own seigneurial court (*curia domini*), which was distinct from the portmoot. It is the existence of this court, Tait tells us, which explains the appearance of the *vavasor*:

> Whatever may be the true meaning of this (in England) rare term, there can hardly be a question that the reference here is to the great feudal tenants of the baron of Manchester, who constituted his baronial court. In the absence of any special provision they would no doubt have insisted on drawing disputes between themselves and their burgesses into their own court.[67]

The *vavasores* of Grelley's charter are, in effect, his own honorial barons, and their position accords well with the evidence given above. These instances can hardly be explained away as either occasional borrowings or as part of a literary or a legal tradition. There is now a strong probability that we are dealing with a term of contemporary parlance. Before turning to the implications of this for the study of thirteenth-century society, however, we must look more closely at the *Chronicle of Pierre de Langtoft*.[68] Vavasours are to be found on three occasions in the

66 James Tait, *Medieval Manchester and the Beginnings of Lancashire* (Manchester, 1904), pp. 73–6, 114–16. I have followed Tait's translation.

67 *Ibid.* pp. 75–6.

68 For discussions of the value and content of Langtoft's Chronicle, see Legge, *Anglo-Norman in the Cloisters*, pp. 70–4, and, more recently, Robert Stepsis, 'Pierre de Langtoft's Chronicle: An Essay in Medieval Historiography', *Medievalia et humanistica*, new ser., iii (1972), pp. 51–73.

final and contemporary part of his work. On each occasion they
are found within that hierarchy of social grades which we have
seen elsewhere in Anglo-Norman literature but here, once again,
occupying a position between baron and knight. Under 1294
Langtoft speaks of those who have gone to Gascony:

> Barouns e vavasours de gentil lynage,
> Chuvalers et serjauns of lur cosinage,
> Gens à pé sanz noumbre de more et boscage

> (Barons and vavasours of noble descent,
> Knights and serjeants with their kindred,
> People on foot without number from moor and bush)

In 1296 we hear of the siege of Dunbar:

> Barouns et vavassours, chuvaler, esquyer,
> Surays et Norays, i alaynt de bon quer

> (Barons and vavasours, knights and esquires,
> Southerners and Northerners, went there with good will)

And later, when recounting the disaster at Stirling in 1297, he
writes how:

> A cele mesavenue estaient tuez
> Vavassours curtoys de gentil parentez,
> Robert de Somerville et sun fiz aynez;
> Chuvalers et sergauns i pristrent congez

> (At this misfortune were slain
> Courteous vavasours of noble kindred,
> Robert de Somerville and his eldest son;
> Knights and serjeants took there their leave)[69]

It seems more than likely that the author intended Robert de
Somerville and his son to be included among, if indeed they are
not synonymous with, those 'courteous vavasours of noble
kindred'. If this is so, then we have an interesting piece of
evidence, for Robert de Somerville was a very substantial Staffordshire knight, with further estates in at least three other
counties and half the barony of Morpeth in Northumberland in

---

[69] *The Chronicle of Pierre de Langtoft*, ed. Thomas Wright, 2 vols. (Rolls Ser.
London 1866–8), ii, pp. 230–1, 240–1, 298–9. I have used the editor's translations.

right of his wife.[70] Moreover, his Staffordshire manor of Alrewas was held in chief, giving us confirmation of what is implied by the writ of 1255 when it speaks of 'other vavasours and knights' who do not hold of the crown. A vavasour may be a tenant-in-chief; he is a substantial landowner and no longer, necessarily, a mere *vassus vassorum*.

The middle part of Langtoft's *Chronicle* affords us an even more startling example. When relating the defeat of the Disinherited in 1266, he includes among their number:

> Baldewyn le Vavasour,
> Ke de Cestrefeld cel houre fu seygnur.

> (Baldwin the Vavasour,
> At that time lord of Chesterfield.)[71]

Now the lord of Chesterfield in 1266 was none other than Baldwin Wake. Lord of the honour, and probable barony, of Bourne in Lincolnshire, Baldwin was one of Simon de Montfort's leading lieutenants, and a more substantial man even than Robert de Somerville.[72] Could the ranks of the vavasours be stretched to include such as him? It would appear so.

One must, however, be wary. Although they are drawn from a range of sources and their cumulative effect is clear enough, none the less the number of instances given above remains relatively small. We may not conclude from them that the word 'vavasour' was on every man's lips in the thirteenth century nor, necessarily, that it was capable of a single and precise definition. The ancient meaning of *arrière-vassal* may have lingered (for example, in

---

[70] An idea of the extent of Somerville possessions can be gained from the following: *Cal. Inquisitions Post Mortem*, iii, no. 392, and viii, no. 140; *Cal. Charter Rolls*, ii, 1257–1300, p. 342; *Book of Fees*, pp. 142, 520, 545, 593, 947, 967, 970, 974–5, 998; and *Feudal Aids*, i, pp. 248, 252, and ii, pp. 7–8, 181–2. For the barony of Morpeth, see I. J. Sanders, *English Baronies: A Study of their Origins and Descent* (Oxford, 1960), p. 66. A Somerville was in the highest grade of lay landowner, below the earls of Lancaster and Derby, in an assessment for taxation purposes made in Staffordshire in 1337: R. H. Hilton, 'Lord and Peasant in Staffordshire in the Middle Ages', in *The English Peasantry in the Later Middle Ages* (Oxford, 1975), p. 218; repr. from the *N. Staffs. Jl. Field Studies*, x (1970).

[71] *Chronicle of Pierre de Langtoft*, ed. Wright, ii, p. 149.

[72] Sanders, *English Baronies*, pp. 107–8; F. M. Powicke, *King Henry III and the Lord Edward*, 2 vols. (Oxford, 1947), ii, p. 523; *Documents of the Baronial Movement of Reform*, ed. Treharne and Sanders, pp. 284–5.

vernacular literature), much as the older meanings of baron tended to linger.[73] We *may* conclude, however, that it *was used*, and used to give expression to a perceived difference among landowners below the highest rank, in terms of wealth and social standing. This being so, it does seem unsafe, to say the least, to assume that the vavasour of the Provisions of Oxford stands for the county knight *per se*. In all likelihood what the reformers intended in the summer of 1258 was that the sheriffs should be drawn from among the more (possibly the most) substantial county landowners.[74]

The changing meaning of vavasour has an importance, however, which transcends the interpretation of a single, though significant, clause in the baronial reform programme. That the mid-thirteenth century was an important stage in the formation of the English gentry is generally agreed. Treharne, in particular, has stressed the growth of political awareness and participation on the part of the lesser landowners at this time,[75] and the reasons for this are well enough known. The great Angevin reforms, the gradual (and allied) decline in the role of the honour court and the development of 'self-government at the king's command' all played their part. The thirteenth century, moreover, was to experience a relative decline in the importance attached to tenure, a decline manifested

---

[73] For the various meanings attached to the word baron, see Round, 'Origin of the House of Lords', pp. 339–42, and for the general evolution of the word, the works given in n. 84 below. Since literature does not necessarily reflect social reality in a direct way, there may often be a time-lag before it registers a change in the meaning of a social term.

[74] Of the sheriffs appointed in Oct./Nov. 1258 for the ensuing year, Treharne noticed three who he considered 'may have been of standing higher than that of vavassours': Treharne, *Baronial Plan of Reform*, p. 122. In fact, these may have been closest to what was originally envisaged. There are indications, moreover, that the Council found difficulty in securing the services of the sort of men they required. Some of those selected either failed to act or delayed taking up office, while at least one was appointed without consultation: *ibid.*, pp. 122–5. The subject warrants further research. For a recent discussion of the sheriff in the immediately preceding period, see D. A. Carpenter, 'The Decline of the Curial Sheriff in England, 1194–1258', *Eng. Hist. Rev.*, xci (1976), pp. 1–32. Ironically, one of the most notorious of thirteenth-century sheriffs was Robert le Vavassur, sheriff of Nottingham and Derby in 1246–55, whose misdeeds warranted a royal inquiry: *Cal. Patent Rolls*, 1247–58, pp. 430–2, 459, 507; see also Jacob, *Studies in the Period of Baronial Reform*, p. 26 n., where, however, he is erroneously called Richard.

[75] R. F. Treharne, 'The Knights in the Period of Reform and Rebellion, 1258–67: A Critical Phase in the Rise of a New Class', *Bull. Inst. Hist. Res.*, xxi (1946), pp. 1–12.

in numerous ways. Barony, for example, was becoming more a matter of tradition, whilst by the 1240s the crown was moving away from military tenure to minimum (landed) wealth qualification in its distraint of knighthood.[76] All of this was bound to transform the lesser landowners' perception of their relationship to the central government. But it must also have altered their perception of themselves, and not only in the sense of their corporate identity. There must surely have emerged a stronger awareness of differences in their own ranks than ever before. Though there could be no sharp dividing lines it seems highly likely that men will have perceived more than a mere continuum. Some, to take an obvious point, had interests which transcended county lines. The new meaning attached to vavasour may well represent this changed perception. In the fullness of time this perception was to help create the series of fairly clearly defined gradations with which the mature gentry came to be comprised.

The thirteenth-century knightly class, however, has been credited with a degree of cohesion, and even capacity for concerted action, which it almost certainly did not possess; and rather too much, arguably, has been made of single occurrences in the sources: the vavasour in the Provisions of Oxford; the community of the bachelry of England (*communitas bacheleriae Angliae*) in the Annals of Burton for 1259.[77] On the other hand the effect of

---

[76] M. R. Powicke, 'Distraint of Knighthood and Military Obligation under Henry III', *Speculum*, xxv (1950), pp. 457–70.

[77] According to the Burton annalist the community of the bachelry of England forced the hand of the baronial reformers causing the publication of what became known as the Provisions of Westminster in October 1259: *Annales Monastici*, ed. H. R. Luard, 5 vols. (Rolls Ser., London 1864–9), i, p. 471. The interpretation of this phrase has occasioned much debate. Tout argued, against Stubbs, that *bachelor* denoted little more than young man or young warrior and that the community of the bachelry of England meant no more 'than a chance number of rash young gentlemen': T. F. Tout, 'Communitas Bacheleriae Angliae', *Eng. Hist. Rev.*, xvii (1902), pp. 89–95. Jacob, on the other hand, reaffirmed the traditional line and urged that the bachelry was 'a body which had corporate interests and perhaps even a corporate policy', and that 'the bachelors were the mouthpiece of the vavasour class': Jacob, *Studies in the Period of Baronial Reform*, pp. 126–34. For him, the bachelors were knights in the retinues of the magnates, many of them landowners in their own right. Treharne and Powicke followed Jacob rather than Tout: Treharne, *Baronial Plan of Reform*, pp. 160–4; Powicke, *King Henry III and the Lord Edward*, p. 407; Powicke, *The Thirteenth Century*, pp. 153–4. A recent study of the term *bachelor* concludes that 'throughout the thirteenth and fourteenth centuries the "bachelor" was a special kind of retainer associated . . . with service in the

words used to express differences in status or influence has sometimes been blunted. One thinks of the *buzones* of the county court 'on whose nod', 'Bracton' tells us, 'the votes of the others depended'.[78] This term has been extended to the administrator knights as a whole and, more recently, to the entire social class from which they sprang.[79] Another example would appear to be vavasour.

It is paradoxical, though, that it should have been vavasour, with its clear tenurial connotations, which was adapted to meet this new perception. And yet it ought not really to surprise us, for as Sir Frank Stenton wrote of the Normans, these men had 'no great store of words from which to draw indefinite terms of social significance.'[80] Regarding the process by which the change in meaning occurred, a clue is provided by Walter Map. Looking back from the court of Henry II to that of his grandfather, he pictures Henry I in the company of his earls, his barons and his chief vavasours (*proceres vavassores*).[81] From here it was but a short step to confining the term vavasour to the greater among them. The sense will have shifted somewhat in consequence. It is worth recalling that the same period saw the emergence of expressed differentiation within the baronage, as terms like

household, and enjoying a more intimate relationship with his lord than did other knightly retainers who did not have his status': J. M. W. Bean, 'Bachelor and Retainer', *Medievalia et humanistica*, new ser., iii (1972), pp. 117–31. Though Tout's discussion of *bachelor* has been superseded, his scepticism over the high-flown interpretation of what is, in any case, a single statement by a single chronicler remains salutary.

[78] *Bracton on the Laws and Customs of England*, ed. Woodbine, trans. Thorne, ii, p. 327; Gaillard Lapsley, 'Buzones', *Eng. Hist. Rev.*, clxxxvi (1932), pp. 117–93.

[79] R. F. Hunnisett, *The Medieval Coroner* (Cambridge, 1961), pp. 170–1; N. Denholm-Young, *The Country Gentry in the Fourteenth Century* (Oxford, 1969), pp. 2–3; K. S. Naughton, *The Gentry of Bedfordshire in the Thirteenth and Fourteenth Centuries* (Leicester, 1976), p. 54.

[80] Stenton, *First Century of English Feudalism*, p. 23. The Normans carried the word 'vavasour' with them on their travels. As we have seen it penetrated into England in the wake of the Conquest. In Norman Italy it was used to describe the lightly armed cavalryman owing what was essentially public military service, and eventually less discriminately as a synonym for *miles* whether Norman or Italian, enfeoffed or not: Claude Cahen, *Le régime féodal de l'Italie Normande* (Paris, 1940), pp. 29–30, 53–4.

[81] *De nugis curialium*, ed. Thomas Wright (Camden Soc., I, London, 1850), p. 225. On another occasion Walter Map tells the story of Raso Christianus, builder of a fortress and 'one of those who are commonly called *vavassores* (unus ex hiis quos vulgo vavassores aiunt)': *ibid.*, p. 131.

'greater barons' (in *Magna Carta*) and 'chief barons' (in Glanvill's treatise) testify.[82] 'The goal therefore to which the "baro" was tending was that of *a member of the more important class* ("ba-rones *majores*") of *tenants-in-chief not distinguished by any higher title*'.[83] Developments here, however, were foreshortened by the interests of the crown, which resulted in barony by tradition and, ultimately, in barony by writ.[84]

Similar shifts in meaning occurred in other provinces. In Lombardy, for example, *valvassor* as a term of social definition travelled downwards. The *Consuetudines feudorum*, compiled towards the middle of the twelfth century, complains repeatedly of the usurpation of the title *capitaneus*, once reserved for marquises and counts, by the *valvassores majores* or *valvassores regis*.[85] This older class of *valvassores* appear, in fact, to have become known as *valvassores majores* in order to distinguish them from their vassals, the *valvassores minores* whose vassals in turn were *valvassores minimi*. The usurpation of *capitaneus* by the *valvassores majores* left the designation *valvassor* as the prerogative of the erstwhile *valvassores minores*, so that the *valvassores minimi* now became *valvassores minores* or *valvasini*.[86] A combination of subinfeudation and social aspiration had thus resulted in first an extension and then a renarrowing of an ancient term.

Once it is recognized that the term was an evolving one, and that it was liable to evolve peculiarly in any given region, then the

---

[82] J. H. Round, ' "Barons" and "Knights" in the Great Charter', in H. E. Malden (ed.), *Magna Carta Commemoration Essays* (Roy. Hist. Soc., London, 1917), pp. 46–77; *Tractatus de legibus et consuetudinibus regni Anglie qui Glanvilla vocatur*, ed. G. D. G. Hall (London, 1965), p. 110. Glanvill speaks also of chief baronies: *ibid.*, p. 108, whilst the *Dialogue of the Exchequer* refers to greater and lesser baronies: *Dialogus de Scaccario*, ed. C. Johnson (London, 1959), p. 95.

[83] Round, 'Origin of the House of Lords', pp. 341–2 (Round's italics).

[84] On this whole question, see in particular I. J. Sanders, *Feudal Military Service in England* (Oxford, 1956), pp. 1–27; Sanders, *English Baronies*, pp. v–vi; Round, 'Origin of the House of Lords', *passim*; J. E. Powell and K. Wallis, *The House of Lords in the Middle Ages* (London, 1968), pp. 223–31.

[85] *Das Langobardische Lehnrecht*, ed. Karl Lehmann (Göttingen, 1896), pp. 83, 93, 101.

[86] *Ibid.*, pp. 83, 85, 93, 127–8; Guilhiermoz, *Essai sur l'origine de la noblesse*, p. 151 and nn. 40–41, pp. 264–5 n. 29; R. Boutruche, *Seigneurie et féodalité: le premier âge des liens d'homme à homme* (Paris, 1968), pp. 392–4; Boutruche, *Seigneurie of féodalité: l'apogée*, p. 271 n. 48. For the vavasour in Spain, see n. 12 above.

search for a single definition becomes fruitless and vavasour loses some of that imprecision which historians have diagnosed.

III

Did vavasour retain its thirteenth-century value through to the time of Chaucer, as Gerould suggests? To answer this we must turn to the literature in Middle English. The first observation to be made here is that the incidence of vavasour is, in fact, very low. There is, however, one cluster of occurrences: in three of those four romances written in the London area, most probably around 1300, and known collectively as 'the *Kyng Alisaunder* group'. *Kyng Alisaunder* itself is a fairly free adaptation of *Le roman de toute chevalerie*.[87] It employs vavasours on two occasions, neither of them corresponding to any of the four occasions when it is found in the Anglo-Norman work. They occur in fact, at expansions of the Anglo-Norman model. In the account of Alexander's second battle against Darius we find the following:

> Egipte justed wiþ hem of Tyre,
> Symple kniȝth wiþ riche syre
> þere nas foreȝift ne forberying
> Bituene vauasoure ne kyng
> Tofore men miȝtten and byhynde
> Cuntek seke and cuntek fynde

> (Egyptians jousted with those of Tyre,
> Simple knight with rich sire.
> There was no giving of quarter nor showing of mercy
> Between vavasour nor king.
> Men might before and behind
> Conflict seek and conflict find)

While the discussion of the preparations for the battle includes:

> Noot Ich no tale of his squyers,
> Ne of vavasoures ne of bachilers,
> Ne of b[o]wers ne of arblasters

---

[87] *Kyng Alisaunder*, ed G. V. Smithers, 2 vols. (Early English Text Soc., original ser., ccxxvii, ccxxxvii, London, 1952–7).

(I know not the tally of his squires,
Nor of vavasours nor of bachelors,
Nor of archers nor of crossbowmen)[88]

There may be an echo, here, of the account of the preparations made by Porrus before a later conflict in the Anglo-Norman work, though shorn of its more outlandish terms.[89]

Of Arthour and Of Merlin is an adaptation of the *Estoire de Merlin*.[90] It boasts three vavasours, though again not in places where one would expect to find them from the Old French text. Whereas in the Middle English version Arthur's host in *Carohaise* is Blaire a 'good and jovial burgess' (*fair buriays and ioliif*), in the French he is 'a vavasour, a very valiant man, a young and rich bachelor' (*un vauassor moult preudomme & iouene bacheler & riche*).[91] Nevertheless we do find:

Chasteleins sones and vauasours

(Châtelains' sons and vavasours)[92]

Boþe kniȝtes and vauasour
þis damiesels loue par amour.

88 *Ibid.*, ll. 3820–5; 3300–2.
89
　　　Assemble a ly ses fiz e soud[i]ers,
　　　Dux, princes e contes, vavasors e terrers,
　　　Serganz e bachelers, arblasters e archers

　　　(He assembles his sons and soldiers,
　　　Dukes, princes and earls, vavasours and lords holding land,
　　　Sergeants and bachelors, crossbowmen and archers)
　　(*Anglo-Norman Alexander*, ed. Foster, ll. 5210–12).

90 *Of Arthour and of Merlin*, ed. O. D. Macrae–Gibson, 2 vols. (Early Eng. Text Soc., original ser., 1973–9).

91 *Of Arthur and of Merlin*, ed. Macrae-Gibson, 1. 5562; *The Vulgate Version of the Arthurian Romances*, ed. H. O. Sommer, 7 vols. (repr. New York, 1969), ii, *Histoire de Merlin*, p. 142.

92 *Of Arthur and of Merlin*, ed. Macrae-Gibson, 1. 4761. Comparison between extant Middle English and Old French texts is, of course, hazardous. We cannot always be sure that the line in question was not in the particular manuscript which served as the model. Of the passage in which this particular line occurs, the editor states that none of the manuscripts of the *Estoire de Merlin* which he has consulted has an equivalent passage but that Kölbing quotes the following from the printed version of 1528; 'who were sons of châtelains and of noble men of the country of Logres' (*qui estoient filz des chastelains et des gentils hommes de la contree de Logres*): *ibid.*, ii, p. 120. The phrase *Castelleins and vauasours of the londe* is found at this point, moreover, in the English Prose Merlin, itself a close translation of the *Estoire de Merlin*: Merlin, ed. H. B. Wheatley (Early Eng. Text Soc., original ser., x, xxi, xxxvi, cxii, London, 1865–99; repr. in l vol. 1973), p. 192.

> (Both knights and vavasours
> These damsels love passionately.)

And:

> Hou he dede Sagremor soccour
> þurth an eld vauasour.

> (How he did support Sagremor
> Through an old vavasour.)[93]

In the *Seven Sages of Rome* the queen relates the story of the evil steward and warns her husband that he too may suffer a malign fate though she will survive:

> No forse on me, after an emperour
> Mai me wedde a vauasour
> I mai liue a wel god lif,
> þai i be nowt an emperours wif.

> (It matters not to me, after an emperor
> I may wed a vavasour.
> I can live a very good life,
> Though I be not an emperor's wife.)[94]

What the authors (or possibly author) of these works understood by the word 'vavasour' is, perhaps, another matter, but at least they were prepared to employ it.[95] This is hardly true of the

---

[93] *Of Arthur and of Merlin,* ed. Macrae-Gibson, ll. 8660–1, 8557–8.

[94] *The Seven Sages of Rome (Southern Version),* ed. K. Brunner (Early Eng. Text Soc., original ser., cxci, London, 1933). ll. 1655–8. This passage does not appear to correspond to anything in the source, the French prose version, but again there are numerous manuscripts and it could be derived from a variant: *Deux rédactions du roman des sept sages,* ed. Gaston Paris (Société des Anciens Textes Français, Paris, 1876).

[95] G. V. Smithers, following Kölbing, argued that the four romances had a single author: *Kyng Alisaunder,* ed. Smithers, ii, p. 41. Professor Pearsall accepts this, but both Dieter Mehl and Mrs Loomis have had doubts: *The Auchinleck Manuscript,* ed. D. Pearsall and I. C. Cunningham (London, 1977), p. xi; D. Mehl, *The Middle English Romances of the Thirteenth and Fourteenth Centuries* (London, 1968), p. 242; L. H. Loomis, *Medieval Romance in England* (New York, 1924; repr. 1963), pp. 147–8, 177. The recent editor of Arthur and Merlin is also sceptical and would particularly exclude *Richard Coeur de Lion: Of Arthour and of Merlin,* ed. Macrae-Gibson, p. 75. Interestingly, this is the only one of the four which has no vavasour. The possibility that we may have a single author, steeped in French literature, however, prevents us from readily concluding that the term 'vavasour' was well known to, and understood by, the audience.

writers of the next generation. The romances of 'the *Kyng Alisaunder* group' are all to be found in the famous Auchinleck manuscript, produced in a London bookshop shortly after the accession of Edward III. Their composition, though, is placed a generation or so earlier. Many of the other romances in the volume, however, were composed nearer to the date of the manuscript, and some at least in the bookshop itself.[96] Two of them are adaptations of Anglo-Norman romances which have already been discussed. It is interesting to observe what has happened to the vavasours in them. In *Boeve de Haumtone*, it will be recalled, a messenger in search of the emperor meets with a vavasour. In the Middle English *Sir Beves of Hamtoun*:

> þo he com in to Al-mayne,
> þar a mette wiþ a swain
>   And grette him wel:
> 'Felawe,' a seide, 'par amur
> Whar mai ich finde þemperur?
>   þow me tel.'

> (Then he came to Germany,
> Where he met a swain
>   And greeted him well:
> 'Fellow', he said, 'for love
> Where may I find the emperor?
>   Do tell me.')[97]

The composer of the Auchinleck *Guy of Warwick* worked from a manuscript which was undoubtedly close to the extant Anglo-Norman manuscript. And yet, whereas Gui sees the Greeks complaining that the son of a poor vavasour will become their emperor, Guy says rather:

> For, ȝif þou haddest me hir ȝiue,
> & ich hir toke þer whiles y liue,
> þan wold þi men anon,

[96] On the 'Auchinleck Bookshop', see in particular L. H. Loomis, 'The Auchinleck Manuscript and a Possible London Bookshop of 1330–1340', *Pubns. Mod. Language Assoc. America*, lvii, no. 3 (1942), pp. 595–627; *Auchinleck Manuscript*, ed. Pearsall and Cunningham, pp. vii–xi.

[97] *The Romance of Sir Beues of Hamtoun*, ed. E. Kölbing, 3 vols. (Early Eng. Text Soc., extra ser., xlvi, xlvii, lxv, London, 1885–94; repr. in 1 vol. 1973), ll. 115–20.

þat wonderful be mani on,
þe seggen wiþ deshonour
þou haddest made a pouer man emperour.

(For, if you were to give her to me,
And I took her for my lifetime,
Then your men, many of them excellent,
Would soon say that with dishonour
You had made a poor man emperor.)[98]

For the barons' complaint that Adelstan shamed them in honour-
ing Heralt, the son of a poor vavasour, Auchinleck has only:

Oþer hadde þer-of envie,
And þouȝte hii wolde on hym lye,
þat a wer y-schent.

(Others were envious thereof,
And thought they would lie about him
So that he would be disgraced.)[99]

The same impression – of avoidance of the word vavasour – is
given by Robert Mannyng of Brunne in his *Chronicle of England*,
written at the priory of Sixhill in Lincolnshire and completed in
1338. The second part of it is a translation of Pierre de Langtoft's
Chronicle.[100] Robert Mannyng omits vavasour on two of the three
occasions when it is found in Langtoft's contemporary section.

---

[98] *The Romance of Guy of Warwick*, ed. J. Zupitza, 3 vols. (Early Eng. Text Soc.,
extra ser., xlii, xlix, lix, London, 1883–91; repr. in 1 vol. 1966), ll. 4435–40.

[99] *Ibid.*, Reinbrun, Gii sone of Wawike, v. 15, ll. 7–9.
Another Middle English version (Gonville and Caius MS. 107) has here:

. . . the kyng did an-ryght
To honoure so pore a knyght
That was no better than a page:
To hys barons he did outerage.

(. . . the king was unjust
To honour so poor a knight
That was no better than a page:
To his barons he acted wrongly.)

(ll. 8780–3; *Romance of Guy of Warwick*, ed. Zupitza, p. 495).

[100] For Robert Mannyng, see K. Sisam, *Fourteenth-Century Verse and Prose*
(Oxford, 1921), pp. 1–3; D. Pearsall, *Old English and Middle English Poetry*
(London, 1977), pp. 117–18. The first part of the chronicle is based on Wace
and was edited for the Rolls Series: *The Chronicle of Robert of Brunne*, ed. F.
J. Furnivall, 2 vols. (London, 1887). The second part is available only in an
eighteenth-century edition by Thomas Hearne.

Though we do find 'Barons & vavasours, knyghtes & squiere', the phrase 'barons and vavasours of noble descent' (*Barouns e vavasours de gentil lynage*) has been lost by contraction, while for 'courteous vavasours of noble kindred' (*vavassours curtoys de gentil parentez*) we have 'God men of honour, that would to the bataile bide'.[101]

In the romance *Ywain and Gawain* the avoidance is total. An abridged free translation of the *Yvain* of Chrétien de Troyes, this was written in the north of England, most probably in the second quarter of the fourteenth century.[102] As P. J. Frankis has pointed out, for Chrétien's hospitable vavasour the Middle English version invariably substitutes knight. 'It is therefore likely', says Frankis, 'that the word *vavasor* did not mean anything very specific to the fourteenth-century English translator, even though he was evidently a northerner'.[103]

It has to be admitted, however, that the term 'vavasour' does come through very occasionally in works written after this date.[104]

---

[101] *The Works of Thomas Hearne*, 4 vols. (Oxford, 1725), iv, pp. 271, 274, 297. From the second part of Langtoft's Chronicle, Mannyng took over *Baudewyn the vauasoure* and the story of Statin, the *vavasoure* of King Isaac: *ibid.*, pp. 166, 223. In the first part of Mannyng's chronicle the following comes through from Wace (see n. 21 above):

> He gaf giftes of honurs
> & lands & rents to vauasours

> (He gave gifts of honours,
> And lands and rents to vavasours)

> (*Chronicle of Robert of Brunne*, ed. Furnivall, ll. 10995–6).

[102] *Ywain and Gawain*, ed. A. B. Friedman and N. T. Harrington (Early Eng. Text Soc., original ser., ccliv, London, 1964).

[103] P. J. Frankis, 'Chaucer's "Vavasour" and Chrétien de Troyes', *Notes and Queries* (Feb. 1968), pp. 46–7.

[104] Most notably in *Sir Ferumbras*, a free translation of a manuscript similar to the extant Old French *Fierabras*, written, according to its editor, in southern dialect early in the reign of Richard II: *The English Charlemagne Romances I: Sir Ferumbras*, ed. S. J. Herrtage (Early Eng. Text Soc., extra ser., xxxiv, London, 1879); *Fierabras: chanson de geste*, ed. A. Kroeber and G. Servois (Paris, 1860). In both works the term has a strong 'pejorative value'. Compare, for instance:

> Litel prowesse for me it were wiþ a vauasour for to melle

> (For me there would be little valour in fighting with a vavasour)
> (*Ferumbras*, ed. Herrtage, l. 430)

with:

> Certes, ains en seroit laidement avillés,
> K'au fil de vavasour seroie en canp mellés.

This is no more then we would expect from a literature which is essentially derivative. On these grounds even the evidence of 'the *Kyng Alisaunder* group' must be treated with just a little caution. If one were to discount it, it might then be argued that the term lost currency a little earlier in the south than in the north and the north midlands. Taking the Middle English evidence as a whole, though, it does look as if the early fourteenth century was crucial and that vavasour hardly survived as a living term beyond that date. An objection to the evidence on the grounds of the relative audiences for Anglo-Norman and Middle English literature ought not to detain us for long. It is being increasingly realized that the social distance between the two wings of vernacular literature has been exaggerated in the past, and that the differences between

> (Rather indeed would he be meanly degraded,
> Who would engage in battle with the son of a vavasour.)
> > (*Fierabras*, ed. Kroeber and Servois, p. 15).

See also *Ferumbras*, ed. Herrtage, ll. 562, 1180, 1184; *Fierabras*, ed. Kroeber and Servois, pp. 14, 15 (*bis*), 59. There is one occurrence in *Octovian Imperator*:

> And everych was yong vauyssour
> With good gysarmes.

> (And everyone was a young vavasour,
> With good halberd.)
> > (ll. 1613–14)

(H. Weber, *Metrical Romances of the Thirteenth, Fourteenth and Fifteenth Centuries*, 3 vols., Edinburgh, 1810, iii); and one occurrence in the Gonville and Caius *Guy of Warwick*, though surprisingly not in a place where it is found in the extant Anglo-Norman which it seems to follow quite closely:

> Hys lord he hath be-trayed are,
> That made hym knyght of gret honour
> From a pore vavyssoure.

> (He has betrayed his lord,
> Who made him a knight of great honour
> From a poor vavasour.)
> > (ll. 8837–9; *Guy of Warwick*, ed. Zupitza, p. 496)

It is also to be found in the English Prose Merlin: *Merlin*, ed. Wheatley, p. 24, l. 19, and p. 307, l. 15. Two occurrences in fifteenth-century Scottish literature are also derivative: *Lancelot of the Laik*, ed. M. M. Gray (Scottish Text Soc., Edinburgh, 1912), l. 1729; *Gilbert of the Haye's Prose Manuscript (1456)*, ed. J. H. Stevenson, 2 vols. (Scottish Text Soc., Edinburgh, 1901–14), ii, *The Buke of Knychthede*, pp. 20–1.

Anglo-Norman and Middle English romances are to be explained more by the latter's catering for a wider than for an exclusively lower-class audience.[105] The quality of some of the Middle English romances, for example *Kyng Alisaunder* and *Ywain and Gawain*, suggests moreover that we ought not to be seeking a uniform audience for them. In any case vavasour is hardly found at all in a language other than English after the early fourteenth century. In French, after Langtoft and his contemporary Nicholas Bozon,[106] we do not meet with it again until it appears, fleetingly, in the work of Chaucer's friend John Gower. It is not to be found in works like Thomas of Heaton's *Scalacronica*, nor the *Life of the Black Prince* by the Chandos Herald. It does not figure in the *Statutes of the Realm* nor, with one curious exception, in the *Parliament Rolls*, despite items which reveal contemporary social terminology such as the Sumptuary Laws of 1363 or the poll tax preamble of 1379.[107]

---

[105] Legge, *Anglo-Norman Literature and its Background*, pp. 370–1; Mehl, *Middle English Romances*, pp. 7–13; Pearsall, *Old English and Middle English Poetry*, pp. 87–9, 113–18.

[106] Bozon was a Franciscan, probably of Nottingham Friary. Vavasour occurs in his *Lettre de l'Empereur Orgeuil* produced, most probably, between 1291 and 1310. There the Emperor Pride instructs the various classes on how they are to behave. The vavasours who keep house and retinue should make themselves difficult to serve; they should find fault with their servants whether they do well or ill: *Deux poèmes de Nicholas Bozon*, ed. Johan Vising (Göteborgs Högskolas Arsskrift, xxv, Göteborg, 1919), p. 66. For Bozon, himself, see Legge, *Anglo-Norman Literature and its Background*, pp. 229-32. See also J. Mann, *Chaucer and Medieval Estates Satire* (Cambridge, 1973), pp. 155, 307.

[107] *Statutes of the Realm*, 11 vols. (London, 1810–28), i, p. 380; *Rotuli Parliamentorum*, 6 vols. (Rec. Comm., London, 1783), iii, pp. 57–8. The exception is during the formal 'record and process' of Richard II's deposition in 1399. In his renunciation Richard absolved the following from their oath of fealty, their homage and all bond of allegiance: 'Archbishops, bishops and all other prelates of churches secular or regular . . ., and dukes, marquesses, earls, barons, knights, vassals, and vavasours (*Vassallos, et Valvassores*) and all my liegemen'. The same words were used by the committee of deposition in forbidding any future obedience or submission to Richard as king: *Rotuli Parliamentorum*, iii, pp. 416, 422. It cannot be without significance, however, that the form *valvassor* is not found elsewhere among the instances of the usage of this term in England, whereas it is the common form in documents emanating from northern Italy. It is worth recalling here that the committee set up to advise on the best way of deposing Richard, on which sat civil and canon lawyers, had taken as its major precedent not the deposition of Edward II but that of Frederick II by Pope Innocent IV in 1245: *Chronicon Adae de Usk*, ed. E. M. Thompson (London, 1812), pp. 29–30; B. Wilkinson, 'The Deposition of Richard II and the Accession of Henry IV', *Eng. Hist. Rev.*, liv (1939), p. 231.

It would be foolhardy, given the limitations of the evidence, to offer absolute reasons as to why the term should have been superseded, but a plausible hypothesis would be to connect it with the increasing definition of grades within the gentry. The early fourteenth century saw, after all, the emergence of a closed, or at least closing, parliamentary peerage, and the real beginnings of a recognized squirearchy below the knights. The knights themselves were becoming a relatively small élite, occupying a position not dissimilar from that suggested here for the thirteenth-century vavasour.[108] The latter belonged to an early and transitional phase in the formation of a graded English gentry.

What, then, of Chaucer and John Gower? It has been shown recently that there existed in the capital in the latter part of the fourteenth century what can only be described as 'the Chaucer circle', a sophisticated group of 'littérateurs' whose members included courtiers, diplomats and civil servants.[109] This circle probably constituted the primary audience for the *Canterbury Tales* and, no doubt, for the works of other members of the group, including Gower. Though their main interests lay with contemporary and with classical literature, these men will have had some acquaintance, at least, with the literature of the more recent past. It is not, therefore, altogether surprising that the archaic vavasour should be found in their work. Gower's vavasour occurs in his *Mirour de l'Omme*, a work in the estates satire tradition. In his portrayal of Usury he speaks of her brokers and procurers who search for *chivaliers, vavasours* and *escuiers* who have mortgaged

---

[108] The classic statement on the retreat from knighthood is N. Denholm-Young, 'Feudal Society in the Thirteenth Century: The Knights', repr. in his *Collected Papers* (Cardiff, 1969), pp. 83–94. In his, unfortunately, unpublished thesis, A. R. J. Jurica has shown that for Somerset, at least, the decline in the number of knights became serious only from 1292: 'The Knights of Edward I' (Univ. of Birmingham Ph.D. thesis, 1976), esp. ch. 3, 'Knights and Men at Arms'. The chronology and pace of the retreat from knighthood requires further attention, as does the rise of esquire as a social grade. On this last point, see Denholm-Young, *Country Gentry in the Fourteenth Century*, ch. 1, esp. pp. 5, 17–19. The growing importance of the banneret, or knight leading a troop as opposed to a knight bachelor, may also be important in this context, in that it produced a division within the already thinning knightly ranks. For the peerage, see n. 84 above.

[109] D. Pearsall, 'The Troilus Frontispiece and Chaucer's Audience', *Year Book of English Studies* (Mod. Humanities Research Assoc., 1977), pp. 68–74; Pearsall, *Old English and Middle English Poetry*, pp. 194–7; Paul Strohm, 'Chaucer's Audience', *Literature and History*, v (Spring 1977), pp. 26–41.

their lands and come to borrow of necessity. They are led to usurers so that there may be arranged what is newly called a 'money contract' (*la chevisance des deniers*).[110] The order *chivaliers, vavasours, escuiers* is reminiscent of the order *bachelers, vavasours, esquiers* found in Nicholas Bozon's *Lettre de l'Empereur Orgeuil*, whilst the separation of vavasour from knight (that is, knight-errant) has considerable significance in French literature.

That the Franklin should be a vavasour has often been found puzzling. In 1968 Frankis broke rather with tradition in suggesting that the 'solution of the problem is to be found . . . not in any technical application the word may have had to legal or social organization but in a specifically literary usage'. He proceeded to trace Chaucer's hospitable vavasour to Chrétien de Troyes pointing, in particular, to the equally hospitable vavasour of *Eric and Enide* who also shares some of the Franklin's other characteristics: he is snow-white haired and he employs a diligent and resourceful cook. There is, Frankis admits, no evidence that Chaucer knew the work of Chrétien but a strong possibility that he did.[111]

More recently, R. J. Pearcy has found in the Franklin echoes not only of the French romance tradition but also of the conflict of values between knight-errant and vavasour seen in some of the French *fabliaux*, where the vavasour is imbued with a strong materialistic strain.[112] The Franklin, too, reveals on occasions a decidedly practical frame of mind and, worse, is found riding with the Man of Law. For Pearcy, Chaucer's vavasour:

> While sharing all the mature dignity and generous hospitality of the romance portraits, and none of the grossness of the fabliau portraits, is nevertheless a product of his time, whose conformity to the pattern of the ideal romance vavassor is compromised by his inextricable involvement with a fourteenth-century civil-servant's world.[113]

A third literary parallel is provided once again by Nicholas Bozon whose vavasour treats his servants in a haughty manner which

---

110 *Mirour de l'Omme*, ll. 7225–36, *The Complete Works of John Gower*, ed. G. C. Macaulay, 4 vols. (Oxford, 1899–1901), *The French Works*, p. 84.

111 Frankis, 'Chaucer's "Vavasour" and Chrétien de Troyes', pp. 46–7.

112 R. J. Pearcy, 'Chaucer's Franklin and the Literary Vavasour', *Chaucer Rev.*, viii, no. 1 (1973), pp. 33–59.

113 *Ibid.*, p. 53.

recalls the Franklin's treatment of his own cook.[114]

There is, however, one other possible literary source which ought to be considered. Some time ago L. H. Loomis suggested that Chaucer not only knew the Auchinleck manuscript but actually made use of it in his Tale of Sir Thopas. She further suggested that his notion of a Breton lay may have been derived from the same source. Now, if his idea of calling the Franklin's Tale a Breton lay came from his reading in these 'olde bokes' then perhaps his idea of calling the Franklin a vavasour came from there too, especially if he really did wish to give the teller an old-fashioned air as Loomis suggests.[115] Though this is quite possible, it has to be acknowledged that the Auchinleck vavasours are devoid of personality. If the Franklin's traits are intended to be those normally associated with a vavasour then they would seem to have been derived from French literature.

It is not my purpose, however, to suggest a priority among these apparent literary allusions, still less to offer an interpretation of the Franklin, but only to reaffirm that the meaning of 'swich a worthy vavasour' must lie within a literary tradition. This is not to deny that we have in Chaucer's Franklin a figure of great social, and hence historical, significance. That significance, however, will not be grasped by seeking a value for the word 'vavasour' within the contemporary social order, and still less by uncritically invoking earlier instances of this rather mutable social term.

Before concluding it is necessary to dispose of a myth. In his *New Light on Chaucer*, J. M. Manly argued for the identification of the Franklin with the courtier Sir John Bussy.[116] Now, although Manly's identification has not stood the test of time, some of his supporting evidence has passed into tradition. Chaucer's choice of the word 'vavasour', he suggested, points to Lincolnshire, Bussy's

---

[114] This point is made by Jill Mann, in her *Chaucer and Medieval Estates Satire*, p. 155.

[115] L. H. Loomis, 'Chaucer and the Auchinleck MS: "Thopas" and "Guy of Warwick" ', in *Essays and Studies in Honor of Carleton Brown* (New York, 1940); L. H. Loomis, 'Chaucer and the Breton Lays of the Auchinleck MS.', *Studies in Philology*, xxxviii (1941), pp. 14–33. A different explanation is suggested by K. Hume, 'Why Chaucer Calls The Franklin's Tale a Breton Lai', *Philological Quarterly*, li (1972), pp. 365–79. Of course Chaucer may well have known another product, or products, of the Auchinleck bookshop rather than the extant manuscript itself. See *Auchinleck Manuscript*, ed. Pearsall and Cunningham, p. ix.

[116] J. M. Manly, *Some New Light on Chaucer* (New York, 1926), pp. 157–68.

home. His method of determining this is interesting: 'As I was unable to obtain much evidence for the use of "vavasour" as a technical term in fourteenth-century England, a brief study was made of the occurrence of the word as a family name'. On the basis of this study he concluded that vavasour was 'a northern, and particularly a Lincolnshire, institution'.[117] On closer examination, however, we find that the majority of the northern instances of the surname come either from the main line or from a collateral of one prolific Yorkshire family, the Vavasours of Hazlewood. They were descended from a royal judge, William le Vavasour, grandson of a Domesday under-tenant called Mauger. A later William was to become Lord Vavasour by virtue of parliamentary summons.[118] Some of the more southerly instances of the name also come from this family,[119] while the Vavasours of Hazlewood and the Vavasours of Cockerington, Lincolnshire, were one and the same.[120] Leaving this family aside we find the surname spread thinly across England with examples coming, in the thirteenth century, from Kent, for instance, from the Isle of Wight, Devon, Gloucestershire, Buckinghamshire, Leicestershire, Derbyshire and Nottinghamshire.[121] There is in reality no significant northern

---

[117] *Ibid.*, p. 166.

[118] For details of this family and its interests, see G. E. Cokayne, *The Complete Peerage*, ed. V. Gibbs *et al.* (London, 1910–59), xii (ii), pp. 230–8; *Early Yorkshire Charters*, vols. 4–11, ed. C. T. Clay (Yorkshire Record Society, 1914–63), vii, pp. 166–77, and xi, pp. 118–37; W. Paley Baildon, *Baildon and the Baildons: A History of a Yorkshire Manor and Family* 3 vols. (1912–27), i, pp. 505–52.

[119] Mauger le Vavasour who held the manor of Weekley, Northants., for instance, represented a collateral; whilst John le Vavasour who held a half fee at Narborough, Leics., in 1242–3 was of the main line, as was probably the Robert le Vavasour who claimed land at Westwick and Oakington, co. Cambridge in the early thirteenth century: Clay, *Early Yorkshire Charters*, vii, p. 168, and xi, p. 130; Baildon, *Baildon and the Baildons*, i, pp. 508–9.

[120] Clay, *Early Yorkshire Charters* vii, pp. 170–1. Most of those called Vavasour in Lincolnshire, at least in the twelfth- and thirteenth-century sources, come from this same area, north-east of Louth.

[121] Hardy, *Rotuli litterarum clausarum*, i, p. 327; *Victoria Histories of the Counties of England: Hampshire*, v (London, 1912), pp. 191–2; *Curia Regis Rolls*, x, 1221–2, p. 96; *Pipe Roll 28 Henry II* (Pipe Roll Soc., xxxi, London, 1910), p. 27; *Curia Regis Rolls*, v, 1207–9, pp. 176, 194, and vii, p. 24; *Book of Fees*, pp. 976, 983, 1001. The last refers to Robert le Vavassur, sheriff of Nottingham. He seems to have come originally from Shipley (in Heanor), Derbyshire: *Cal. Close Rolls*, 1227–31, p. 254; 'The Willoughby Deeds', ed. J. C. Holt, in *An Early Medieval Miscellany for D. M. Stenton* (Pipe Roll Soc., new ser., xxvi, London, 1962), pp. 172–3. No evidence has been found, as yet, to connect him with the Vavasours of Hazlewood.

bias. Moreover, it is extremely doubtful whether the surname has any bearing at all on Chaucer's use of the word. Although the social position of the Vavasours of Hazlewood seems to correspond to that envisaged in 'Bracton' and Langtoft, they were in truth more exalted than most thirteenth-century bearers of the name. We find, as we should expect, considerable variation in wealth among these, for the surname has its origin in the twelfth century when the word meant little more than sub-vassal. By the mid-thirteenth century a more elevated and less technical usage had evolved. Surname and social term now inhabited different planes.

6. The Struggles between the Abbots of Halesowen and their Tenants in the Thirteenth and Fourteenth Centuries*

ZVI RAZI

In 1949 Professor R. H. Hilton published an article in the *Economic History Review* in which he demonstrated that the 'Great Revolt' of 1381 was not a unique event in English history since already in the thirteenth century the peasants were waging a fierce struggle against the landlords who tried to exact from them more of their surplus produce.[1] Although Hilton has analysed the relationship and the conflict between tenants and landlords in Marxist terms, it has been generally accepted by historians, not only because his observations are based on solid evidence, but also because they tally with the works of Seebohm, Maitland, Vinogradoff, Postan and Homans, who could hardly be labelled as Red Marxists. In recent years, however, Hilton's interpretation has been challenged by some North American historians. Using the records of royal and Ramsey Abbey manorial courts, they have claimed, that although there were some aspects of the manorial system, like fines, which impinged upon the village community, their negative effects were somewhat limited. The fines, tallages and rents the peasants had to pay were both modest and reasonable, considering the amount of capital accumulated by them. Even the frequent evasion of labour services and other seigneurial exactions are not regarded as an indication of a struggle against the landlords, in that there is no evidence in the court rolls that the landlords employed any physical coercion, or even threatened to do so, in order to compel the peasants to

---

* I wish to thank Dr David Katz, Marianne Zuckermann and Marianne Kopel who helped me with this essay.

[1] R. H. Hilton, 'Peasant Movements in England before 1381', *Econ. Hist. Rev.*, 2nd ser., ii (1949), pp. 117–36. For previous accounts of the struggles at Halesowen, see G. C. Homans, *English Villagers of the Thirteenth Century* (Cambridge, Mass., 1941), pp. 276–84; R. H. Hilton, *A Medieval Society* (London, 1966), pp. 159–61.

perform labour services.[2] This new interpretation of the relationships between landlords and tenants in medieval England is based
on a preconceived idea that the peasants and their landlords under
the seigneurial regime formed organically interrelated groups, and
that their mutual relationship was not of oppressor and oppressed,
but that of two different interest groups between which concilia-
tion was more common than conflict.

This interpretation is based on the organic theory of society and
has found few adherents among English medieval historians,
perhaps because the knowledge gained from hard work in the best
medieval archives of Europe rather inhibits far-reaching specula-
tions. In France, however, the organic theory is currently very
popular. This is due to the influence of one of the great historians
of the *ancien régime*, Roland Mousnier, and to the conservative
political views of many other French specialists. Professor Mousnier has argued that before the Industrial Revolution the economy
never played a determining role in any social formations, and that
therefore pre-industrial societies had no classes and were consequently free from the class conflicts which infested industrial
societies. He has claimed further that stratification before the
nineteenth century did not result from economic differentiation
but from social evaluation. The different strata, which he calls
'orders' or 'estates', are distinguished from each other not by the
income and consumption capacity of their members, nor by their
position in the production of material goods but by the esteem,
honour and diginity attached by society to social functions which
have nothing to do with the production of material goods.[3]

The acceptance of Mousnier's *société d'ordres* theory is bound
to lead, even if there is good evidence to the contrary, to the
conclusion that in pre-industrial societies co-operation between
social groups was a more pervasive relationship than conflict. In a
society in which different groups are stratified on the basis of a
common evaluation of the social role of each group, contrasting
interests and conflicts between the various strata cannot possibly

---

[2] E. Britton, *The Community of the Vill* (Toronto, 1978), pp. 111–33; E. B.
Dewindt, *Land and People in Holywell-cum-Needingworth* (Toronto, 1971), pp.
264–8; A. Dewindt, 'Peasant Power Structures in Fourteenth-Century King's
Ripton', *Medieval Studies*, xxxviii (1976), pp. 236–44.

[3] R. Mousnier, J.-P. Labatut and Y. Durand, *Problèmes de stratification sociale*
(Paris, 1965); R. Mousnier, *Les hierarchies sociales de 1450 à nos jours* (Paris,
1969); R. Mousnier, *La plume, la faucille et le marteau* (Paris, 1970).

be severe or long lasting. If there were serious conflicts in such societies they must have been temporary and caused neither by the greed and the brutality of the mighty and the rich, nor by the suffering of exploited masses, nor by the assertiveness of economically strong but nevertheless unprivileged and politically crippled groups, but always by a combination of a long spell of bad weather, wars, plagues, and the excessive taxation of the absolutist state.[4]

More recently Mousnier's theory has been applied to Europe in the middle ages by Professor Fourquin.[5] This attempt is theoretically clumsy and rather thin empirically and consequently does not merit a full discussion. However, he has claimed that the Marxist assumption that latent revolt is always present and is only waiting for an opportunity to erupt, has never been successfully shown to be true for the medieval period.[6] Marc Bloch, who probably knew some French and European rural history and who was certainly not a Marxist, wrote : 'To the historian, whose task is merely to observe and explain the connections betwen phenomena, agrarian revolt is as natural to the seigneurial régime as strikes, let us say, are to large-scale capitalism'.[7]

Despite the fact that Bloch's observation has been shown to be true for England in the thirteenth and fourteenth centuries, it is useful to test the validity of the organic theory of medieval society against the history of a well documented west-midland manor.

The manor of Hales, or Halesowen as it was later called, is located west of Birmingham, upon which it now borders. The parish of Halesowen was coterminous with the manor which was eight miles long and about two and a half at its greatest width : its area amounted to some 10,000 acres. The manor is situated in a broken, hilly terrain of mixed heavy and light clays. The uneven landscape of the manor shaped the structure of the local settlement which was not concentrated in large nucleated villages but scattered in small hamlets. In addition to the small market town of Halesowen there were twelve rural settlements or townships in the manor : Oldbury, Langley-Walloxhall, Warley, Cakemore, Hill,

---

[4] R. Mousnier, *Fureurs paysannes: les paysans dans les révoltes du XVIIe siècle* (Paris, 1967).

[5] G. Fourquin, *Les soulèvements populaires au moyen âge* (Paris, 1972).

[6] *Ibid.*, pp. 56–7.

[7] M. Bloch, *French Rural History*, trans. J. Sondheimer (London, 1966), p. 170.

Ridgeacre, Lapal, Hawne, Hasbury, Hunnington, Illey and Romsley. Oldbury in the north and Romsley in the south were the
largest settlements in the parish; each had about thirty to thirty-
five families in *circa* 1300. The other hamlets had only between ten
and twenty families each, and Illey had no more than six.

After the Norman Conquest the manor was given to Roger, earl
of Shrewsbury, who also held it in 1086. In 1102 the manor
escheated to the crown. It remained crown property for seventy-
five years, until Henry II granted it to David ap Owen, prince of
Wales, in 1177. In 1204, after the death of the prince, the manor
reverted again to the crown. In 1214, King John granted the
manor to Peter des Roches, bishop of Winchester, for the purpose
of establishing a religious house, and in the next year confirmed
the grant to the Premonstratensian Canons, who in 1218 took
possession of the new abbey of Halesowen.[8]

When the manor was in the hands of King John the customary
tenants, who probably constituted about 70 per cent of all the
tenants, paid a rent of 40d. for each yardland and had to plough
the demesne lands for six days and sow for ten days.[9] They owed
one day's 'boon work' for which they were given food at the lord's
expense. They also had to mow the lord's grass and fence his
garden. The tenants owed suit of court every three weeks, but
were exempted from suit of mill, as the king had no mills in the
manor. On the death of a villein his best beast was taken as a
heriot and the heir had to pay as a relief a sum of money
equivalent to two years' rent, 6s. 8d. for a yardland, 3s. 4d. for a
half yardland and 1s. 8d. for a quarter yardland. The customary
tenants each had to pay 2s. 0d. for permission to marry off their
daughters inside the manor and 12s. 0d. if they married out of the
manor. They also paid tallage when the king tallaged his demesnes.[10]

The new lord of Halesowen tried almost immediately to exact
more money and services from his tenants. As in many other

---

[8] *Court Rolls of the Manor of Hales, 1272–1307*, ed. J. Amphlett, S. G. Hamilton
and R. A. Wilson, 3 vols. (Worcs. Hist. Soc., Worcester, 1910–33), i, pp. v–xiii.

[9] Z. Razi, *Life, Marriage and Death in a Medieval Parish: Economy, Society and
Demography in Halesowen, 1270–1400* (Past and Present Pubns., Cambridge,
1980), p. 10.

[10] This list of customs and services was reported by a jury in 1275 during an inquiry
held by the sheriff of Shropshire: T. R. Nash, *Collections for a History of
Worcestershire*, 2 vols. (London, 1799), i, p. 512.

contemporary manors, such an attempt was resisted by the tenants of Halesowen. Since they were for a long time part of the royal demesne, they appealed to the protection of the king against arbitrary change in the level of their rents and services. In an agreement between the parties, which is enrolled in 1243 in the exchequer, the villeins of Halesowen made significant concessions. They agreed to grind their corn at the abbot's mill in Halesowen. This was not a negligible concession since it was more expensive to use the abbey's mill, as the frequent evasions of tenants from 1270 onwards indicate. They agreed to pay marriage fines and reliefs at the will of the abbot and fines in his court according to the quality of offences instead of the fixed sum they had previously paid. They also agreed to pay tallage according to the custom of the manor, but only when the king himself tallaged his manors. All these concessions meant that the tenant gave in to the abbot's demand to pay him more than in the past. Admittedly, the labour services which they promised remained on their former level. However, they undertook to 'render to the abbot all other services which they ought to render, and which lawfully they owe'. This was a dangerous undertaking because it could have been used, and probably was later used, by the abbot to demand more services from his tenants. The abbot on his part also made some concessions. He promised that neither he nor his successors would exact more services than those agreed; that he would not force his tenants to attend his market in the town of Halesowen; that if he obstructed any entrance to or exit from the common pasture of the tenants he should, in the view of legal men, make amends. Eventually, the abbot remitted £8. 6s. 8d. which they had guaranteed in the name of tallage.[11]

If the customary tenants of Halesowen thought that their landlord would be content with their concessions and would not raise new demands they were mistaken. In 1252 the abbot secured a royal writ ordering the sheriff of Shropshire, since the king was tallaging his demesnes, to see that the abbot had reasonable tallage of his tenants of Hales.[12] The words 'reasonable tallage' suggest that the tenants objected to the abbot's demand because he wanted them to pay unusually high tallage. It would seem that the abbot made other demands from his tenants and, as they

---

[11] *Ibid.*, pp. 511–12.   [12] *Cal. Close Rolls, 1251–3*, p. 108.

refused, their beasts were taken from them as gage and pledge. In 1255 the villagers of Halesowen complained to the king, but a royal inquest rejected their complaint because the foundation charter freed the abbot and convent from suits to the courts of hundred and shire.[13]

The results of the pressure put by the abbey of Halesowen on its tenants can be learned from the court rolls which start in 1270. It appears that they were required to pay rents twice as high as they had previously paid, namely 6s. 8d. instead of 3s. 4d. for a yardland. Entry fines were similarly raised from 6s. 8d. for a yardland to 13s. 4d. At the same time labour services were also raised considerably. In 1243 it was agreed between the abbot and the tenants that a yardlander would do twelve days' labour service a year, but in 1301 a yardlander in Romsley had to do eighteen days' labour service a year.[14] However, the true extent of the abbot's pressures on the tenants to comply with his demands, the methods used by him and his servants against those who tried to resist them, the high sums of money he extracted from them through his seigneurial and public jurisdiction in addition to their rents and services, are also clearly told in the manorial court rolls.

In the court held on 30 April 1270 William Modi was amerced 12d. probably because his dogs had been guilty of sheep-worrying.[15] At the same court Richard de Teonhale raised a dyke (or dug a ditch) wrongfully, and though he had been ordered to take it away before last Whit-tide, he had not done so. For this he was amerced 6s. 8d. John son of Walter, however, not only wrongfully placed a fence, but he also wrongfully took it away and for this the abbot's court amerced him 8s. 0d.[16] In the court held on 26 April 1280 Robert Cocus and Margaret le Wyte were amerced 4s. 0d. because they ploughed badly the abbot's demesne land.[17] At the same court William de Teonhale and Henry his son fished inside their lord's enclosure; for this, each was amerced 12d. Thomas son of Henry Sigrim, who was a poorer tenant than the rich Teonhales, was, nevertheless, amerced 2s. 0d. for the same offence.[18] In the court held on 1 July 1282 'Peter of Hales

13 *Rotuli hundredorum temp. Hen. III et Edw. I,* ed. W. Illingworth, 2 vols. (Rec. Comm., London, 1812–18), i, p. 10.

14 Razi, *Life, Marriage and Death,* p. 9.

15 *Court Rolls of the Manor of Hales,* i, p. 9.

16 *Ibid.,* pp. 9–10.   17 *Ibid.,* pp. 133–4.   18 *Ibid.,* p. 135.

was impleaded to make amends to the abbot for a trespass upon him by depriving him of four days of ploughing at the spring sowings, which ploughing is valued at 16d. and the damage the lord sustained at 16s. 0d'.[19] It is interesting to note that in other parts of Worcestershire the values of a day's ploughing in various places varied from 1d. to 2d., according to the season, the spring ploughings usually seeming to be less valuable.[20] Collective fines were even higher : in February 1276, for example, the men of Halesowen were fined £10 for refusing to elect a reeve and for other offences.[21] These individual and collective fines and amercements were exceedingly high : a good ox in Halesowen at that time could have been bought for between 10s. 0d. and 13s. 4d. The fines were high not only in absolute but also in relative terms since in the late 1290s and in the 1300s when the abbots were compelled by the tenants' resistance to ease their pressure, the villagers had to pay only between 2d. and 6d. for the same types of offence mentioned above.

The abbots also levied very high marriage fines and heriots on their tenants during the period under discussion. In the court held on 11 December 1279, Juliana, the daughter of Thomas Simon, a yardlander from Oldbury, had to pay 10s. 0d. as a marriage fine.[22] In the court which sat on 14 January 1276 William le Hyne was amerced 4s. 0d. for marrying his daughter without permission. But it was not enough; the cellarer who was present at the court ordered that William should be distrained until he would 'satisfy the abbot according to the custom of the manor', that is until he would pay merchet.[23] In 1278 Thomas, son of Thomas Sibille, a well-to-do villein, had to give as a heriot two good oxen valued at 20s. 0d., a colt valued at 6s. 8d. and two hogs valued at 2s. 0d., in addition to an entry fine of 26s. 8d.[24] On 27 April 1276 William de la Penne was distrained to bring his wife 'to answer for concealing a half share of a sow which ought to be the lord's portion and for not giving the beast as heriot on the death of her former husband'. For concealing the half sow she was required to pay the abbot 20s. 0d. as damages.[25]

---

[19] *Ibid.*, p. 200.
[20] This estimate is based on data obtained from the contemporary *Inquisitiones post mortem* for Worcestershire. See *ibid.*, p. 200 no. 2.
[21] *Ibid.*, ii, p. 5.   [22] *Ibid.*, i, p. 121.   [23] *Ibid.*, p. 77.
[24] *Ibid.*, p. 104.   [25] *Ibid.*, ii, p. 13.

Like other contemporary landlords the abbots of Halesowen kept a very tight control on the inter-tenant land market. In the court held on 23 October 1274 it was ordered that no one 'shall hand over or sell his land for any length of time at all except for a year without permission of the abbot under a penalty of 20s. 0d.'[26] In 1281 Richard de Notwyke recognized in the court that he sold land without permission. But since he did not want to compensate the abbot for this, his land was seized by the bailiff.[27] Usually the tenants were required to pay between one and four shillings for the sale of a small plot of customary land and often the abbot increased the annual rent the buyer had to pay for the land.

The tenants tried as much as possible to evade doing services and paying the excessive rents, merchets, leyrwytes (fines for fornication), licences to leave the manor and other seigneurial exactions. For example, although the customary tenants agreed in 1243 to grind their corn in the abbot's mills, they tried to avoid doing it as much as possible, probably because he charged them so much. In the court held on 30 April 1270 five tenants were amerced 12d. each for grinding their corn 'privately' instead of taking it to the abbot's mill.[28] On 11 March 1275, the abbot's bailiff intercepted a man coming from Frankley Mill, south of Halesowen, with a sack full of flour, and took it from him.[29]

However, it was very difficult to cheat the abbot and the canons of Halesowen, despite the fact that the peasants were quite cunning. The abbot and the canons lived in the same community, they knew everybody and they had their spies everywhere. On 7 January 1280, Alice de Hiddley was distrained to answer the abbot for her daughter Matilda, for whom she was responsible, because she insulted the abbot in the privacy of her mother's house. Later Alice had to pay 3s. 0d. for her daughter's lack of respect towards her lord.[30] In order to compel the peasants to render services and to pay fines and seigneurial charges, the bailiffs and the abbey's servants distrained and seized the tenants' beasts, chattels and holdings. On 11 December 1279, Matilda, daughter of William la Leche, was distrained by her land and chattels to answer some charges against her. But she preferred to flee rather than to appear in the court.[31] At the same court two tenants who probably left the

[26] *Ibid.*, i, p. 62.   [27] *Ibid.*, p. 163.   [28] *Ibid.*, p. 9.
[29] *Ibid.*, p. 103.   [30] *Ibid.*, pp. 122, 124.   [31] *Ibid.*, p. 120.

manor for a time were also distrained. Richard Heath was distrained by his chattels in the house of William Heath, his brother, who was forbidden 'to allow them to go away'. Adam, son of William Smith of Hill, the second customary tenant, was distrained by his chattels and especially by a cow and twenty sheaves of wheat. His pledge Philip Balismith was ordered to produce at the next court either Adam Linsely or his chattels, and in the next court he brought Adam's cow.[32] On 3 June 1282, the holding of John le Squire was seized by the lord until 'he will satisfy him for many transgressions'. In the court held on 1 July of the same year, John le Squire was distrained for working his own holding which the lord seized.[33]

Very often the oppressed tenants, both customary and free, resorted to verbal and physical assaults against their oppressors. On 24 June 1275, 'Thomas Linacre was charged with fishing in the abbot's waters, and with saying scandalous things about the abbot and his brethren of the abbey'.[34] On 25 May 1281 it was reported in the court that the abbot had taken seizin of the house where Roger Ordrich used to live and of his whole tenement, by William the bailiff. Philip Hill, Thomas Richard of Oldbury and John Bovri, probably the deceased's sons-in-law, came and turned the bailiff out, and prevented him from raising the hue by taking the horn from his mouth. The abbot put his loss at 20s. 0d. and his shame at 20s. 0d.[35] In 1287 Nicholas Broome, a newcomer to the manor, married a local widow of a free status. The abbot objected since his permission was not asked and sent his servants to evict him. Nicholas and his own servants resisted the eviction by force. While Nicholas probably kept watch at the door, his two servants stood at the windows and slashed the abbot's servants with swords.[36]

Individual and even group resistance did not hinder the abbots and their men. They were brutal, well-armed, rich and had the law on their side, as we shall presently see. Even those bondmen and bondwomen who fled were persecuted through their relatives who remained in Halesowen. For example, on 7 January 1280, Margaret, the daughter of Henry Koc, who was married in Coventry, gave the abbot 2s. 6d. as a merchet, 'to have peace' (*pro pace*

---

[32] *Ibid.*, pp. 120–2.   [33] *Ibid.*, pp. 196, 201.
[34] *Ibid.*, p. 65.   [35] *Ibid.*, ii, pp. 99–100.   [36] *Ibid.*, i, pp. 184–5, 196.

habenda).[37] In order to defend themselves against their tenants' fury, the abbot and the canons obtained in 1273 permission from Edward I to fortify certain newly-built rooms within the abbey.[38]

As the abbey of Halesowen was so strong and oppressive the tenants organized and appealed to their king's help. It would seem that they were well aware of the king's attempt to restore the crown rights and property alienated without warrant and consequently they appealed to the king against the abbot. In November 1275 a royal inquest which sat at Shrewsbury found that the abbot and convent of the house of Halesowen increased the customs and services 'greater than they were accustomed to do in the time of King Henry'. The jury referred to the fact that the abbey did not keep the 1243 agreement with the tenants. In the next year the tenants scored another success. A writ was issued directed to the sheriff of Shropshire 'on part of the tenants of the abbot of Halesowen', requiring the sheriff to make an inquisition by jury into the wrongs complained of by the tenants.[39] The inquest was held in June 1276 and drew up a list of customs and services which the customary tenants rendered in the time of King John before the foundation of the abbey. The jury ended their statement by declaring that 'the said King John granted the manor subject to the same services by which the lands were held of him'.[40] From the records of the royal court of Shropshire held in 1292 we learn that the tenants' appeal of 1275 against the abbey was pleaded on the grounds that Halesowen was an ancient demesne before its alienation to the abbey which entitled them to royal protection against any increase in their customs and services.[41] At the same time the customary tenants became more difficult to control and less co-operative. In February 1276, for example, 'the men of the manor of Halesowen' were fined ten pounds 'for refusing to elect a reeve to the use of the abbot and for many despites and disputes against the abbot and the convent'.[42]

The abbot and the convent reacted to the tenants' action by

---

[37] *Ibid.*, p. 122.
[38] Nash, *Collections for a History of Worcestershire*, ii, appendices, p. xxiv.
[39] *Rotuli hundredorum*, ii, p. 98.
[40] Nash, *Collections for a History of Worcestershire*, i, p. 512.
[41] *Select Bills in Eyre, A.D. 1292–1333*, ed. W. C. Bolland (Selden Soc., xxx, London, 1914), p. 25.
[42] *Court Rolls of the Manor of Hales*, ii, p. 5.

presenting a petition to the king and his council in 1278. They argued that the tenants wrongly impleaded them in the royal court, claiming that they were of the ancient demesne of the crown, but the Domesday Book showed that they were not. The abbot also claimed that the convent lost services and customs as a result of the king's writ in favour of the tenants. He asked for a remedy and seizin of services until the case was heard. The king's answer to the petition was that the canons had to bring their case before the court.[43] This the abbot immediately did, and in the plea roll of the Easter term of the King's Bench in 1278 it was recorded that the abbot was allowed to go *sine die* because his tenants failed to appear to prosecute their writ against him.[44]

The tenants who failed to appear in Westminster, probably because they had insufficient time or money to do so, reacted angrily against the abbot and the canons. In the spring of 1278 they assaulted the abbot and a group of canons from the abbey near Beoley, possibly on their way back from Westminster to Halesowen. As a result in December 1278 the bishop of Worcester sent an order to the deans of Warwick, Pershore, and Droitwich to excommunicate those who had assaulted the abbot and his canons.[45] The tenants of Halesowen, however, were determined to resist the court's decision which implied that they were villeins at the will of the lord. Consequently, in order to break the tenants' resistance, the abbot decided to take action against their leader, Roger Ketel, a rich villager from the township of Illey. In December 1279 Roger Ketel was fined five pounds in the manor court to be paid in five years, 'because he impleaded the abbot unjustly in the court of the lord king and was in aid and council with his other neighbours impleading the abbot'. Roger was allowed to hold his tenement 'in that condition which is stated in the writ of judgement, namely servile at the will of the lord'.[46]

The career of Roger Ketel is well documented in the court rolls and it suggests that it was not by chance that he became their leader. If Roger held the same holding in Illey which his descendants held in the fourteenth century, it amounted to some twenty

---

[43] *Rotuli parliamentorum*, 6 vols. (Rec. Comm., London, 1783), i, p. 10.

[44] Nash, *Collections for a History of Worcestershire*, i, p. 513.

[45] *Episcopal Registers, Diocese of Worcester: Register of Bishop Godfrey Giffard*, ed. J. W. Willis Bund (Worcs. Hist. Soc., Worcester, 1902), p. 103.

[46] *Court Rolls of the Manor of Hales*, i, pp. 119–20.

acres. Like other well-off villagers at that time, Roger had livestock and even horses. He often pledged his neighbours and served like other rich villagers as a juryman many times.[47] Already in 1274 Roger showed that he was not an obedient tenant when he refused to pay heriot on the death of his mother-in-law, and he and his pledges were distrained several times until he came to an agreement to pay 4s. 0d. as heriot.[48] He and his son Roger II broke into the lord's pound several times to release their beasts. In November 1279, a month before he was amerced £5, the vill of Illey presented that he raised the hue and cry on the abbot's servants and that both sides were to blame for the affray.[49] Despite the defeat in the royal court and the huge fine Roger Ketel had to pay, he did not give in, and did not pay a penny.[50]

The other tenants of the manor followed their leader's example and continued their struggle against the abbot, individually as well as collectively. Again they pleaded their case in a royal court, this time in the county court of Shropshire. Once more the basis of their appeal was that they were tenants of the ancient demesne. The exact date of this appeal is not known, but from later records of the county court it appears that they failed. The court decided that 'because it could not be found in Domesday that they were men of the ancient demesne . . . they should continue in a state of servile and villein condition'.[51]

In order to put the court's verdict into effect, this time the abbot decided to crush the tenants' resistance once and for all. To achieve this, physical, coercive power was used, mainly against the tenants' leaders. In 1282 an armed group of canons and servants from the abbey seized Roger Ketel, John Edrich of Cakemore (who like Roger was a rich and obstinate villein) and another villein whose name is not given, and put them into the stocks. Alice, the wife of John Edrich, probably tried to resist her husband's arrest and as a result she was beaten and molested. The violence used by the canons and their servants caused the death of Alice, who was pregnant, and of Roger Ketel.[52] In the same year

---

[47] *Ibid.*, pp. 29–119.   [48] *Ibid.*, pp. 52–4.

[49] *Ibid.*, ii, pp. 33–4, and i, pp. 102–3, 114.

[50] *Ibid.*, i, p. 215.   [51] *Select Bills in Eyre*, ed. Bolland, p. 26.

[52] A copy from the proceedings of the royal court in Shropshire in October 1292 is deposited in Birmingham Reference Lib. (hereafter B.R.L.), 383853.

another armed group from the abbey came to Oldbury and seized all the goods and chattels, worth £10, of John, the son of Walter of Oldbury. In 1283 an undisclosed number of villeins who still refused to submit were taken forcibly by the canons to the town of Halesowen and were imprisoned there.[53]

These cases were brought before the royal justices in the Shropshire county court only some ten years later, in 1292. It is possible that the justices in 1292 had a special instruction to hear the complaints of local tenants against their landlords. But even when the tenants were encouraged to bring their complaints to the court their chances of obtaining justice were very slim. The abbot and the canons were acquitted since they had acted against rebellious tenants. The canons had not used arms against the tenants, but according to the jurymen only axes and staves, which any person travelling through the countryside was allowed to carry. The jury rejected the tenants' claim that they were detained in prison, and ruled that the abbot had acted within his rights when he put his rebellious tenants in stocks. Those who had died, like Roger Ketel, died as a result of natural causes and not because of the acts of the canons and their servants.[54]

In 1285 the abbot appealed to the royal court against his tenants. Unfortunately, very little information can be obtained about this case and the court rolls between 1283 and 1291 are missing. Nevertheless, this time the abbot obtained a decisive judgement in his favour when the royal court declared that 'the tenants are villeins for ever'.[55]

With this judgement the tenants of Halesowen ceased to resort to the royal court. Moreover, it would seem that in the late 1290s the struggle between the abbey and its tenants subsided. It is true that during the period from the 1240s to the 1290s the abbots succeeded in exploiting their tenants, managed to double the rate of rents and entry fines, to increase the tenants' labour services and to prevent their tenants from securing the status of privileged

[53] *Select Bills in Eyre*, ed. Bolland, pp. 24–6.
[54] B.R.L., 383853; *Select Bills in Eyre*, ed. Bolland. For further information about the use of coercive force by landlords against their tenants, see E. Miller and J. Hatcher, *Medieval England: Rural Society and Economic Change, 1086–1348* (London, 1978), pp. 115–17; P. R. Hyams, *King, Lords and Peasants in Medieval England* (Oxford, 1980), pp. 40–1; R. B. Pugh, *Imprisonment in Medieval England* (Cambridge, 1970), pp. 52–5.
[55] Nash, *Collections for a History of Worcestershire*, i, p. 513.

villeins. However, the peasants' resistance was not in vain, as the abbey had to be content with what it had achieved between 1243 and 1285. The court rolls show clearly that for a very long time after this date, not only were rents, services and other seigneurial exactions not raised any more, but also that the abbey had to lower fines and amercements considerably.[56]

In the post-plague period the abbots of Halesowen made a new attempt to change the *status quo*. Their income, like that of many contemporary landlords, fell as a result of the steep rise of wages and the decline, especially from the 1370s, of prices and rents. In common with other landlords the abbots of Halesowen attempted to make good their losses by exploiting the financial side of their seigneurial rights.[57] They were much more assiduous than ever before in collecting fines from customary tenants who did not grind their corn in their mills, who sold livestock outside the manor, or failed to attend the 'three weekly courts'. The abbots also raised marriage fines and leyrwytes from 12d. or 2s. 0d. to 5s. 0d. and 6s. 8d. Tenants who took good holdings to which they had no hereditary right were made to pay through the nose. In 1370, for example, for half a yardland, a tenant had to pay as an entry fine £2. 6s. 8d. instead of 6s. 8d.[58] Moreover, the abbot began to demand that bondwomen who married outside the manor should quitclaim all their rights in their parental holdings before obtaining his licence.[59] He did this because many descendants of emigrating Halesowen bondwomen returned to the manor and took their family land; thus more and more customary land passed into the hands of freemen. It would seem that the villagers saw in the abbot's demand from bondwomen another manifestation of seigneurial exploitation which prejudiced their deep-rooted belief in the bond between land and blood.

As in the thirteenth century, so in the post-Black Death period, the peasants of Halesowen actively resisted their lord's attempt to take more of their surplus produce. Initially they reacted by

---

[56] On 20 September 1301, for example, three tenants were amerced 2d. each for not performing a day of ploughing. Whereas in 1282, as we saw on pp. 156–7 above, a tenant was amerced 16d. for not performing four days of ploughing, in addition to 16s. 0d. he was required to pay to the abbot in compensation: *Court Rolls of the Manor of Hales*, i, p. 422.

[57] R.H. Hilton, *The English Peasantry in the Later Middle Ages* (Oxford, 1975), pp. 60–73.

[58] B.R.L., 346349.   [59] B.R.L., 346357.

individual or group acts of insubordination and defiance. The abbey's servants and officials were assaulted and abused, and there was a widespread plundering of the abbey property by almost all the peasants, ceaselessly and shamelessly, day and night. Never in the recorded history of the manor had so many peasants trespassed so openly on the abbey crops, pastures, fish-ponds and warrens.[60] In the 1380s the tenants undertook more collective and organized action. We do not know exactly what happened, but in the court held in September 1380 all the tenants in the manor, free as well as bond, were declared to be in mercy except a small number of villagers who had bought their peace.[61] Late in 1385, Thomas Harboury, a bond tenant from Hasbury, sneaked into the abbey courtyard under the cover of darkness, and released all the doves from their dovecotes: 'Maliciously', it says, 'with an intent of causing the lord a damage'.[62] This incident suggests that the peasants were in a very ugly mood and indeed some months later the abbot was faced with a rebellion.

The villeins of Romsley, the largest village in the manor, were not disheartened by the failure of the Peasants' Revolt of 1381. In October 1386, when they were expected to do fealty and to recognize their services, they refused to do so, and declared that they would neither perform any more services nor be the abbot's bondmen. As in the struggle against the abbey in the second half of the thirteenth century, so in the rebellion of 1386 the villeins were led by villagers who belonged to the richest families in the parish, Thomas Puttway, John atte Lythe and his sister Agnes, the wife of John Sadler. This time the abbot probably did not dare to use coercive power against his rebellious tenants. Instead he appealed to the king for help. Richard II sent a commission of *oyer* and *terminer* to deal with the crisis.[63] In February 1387 the commission sent in a report and the sheriff of Shropshire was ordered to take action. In May 1387 the sheriff announced that

---

[60] In the period between 1312 and 1348 each of the males identified in the court rolls performed on average 0.32 trespasses against the lord per year. While in the period from 1350 to 1386 the mean was 0.73.

[61] B.R.L., 346357.   [62] B.R.L., 346365.

[63] The abbey of Halesowen kept a copy of a report of a commission of *oyer* and *terminer* from February 1387 and a report of a royal inquiry held in Bridgnorth in May 1387: B.R.L., 347156.

one of the leaders who was imprisoned had died, and the other two could not be found.[64]

It seems the abbot recognized that in a period in which each landlord was seeking tenants for vacant holdings, he could not use physical coercive power as his predecessors did. Instead he probably searched for a compromise with his tenants. The holding of John atte Lythe, who had died in prison, was not escheated to the abbot, but was given to his daughters.[65] The other leaders of the Romsley rebellion, Thomas Puttway and Agnes Sadler, were allowed to return to the manor.[66] The evidence available in the court rolls suggests that the conflict was resolved in 1387 when the abbot made concessions to his tenants. After 1387 there was a substantial fall in the number of fines for default of court, for not grinding corn in the abbey mills, and for selling livestock outside the manor. The rate of marriage fines and leyrwytes, which were especially hated by the peasants, not only went down to the pre-plague level, but also almost completely ceased to be levied by the abbey. After 1387 very few such fines were recorded in the court rolls. The abbey continued to demand high entry fines for good holdings from tenants who had no hereditary claim to them, but such fines were usually not as high as before the rebellion. The villeins of Romsley on their part probably recognized their rents and services, and co-operated again with the abbot. At the same time, all the tenants in the manor stopped their systematic plundering of abbey property, for the annual number of trespasses against the lord fell considerably after 1387.

Struggles between landlords and tenants, like the one studied here, can be found in many other places in thirteenth- and fourteenth-century England. Although not all the landlords were as oppressive and efficient as the abbots of Halesowen and although lords and tenants sometimes co-operated to their mutual benefit, it was inevitable that in a seigneurial regime conflicts of interest often arose, because the ruling class derived their income largely from the toil of the peasantry. Moreover, the present study

[64] *Cal. Pat. Rolls, 1385–9*, p. 317.

[65] B.R.L., 347156.

[66] According to a report by the sheriff of Shropshire the villager who died was Thomas Puttway. But Thomas appears in the court records frequently from 1388, while it is reported in the manor court that John atte Lythe died and his holding was given to his daughter, Alice: B.R.L., 346822. They appear in the court records from 1388 onwards: B.R.L., 346367.

suggests that although the level of feudal rent was affected by changing economic and demographic conditions, it was ultimately determined by the pressure brought to bear by the landlords, and by the ability of the village community to resist such pressure. In the second half of the thirteenth century, when the population was rising and land was in short supply, the abbots of Halesowen succeeded in raising the level of the feudal rent, but in face of the fierce resistance from their tenants they did not raise it any more, and it remained fixed for a very long period. In the second half of the fourteenth century as the population fell considerably and land became abundant, the conditions of the peasants of Halesowen improved considerably. But this trend was not reversed mainly because they, like other contemporary villagers, successfully resisted the seigneurial reaction of the 1370s and 1380s.

The Marxist use of the notion 'class' as an analytical tool is problematic, but so is any other system of stratification. It would seem to me, however, that the adoption of a system of social classification based on real economic and political differentiation is better than the adoption of a system based on the social evaluation of the society under study, because it helps us to understand better the behaviour and actions both of the ruling feudal élite and the peasantry in medieval Europe. Those who apply Mousnier's system of stratification to analyse medieval society are not only led inevitably to describe an idyllic society which never existed, but also often fail to understand the behaviour and actions of landlords and peasants. This is why both Marc Bloch and M. M. Postan, who were certainly not Marxists, adopted in fact a Marxist system of stratification in order to analyse feudal society.

7. *Poverty in* Piers Plowman

GEOFFREY SHEPHERD

The argument of the opening Passus of the *Visio* of *Piers Plowman* concerns the renovation of contemporary society. All round him the Dreamer sees confusion in which everybody is seeking individual advantage. Society is fragmented and corrupt through a driving acquisitiveness. He sees that the times demand the enforcement of a new order of distributive justice. To this end a co-operative commons must submit to and support a just king. There must be recognition of what has gone wrong, then society must commit itself wholeheartedly to a purer intention and devise and pursue just and effective policies.

At this point the Pardon from a supreme authority arrives.[1] Such a Pardon, however unexpected its arrival, should cancel the past, annul the sense of guilt, give hope and some ultimate promise and suggest an appropriate programme for the future. This Pardon is a disappointment and a bafflement. It has the portentousness but also the banality of a dream-message remembered on waking. Indeed we may take it that this Pardon scene is some sort of record of actual dreams – one of the moments of vision which form the narrative skeleton of the poem.[2] But constructional puzzles do not concern us here, save in so far as we can understand Langland's own puzzlement with the content of

---

1 *Piers Plowman by William Langland: An Edition of the C-Text*, ed. Derek Pearsall (York Medieval Texts, 2nd ser., London, 1978), Passus IX, lines 1 ff.; *The Vision of William concerning Piers the Plowman in Three Parallel Texts*, ed. W. W. Skeat, 2 vols. (Oxford, 1886; reprinted), i, Passus X, p. 227. In this article prime reference to the C text is to Pearsall's valuable edition (which contains a useful glossary at pp. 386–416); page references to volume i of Skeat's standard edition are added. The best general treatment of the poem in its latest revised form (C text) is still E. T. Donaldson, *Piers Plowman: The C-Text and its Poet* (New Haven, 1949).

2 See G. Shepherd, 'The Nature of Alliterative Poetry in Late Medieval England' (Sir Israel Gollancz Memorial Lecture), *Proc. Brit. Acad.*, lvi (1971), pp. 19–20.

the Pardon to which his own narrative exposition of his series of dreams has given such weight and expectancy.

For the Pardon is no amnesty, no statement of forgiveness; it ends nothing, it seems to start nothing new, except the prolonged puzzlement. It offers a hard and familiar commonplace, known by a child as soon as he has the first glimmer of sense: 'if you are good you will get on and go to heaven; if you do wrong you will be most certainly punished'. It is of course, as Langland presents it, the last expository sentence of the Athanasian Creed.

The Dreamer worries about the Pardon. All the rest of the poem turns on it, with the Dreamer seeking to discover what exactly is implied by this commonplace delivered to him in his own dream. He is persuaded of the authenticity of the revelation but cannot readily accept that a genuine revelation should be only an inscrutable and banal commonplace.

What does doing good mean? The Dreamer understands well enough that it is in part a matter of training, not related to self-advancement, but to the proper exercise of a social role. The terms of the Pardon refer specifically to kings, knights, bishops and honest workers. Where men recognize their estate and fulfil their obligations accordingly, the Pardon is fully effective. But the theory of the three estates is neither comprehensive nor realistic, as Langland knows; and the social unease of the times is generated and the corruption has developed through the interaction of the three estates with new groups outside the traditional analysis. He identifies three such groups. All of them are socializing and institutionalizing the characteristic acquisitiveness of the times: merchants first, who, if they buy and sell fairly, are covered by the terms of the Pardon; then lawyers, less securely based, who manipulate the dangerous machinery of distributive justice; finally beggars, who live off society and contribute nothing to it; and these are totally excluded from the Pardon.[3]

Throughout *Piers Plowman* Langland speaks of professional beggars as harshly as the Statute of 1388 sought to treat them. Public attitudes often associated with the later history of the Poor Law go back a long way. Langland clearly believes that making a

---

[3] Pearsall, C IX, lines 22–42 (on merchants), 43–57 (on lawyers), 61–281 (on beggars); Skeat, pp. 228–42.

trade out of poverty is one of the clearest symptoms of the social disease. Professional beggars defraud the needy and cheat the giver. They observe neither social nor legal obligations. They live as irresponsible animals casually begetting children to use unnaturally as the tools of their profession, breaking their backs and limbs in infancy to make them later on more profitable objects of pity. It is as hateful a passage as any in the poem.

In the C version at this point in the account of the Pardon there is a substantial insertion. It is generated by material of the earlier versions. Of course beggary is damnable but there are we know poor people who need and deserve our help. From the schoolroom onwards you learn how careful you should be in giving. Only God knows the real needs of those that seem needy. How then to discriminate? You give to those you know:

The most needy are our neighbours if we take proper notice: not only captives in dungeons, but also poor people in cottages, burdened with children and with a quitrent to find. What they can make by spinning they spend on the house rent, what they can save up in milk and meal they use for porridge to fill the bellies of their children who cry out to be fed. They themselves endure sharp hunger and misery in winter-time; they are kept awake at nights to get out of bed to rock the cradles along the wall. How they card and comb, patch and wash, scrape flax and wind it, and peel rushes would be distressing to read about or put into verses – the misery of the women who live in the cottages; and of many other people suffering hardship, short of food and drink, who yet keep up appearances and are ashamed to beg and do not want to make known what they could well do with from their neighbours for breakfast or supper.

Familiar experience shows what are the needs of people who have many children but have nothing to live on but their own labour with which to clothe and feed them, when they have many to provide for and few pennies to go round. There, bread and penny ale would be regarded as a feast and cold flesh and fish taste like roast venison. On Fridays and fast-days a farthing's worth of mussels or the same again of cockles would be a special treat for such people. To help this sort of people with dependants to support, cottagers like these and cripples and the blind, this would be almsgiving.[4]

It is to the decent employed and employable poor that alms should be given (in particular the new urban poor of the fourteenth century, but the policy is familiar) not to professional beggars with their bags, who haunt brewhouses as if they were churches. Rich men would do well to let such rascals starve.[5]

Langland is of course recommending local acts of kindness, not a programme of relief or a policy. This insertion is probably the earliest passage in English which conveys the felt and inner bitterness of poverty, just as throughout the poem we first catch that uncompromising aversion to public beggary which in the post-medieval centuries has remained the normal response of

[4] The insertion in C begins:
> Woet no man, as y wene, who is worthy to haue;
> Ac þat most neden aren oure neyhebores, and we nyme gode hede,
> As prisones in puttes and pore folk in cotes,
> Charged with childrene and chief lordes rente;
> þat they with spynnyng may spare, spenen hit on hous-huyre,
> Bothe in mylke and in mele, to make with papelotes
> To aglotye with here gurles that greden aftur fode.
> And hemsulue also soffre muche hunger,
> And wo in wynter-tymes, and wakynge on nyhtes
> To rise to þe reule to rokke þe cradel,
> Bothe to carde and to kembe, to cloute and to wasche,
> And to rybbe and to rele, rusches to pylie,
> That reuthe is to rede or in ryme shewe
> The wo of this wommen þat wonyeth in cotes;
> And of monye oþer men þat moche wo soffren,
> Bothe afyngred and afurste, to turne þe fayre outward,
> And ben abasched for to begge and wollen nat be aknowe
> What hem nedeth at here neyhebores at noon and at eue.
> This I woet witterly, as þe world techeth,
> What other byhoueth þat hath many childrene
> And hath no catel but his craft to clothe hem and to fede,
> And fele to fonge þer-to, and fewe panes taketh.
> There is payne and peny-ale as for a pytaunce ytake,
> And colde flesche and fische as venisoun were bake.
> Fridays and fastyng-days a ferthing-worth of moskeles
> Were a feste with suche folk, or so fele cockes.
> These are almusse, to helpe þat han suche charges
> And to conforte such coterelles and crokede men and blynde.
> Pearsall, C IX, lines 70–97.

[5] Ac beggares with bagges, þe wiche brewhous ben here churches,
> But they be blynde or tobroke or elles by syke,
> Though he falle for defaute þat fayteth for his lyflode,
> Reche ȝe neuere, ȝe riche, thouh suche lollares sterue.
> Pearsall, C IX, lines 98–101; Skeat, p. 234.

northern Europeans. Beggars are shocking, beggary is somehow obscene. A bond of shame unites public giver and public recipient. Beggars are parasites upon and enemies and betrayers of society, the dangerous drones who according to the prosperous Franklin in *Mum and the Sothsegger* should be nipped out of the busy commonwealth of bees and destroyed utterly.[6] Langland knows them all, the guilers, lubbers, lollers, gadelings, false hermits, fobbes, faitors, bidders, leapers, lordains, lorels, mendinants, and their criminal associates the pissares, Robardsmen, Britonners, draw-latches, and so on, creatures familiar enough in national and local ordinances and records. The whole gallery has nothing of the charm for Langland that it had for bourgeois writers of the Elizabethan age. In Langland's ideal commonwealth, as in More's *Utopia*, professional beggary would be eliminated by strict control of employment and by careful surveillance.

In his own world apparently he looks for stricter policing, relief for the local and resident poor, and for moving outsiders back to where they belong. He sees that it is vagrancy that has made the problem of large-scale poverty difficult to grasp and solve. The new mobility in society astonishes him. He is aware of it through-out the poem and of its consequences in rootlessness, anomy and confusion. The fair field between the Tower of Truth and the deep dale of Death is crowded with moving people, working and wandering as the world asks. The Dreamer knows he is something of a vagrant himself, living in London and in the country (*yn London and opelond both*), and is uneasy about it. He would prefer to live in the Barn of Unity, or in the established orchard where the Tree of Charity can grow. Instead he inhabits the wilderness, an urbanized wilderness where order is replaced by agglomeration and purpose by chance encounter. Even in the renovated society envisaged in the penultimate Passus the Barn cannot be made secure, and the *viator* can only seek a lasting order in the movement of his own mind.

The poet's sympathies are with the stable and industrious poor who survive among this frantic confusion. Of them he speaks in terms of affection such as popular preachers used. They are God's people, God's minstrels, poor folk sick, poor patient, the needy

---

6 *Mum and the Sothsegger*, ed. Mabel Day and R. Steele (Early Eng. Text Soc., cxcix, London, 1936), pp. 57–8, lines 1044–86 – a passage reminiscent of Seneca, *De Clementia*, i. 19.

poor sib to Christ. To them Christian men show pity and give help. The worthy poor are carefully categorized:

> Ac olde and hore, þat helples ben and nedy,
> And wymmen with childe þat worche ne mowe,
> Blynde and bedredne and broken in here membres,
> And alle pore pacient, apayed of goddes sonde,
> As mesels and mendenantes, men yfalle in meschief,
> As prisones and pilgrimes and parauntur men yrobbed
> Or bylowe thorw luther men and lost here catel after,
> Or thorw fuyr or thorw floed yfalle into pouerte,
> That taketh thise meschiefes mekeliche and myldeliche at herte,
> For loue of here lower hertes oure lord hath hem ygraunted
> Here penaunce and here purgatorye vppon this puyre erthe
> And pardon with the plouhman *a pena et a culpa*.
> And alle holy eremytes haue shal þe same.[7]

comprising then, the old and infirm, expectant mothers, the maimed and disabled, the incurables, those who have suffered accidental misfortune, captives and homeless men, victims of robbery or unjust litigation, those who have lost all in fire or flood – if they take their losses humbly – such men are the poor to whom properly alms can be given. Such men individually may take their poverty as a penance which can win them full pardon in heaven; but they also exist collectively in a kind of contractual relationship with society as a whole. The full and careful list identifies and consolidates almost with legal precision a class with a role and status in society. A well-ordered society needs justice and the fruits of labour; for its full health it also need to exercise charity. The rich need the poor as much as the poor need the rich. It is a position that the Dominican author of the early fifteenth-century *Dives and Pauper* argues with some wit and vigour.[8]

Langland is not offering easy speeches to comfort cruel men. His interest in and sympathy for the honourable poor shines constantly and repeatedly through the poem. On this theme his

---

[7] Pearsall, C IX, lines 175–86; cf. Skeat, pp. 238–9.

[8] *Dives and Pauper*, ed. Priscilla H. Barnum, 1 vol. in 2 pts (Early Eng. Text Soc., cclxxv, lxxx, London, 1976, 1980), pt. 1, p. 63, 'Holy Poverty', ch. 7. Bishop Brinton uses the same argument to urge the unity of the realm: *The Sermons of Thomas Brinton, Bishop of Rochester, 1373–1389*, ed. Mary A. Devlin, 2 vols. (Camden Soc., 3rd ser., lxxxv–lxxxvi, London, 1954), i, pp. 194–200, Sermon 44.

verse often acquires a surge and tender rapture, that sharply articulated concentrated utterance once counted the signal of sincerity in a writer. Worldly poverty is not an infrequent theme of medieval composition particularly in satire and complaint, or among client writers seeking reward from powerful patrons; and in such situations poverty is treated as a form of non-existence, a topic to be exploited in an argument for affluence.[9] And Langland can write like this: he is not writing for the poor. But he is precocious in that often he presents the inner life of the unvocal unassertive people who live in powerlessness and poverty and he draws them into the cultural reality of his time. This voice is not heard so clearly again for another four hundred years, not until Crabbe delineates his Village or more powerfully Wordsworth acculturizes the individual distinctiveness of the Cumbrian poor: his Cumberland beggar, the afflicted mother, the disabled pensioner, Simon Lee himself or Goody Blake. Wordsworth's Leech-gatherer accurately exemplifies Langland's Patient Poverty; the Idiot Boy is none other than one of God's boys, a merry-mouthed man, a minstrel of heaven.

What Langland has to say about poverty, the poor and vagrancy is born of reflection on experience and clear-eyed observation. At the same time discussion and opinion about poverty must have been a substantial part of his intellectual education, as a cleric hearing or overhearing much of the conventional wisdom of the church on this theme; as a clerk with some interest in the law, acquiring fragments of a systematic body of law dealing with the poor.[10] Christian concern in theory and in practice with poverty

---

[9] Involuntary poverty and unregarded merit are bitterly (and wittily) linked in Goliardic verse, for example, by Hugh Primas, the archpoet, and Walter of Châtillon: see F. J. E. Raby, *A History of Secular Latin Poetry in the Middle Ages*, 2 vols. (Oxford, 1934), ii, pp. 172, 182, 196. On vernacular composition, see J. Peter, *Complaint and Satire in Early English Literature* (Oxford, 1956); Claus Uhlig, *Chaucer und die Armut: zum Prinzip der Kontextuellen Wahrheit in der Canterbury Tales* (Weisbaden, 1973). An obvious motif in many romance stories is that of an aspiring young man brought up in poverty: so Havelok (among fishermen), William of Palerne (by a cowherd), Perceval and Tristram (among woodmen), In *Chevelere Assigne*, *Degaré*, the heroes are reared by hermits; many *en route* to success survive episodic poverty, voluntary or enforced, and emerge apparently neither wiser nor sadder: so Sir Isumbras, Emaré, Sir Launfal, Sir Gowther, Horn *et al.*

[10] See Brian Tierney, *Medieval Poor Law: A Sketch of Canonical Theory and its Application in England* (Berkeley and Los Angeles, 1959). On Langland's interest in law, see Skeat, ii, preface, p. xxxvi.

touches very many aspects of social behaviour throughout the
medieval centuries as has been demonstrated by Michel Mollat
and his collaborators in their *Études sur l'histoire de la pauvreté*.
Having already made the point (as all writers on poverty must do)
that poverty must always be treated as a matter of relativities,
Mollat writes:

> But the different kinds of poverty are so relative that the final
> characteristic is one of ambiguity. The most elementary ambigu-
> ity is between the actual experience of being poor and the
> choice of poverty as a way of life. But beyond that, ambiguity
> turns into an ambivalence where terms are in strong opposition.
> Material distress can degenerate into total collapse, sanctifying
> humility can turn into humiliation, instead of being an honour-
> able distinction, poverty can become disgrace. Poverty is ac-
> quainted with patience, is familiar with envy. It stirs charitable
> comparison and philanthropic sympathy or else provokes revul-
> sion, contempt, fear and condemnation. Poverty is bound to
> charity but also to hatred. It always produces shock and alarm.
> As a stumbling-block of paradox the presence of a poor man is
> embarrassing, for it troubles men's consciences, upsets the
> ordinary assurances of life and flouts the sense of self-esteem.
> One aspect arising from the study of medieval poverty is the
> emergence of the dilemma of modern times between the
> evangelical requirement of poverty and the need to overcome it
> in order to eliminate it in its extreme forms.[11]

Even to this last sentence Mollat's words are relevant to the
treatment of poverty in *Piers Plowman*. No work dealt with in the
Études so comprehensively demonstrates the complexity of the
subject as *Piers Plowman*. It would seem that there is scarcely a
general argument about poverty or any characteristically medieval
reflection about the treatment of the poor which is not drawn on
or alluded to somewhere in the three texts of the poem.[12] Langland knows that some virtuous form of poverty is enjoined by

---

[11] M. Mollat (ed.), *Études sur l'histoire de la pauvreté, moyen âge – XVIe siècle*, 2
vols. (Paris, 1974), i, p. 13 (my translation).
[12] No one has dealt with the plentiful English material comprehensively as Mollat
and his collaborators have dealt with medieval poverty on the Continent (taking
French society as a norm). The fullest treatment in English appears to be *Piers
Plowman* itself. Pearsall's brief line notes are often useful in identifying topics
and issues.

Scripture. He understands also very well that to be a poor man is a misery. He knows that it is an absolute Christian obligation to relieve this misery of the poor. Yet the poem gives the sense that Langland believes that poverty is permanent and the poor are always with us. Poverty is a mystery.

Langland does not simplify the mystery into the almost meaningless paradox that Hoccleve offers once; in the end:

> Than schal men see how in this world, I gesse,
> Richesse is pouert, and pouert richesse.[13]

Langland's treatment does not seek paradox but he produces a confusion that does not impair his achievement or deny his intention. On many issues beside poverty, confusion is his subject-matter. The poem is this struggle towards understanding, not a statement of discovery and solutions. Poverty is an important and recurrent but contingent issue; and Langland does not need to avoid the confusion that it breeds. Often his irony and his dramatic presentation will stir up again what seems to have already been almost settled. For us poverty will remain perhaps an economic problem with sociological implications; for Langland a religious mystery which continues to ask diffuse and complicated questions.

The ambiguities that inhere in poverty reflect the essential Christian paradox of the Incarnation, the incredible challenge at the centre of the religion. This lowering which was a raising, this impoverishment which was a redeeming, a foolishness to the Greeks and a stumbling-block to the Jews had been brought into intellectual prominence again in Anselm's Christology. It remained a large and important theme of all the theological Summas of the later middle ages. The divine Christ was also of course the exemplary figure for men; and in consequence the how and the why of the Incarnation made moral and social demands. With the unexpected intrusions of Piers the Plowman, Langland is acknowledging subtle points of juncture between theology and ethics, between doctrine and behaviour.

The New Testament itself dealt with these moral consequences: to save his life a man must lose it; possessiveness is a force of destruction; renunciation is the means of permanent possession.

---

[13] Thomas Hoccleve, *The Regement of Princes . . . and Fourteen of Hoccleve's Minor Poems*, ed. F. J. Furnivall (Early Eng. Text Soc., extra ser., lxxii, London, 1897), p. 158.

The ultimate rewards are still proclaimed in terms of riches and power, of kingdoms, of honour and of bliss, of the very goods which characterize the rich of this world. The poor are defined as those lacking these goods – the powerless, the men of no repute, the miserable and the deprived. Yet salvation is not effected simply by the poor becoming rich and the rich, poor. Christian means to true riches are the poverty and the pain and the powerlessness which seem the permanent enemies of men. Such contradictions can be accommodated at different times in a somewhat unstable orthodoxy but they could never be reduced to clear conduct for moral behaviour. The Gospels themselves do not speak with one voice. According to Luke vi. 20, 'Blessed be ye poor: for your's is the kingdom of God!', which may be used to support a theology of liberation; Matthew extends the Beatitude 'Blessed are the poor in spirit . . .' in v. 3; and most medieval commentators follow Matthew's sense.[14] Perhaps the discordance is more striking to us if we insist that poverty is a function of economies. Following the Gospels generally Christians regarded poverty as material as well as spiritual and looked for the Kingdom to exist in human history as well as in heaven. Material poverty was a marginal disability but it could be used as a condition of virtue in this life and as a preparation for and even as a penance paid for a better life hereafter.

It was the promise that was accepted by Christian monasticism; and what monasticism made of poverty is almost a sufficient and characterizing index of the changing history of monasticism and of the fortunes of new religious orders. Langland summarizes this development: the Desert Fathers sought a total independence of the world, apathy and autarchy, counting it a vice and foul shame to beg or borrow but of God alone, aspiring through voluntary renunciation to attain to a vision of God and a control and authority over spiritual forces. Langland recalls such men, Antony and Arseny and Paul *primus heremita*.[15] He observes that their heroic days are gone. Such men live now only in legend.

A tradition of a more modest ideal of scriptural poverty remains

---

[14] See J. Leclercq, 'Aux origines bibliques du vocabulaire de la pauvreté', in Mollat (ed.), *Etudes sur l'histoire de la pauvreté*, i, pp. 35–43, esp. pp. 41–2 and nn. 21–9.

[15] Pearsall, C XVII, lines 6–15; Skeat, pp. 452–5.

however, and had been institutionalized in western monasteries. The religious should follow:

> Benet and Bernarde the which hem first tauȝte
> To lyue bi litel and in lowe houses by lele mennes almesse[16]

This was the general limit of monastic ambition, although each reforming movement struggled in turn to redefine a new and acceptable standard of poverty: the Cluniacs by heavy insistence on communal ownership, the Cistercians by renunciation of all movable wealth. By the twelfth century the evangelical appeal had touched the laity. The Franciscan ideal gave a new glamour to Lady Poverty. Still in Langland's field of folk, hermits, anchorites, pilgrims are numerous, even conspicuous. The degree of commitment to holy poverty strikes Langland as everywhere uncertain; for everybody is enclosed in that acquisitive context described in the first Passus. He testifies later:

> Ich haue yleued in Londone monye longe ȝeres . . .
> I knewe neuere, by Crist, clerk noþer lewed
> That he ne askede aftur his and oþerehwiles coueytede
> Thyng that nedede hym nauhte, and nyme hit, yf a myhte![17]

Possessiveness deeply infects lives of professed poverty: indeed it may be noted that throughout the Confessions most of the occasions for all sin relate to acquisitiveness. The full openheartedness can be exemplified in very few men; by St Lawrence who gave God's men (the poor) God's goods (church treasure); by other individual men to be found in all ranks of society.[18] These are the few who can dissolve the sinful temptations of poverty into self-forgetfulness and exalt the sense of a human solidarity into the exercise of a most excellent charity.

But all this teaching on the virtues of spontaneity and generosity of spirit and the life of love which transcends self-regard comes from Recklessness. And from Recklessness Langland in C text seems reluctantly, almost surreptitiously, eventually to disassociate himself. The C text does not present a deeper degree of

---

[16] Skeat, p. 464, B XV, lines 414–15. This passage is not in the C text.

[17] Pearsall, C XVI, lines 286, 290–2; Skeat, p. 447.

[18] Pearsall, C XVII, line 64; Skeat, p. 457; Pearsall, C XVI, lines 340–65; cf. Skeat, pp. 450–3. The passage is apparently linked with Gerard of Abbeville, 'Contra adversarium perfectionis christianae', ed. Sophronius Clasen, *Archivum franciscanum historicum*, xxxii (1939), p. 139.

disillusionment about doing good. It emphasizes rather the difficulty of knowing clearly what that good is, how circumscribed it may be under the harsh compulsions of life. The poor have a role imposed upon them by society: at the same time what can be done to help them is limited by other obligations that society must lay upon itself if it is to survive.

The grounds for the quarrel among Franciscans between the Spirituals who sought indeed to pursue holy poverty recklessly and the Coventuals who admitted the need to organize for survival were familiar. A visible adjustment between salvation and social order was as old as western monasticism, symbolically expressed in the Donation of Constantine which in the fourteenth century was still accepted as an authorization for the peculiar medieval enmeshment of religion and politics that only humanist scholarship and radical thought and action was to disentangle. But some churchmen had always been wary of it: the legitimization of possession was the draught of poison which had been a reproach to the church at least from the twelfth century. Langland like the Lollards would abate the effects of the old poison by taking church lands back, not for direct economic reasons, but because as he saw it the church's exploitation of their possessions disturbed the peace of Europe and grossly enfeebled the proper work of bishops as teachers.[19]

But Langland could not and would not evade the consequences of the old settlement. It guaranteed the base and the independence of the clerical class. In the well-known defence of a life in minor orders inserted into the C text at the beginning of Passus V, and understood by most readers as having a close relation to Langland's view of his own career, he finds it entirely reasonable that no clerk should be constrained to knave's work. A man should live and work in the estate to which he is called and should be paid according to what he does. The clerisy can rightfully expect to be supported by good men's alms. 'A perfect priest to poverty should draw', but yet keep so far from actual poverty that he never lack a subsistence, nor woollen, nor linen.[20] Like the injunction to monastics 'to live by little in low houses' it is a modest, sensible and traditional claim but one far removed from any counsel that there is a perfection in poverty itself.

[19] Pearsall, C XVII, lines 220–38, 283–96; cf. Skeat, pp. 470–7.
[20] Pearsall, C XIII, lines 99–102; cf. Skeat, pp. 356–7.

But in the long run over the medieval centuries the most morally awkward consequence of the separation of the secularizing values of the ecclesiastical institution from the monastic ethic based on a rigorist understanding of Christian doctrine was the emergence of what was accepted as a Double Standard.[21] The church adopted a system of worldly rewards; on the other hand the world came to accept the ultimate validity of monastic morality. The monastic ideals were fierce and strict and remained so, even if in application they were tempered somewhat by Benedict. Monks consciously aimed higher and looked for the greater reward. Monks it was agreed had an excellent chance of getting to heaven. The odds against any layman getting there were quoted by popular preachers as extremely long. In the monastic scheme the contemplative life was different and absolutely better than the active: humility was better than ambition, virginity than marriage, the fruits of peace than the glory of war, learning than power, obedience than authority; and of course holy poverty better than worldly wealth. The alternatives were better because they more securely guaranteed salvation. Langland is committed to deal with these issues in old familiar terms when he considers the nature of the Pardon and what is meant by doing well, and doing better and doing best.

These may have been ideals by which in each generation only a few ardent and simple souls could live, but the monastic ethic taken as a standard, coherently and persuasively presented by dozens of intellectually gifted monastics in the twelfth century, relayed to laymen from pulpit and in catechism, and confession, established the value system of the later middle ages. There was no other scheme available (the chivalric code was a derivative) and even those men – the majority of men – who did not live by it nevertheless acknowledged its ultimate validity; many of them, knights, merchants, peasants, were eager enough to gather, in Burke's phrase, 'the useful fruit of late penitence', by deathbed gifts, by works of mercy and charity, by seeking 'to die under the frock'. Langland complains that money that by right should have gone to the poor was wastefully spent on glazing conventual windows.[22] Outside the gates of paradise no doubt there was often an unholy scramble. By Langland's time there were many voices

---

[21] See Kenneth E. Kirk, *The Vision of God* (London, 1931), esp. pp. 240–57, and note N, pp. 526–34.
[22] Pearsall, C III, lines 50–76; cf. Skeat, pp. 66–9.

protesting at the inferior and dependent role of the laity in the work of salvation, and at the identification of the church (outside which there was no salvation) with the estate of the clergy. It took centuries to establish an alternative moral order and a system of values which would accommodate the aspirations of laymen. But Langland (like Thomas More in *Utopia*) still thinks that the monastic ideal gives the best model for communal life:

> For yf heuene be on this erthe or eny ese to þe soule
> Hit is in cloystre or in scole, by many skilles y fynde.
> For in cloystres cometh no man to chyde ne to fyhte.[23]

But there is no suggestion in the poem that the monasteries of the time offer such satisfactions: the monastery is indeed the locale of Wrath.[24] The milieu depicted in *Piers Plowman* is distinctly lay. Only the underlying pervasive morality is still monastic. The transformation of this morality is usually regarded as an achievement of the northern Renaissance in the sixteenth century. Within Langland's conservatism there are sympathetic anticipations of things to come.

His treatment of poverty on many points illustrates this foresight. Much of what is said is put into the mouth of Recklessness, this curious wavering composite creature speaking apparently for aspects of Langland's consciousness. In some sense Recklessness certainly means 'throwing oneself upon God'. But Recklessness, who is a hugely extended figure in the C version, is first presented also as the over-hasty voice of contemporary progressivism. He is made to sound like an excited spiritual drop-out with decided views on reforming society. If there were a philosopher behind the Great Revolt his name could be Recklessness. Langland presents him with a sympathetic understanding that changes to wariness.

Recklessness argues strongly that all men are brothers as long as they maintain 'love and loyalty'; indeed it might be inferred that he accepts a universalism in salvation (an apocotastasis in the term of the old theology). All men have a common destiny as they have a saviour in common. Our common brotherhood sealed in the

---

[23] Pearsall, C V, lines 152–4; cf. Skeat, pp. 126–7. See Morton W. Bloomfield, *Piers Plowman as a Fourteenth-Century Apocalypse* (New Brunswick, N. J., 1963), p. 72 and nn.

[24] 'Confessio Ire', Pearsall, C VI, lines 115–63; Skeat, pp. 140–5.

blood of Christ makes us all gentlemen. Only sin produces inferiors. But gentlemen are not to be identified simply by their appearance. Christ himself never looked rich; born a bourgeois in the best house in the town, the longer he lived the poorer he became.[25] This poor Christ we may recall had long been the model for a monk. The counsel of perfection to the rich young man in Matthew xix, 'If thou wilt be perfect, go and sell what thou hast, and give to the poor, and thou shalt have treasure in heaven: and come and follow me', presented the postulant monk with the decisive challenge. Taken as a monastic challenge it gave the Double Standard its warrant. Mary also who chose the better part was likewise taken as type of the monk. *Dives and Pauper* uses the same texts in the old sense and, though the author does not directly apply them to the life of monks, he regards the better part as the life of contemplation, a life which Dives, the partner in the dialogue, may hear about but is not expected to follow.[26] But Recklessness explains the better part that Mary chose not as the life of religious contemplation but as poverty – that degree of modest poverty that induces quietness of mind. When Recklessness follows on with the counsel to the rich young man he turns it to a general application:

ȝut conseileth Crist in commen vs all.[27]

A call to a kind of poverty is made to all men, not exclusively to monks. It is not a challenge to specialists but rather an ethical doctrine taught in proverbs and made familiar by philosophers at all times, by:

Porfirie and Plato,
Aristotel, Ennedy, enleuene hundred,
Tulius, Tolomeus, Y can not tell here names . . .[28]

It is the demand made by what Langland calls 'patient poverty'. It is the renunciation made within a clear recognition of limits of an active pursuit of wordly goods and satisfaction. Perhaps it should not surprise us that when the authorities adduced are pagan

---

25 Pearsall, C XIV, lines 90–1, and C XIII, lines 3–4; cf. Skeat, pp. 374–5, 352.
26 *Dives and Pauper*, ed. Barnum, i, pt 1, pp. 67–9, 'Holy Poverty', ch. 10.
27 Pearsall, C XII, line 166; Skeat, p. 349.
28 Pearsall, C XII, lines 172–4; Skeat, p. 349.

philosophers the ideal of 'patient poverty' is highly reminiscent of the Stoic idea of the conditions of a virtuous life.

This emphasis remains during the rest of the C text insertion. Recklessness no longer speaks as an eager spontaneous youth assuming that high ideals constitute a programme of action. Now he speaks like an old prudent man. Modest poverty is recommended as simple good sense. The pursuit of riches is tedious, burdensome and ultimately unproductive. The rich are fools, chasing an illusion, painfully amassing that which corrupts, as well as corrupting others. It is the counsel of an old man aware of death perhaps. Even thus it is an adaptation of a familiar monastic theme of contempt of the world, but in Langland it is presented here as a means of accepting the world. Poverty endured with patience is a way of living tranquilly in this life with some hope for the next. Possessions are not bad; they can be dangerous; they are certainly a nuisance. Riches as well as poverty can be turned to good ends, but there is finally a real advantage in poverty. It gets you through purgatory quicker.[29]

But as is not unusual in Langland's exposition, conclusions outrun arguments. The diluted monastic ethic that Langland is sketchily developing is tested upon a 'mynstral' by name *Activa Vita*, the apprentice of Piers Plowman himself, but one not very far advanced in his master's mystery. He is represented as a type of paid employee in service activities primarily concerned with provisioning. He does not readily understand that the bread men need includes supersubstantial bread. He is much too busy in supplying the world's needs to see that all human effort and achievement dissolves into an acceptance that 'Thy will be done'. He has still to learn the proper balance between this world and the next:

And yf men lyuede as mesure wolde sholde neuere be defaute[30]

Why then asks *Activa Vita* if supplies must be fitted to demand should patient poverty, a negative principle surely, please God more:

Then rihtfullyche rychesse and resonablelyche to spene?[31]

---

[29] Pearsall, C XIII, lines 25–31; Skeat, pp. 352–3.
[30] Pearsall, C XV, line 272; Skeat, pp. 418–19.
[31] Pearsall, C XV, line 280; Skeat, pp. 420–1.

Patience has a deeper insight. There is a measure, an equity within
nature itself. It is not that rich men are to be condemned; in a
sense they condemn themselves by being unlike the poor. Very
few men can successfully carry the burden of riches. The rich have
never had an equal opportunity of heaven. The poor who have
never known in this world the satisfaction of the rich can fairly
claim a better balance, 'either here or elsewhere'. If this life seems
perpetual fair weather for the rich, sometimes surely the patient
poor must also know their days of summer.

The B version is cut here and in C a new Passus begun to enable
Patience to develop this theme:

Alas that riches should steal and snatch a man's soul . . .
Servants that get their pay in advance are ever after poor and
rarely die unencumbered, and those who eat their dinner before
they have earned it rarely die out of debt. When a man's service
is done and a full day's work, then men can tell what he is worth
and what he is to be paid. But payment is not to be taken in
advance for fear of not giving satisfaction. So I say to you rich
men it is not fitting that you should have two heavens just
because of your present situation . . . Now Lord send summer
sometime to their comfort and the delight of all those who lead
a life in abject poverty. For you might have made all men men
of great wealth and all equally clever and wise to live beyond
want; but yet it is for the best I expect that some are poor and
some rich.[32]

No doubt it is a poor man's view of prosperity. Here again
Langland reveals that characteristic eloquence, and the voice that
appeals to a divine sense of fair play curiously touches the heart.
Unless we catch this dry but loving tone, what Langland has to say

---

[32] Allas! þat rychesse shal reue and robbe mannes soule
     Fro þe loue of oure lord at his laste ende.
     Hewen þat haen here huyre byfore aren eueremore pore
     And selde deyeth oute of dette þat dyneþ ar he deserue hit.
     When his dyuer is doen and his dayes iourne
     Thenne may men wyte what he is worth and what he had deserued,
     Ac nat to fonge byfore for drede of dessallouwynge.
     So y sey by ȝow ryche, hit semeth nat þat ȝe sholle
     Haue two heuenes for ȝoure here-beynge.
     Muche murthe is in May amonge wilde bestes
     And so forth whiles somur laste here solace duyreth,
     And moche murthe among ryche men is þat han meble ynow and hele.
     Ac beggares aboute myssomur bredles they soupe,

will sound outrageous or superficial or merely sentimental. Rich and poor are bound together in one society on this earth and hereafter and they need each other: even their salvation is linked. Christians should be rich in common and individual shares are of little account. This is counsel for the rich in this world to take notice of, and it is also a justification for the poor who enjoy more security and the greater hope.

This kind of pious talk is not to the taste of *Activa Vita*, who in some exasperation asks Patience then to define poverty. Poverty is, says Patience, 'a disagreeable advantage, a remover of worries, ownership beyond reproach, the gift of God, mother of health, a career without anxiety, a judicious standard of reference, a transaction which involves no loss, a future with possibilities, a happiness free from anxiety'.[33]

So from an eloquent and subtle analysis of the moral and spiritual consequences of poor men's experience, Langland reads off schoolroom commonplaces and through their context gives them power. The Latin phrases often ascribed to the apocryphal Second Philosopher, counsellor to the Emperor Hadrian, in part derived from Seneca, appear to sum up what Langland has to say. This poet was never afraid of commonplaces.

The presentation of the Nine Points draws the discussion on poverty to a close. In a sense nothing is concluded concerning poverty. To seek to understand poverty is to transcend its ambiguities. Poverty remains an ill for it blights men's lives, but it must be good because it is a characteristic of common humanity, a mark of brotherhood. Poverty again elicits a dual response; from the poor in their begging; and begging is a bad thing because it destroys the sense of mutual responsibility, because the unspiritual poor can offer nothing in return and thus a genuine interdepen-

---

And 3ut is wynter for hem worse, for weet-shoed þey gone,
Afurste and afyngered and foule rebuked
Of this world-ryche men, þat reuthe is to here.
Now lord, sende hem somur somtyme to solace and to ioye
That at here lyf leden in lownesse and in pouerte!
For at myhtest þou haue ymad men of grete welthe
And yliche witty and wys and lyue withoute nede –
Ac for þe beste, as y hope, aren som pore and ryche.
Pearsall, C XVI, lines 1–21; Skeat, pp. 422–5.

[33] Pearsall, C XVI, line 116; Skeat, pp. 430–1. Langland then renders this Latin definition (lines 120–54), and gives a commentary omitting *incerta fortuna*: see the notes on this rhetorical definition by Skeat and Pearsall.

dence is destroyed. But begging is good to the degree that it implies an utter and innocent dependence on God. From the other side almsgiving in relief of poverty is a good if properly motivated and strictly measured; but bad, if it is the occasion of self-assertion and injustice. In sum then poverty is only to be understood in the coexistence and interaction of the two great commandments: the love of God and the love of one's neighbour.

What follows in the poem is for most modern readers the culmination and the most effective part, beginning with the account of the Tree of Charity. And up to the end of the poem Langland scarcely adverts to the theme of poverty again save where he uses the story of Dives and Lazarus to reassert the essential and natural brotherhood of all men.[34] In the last Passus, however, appears another mysterious figure, Need. Need is certainly no simple personification of poverty; rather it is a summary of the constraints, economic, social, physical, and moral, human and divine, within which men in society have to work and survive. This is the realm of necessity in which even the earnest Christian has to live. The fundamental virtue which all men of all estates need to exercise in order to sustain society under this pressure is Temperance.[35] Justice may best qualify a king; fortitude the knight; wisdom (*prudentia*) the clergy; but what is required in common by the new society bursting through the old categories of the estates and breaking down the Double Standard of effort and rewards is Temperance understood as a spirit of moderation, self-control, fair compromise and tolerance. Only thus can the chances of fortune, the unequal gifts of nature, the accidents of birth, sickness and age be surmounted. Without Temperance the militant tyranny of Antichrist will triumph absolutely: for Langland seems to apprehend in Antichrist the coming of an age of

---

[34] Pearsall, C XIX, lines 229–49; cf. Skeat, pp. 512–15.

[35] Pearsall, C XXII, lines 4–23; Skeat, pp. 578–81. Temperance is discussed by Morton W. Bloomfield in his *Piers Plowman as a Fourteenth-Century Apocalypse*, pp. 135–51; 'Temperance is the keynote of the poem' (p. 151). Bloomfield seeks to show that Temperance in *Piers Plowman* is a monastic virtue, but neither his authorities nor his arguments are convincing. Indeed he has already admitted that 'the role given to Temperance is most curious and as far as I know unique' (p. 136). The *New English Dictionary, s.v.* 'temperance' in note *ad finem*, observes that it was originally not a Christian word but part of the Latin vocabulary of Platonic and Stoic philosophy. No schoolman appears to give Temperance primacy among the civic virtues; but Cicero regards it as an indispensable common element in all virtue: *Tusculan Disputations*, iii. 8.

total social dissolution when self-regard, acquisitiveness and moral perversity are all-pervasive. Against Antichrist, Conscience still sets a principle of order. Nature itself proclaims:

> That in mesure God made alle manere thynges
> And sette hit at a serteyne and at a syker nombre
> And nempned hem names and nombred þe sterres.[36]

But it is a harmony of the universe and presumably of society only audible to the inner ear. The *viator* needs to free himself from the chances and changes inherent in the realm of necessity to apprehend the permanent order of the inner reality of things.

Perhaps it is almost inevitable that an old reflective man at the end of the fourteenth century, or for that matter at the end of any century, should reach some such conclusions, compounded of a patient pessimism about his society and a hopeful assurance about a better invisible reality. But *Piers Plowman*, if we take it as completed in this last revision, suggests a somewhat firmer system than that afforded by an old man's hopes and fears. Will has made a long and arduous pilgrimage. He has sought the recipe for well-doing in a just society. Of course there is much discussion of Christian doctrine in *Piers Plowman*, but chiefly to the end that doctrine defines intention and conduct; there are also passages of high devotion but again devotion is not the substance of the poem; nor is it concerned with religious doubt. The education of Will is moral. He disentangles Truth in order to do good.

But one Christian doctrine Langland takes as giving the very structure of human thought and action. Even a superficial reading of the poem discloses some of its triads. The most profound reading will observe that Langland's belief in the Trinity shapes the whole work. God in Trinity is in everything, in man and in the mind of man. The reader is aware rather of immanence than transcendence. A human Piers Plowman manifests this divine presence.[37]

The same divine constitution is manifested in the universe and in the order of creation. Imaginatif talks about this unity in Passus XIV. Human society is similarly held together. All men are

---

[36] Pearsall, C XXII, lines 254–6; Skeat, pp. 592–3.

[37] See R. W. Frank, *Piers Plowman and the Scheme of Salvation* (Yale Studies in English, cxxxvi, New Haven, 1957); Barbara Raw, 'Piers and the Image of God in Man', in S. S. Hussey (ed.), *Piers Plowman: Critical Approaches* (London, 1969), pp. 143–79.

brothers. The social order reflects the stability of the cosmos. There is a single intelligible order governed by a common morality. There is no Double Standard which can be validated; men are essentially equal.

The wise man who understands and penetrates in thought into this order and unity acquires a kind of detachment from worldly affairs – as Piers does. Will's pilgrimage, which is no more than a succession of rational and moral arguments, moves to the same end – to a discovery of principles, to a rejection of accidentals. The wise man comes to make a clear difference between the inner important things and those things which are not under a rational control. An educated will concerns itself with the former; poverty and riches, gifts of fortune, are irrelevant. So are most events in the world of human time and space. The end of the poem suggests a quiet extrication from apocalypse. There may be a nostalgia for an ideal and imaginary past order of the world; but the wise man will transcend in thought and will the conditions of his present.

Is this how to read *Piers Plowman*? If so, it is markedly Stoic.[38] The entry of Need in the last Passus with his message of Temperance may seem to give confirmation of some strength. But where or how Langland came by such ideas it would be difficult to say: medieval Stoicism has never yet been fully investigated. What is clear however is that on social and institutional issues Langland's revisions of his poem, in both the B and C texts, show him moving in reaction to the revolutionary excitements of the 1380s and thoughtfully embracing a cosmic Fabianism.

---

[38] But see William J. Bouwsma, 'The Two Faces of Humanism: Stoicism and Augustinianism in Renaissance Thought', in Heiko A. Oberman and Thomas A. Brady (eds.), *Itinerarium Italicum* (Studies in Medieval and Reformation Thought, xiv, Leiden, 1975), pp. 3–60, esp. pp. 14 ff. What is required is systematic study of the moral writings of Cicero – cf. Charles B. Schmitt, *Cicero scepticus* (The Hague, 1973) – and of Seneca – see G. M. Ross, 'Seneca's Philosophical Influence', in C. D. N. Costa (ed.), *Seneca* (London, 1974), pp. 116–65 – to establish their roles in the transmission of Stoicism to the middle ages.

8. *English Diet in the Later Middle Ages*

CHRISTOPHER DYER

The study of diet used to be left to antiquarians, 'relegated to the level of anecdotal curiosities', in Marc Bloch's words, but it is now recognized as a subject of central importance for our understanding of the pre-industrial past.[1] The systematic historical study of food and nutrition in the middle ages has been actively pursued on the Continent, notably by the *Annales* school, but the subject has been neglected in England.[2] This essay will define the main characteristics of the diet of different sections of (mainly rural) society, from the nobility to wage-earners, with the aim of assessing the quality of late medieval nutrition, and examining some of the implications for the wider problems of the demographic and economic history of the period.

I

Food and drink formed a major item in the expenditure of the upper classes. At the highest social level the provisioning of the household could cost about a third of total income. For example, Thomas earl of Lancaster in 1313–14 spent £3,405 on food and drink from revenues of about £11,000, and feeding the household

---

[1] Quoted in P.-A. Amargier, 'Questions d'hygiène alimentaire et de panification aux Saintes-Maries-de-la-Mer en 1286', *Annales du Midi*, lxxxi (1969), p. 73.

[2] Examples of Continental work are L. Stouff, *Ravitaillement et alimentation en Provence aux XIVe et XVe sièctes* (Paris, 1970); *Bulletin philologique et historique du Comité des travaux historiques et scientifiques*, vol. i for 1968 (1971), 'Les problèmes de l'alimentation'; B. Bennassar and J. Goy, 'Contribution à l'histoire de la consommation alimentaire du xive au xixe siècle', *Annales. E.S.C.*, xxx (1975), pp. 402–30. Useful English works are W. Ashley, *The Bread of our Forefathers* (Oxford, 1928); J. C. Drummond and A. Wilbraham, *The Englishman's Food* (London, 1939); C. Anne Wilson, *Food and Drink in Britain* (London, 1973). The best summary of our knowledge of lower-class diet is R. H. Hilton, *A Medieval Society: The West Midlands at the End of the Thirteenth Century* (London, 1966), pp. 110–13.

of Bishop Bourgchier of Worcester in 1435–6 cost about £300 when total income was £900–£1,000.[3] However, spending on foodstuffs could take up as much as two-thirds of revenues, so that Battle Abbey's food bill accounted for £750 to £830 out of an income of about £1,200 in the late fourteenth century. The two priests of Munden's chantry of Bridport (Dorset), whose household may be regarded as representative of the lesser beneficed clergy, bought food and drink for £8 or £9 per annum in the mid-fifteenth century, when their total spending varied in most years between £12 and £17.[4]

It might be thought that these high rates of spending on food resulted from the consumption of esoteric delicacies at noble and clerical tables.[5] However, a good deal of the cost in the case of the magnates can be attributed to the large number of people accommodated in the households, which could be in excess of a hundred for earls and dukes, and between twenty and eighty for barons and bishops, while in most monasteries the servants, corrodians and guests outnumbered the monks. A large entourage performed domestic, administrative, and religious duties, but their function was also to display their lord's status, and to enable him to demonstrate publicly the virtue of *largesse*. Contemporary writers on the conduct of the household emphasized that all members should eat together, partly in the interests of economy (to prevent corruption or theft), and partly to reinforce the social solidarity of a group bound to the lord by ties of loyalty and service, and in turn rewarded with a generous provision of good things.[6] This ideal showed signs of breaking down because of a growing sense of social divisions in the late medieval period.[7]

The diet provided in lordly households, that is from the gentry and lesser beneficed clergy upwards, seems to have been based on a common standard in the quantities of bread and ale. Each

[3] J. R. Maddicott, *Thomas of Lancaster* (Oxford, 1970), pp. 22–7; C. Dyer, *Lords and Peasants in a Changing Society: The Estates of the Bishopric of Worcester, 680–1540* (Past and Present Pubns., Cambridge, 1980), p. 200.

[4] E. Searle, *Lordship and Community: Battle Abbey and its Banlieu* (Toronto, 1974), p. 256; *A Small Household of the XVth Century*, ed. K. L. Wood-Legh (Manchester, 1956), *passim*.

[5] This aspect is emphasized in W. E. Mead, *The English Medieval Feast* (London, 1931), and in B. A. Henisch, *Fast and Feast* (Pittsburgh, 1976).

[6] *Walter of Henley*, ed. D. Oschinsky (Oxford, 1971), pp. 402–7 (from the Rules of Bishop Grosseteste).

[7] Henisch, *Fast and Feast*, p. 17.

member was allowed daily between two and three pounds of wheat bread and about a gallon of ale. Such a standard can be calculated from household accounts; it also formed the basis of estimates for the provisioning of castle garrisons in the Scottish wars of Edward I; it was stipulated in the grants of corrodies by monasteries to laymen; and it was even laid down for the inmates of hospitals.[8] This led to the wealthiest households spending about a third of their food budget on cereals, and the proportion rose to a half in the case of the less well-off, such as the Bridport priests, and the household of a member of the lesser Northamptonshire gentry, Thomas Bozoun of Woodford, in 1328.[9]

The distinguishing characteristics of upper-class diet lay in the ample amounts of meat and fish, which were eaten in almost equal quantities because of the generally strict observance of fish days on three days of each week, and throughout Lent. A third to a half of expenditure on food, depending on the wealth of the lord, went on meat and fish, so that the average per capita consumption in magnate households was in the region of two or three pounds per day. The myth of a mass 'autumn slaughter' of animals, followed by a diet of salt meat throughout the winter, deserves to be corrected. It is true that animals needed for salting down were traditionally killed around Martinmas (11 November), but households were usually able to obtain supplies of some fresh meat and fish throughout the year.[10] The bulk of the meat came from the

---

8   For example, 'Household Roll of Bishop Ralph of Shrewsbury, 1337–8', ed. J. Armitage Robinson, in T. F. Palmer (ed.), *Collectanea*, 2 vols. (Somerset Rec. Soc., xxxix, xliii, Frome and London, 1924–8), i, pp. 72–178; *Household Book of Dame Alice de Bryene*, ed. M. K. Dale and V. B. Redstone (Suffolk Inst. Archaeol. and Nat. Hist., Ipswich, 1931), *passim*; M. Prestwich, 'Victualling Estimates for English Garrisons in Scotland during the Early Fourteenth Century', *Eng. Hist. Rev.*, lxxxii (1967), pp. 536–43; *Cartulary of the Abbey of Eynsham*, 2 vols., ed. H. E. Salter (Oxford Hist. Soc., xlix, li, Oxford, 1907–8), i, pp. 186–7, 332; P. Richards, *The Medieval Leper and his Northern Heirs* (Cambridge, 1977), pp. 125–8. But not all corrodies or hospital rations were as generous; see A. G. Little and E. Stone, 'Corrodies at the Carmelite Friary at Lynn', *Jl. Eccles. Hist.*, ix (1958), pp. 8–29; A. Wyczanski, 'Structure sociale de la consommation alimentaire en Italie au XVIe siècle', in *Mélanges en l'honneur de Fernand Braudel*, 2 vols. (Toulouse, 1973), p. 679.

9   G. H. Fowler, 'A Household Expense Roll, 1328', *Eng. Hist. Rev.*, lv (1940), pp. 630–4 (the value of cereals in this document has to be reconstructed from contemporary price data).

10   For the slaughter of some animals in November, see *A Roll of the Household Expenses of Richard de Swinfield, Bishop of Hereford*, ed. J. Webb (Camden Soc., old ser., lix, London, 1854), pp. 19–24.

normal domestic animals, and game, venison and smaller animals and birds, were not major items of consumption. For example, Alice de Bryene, the widow of a lesser baron, maintained in Suffolk a substantial household which, in the year 1418–19, ate 46 cattle, 44 pigs, 97 sheep and much poultry, but the total of game consumed amounted to 3 pheasants, 13 partridges and 5 herons, to which might be added from semi-domesticated animals 102 conies and 5 cygnets.[11] The game was reserved for special occasions, and was then presumably served only to those on high table. Similarly the mundane products of commercial fisheries, mainly herrings, cod and haddock, formed the bulk of the fish eaten, and luxuries such as salmon, pike and sturgeon were comparatively rare.

The most prized constituents of aristocratic consumption were the imported luxuries, wine and spices. In magnate households expenditure on these could be as high as 16 per cent of the total, but a lower percentage is often found. Magnates like Battle Abbey or the countess of Warwick (in 1420–1) bought 2,000 and 3,000 gallons of wine per annum respectively, which would enable the superior members of the household each to drink two or three pints each day.[12] Spices, which included dried fruits or rice as well as condiments such as pepper and ginger, were again used mainly in the preparation of dishes for the inner circle of family, friends and top officials, and normally accounted for less than 5 per cent of expenditure. Their use is commonly associated with the consumption of poor quality meat; but the explanation of the nobility's attachment to spices is more likely to be cultural – they provided a link with the sophisticated Mediterranean world. Regular enjoyment of wines and spices was confined to the very wealthy, so that lesser gentry and clergy seem to have bought them only sporadically. The Bridport priests, for example, seem to have used wine in small quantities for liturgical purposes, and to entertain exceptionally important guests; their spice bill in 1456–7

---

[11] *Household Book of Dame Alice de Bryene*, ed. Dale and Redstone, pp. 128–35.
[12] *The Cellarers' Rolls of Battle Abbey, 1275–1513*, ed. E. Searle and B. Ross (Sussex Rec. Soc., lxv, Lewes, 1967), *passim*; C. D. Ross, 'A Household Account of Elizabeth Berkeley, Countess of Warwick, 1420–1', *Trans. Bristol and Gloucs. Archaeol. Soc.*, lxx (1951), p. 97.

of 1s. 6d. represented less than 1 per cent of a total of £8 expenditure on food.[13]

Upper-class nutrition clearly lacked for nothing in terms of quantity. The individual intake of calories in households of all kinds would have been in the region of 4,000 to 5,000 per day, similar to those found on the Continent, for example in the households of the archbishop of Arles or the seigneur of Murol (in the Auvergne).[14] Presumably in reality the daily intake was rather less than this, and a good deal of food was wasted, or at least handed out to the poor gathered at the gates. Judged by modern nutritional standards, the diet of the upper ranks of medieval society shows serious deficiencies in quality. Consumption of dairy produce and fresh fruit and vegetables was minimal. In a fortnight in 1337 in the household of the bishop of Bath and Wells, milk worth 1½d, cheese worth 3d., and vegetables worth 10d. were accounted for in a total budget of £18. 11s. 3d.[15] Such figures are by no means exceptional, and must mean that on many days none of these foodstuffs were eaten. It is sometimes argued that fruit and vegetables were in reality available, but do not appear in the records because they came from gardens attached to the manor-houses, castles or monasteries in which the households were accommodated. Such reasoning underestimates the sophistication of late medieval accounting techniques, which would, for example in the case of the accounts of the bishop of Bath and Wells just mentioned, lead to the valuation of garden produce used in any quantity. Seigneurial gardens could be large, but they were often used to grow flax and hemp, and usually contained an area under grass. The most commonly grown fruits, apples and pears, were often used for cider and perry making. The vegetables that were

---

[13] *A Small Household of the XVth Century*, ed. Wood-Legh; a similar picture emerges, especially in respect of wine, from the records of a rather more prosperous lay family, the le Stranges, in the fourteenth century; see H. Le Strange, 'A Roll of Household Accounts of Sir Hamon Le Strange of Hunstanton, Norfolk, 1347–8', *Archaeologia*, lxix (1917–18), pp. 111–20; G. H. Holley, 'The Earliest Roll of Household Accounts in the Muniment Room of Hunstanton for the 2nd Year of Edward III', *Norfolk Archaeol.*, xxi (1920–2), pp. 77–96.

[14] Stouff, *Ravitaillement et alimentation en Provence*, p. 237; Bennassar and Goy, 'Contribution à l'histoire de la consommation alimentaire du xive au xixe siècle', p. 408.

[15] 'Household Roll of Bishop Ralph of Shrewsbury', ed. Armitage Robinson, pp. 85–100. See also the calculations in I. Kershaw, *Bolton Priory* (Oxford, 1973), p. 158.

grown – notably leeks, onions, garlic and herbs such as pars-
ley – were appreciated mainly for flavouring rather than as a
major constituent of meals.[16] Medieval dietary theory distrusted
greenstuff as a danger to health, reinforcing a widespread prejudice.[17] There is evidence, from the analysis of the contents of
urban cess pits, that better-off townsmen ate a great variety of
both cultivated and wild fruits, but we cannot tell over how long a
period the cess pits were in use, so they do not provide information on how frequently fruits were eaten by individuals.[18]

We must conclude that the late medieval upper classes provided
themselves with a diet rich in carbohydrate and protein, but
deficient in vitamins. The many herrings eaten contained vitamin
D, but without much milk, cheese, fruit and vegetables there
would have been a lack of adequate amounts of the vitamins A
and C.[19] This factor must be taken into account in explaining the
rate of mortality and low expectation of life among people who
otherwise might be expected to have enjoyed many advantages.

There were apparently no great changes in aristocratic diet
during the later middle ages. The system of victualling households
was affected by developments in estate management. Although
some landlords in the thirteenth century sold their estate produce
and bought foodstuffs on the market, many lived directly off their
own manors, and turned more to purchasing supplies when their
demesnes were leased out in the fourteenth and fifteenth centuries. Any rise in costs incurred because of this change were
probably offset by the underlying downward movement in
food prices. The magnates would have suffered in the late
fourteenth and fifteenth centuries from the increasing price of
spices and wines, and the reduced level of wine imports in the

---

[16] T. J. Hunt and I. Keil, 'Two Medieval Gardens', *Proc. Somerset Archaeol. and
Nat. Hist. Soc.*, civ (1959–60), pp. 91–101; P. D. A. Harvey, *A Medieval
Oxfordshire Village* (Oxford, 1965), pp. 38–9; T. McLean, *Medieval English
Gardens* (London, 1981), pp. 26–8, 38–41, 72–5, 116–17, 219–20. This latter
work gives examples of gardens with a greater variety of produce, for example on
pp. 81–3, but we can suspect that overall quantities were small.

[17] Henisch, *Fast and Feast*, p. 109.

[18] C. P. S. Platt and R. Coleman-Smith, *Excavations in Medieval Southampton,
1953–69*, 2 vols. (Leicester, 1975), i, pp. 344–6.

[19] A similar deficiency of A and C has been tentatively suggested for an aristocratic
household in Provence; see Stouff, *Ravitaillement et alimentation en Provence*,
pp. 237–8.

fifteenth century shows that there was a considerable drop in consumption.[20]

The wider economic importance of aristocratic food consumption lies firstly in the stimulus that it gave to the market. The magnates bought their imported luxuries from merchants in the major ports, or at the large fairs, while lesser lords were more likely to patronize small towns, like the Bozoun family, who shopped regularly at Higham Ferrers. Secondly, the aristocratic life style depended on the organization of demesne production and rent payment in order to concentrate large quantities of victuals into over-fed households, which must be judged, in an underdeveloped economy, to have amounted to a form of conspicuous waste.

II

Once we leave the relatively fully-documented nobility and turn to the majority of the population, the task of even describing diet adequately becomes problematic. The best sources for the diet of the peasants, which allow us to break into their normally hidden cycle of production and consumption, are the maintenance agreements found in manorial court rolls. Maintenance agreements normally followed from the surrender of a customary holding by an elderly tenant (often a widow) to an heir or a successor who was not a relative. In exchange for the holding the newcomer would promise to keep the former tenant in his or her retirement, and the details of the agreement might be written into the court rolls along with the record of the transfer of the land. Less often, maintenance might be agreed for a ward, or for a non-inheriting sibling. Often these agreements are recorded in the most general terms, with no more than a reference to 'food and drink', but many give specific quantities of grain and legumes.

Using this information is fraught with difficulties. The agreements were no more than promises, and we know from both contemporary literature and the court rolls themselves that new tenants neglected their responsibilities.[21] The detailed entitlement to grain is sometimes given as an alternative to a share in the food

---

[20] M. K. James, *Studies in the Medieval Wine Trade* (Oxford, 1971), pp. 38–63.

[21] R. H. Hilton, *The English Peasantry in the Later Middle Ages* (Oxford, 1975), p. 29; G. C. Homans, *English Villagers of the Thirteenth Century* (Cambridge, Mass., 1942), p. 155.

and drink of the new tenant's household, as if they represent a poorer version of the normal dietary regime. On the other hand, the bulk of the agreements are recorded in a period of land-hunger, in the century before 1349, when old people would have been able to drive a hard bargain for a generous allowance of food. We cannot be sure that the specified foodstuffs were the sole means of support of the retired peasant, who may have been able to earn wages or keep animals, but although some agreements do concede pasture for stock to the outgoing tenant, most, which in respect of housing or clothes can be very detailed, make no reference whatever to supplementary sources of income or food. In justification of the use of the maintenance agreements, it should be emphasized that the parties only troubled to record the details when there was an element of distrust between them. Many retirements were agreed informally and so leave no record, and it is comforting to find occasionally that the quantity of food was 'according to the custom of the vill', and therefore represents a normal and customary allowance, not a unique or exceptional arrangement.[22] Similarly we are told in some agreements that the food granted was 'according to that which her status requires', suggesting that we are justified in generalizing from our examples, which can tell us something about the standards of diet among the peasantry as a whole.

Having made these reservations and qualifications, what can be learnt from the maintenance agreements? This analysis is based on a total of eighty-three examples collected from manorial records from sixteen counties, mainly in the midlands, East Anglia and the south.[23] They range in date from 1240 to 1458, but seventy of them

[22] J. A. Raftis, *Tenure and Mobility* (Toronto, 1964), p. 46.

[23] The maintenance agreements are from the following sources: *Court Rolls of the Manor of Hales, 1270–1307*, ed. J. Amphlett, S. G. Hamilton and R. A. Wilson, 3 vols. (Worcs. Hist. Soc., Worcester, 1910–33), i, pp. 166–8; and iii, p. 52; F. M. Page, 'The Customary Poor-Law of Three Cambridgeshire Manors', *Cambridge Hist. Jl.*, iii (1930), p. 132; F. M. Page, *The Estates of Crowland Abbey* (Cambridge, 1934), pp. 361–2, 364–5; A. E. Levett, *Studies in Manorial History* (Oxford, 1938), p. 306; *Court Roll of Chalgrave Manor, 1278–1313*, ed. M. K. Dale (Beds. Hist. Rec. Soc., xxviii, Streatley, 1950), p. 10; *Chertsey Abbey Court Roll Abstracts*, 2 vols., ed. E. Toms, 2 vols. (Surrey Record Soc., xxxviii, xlviii, 1937–1954), i, pp. 9, 23, 37, 76, 81 and ii, p. 115; Raftis, *Tenure and Mobility*, pp. 43–6, 72, 74, 81; Homans, *English Villagers of the Thirteenth Century*, pp. 152–3; *Registrum prioratus beatae Mariae Wigorniensis*, ed. W. H.

fall within the crucial pre-plague century, between 1248 and 1349. The sizes of the holding transferred as part of the agreements are recorded in sixty cases, which are analysed in Table 1.

This suggests, with its clear majority of holdings of below fifteen acres, and substantial minorities with half and full yardlands, that we are dealing with a representative cross-section of customary tenements.

The quantities of grain specified in the agreements varied a good deal, from one bushel to 9 quarters (72 bushels). The range of quantities is indicated in Table 2.

The agreements do not always tell us how many people were to be supported by the grain allowances. The retired couple or widow might be supporting non-inheriting children; one widow even had an unspecified number of servants. At least nine of the largest allowances were intended to provide for two or more people. Taking this into account, there seem to have been at least thirty agreements allowing twelve to sixteen bushels ($1\frac{1}{2}$–2 quarters) per person, but with almost as many receiving eight bushels or less, while some individuals were apparently promised a good deal in excess of two quarters. There is some correlation, but by no means an exact one, between the size of the holding and the quantity of grain allowed. The largest allowances of grain tended to come

Hale (Camden Soc., old ser., xci, London, 1865), p. 7; Hilton, *English Peasantry in the Later Middle Ages,* pp. 29–30; R. K. Field, 'The Worcestershire Peasantry in the Later Middle Ages' (Univ. of Birmingham M. A. thesis, 1962), p. 155; *Court Rolls of the Wiltshire Manors of Adam de Stratton,* ed. R. B. Pugh (Wilts. Rec. Soc., xxiv, Devizes, 1970), pp. 104–5; *Halmota prioratus Dunelmensis,* ed. W. H. Longstaffe and J. Booth (Surtees Soc., lxxxii, Durham, 1889), p. 84; J. S. Drew, 'The Manor of Michelmersh' (unpublished typescript, copy at Inst. Hist. Research, London), p. 288; Gloucestershire County Record Office D678/96; Worcestershire Cathedral Lib., E15; East Sussex Record Office, 18/6a; Glynde MSS. 973, 976; Worcestershire County Record Office (hereafter Worcs. C.R.O.), ref. 009 : 1, B.A. 2636/158; ref. 705 : 56, B.A. 3910/24; ref. 899 : 95, B.A. 989/2/23; East Suffolk Record Office, HA 12/C 3/5; Essex Record Office, D/DP M15, M19; West Suffolk Record Office, HA 504/1/7,8; Norfolk Record Office, Dean and Chapter muniments 4970, 5282, 5284; ING 4 (I am grateful to Dr J. Williamson for these Norfolk examples); Lincolnshire Record Office, 6 ANC 1/29 (I am grateful to Dr G. Platts for these examples); Brit. Lib., Add. Ch. 63407, 63409; Public Record Office (hereafter P.R.O.), D.L. 30/62/785, 795–6, 798–801; D.L. 30/64; Essex Record Office, D/DTu 239, D/DK M108; East Suffolk Record Office, V5/6/1; Univ. of Chicago Lib., Bacon MSS. 3,4,5,117 (I am grateful to Dr R. Smith for these examples).

Table 1. Sizes of holdings recorded in sixty maintenance agreements (size unknown in twenty-three cases)*

	5 acres or below	6–14 acres	15 acres/ ½ yardland	16–29 acres	30 acres/ 1 yardland	Above 30 acres	Total
Number of holdings	19 (32)	13 (22)	8 (13)	8 (13)	10 (17)	2 (3)	60 (100)

* Figures in brackets denote percentages.

Table 2. Quantities of grain recorded in eighty-three maintenance agreements

	1–8 bushels	10–14 bushels	16 bushels	12–24 bushels	25 bushels or above	Total
Number of agreements	25	16	9	11	22	83

Table 3. *Types of corn in eighty-three maintenance agreements**

	Wheat	Maslin	Rye	Barley	Dredge	Oats	Pulse	Unspecified	Total
Cumulative quantity	92 qrs. 4½ bs.	4 qrs.	13 qrs. 4 bs.	39 qrs. 4 bs.	5 qrs. 5 bs.	21 qrs. 7 bs.	18 qrs. 3 bs.	2 qrs. 5 bs.	198 qrs. ½ bs.
	(47)	(2)	(7)	(20)	(3)	(11)	(9)	(1)	(100)

* Figures in brackets denote percentages. Maslin was a mixture of wheat and rye, dredge was a mixture of barley and oats.

Table 4. *Combinations of corn in eighty-three maintenance agreements**

wheat only	barley only	winter corn + barley	winter corn + oats	winter corn + dredge	winter corn + pulse	winter corn + barley + pulse
12	5	20	9	3	6	12

winter corn + oats + pulse	winter corn + dredge + pulse	winter corn + barley + oats	winter corn + barley + pulse + oats	barley + oats	'all types'
6	3	2	1	1	3

* Winter corn is wheat, rye or maslin.

from holdings of a yardland or more, though some smaller holdings seem to have been very heavily burdened.[24]

Most agreements specify more than one type of grain or legumes (for the sake of brevity, corn will be used to cover both). Tables 3–4 classify the amounts of different types of corn, and indicate the variety of combinations.

On the basis of this sample it would be very wrong to assume that peasants grew wheat only for sale. A good deal of wheat, the most highly priced and nutritious of grains, was clearly consumed by the peasants themselves. The most frequent combination was of winter corn (wheat and/or rye) with a single type of spring corn; this is found in thirty-eight (46 per cent) of the agreements. Another twenty-two (27 per cent) involved a combination of winter corn with both a spring grain and pulses. These combinations must partly reflect the crops grown on the holding, but they also give us some insight into the dietary regime. It was clearly expected that part of the food eaten would consist of bread made from winter corn, mainly wheat. Spring corns were also used to make bread, especially barley, which in five examples was the only grain in the allowance; they could also, especially oats and pulses, have been boiled in pottages. Barley, dredge and oats might alternatively have been made into malt for brewing. The choice of consuming spring corns either as food or drink would have depended on the total quantity of corn available, as much of the nutritional value of the corn would have been lost in the brewing process. So the different types of peasant diet can be distinguished only by examining both the quality and quantity of corn mentioned in individual agreements.

Among the peasants there was undoubtedly a superior type of dietary regime represented in the maintenance agreements by those who had enough grain to enable them both to eat wheat bread and drink ale. An example is Margaret atte Green of Girton (Cambridgeshire), who in 1291 was to receive annually two quarters of wheat, enough to make about 840 lbs. of bread (2.3 lbs. per day), and two quarters of barley, which if brewed would have given 120 gallons of ale (2.6 pints per day). This bread

---

[24] For example, three quarter-yardland holdings in Waltham and High Easter, Essex, were expected to provide maintenance allowances of 4 quarters 2 bushels, 5 quarters 7 bushels, and 6 quarters 3 bushels, which would have left little produce for the succeeding tenants.

and ale together would have provided a calorific intake of about 3,000 per day, more than sufficient according to modern assumptions of the needs of an elderly sedentary woman.[25] That spring corn was used for ale is shown by a late agreement (1458) from Elmley Castle (Worcestershire) in which a widow was given access to the brewhouse of the tenement.[26] Because of uncertainties about the number of people involved in the agreements, we cannot be sure how many of our sample would have allowed the retired peasants such a diet, but a reasonable estimate is that at least a dozen lived as well as Margaret atte Green.

A more numerous group, more than thirty, were to receive individual allowances of twelve to sixteen bushels of corn (1½–2 quarters). They would have needed to gain the maximum nutritional value from their corn by eating it in the form of bread, or boiled in pottages or puddings. For example, Sarra Martin of Wistow (Huntingdonshire), who received 4 bushels each of wheat, barley and pulse, could have maintained an intake of about 2,000 calories per day, adequate by modern standards, if she confined herself to eating bread and pottage accompanied by water.[27] Was such a diet found only among the retired and elderly? There is no direct evidence of cereal consumption in a normal peasant household, but a tentative calculation of the budget of a customary half-yardlander in the late thirteenth century, burdened with an annual rent of 10s. 0d., suggests that corn would have had to be used to feed a family in the most economical form, which would leave little for brewing.[28]

[25] This calculation is based on the assumptions that: (1) A quarter of wheat would make about 420 lbs. of coarse bread; see *The Account-Book of Beaulieu Abbey*, ed. S. F. Hockey (Camden Soc., 4th ser., xvi, London, 1975), pp. 290–1 (this gives the weight of servants' bread baked from a quarter of corn as 560 lbs., but using Tower pounds; in pounds avoirdupois the weight would be 420 lbs.). (2) That a quarter of barley would make about 60 gallons of ale; see *Documents Illustrating the Rule of Walter de Wenlok, Abbot of Westminster, 1283–1307*, ed. B. F. Harvey (Camden Soc., 4th ser., ii, London, 1965), p. 248. (3) That medieval bread, like modern bread, had a calorific value of about 70 calories per ounce, and ale of about 7 per ounce; see Ministry of Agriculture, Fisheries and Food, *Manual of Nutrition* (London, 1970), pp. 90–1. (4) That the recommended daily intake of calories for an elderly, sedentary woman is 2,100–2,350; see *ibid.*, p. 42.

All of these assumptions can be questioned, so that there is a considerable margin of error in any arithmetic based on them.

[26] Worcs. C.R.O. ref. 899 : 95, B.A. 989/2/23.

[27] Raftis, *Tenure and Mobility*, p. 46.

[28] This assumes that a 15-acre holding, on a three-course rotation, would yield in an average year 12 quarters of grain from 10 acres. 3 quarters 5 bushels would be

The prevalence of boiled pottages or puddings, probably with a base of cereals or legumes, is indicated by peasants' cooking equipment. Documentary references to tenant bakehouses are quite frequent, but not every holding had one. The archaeological evidence for baking ovens supports this – they are found sporadically, by no means in every house or toft. In some villages there were communal ovens, or bread was bought from specialist bakers. On the other hand ceramic cooking pots are ubiquitous on medieval sites of all kinds, and references in court rolls to tenant possessions suggest that virtually every peasant household owned a brass cooking pot or pan.[29]

That water rather than ale was often drunk is difficult to prove. On the contrary, the constant amercement of brewers in seigneurial courts might suggest an abundance of ale. However, the numbers of people said to have brewed only once or twice in a year implies a sporadic and discontinuous trade, and the noticeable drop in brewing in bad harvest years implies that the occasional ale drinkers had turned to water.[30] It is relevant to note that while many lords provided ale for the tenants performing boon-works, together with food normally regarded as superior in quality to normal peasant fare, at some boons the bread, cheese and meat was accompanied by nothing stronger than water.[31]

If then the middling group of those appearing in the maintenance agreements, corresponding perhaps to the middle ranks of peasant society, consumed an adequate, but by no means generous allowance of cereals, without regular ale-drinking, what of the

---

reserved for seed, leaving 8 quarters 3 bushels; if 1 quarter was sold to help pay the rent (the rest of the rent money could have come from the profits of animal husbandry), this would leave about enough grain to provide for the minimum calorific needs of a family of four – 3 quarters 4 bushels for the husband, 2 quarters for the wife, and 1 quarter each for two children.

[29] M. W. Beresford and J. G. Hurst, *Deserted Medieval Villages* (London, 1971), p. 98; R. K. Field, 'Worcestershire Peasant Buildings, Household Goods and Farming Equipment in the Later Middle Ages', *Medieval Archaeol.*, ix (1965), pp. 137–45.

[30] A correlation between brewing activity and harvest quality is observed, for example, in the records of Hanbury (Worcestershire) in the late fourteenth century: Worcs. C.R.O., ref. 009 : 1, BA 2636/165, 166.

[31] The boon-workers at Denton (Sussex) on the estate of the bishopric of Chichester (1274) were to drink 'water from the king's well'; see *Thirteen Custumals of the Sussex Manors of the Bishop of Chichester*, ed. W. D. Peckham (Sussex Rec. Soc., xxxi, Lewes, 1925), p. 101.

diet of the substantial minority, twenty-five in all (30 per cent of the total) whose 8 bushels or less would have been insufficient to sustain life? A few of them were clearly young, and could have supplemented their grain allowance from their earnings. Others may have had access to a small plot of land. But many of them, retired and elderly, had limited earning capacity, and would have been reduced to gleaning, begging or even stealing to make ends meet. We are surely justified in suspecting that this group of inadequately fed old people represents only part of a large pool of underemployed and undernourished smallholders and landless in the bottom ranks of rural society.

As well as suggesting a hierarchy of dietary standards among the peasantry, the maintenance agreements also reflect regional variations in the consumption of cereals. Rye, rather than wheat, was clearly the main bread corn in parts of Norfolk and Worcestershire, and barley was especially prominent in north Suffolk. If the sample had included agreements from north of the Trent more extreme regional differences would no doubt have been apparent. Oats, a relatively minor constituent of the diet of peasants in the midlands and south, would have figured more prominently in those areas, such as the Pennines and parts of the north-west, where their cultivation constituted a virtual monoculture.[32] The consumption of oats was so prevalent in a district on the Scottish border that in the early fifteenth century an Italian visitor's loaf of wheat bread attracted the awed curiosity of a large crowd.[33]

Peasant diet was based on cereals, but other foodstuffs were available to them. The maintenance agreements sometimes show this. Margaret atte Green, whose allowance of grain has already been mentioned, was also able to keep a cow, a pig and six fowls, so she could add a little milk, cheese, bacon and eggs to her bread and ale. Essex peasants who retired in the early fourteenth century were often given pasture for a cow, or two or three sheep, and in one case a cow, six sheep and two pigs. The most generous

[32] I. S. W. Blanchard, 'Economic Change in Derbyshire in the Late Middle Ages, 1272–1540' (Univ. of London Ph.D. thesis, 1967), pp. 28–9; E. Miller, 'Farming in Northern England during the Twelfth and Thirteenth Centuries', *Northern Hist.*, xi (1975), p. 9.

[33] 'Commentaries of Pius II', ed. F. A. Gragg, *Smith College Studies in History*, xxii (1936–7), pp. 19–20 (I am grateful to Dr A. E. Goodman for this reference).

provision of meat was that of John Stappe of Blackwell (Warwick-shire), a yardlander who retired in 1347 and expected to receive, in addition to wheat and dredge sufficient for a daily 2½ lbs. of bread and 3 pints of ale, a pig and a quarter of an ox carcass each year, so that he could have eaten as much as 8 ounces of meat each day.[34] Turning from the arrangements for retirement to fully active peasant households, the only animals kept entirely for their meat were pigs, and the middling and better-off would have been able to consume one or two carcasses each year. Certainly late medieval writers seem to have regarded bacon as a typically peasant food.[35] To this could be added the meat of sheep and cattle, culled when their useful lives were over as wool and milk producers, or as draught animals in the case of oxen. However, the bones excavated from village sites did not always come from elderly animals, showing that some stock were killed before they reached maturity.[36] But how much meat was eaten–can it be regarded as a regular item in peasant diet? No doubt the prosper-ous minority with substantial flocks and herds could have afforded to slaughter young animals for their own consumption, but this option was surely not open to the many in the late thirteenth century who owned no more than a dozen sheep or four cattle, and certainly not for the 'middling and small man' in thirteenth-century Wiltshire, who often had (in a sheep-farming area) no sheep at all.[37] The bones recovered from excavations are undoubt-

[34] Worcester Cathedral Lib., E15. The calculation of the daily quantity of meat is based on the assumption that a pig weighed about 80 lbs. and a quarter of an ox about 100 lbs: Stouff, *Ravitaillement et alimentation en Provence*, pp. 187–9. Not all of this weight would be edible, which might reduce Stappe's estimated consumption to 5 or 6 ounces per day.

[35] This, and subsequent observations on the literary evidence for peasant diet is based on the following: *The Works of Geoffrey Chaucer*, ed. F. N. Robinson, 2nd edn (Oxford, 1957), p. 199; *The Vision of William concerning Piers the Plowman in Three Parallel Texts*, ed. W. W. Skeat, 2 vols. (Oxford, 1886), i, pp. 220–3, 234–9; *Pierce the Ploughmans Crede*, ed. W. W. Skeat (Early English Text Soc., xxx, London, 1867), pp. 16–17, 29; *Chaucerian and Other Pieces*, ed. W. W. Skeat (Oxford, 1897), p. 147.

[36] The argument that peasant animals were killed at an advanced age is in R. H. Hilton and P. A. Rahtz, 'Upton, Gloucestershire, 1959–64', *Trans. Bristol and Gloucs. Archaeol. Soc.*, lxxxv (1966), pp. 139–43; the presence of younger animals is emphasized in M. L. Ryder, 'Animal Remains from Wharram Percy', *Yorks. Archaeol. Jl.*, xlvi (1974), pp. 42–52.

[37] M. M. Postan, 'Village Livestock in the Thirteenth Century', in his *Essays on Medieval Agriculture and General Problems of the Medieval Economy* (Cambridge, 1973), pp. 214–48.

edly numerous, but they tell us very little about the rate of meat consumption, as they accumulated from the slaughter of animals (or their death from disease) over an unknown number of years, and could represent the demise of, for one household, less than one animal per year. Also, the bones may in some cases mark butchery preparatory to the sale of meat – either to neighbours, or more likely to butchers who catered for a wider market.[38] The bone evidence is most useful in indicating regional variations in the type of animals consumed, with cattle bones predominating on village sites in Berkshire and Northamptonshire, but sheep bones are more numerous on Gloucestershire, Rutland, Wiltshire and Yorkshire sites, though the greater weight of cattle carcasses may mean that even in the latter examples beef was available in rather greater quantity than mutton.[39]   The extent of peasant fish eating must also remain uncertain. Fish bones and shells found at the village of Wharram Percy (Yorkshire) show that sea fish were consumed in inland communities.[40] Peasants everywhere would be familiar with herrings from seigneurial boon-feasts, and their cheapness, especially in the thirteenth century, must have made them available for at least the occasional peasant meal. Freshwater fisheries were used by peasants, though access was often limited through control by lords. Fish would, of course, have been locally plentiful in coastal or fen-edge villages.

'White meat' – milk, cheese, and eggs – was an important source of peasant protein. Literary sources emphasize its place in peasant eating, like Piers Plowman's 'two green cheeses, a few curds and cream', and William Harrison, writing in the sixteenth century, regarded white meat in his day as lower-class food, though he thought that its consumption had once been more widespread.[41] Cheese and milk were scarcely eaten at all in many noble households, except by servants, so dairy produce must have found its main market at a low social level. And yet we should not

---

[38] Butchers sometimes appear as selling meat in villages in late medieval court rolls; see, for Example, E. Britton, *The Community of the Vill* (Toronto, 1977), p. 89.

[39] Beresford and Hurst, *Deserted Medieval Villages*, pp. 137–40; J. M. Steane and G. F. Bryant, 'Excavations at the Deserted Medieval Settlement at Lyveden', *Jl. Northampton Museums and Art Galley*, xii (1975), pp. 152–7.

[40] Ryder, 'Animal Remains from Wharram Percy', pp. 42–52.

[41] W. Harrison, *Description of England*, ed. G. Edelen (Ithaca, N.Y., 1968), p. 126.

overestimate the quantities eaten, as many peasant households owned only one or two cows, which each yielded enough milk to make seventy to ninety pounds of butter and cheese each year, if they were as productive as demesne cattle.[42] So one cow would have provided each member of a family of four daily with one ounce of dairy produce. Sheep milk would rarely have provided a major alternative, as very few peasants owned the dozen ewes needed to equal the milk yield of a cow. The evidence of heriots paid over as death duties suggests that a substantial minority of smallholding households, between 26 and 45 per cent, lacked any animals, even one cow, in the early and mid-fourteenth century.[43]

Contemporaries thought that the consumption of fresh vegetables was especially characteristic of the peasantry and, like dairy produce, they were shunned by the upper classes. Again, it is difficult to regard vegetables as more than a minor supplement to a cereal-based diet. Peas and beans were the only vegetables grown in the fields, and some of the peasant crop, unlike that on the demesne land, was picked green in the summer.[44] Otherwise vegetables such as cabbages, onions and garlic were grown in garden plots, which, judging from the size of the tofts visible in deserted village sites, often averaged less than a half-acre, some of which area was taken up with animal pens and outbuildings.[45] Similarly, although peasant holdings had apple, pear and nut trees, they can rarely have been numerous enough to constitute an orchard.

Finally, we should allow for a small element of hunting and gathering in the peasant economy as a source of dietary supplements. This would be most significant in woodland districts, where both seigneurial and royal court records reveal a good deal

---

[42] Kershaw, *Bolton Priory*, p. 102.
[43] Dyer, *Lords and Peasants in a Changing Society*, p. 323.
[44] W. O. Ault, *Open-Field Farming in Medieval England* (London, 1972), pp. 38–40.
[45] The size of tofts measured from published plans of midland and southern villages is usually in the range 0.2–0.4 acres. Larger enclosures are found, especially in northern villages, but these are often crofts rather than tofts, and may have been used as stock enclosures and not for garden plots. For examples of small tofts typical of the midlands, see G. Beresford, *The Medieval Clay-Land Village: Excavations at Goltho and Barton Blount* (Soc. Medieval Archaeol., monograph ser., vi, London, 1975), pp. 8, 10. Larger northern enclosures are documented in B. K. Roberts, 'Village Plans in County Durham', *Medieval Archaeol.*, xvi (1972), pp. 33–56.

of poaching by peasants. The legal restrictions must have rendered this source of meat irregular and uncertain, but we know from the excavation of one village that lay in a royal forest, Potters' Lyveden (Northamptonshire) that venison provided a substantial element in meat consumption, as deer bones accounted for between 6 and 23 per cent of the total identified.[46] Outside the restricted areas of woodland, in addition to the occasional illicit rabbit or game-bird, small birds could be quite legitimately caught, and one peasant of Claines (Worcestershire) owned a 'barrel of small birds' (presumably pickled). Again, people living in or near woodlands could gather fruits (such as blackberries) or nuts, and keep bees.[47]

To sum up, the contrasts between noble and peasant diet in terms of the quantities of all kinds of foods, but particularly meat and fish, are obvious. Yet in a sense the peasants' food was more varied; their diet reflected local differences in resources; they ate all types of corn, not just wheat; the peasant's table was more likely to carry the dairy produce and vegetables that the nobility despised. There were important differences of dietary standards within the ranks of the upper classes, in the proportions of meat and fish, and in the regular availability of wines and spices. The variations within peasant society were at least as significant; most of our evidence relates to the late thirteenth and early fourteenth centuries, when we can identify an upper rank, yardlanders and above, who could afford wheat bread, regular supplies of ale, meat and cheese. Middling peasants ate more pottage, drank ale only occasionally, and could have had access to a little cheese and meat. At the lowest level were those with difficulties in obtaining adequate quantities of cereals, and for whom ale-drinking and the consumption of animal protein would have been rare luxuries.

Peasant diet changed over time more than that of the nobility. In the very short term they were much affected by the seasonal cycle of the farming year. The summer months would bring fresh

---

[46] Steane and Bryant, 'Excavations at the Deserted Medieval Settlement at Lyveden', pp. 152–7.

[47] Worcs. C.R.O. ref. 009 : 1, B.A. 2636/175, for the little birds. Peasants are quite commonly recorded gathering blackberries and nuts on their lord's behalf, but presumably also did it for their own benefit. Wild plants which may have been eaten include 'fat hen' (now a common weed); see D. G. Wilson, 'Plant Foods and Poisons from Medieval Chester', *Jl. Chester Archaeol. Soc.*, lviii (1975), pp. 55–67.

dairy produce and vegetables but also a scarcity of grain if the previous harvest had been poor; a good harvest and the autumn slaughter of a pig provided an opportunity for temporary indulgence. In the rather longer term the variations in harvest quality were obviously of crucial importance for the poor, and would also affect the consumption patterns of the middling and better-off, such as the extent of their ale-drinking.

The secular changes affecting the late medieval economy are well known, and all would have led to an improvement in peasant diet – in the late fourteenth and fifteenth centuries the shift in the social balance in peasant society increased the proportion of those with large holdings; the expansion in pastoral farming led to greater production of meat and cheese; and the growing plenty of grain is reflected in low prices. There is no direct evidence for the diet resulting from these changes because maintenance agreements disappear from our records in the fifteenth century, but there is a significant change in the literary image of the peasants' life-style. In the late fourteenth century the peasant was either praised for his hardy frugality, subsisting on brown bread, cabbage and cheese, or he was shown as ground down by hunger. By the late fifteenth century Sir John Fortescue was able to depict the English people as enjoying plenty, in contrast with the miseries of the French; and a poem called 'How the Plowman Learnt his Paternoster' describes a peasant, supposedly French, but clearly portrayed in an English context, with his house stuffed with bacon, dairy produce, malt, salt-beef, onions and garlic – traditional peasant fare, but in abundance.[48]

III

Wage-earners cannot be regarded as an entirely separate section of society, as so many peasants needed to find at least part-time employment. However, their diet is documented separately, so it is convenient to treat them as a distinct group.

Employees on manorial demesnes, the *famuli* who acted as ploughmen, carters and stock-keepers, received most of their pay in the late thirteenth or early fourteenth century in the form of

---

[48] *The Governance of England by Sir John Fortescue*, ed. C. Plummer (Oxford, 1885), pp. 114–15; W. Hazlitt, *Early Popular Poetry of England*, 4 vols. (London, 1866), i, pp. 210–11.

grain or pulses. These 'liveries of the *famuli*' were issued in varying quantities, normally at a rate of one quarter every eight, nine, ten or twelve weeks, so that the annual total received by each worker varied from 4⅓ to 6½ quarters. The larger figure would have been enough to feed a family at a meagre subsistence level; but most *famuli* received rather less than this amount. They also received a cash wage, and those with families would often have had a smallholding with which to supplement their earnings.[49] Some *famuli* may have been young and single, and could have contributed their grain to their parents' family budget. The types of grain given to *famuli* are indicated by figures from twenty manors in the west midlands given in Table 5.[50]

Oats do not figure in the liveries, but were eaten by the *famuli* of most manors in the form of oatmeal pottage prepared in the manor-house in the harvest season. In general the types of corn issued to the *famuli* were inferior to those specified in maintenance agreements. Wheat allowances were relatively small, and some made no provision of winter corn at all. For example, on ten manors of the earldom of Cornwall scattered widely over England, in 1296–7 wheat was entirely absent from the liveries of four manors, and in four others appeared only in the form of low-grade *currall*, or as an admixture in maslin.[51] Wage-earners were clearly expected to eat more rye and barley bread than did retired peasants.

Lords usually provided their *famuli* with corn only. When a supplement was given, it most often took the form of a grant of the 'lactage' (milk yield) of a demesne cow, confirming the association noticed above between the lower classes and the consumption of dairy produce. Otherwise the *famuli* could have used their cash wage to buy a little extra food.

The *famuli* enjoyed the double advantage of continuous employment on annual contracts, and payment in kind that was unaffected by either long-term inflation or most short-term fluctuations in corn prices. The majority of wage-earners were em-

[49] Harvey, *A Medieval Oxfordshire Village*, pp. 77–8, shows that *famuli* might have smallholdings or access to a plot in the *curia*.
[50] P.R.O., E. 358/13 (I am grateful to Miss J. R. Birrell for this reference); P.R.O., S.C. 6 850/2; 851/22; 853/13; 854/2; 855/2; 856/15; 859/17; 1038/2; 1039/12; 1040/21; 1068/7; 1070/5.
[51] *Ministers' Accounts of the Earldom of Cornwall, 1296–1297*, ed. L. M. Midgley, 2 vols. (Camden Soc., 3rd ser., lxvi, lxviii, London, 1942–5), *passim*.

Table 5. *Liveries of famuli from twenty manors in the west midlands 1281–1349 (cumulative totals from twenty accounts)**

	Wheat	Maslin	Rye	Barley	Dredge	Pulse	Tollcorn (mixed)	Total
Cumulative quantity	93 qrs.	105 qrs. 5½ bs.	243 qrs. 7½ bs.	150 qrs. 7½ bs.	22 qrs. 1½ bs.	122 qrs. 1½ bs.	52 qrs. 5 bs.	790 qrs. 3½ bs.
	(12)	(13)	(31)	(19)	(3)	(15)	(7)	(100)

* Figures in brackets denote percentages.

ployed on a less permanent basis, and received more of their pay in cash, and consequently led a more precarious existence. For example, a labourer employed on the building of Vale Royal Abbey (Cheshire) in the accounting year 1278–9 could have been employed for as much as 243 days in the year, in which time he would have been paid £1. 11s. 8d.[52] This was near to his maximum earning capacity, as the other days were taken up with compulsory holidays. If he had a family of four, he would have needed to spend £1. 8s. 1½d. on 7½ quarters of barley to provide them with an intake of calories regarded by modern nutritionists as adequate. In more adverse harvest years, his wages would not have covered the cost of so much grain. Clearly extra income, such as the earnings of wife or children, or access to a small plot of land, would have been vitally important to his household economy. Even so, we may suspect that such labourers and their families, like many people in the modern third world, had to make do with much smaller allowances of calories than are regarded as necessary in modern western countries.[53] Skilled workers, such as carpenters and masons, would have been able in normal years to eat wheat bread and afford a greater variety of food.

The long-term improvement in the diet of wage-earners in the later middle ages is more fully documented than for any other social group. Late fourteenth-century writers complained that labourers demanded better bread, ale and meat. John Gower, writing in the 1380s, commented that servants scorned ordinary food and weak ale: 'Oh why should a man whom water drawn from a well has nourished ever since birth demand such delicious drink?'[54] More objective sources show that the wheat content of the liveries of *famuli* increased in the late fourteenth century.[55] A case brought under the labour laws in Lincolnshire in 1394 revealed that a ploughman employed by the abbot of Newbo, instead of the customary livery of 2 quarters of wheat and 2

---

[52] *The Ledgerbook of Vale Royal Abbey*, ed. J. Brownbill (Lancs. and Cheshire Rec. Soc., lxviii, London, 1914), pp. 226–30.

[53] For this argument in relation to the third world, see C. Clark and M. Haswell, *The Economics of Subsistence Agriculture* (London, 1966), *passim*.

[54] *The Major Latin Works of John Gower*, ed. and trans. E. W. Stockton (Seattle, 1962), p. 210.

[55] For example, the *famuli* of Minchinhampton (Gloucestershire) received rye, barley and dredge in 1306–7, but wheat and barley in 1380–1: P.R.O., S.C. 6, 856/15, 24.

quarters of peas each year, received a weekly allowance of fifteen loaves of bread (at least seven made from wheat) and 7 gallons of ale, together with a high cash wage and fodder for a cow.[56]   Records of wage payments in the late fourteenth and fifteenth centuries often add 'with food', but the exact meaning of this is usually unknown. An occasional insight is provided by manorial accounts which include a record of the expenses of feeding harvest workers – not the exceptional, one-day feast provided for tenants performing boon-works, but regular meals provided for employees over a period of three to six weeks. The nuns of Nuneaton gave their harvest workers at Wibtoft (Warwickshire) in 1397 daily fare of about two pounds of wheat bread, four pints of ale, and two pounds of beef and mutton, together with small quantities of herrings, cheese and eggs.[57] No doubt labourers ate better at harvest-time than for the rest of the year, but this type of evidence, combined with calculations of the value of real wages, suggests that meat-eating came within the reach of even unskilled workers in the fifteenth century. This is paralleled by evidence for high quality diets, including substantial amounts of meat, obtained by wage-workers in the same century in Languedoc, Sicily and Germany.[58] The age of 'carnivorous Europe' had begun, so that in the small town of Carpentras in Provence, per capita meat consumption in 1473 has been calculated at a level of 26 kg per annum, which compares favourably with the diet of Mediterranean countries like Spain and Greece in the 1950s.[59] The inhabitants of English towns and villages, judging from the increased activities of butchers in renting land and overburdening commons were probably also experiencing a high level of meat-eating.[60]

---

[56] *Some Sessions of the Peace in Lincolnshire, 1381–96*, ed. E. G. Kimball (Lincs. Rec. Soc., xlix, Lincoln, 1955), p. 32.

[57] Brit. Lib., Add. Roll 49756. Eight workers employed for five weeks were supplied with 1 quarter 2 bushels wheat, 2 quarters 4 bushels malt, ¾ ox carcass and 9 sheep, with herrings worth 10d., cheese worth 14d. and eggs worth 3d.

[58] E. le Roy Ladurie, *The Peasants of Languedoc* (Homewood, Ill., 1974), pp. 40–4; M. Aymard and H. Bresc, 'Nourritures et consommation en Sicile entre xive et xviiie siècle', *Annales. E.S.C.*, xxx (1975), pp. 592–9; W. Abel, *Agricultural Fluctuations in Europe* (London, 1980), p. 71.

[59] Stouff, *Ravitaillement et alimentation en Provence*, pp. 189–91.

[60] See, for example, D. Moss, 'The Economic Development of a Middlesex Village', *Agric. Hist. Rev.*, xxviii (1980), pp. 110–14.

IV

The evidence presented here must eventually be supplemented by a systematic study of price movements and harvest qualities over the whole medieval period. At present we are aware of a concentration of poor harvests in the decades between 1290 and 1370, and of renewed episodes of instability of corn supplies in the early fifteenth century, culminating in a severe famine in the late 1430s. This was followed by an almost uninterrupted series of good harvests until 1520. Bouts of mortality associated with bad harvests have been identified in the decades around 1300, but not in the fifteenth century, except perhaps in the famine of 1437–40.[61]

To sum up, we can identify many variations in the dietary standards of different social groups in the later middle ages. We cannot fail to be impressed by the great quantities of foodstuffs consumed in aristocratic households, and to be appreciative of the significance for the economy as a whole of provisioning on such a scale. Yet, for all its apparent luxury, medieval upper-class diet would shock a twentieth-century nutritionist because of its imbalances and vitamin deficiencies. The standards of food and drink, in terms of both quality and quantity, show similar characteristics throughout upper-class society, from dukes to gentry, though households at the lower end of the scale ate less meat and fish, and consumed much smaller amounts of wine and spices than the magnates.

There is little evidence of any major development in the diet of the upper classes between the thirteenth and fifteenth century. That of the lower orders went through important changes. Certain foodstuffs, notably vegetables and dairy produce, remained firmly associated throughout with the tables of the peasants and labourers. In the period 1250–1350 the indirect evidence of numerous smallholdings, low real wages and poor harvests all point to dietary deprivation for many people in both town and country. Investigation of the direct evidence for food consumption in no way contradicts this hypothesis, but it does emphasize the considerable differences between the richer peasantry and the smallhol-

---

[61] M. M. Postan and J. Z. Titow, 'Heriots and Prices on Winchester Manors', in Postan, *Essays on Medieval Agriculture and General Problems of the Medieval Economy*, pp. 150–85; R. S. Gottfried, *Epidemic Disease in Fifteenth Century England* (Leicester, 1978), pp. 37–9, 96–7.

ders and wage-earners. Those with large holdings could eat wheat bread and drink ale every day, and even expect regular supplies of meat. The more numerous lower ranks of rural society, though by no means deprived of wheat, ate a good deal of the poorer grains, often in the form of pottage, and could not have consumed either ale or meat frequently. In the late fourteenth and fifteenth centuries wheat bread, ale and meat became more generally available. The changes should not be exaggerated, as social divisions remained, in diet as in other indicators of wealth and status. Also, the relatively small quantities of fruits and vegetables consumed prevent us from regarding any dietary regime of the period as healthy by modern standards. In spite of these qualifications we must conclude that the prevalent miseries of the period before 1350 gave way to a 'dietary optimum' in the fifteenth century.

9. Economic Change in Later Medieval England: An Archaeological Review*

G. G. ASTILL

This essay is concerned with the archaeology of the medieval period: it will review some of the material which has accumulated in the last thirty years, and then consider how this body of data can contribute to discussions of economic change between *circa* 1350 and *circa* 1500. Such an approach stems from the belief that the archaeological evidence must be considered in its own right and within its own framework before it can be compared, and possibly integrated, with the hypotheses developed from documentary evidence. This review differs from previous surveys where the archaeological material has been moulded into an historical framework – a framework constructed from a totally different data set.

There are two main objections to the latter approach: firstly, that the results of one discipline are relegated to providing examples for the theories of another; and, secondly, that archaeological evidence by its very nature does not lend itself easily to the solution of specific 'historical' problems.[1] The dating of most archaeological material is too inexact to contribute to many documentary debates; for example some archaeologists have realized, even in regions where medieval pottery has been intensively studied, that they cannot 'make a contribution to . . . the historical debate on the economic condition of English society in the first half of the fourteenth century'.[2] Similarly some historians involved in debating the economic condition of the later medieval town have seen the potential contribution of archaeological mat-

---

* I am grateful to Christopher Dyer, Michael Fulford, David Hinton and Susan Wright for commenting on an early draft of this paper.

[1] See also the reviews of C. Platt, *Medieval England* (London, 1978), by R. H. Hilton in *Times Higher Educ. Supplement*, 11 Aug. 1978, and by C. C. Dyer in *History*, lxiv (1979), pp. 263–4.

[2] D. A. Hinton, '"Rudely Made Earthen Vessels" of the Twelfth to Fifteenth Centuries A.D.', in D. P. S. Peacock (ed.), *Pottery and Early Commerce* (London, 1977), p. 230.

217

erial, but they realize that there are difficulties not only, for instance, in closely dating perpendicular churches, but also in appreciating what such rebuilding implies in terms of the general well-being of towns.[3] These examples illustrate how some archaeological evidence, as it is currently employed, can prove incapable of contributing to medieval 'history' because inappropriate questions are being asked of the material. By adopting a slightly broader approach the same evidence viewed in the context of other archaeological data could give new insights into the late medieval economy, but there has been a noticeable reluctance to attempt this. Indeed there is a trend towards fragmentation of research with the real danger that particular aspects are studied without reference to the whole.

While this trend may be necessary for substantial progress to be made in detail, there is an even greater need for all the data to be considered together so that their full potential can be demonstrated. Only in this way can more wide-ranging questions be posed.[4] Although these questions – and hopefully some answers – may not be of direct relevance to particular historical debates, it should nevertheless be possible to contribute to economic and social history.

At first sight such a revision of archaeological aims would make much published information redundant. For example one of the basic requirements for discerning change within and between sites is an elementary statistical presentation of plentiful data such as pottery or faunal remains. This was lacking from most site reports until a few years ago, so reducing the possibility of making full use of the already excavated evidence. Yet even when inadequately published, these data cannot be ignored; and nor can we take the easy option and postpone asking general questions until there is sufficient evidence of 'high quality'.

Although an independent line of enquiry and synthesis in medieval archaeology is advocated here it is nonetheless important to bear in mind some of the general problems facing students of the late medieval economy. The main point at issue is whether

[3] For example, B. Dobson, 'Urban Decline in Late Medieval England', *Trans. Roy. Hist. Soc.*, 5th ser., xxvii (1977), pp. 8–9; M. M. Postan, 'The Fifteenth Century', *Econ. Hist. Rev.*, 1st ser., ix (1939), pp. 160–7.

[4] Cf. the debate concerning historical archaeology in America: S. South, *Method and Theory in Historical Archaeology* (New York, 1977).

late fourteenth- and fifteenth-century England was experiencing economic growth or contraction. To what extent did the relaxation of pressure on landed resources contribute to the revival or stagnation of the economy; and where did such expansion or contraction take place – is it to be seen in town or countryside, or rather in a changed economic relationship between the two? Much hinges on the part played by the market: was it so sluggish as to encourage a kind of 'self-sufficiency' or did the internal market expand in response to the greater opportunities for increased production?[5]

This essay is an inevitably impressionistic review of the range and potential of archaeological evidence relevant to the problem of the late medieval economy. Out of necessity I will concentrate on and consider in turn those aspects where the evidence is most plentiful – pottery production, rural and urban settlement – although the more recent growth points in the subject, such as the analysis of coinage and of faunal remains, will not be ignored. In the current state of research pottery can most positively contribute to the discussion of the internal economy and will be considered first.

The production and marketing of pottery

One of the most encouraging developments in ceramic studies has been to exploit this, the most plentiful class of archaeological material, for purposes other than as a means of dating stratification. The study of kilns and of the varying distribution of their products through time enables some discussion of the fortunes of the pottery market. Petrological analysis of fabric has set this work on a firmer foundation than previous attempts based essentially on vessel form.[6] Can such ceramic research have a wider economic significance? No-one would deny that pottery production was a

---

[5] For example, M. M. Postan, *The Medieval Economy and Society* (London, 1972); A. R. Bridbury, *Economic Growth: England in the Later Middle Ages* (London, 1962; repr. Hassocks, 1975).

[6] For example, A. Vince, 'The Medieval and Post Medieval Ceramic Industry of the Malvern Region: The Study of a Ware and its Distribution', in Peacock (ed.), *Pottery and Early Commerce*, pp. 257–305; E. M. Jope, 'Regional Character in West Country Medieval Pottery', *Trans. Bristol and Gloucs. Archaeol. Soc.*, lxxi (1952), pp. 88–97; E. M. Jope, 'The Regional Cultures of Medieval Britain', in I. Ll. Foster and L. Alcock (eds.), *Culture and Environment* (London, 1963), pp. 327–54.

comparatively minor aspect of medieval industrial development, nor that pottery was a cheap commodity, so cheap indeed that it failed to be noted in inventories or *principalia* lists. But these are its main virtues for it affords an unparalleled opportunity to illustrate the workings of one of the 'bread-and-butter industries, directed towards the domestic market', which 'are in large measure unknowable'.[7] An additional advantage of pottery is that it can be used to give a quantitative assessment of change in local marketing arrangements. So far the data have been interpreted in terms of competition from other potteries, that is in terms of supply, rather than considering the implications for demand.[8] One of the next goals for ceramic research must be to relate the developments observed in the industry to a broader economic context.[9] While this may be premature, some headway could be made by considering together the changes in local and imported pottery. This is rarely done, but is nevertheless necessary for the changes may be two aspects of the same reorganization in the production and sale of this commodity. In order to answer such questions a broad characterization of ceramic development is necessary, and this may not take full account of minor regional variations.

Imported pottery has frequently been used to illustrate trade routes but its potential for charting the intensity of trade over time or showing the relative importance of those routes is severely limited. Although pottery was imported alongside such major commodities as wine it cannot by itself demonstrate the diffusion

---

[7] H. Blake, 'Technology, Supply or Demand?', *Medieval Ceramics*, iv (1980), p. 4. See also H. E. J. Le Patourel, 'Documentary Evidence and the Medieval Pottery Industry', *Medieval Archaeol.*, xii (1968), pp. 101–26; R. K. Field, 'Worcestershire Peasant Buildings, Household Goods and Farming Equipment in the Later Middle Ages', *Medieval Archaeol.*, ix (1965), pp. 121–45; G. G. Astill, 'An Early Inventory of a Leicestershire Knight', *Midland Hist.*, ii (1974), pp. 274–83; E. Miller and J. Hatcher, *Medieval England: Rural Society and Economic Change, 1086–1348* (London, 1978), p. 248. Local pottery distributions cannot however claim to reflect 'sales areas' of other commodities nor 'economic regions': Jope, 'Regional Cultures of Medieval Britain', pp. 339–40.

[8] Blake, 'Technology, Supply or Demand?', pp. 4–5.

[9] For example, H. Blake, 'Medieval Pottery: Technological Innovation or Economic Change?', in H. Blake, T. Potter and D. Whitehouse (eds.), *Papers in Italian Archaeology: i, The Lancaster Seminar*, 2 vols. (Brit. Archaeol. Repts., supplementary ser., xli, Oxford, 1978), ii, pp. 435–73.

of the other goods within the country.[10] Even the most recent distribution maps of Saintonge polychrome and green glazed jugs (from West France) and Aardenburg wares (Low Countries) continue to show a heavy bias towards the major ports and royal castles whereas the other imports were much more widespread.[11] Wine was consumed in most aristocratic households and there was even a demand for it in parish churches, but the proportion of imported pottery from the Saintonge (or indeed any imported ceramic) to locally produced wares is minimal, less than 1 per cent, in the larger inland towns (for example, Lincoln, Coventry, Oxford, Northampton), at royal palaces (Kings Langley) and aristocratic households (Northolt, Writtle, the Yorkshire moated sites) let alone villages.[12]

Imported pottery then cannot be used to show the distribution of major incoming commodities, and nor can it be used to argue for social and economic differentiation among sites in the settlement hierarchy. Indeed at present it is difficult to demonstrate such differences from assemblages of local pottery. While one gains an impression that more glazed and decorated wares occur on urban sites, major variations cannot be seen for example in the

10 G. C. Dunning, 'Trade in Pottery around the North Sea', in J. G. Renaud (ed.), *Rotterdam Papers* (Rotterdam, 1968), pp. 35–58.

11 G. C. Dunning, 'Inventory of Medieval Polychrome Ware Found in England and Scotland', *Archaeologia*, lxxxiii (1933), pp. 126–34; G. C. Dunning, 'French Imports into Western Britain', in L. A. S. Butler, 'Medieval Finds from Castell-y-Bere, Merioneth', *Archaeologia Cambrensis*, cxxiii (1974), pp.78–112; G. C. Dunning, 'Aardenburg Ware from Manningtree', *Essex Archaeol. and Hist.*, viii (1976), pp. 184–99.

12 For a find of Saintonge polychrome from a churchyard, see B. Green, G. Dunning and P. Wade-Martins, 'Some Recent Finds of Imported Medieval Pottery', *Norfolk Archaeol.*, xxxiv (1966–9), pp. 403–4; L. Adams, *Medieval Pottery from Broadgate East, Lincoln, 1973* (Lincoln Archaeol. Trust, monograph ser., xvii–xviii, Lincoln, 1977), p. 53; J. Williams, *St. Peter's Street, Northampton, Excavations 1973–1976* (Northampton, 1979), pp. 165–224; B. Durham, 'Archaeological Investigations in St. Aldates, Oxford', *Oxoniensia*, xlii (1977), pp. 113–21; J. G. Hurst, 'The Kitchen Area of Northolt Manor, Middlesex', *Medieval Archaeol.*, v (1961), pp. 254–76; D. S. Neal, 'Excavations at the Palace and Priory at Kings Langley, 1970', *Herts. Archaeol.*, iii (1973), pp. 58–65; D. S. Neal, 'Excavations at the Palace of Kings Langley, Hertfordshire', *Medieval Archaeol.*, xxi (1977), pp. 147–57; P. A. Rahtz, *Excavations at King John's Hunting Lodge, Writtle, Essex, 1955–57* (Soc. Medieval Archaeol., monograph ser., iii, London, 1969), pp. 91–111; H. E. J. Le Patourel, *The Moated Sites of Yorkshire* (Soc. Medieval Archaeol., monograph ser., v, London, 1973), pp. 96–108. The distribution could, of course, indicate a greater consumption of wine at some castles and ports.

proportions of table wares between aristocratic and village sites.[13] While this is merely an impression and can only be checked by a quantitative presentation in future pottery reports, such a pattern is in marked contrast to northern Italy: the Mannonis' fieldwork in Liguria has shown consistent differences in the pottery assemblages which correspond to the status of the sites. Such characterization is however easier in Italy where there is a greater range of pottery types.[14]

Yet the lack of imported wares and the comparative homogeneity of local pottery groups on inland British sites may afford insights into the nature of marketing arrangements. It implies for example that within a region the same pottery was used on all sites, and that the market did not allow higher status sites access to a wider range of ceramics.[15] Before the fifteenth century most imported pottery in Britain might be interpreted as being for the use of those merchants who had dealings with the rest of Europe. Three aspects of the distribution of Saintonge and Aardenburg wares, for example, would support this view: firstly, their essentially coastal distribution, with concentrations at the major ports of entry; secondly, to judge from the known repertoire of these continental potteries, mainly the finer table wares, usually jugs, were imported; thirdly, the proportion of imported to local wares varies within the major ports from site to site suggesting that some of the population had greater access to such goods.[16] If this pottery

---

[13] Hinton, '"Rudely Made Earthen Vessels" of the Twelfth to Fifteenth Centuries', p. 231; M. Beresford and J. G. Hurst, *Deserted Medieval Villages* (London, 1971), pp. 141–2; L. A. S. Butler, 'Hambleton Moat, Scredington, Lincolnshire', *Jl. Brit. Archaeol. Assoc.*, 3rd ser., xxvi (1963), pp. 68–78; J. Parfitt, 'A Moated Site at Moat Farm, Leigh, Kent', *Archaeologia Cantiana*, xcii (1976), pp. 186–97.

[14] L. and T. Mannoni, 'La ceramica dal medioevo all'età moderna nell' archeologia di superficie della Liguria centrale e orientale', *Albisola*, viii (1975), pp. 121–36.

[15] This pattern could reflect the different status of pottery among upper-class households where there was an increasing use of vessels in other materials, such as pewter. This however also seems to have been the case in Liguria, where nevertheless the pronounced differences in ceramic assemblages between sites of differing status remained: J. Hatcher and T. C. Barker, *A History of British Pewter* (London, 1974), pp. 41–63; Blake, 'Medieval Pottery', pp. 435–6.

[16] Dunning, 'Inventory of Medieval Polychrome'; Dunning, 'French Imports into Western Britain'; Dunning, 'Aardenburg Ware from Manningtree'; J. A. Trimpe Burger, 'Ceramiek uit de bloeitijd van Aardenburg (13de en 14de eeuw)', *Berichten van de Rijksdienst voor het Oudheidkundig Bodemonderzoek*, xii–xiii

is an indicator of the activity of cosmopolitan merchants, its absence inland suggests that the merchants were not involved in marketing within the country, and that this function was performed by regional traders. The exceptions are sites which although inland were of royal or important religious character, instanced by Saintonge polychrome on Edwardian castle sites and at monasteries such as Lesnes.[17] Here it could be argued that demand was sufficiently high to encourage direct dealing with the consumer.

The 'non-distribution' of imports then could reflect the localized nature of the marketing system in the thirteenth and early fourteenth centuries. A similar pattern is found for the twelfth century when most imported wares came from Normandy.[18]

The fifteenth century however saw a complete transformation in the distribution of imports. In the second half of that century, while not abundant, imports start to be found inland and on all types of site in the settlement hierarchy. The most common are the German stoneware jugs from Langerwehe, Siegburg and Raeren, so common indeed that they are often referred to as 'type fossils' for pottery assemblages of this period.[19] To regard this pottery as a 'belated tribute' to the strength of the trade with the Low Countries is to relegate it to the role of reinforcing other evidence.

(1962–3), pp. 495–548. For example, Hull: G. Watkins, 'Pottery from Excavations in Hull', *Medieval Ceramics*, ii (1978), pp. 43–4. Bristol: P. A. Rahtz, 'Excavations by the Town Wall, Baldwin Street, Bristol, 1957', *Trans. Bristol and Gloucs. Archaeol. Soc.*, lxxix (1960), p. 236; K. J. Barton, 'A Group of Medieval Jugs from Bristol Castle Well', *Trans. Bristol and Gloucs. Archaeol. Soc.*, lxxviii (1959), pp. 169–74; Barton, 'Excavations at Back Hall, Bristol, 1958', *Trans. Bristol and Gloucs. Archaeol. Soc.*, lxxix (1960), pp. 251–86. Southampton: C. P. S. Platt and R. Coleman-Smith, *Excavations in Medieval Southampton, 1953–1969*, 2 vols. (Leicester, 1975), ii, *The Finds*, pp. 23–50. Dover: M. M. Rix and G. C. Dunning, 'Excavation of a Medieval Garderobe in Snargate Street, Dover', *Archaeologia Cantiana*, lxix (1955), pp. 132–58; S. E. Rigold, 'Excavations at Dover Castle, 1964–66', *Jl. Brit. Archaeol. Assoc.*, 3rd ser., xxx (1967), pp. 87–121.

17 Dunning, 'Inventory of Medieval Polychrome'; Dunning, 'A Group of English and Imported Medieval Pottery from Lesnes Abbey, Kent, and the Trade in Early Hispano-Moresque Pottery to England', *Antiq. Jl.*, xli (1961), pp. 1–12.

18 Dunning, 'Trade in Pottery around the North Sea', pp. 44–5.

19 For example, J. G. Hurst, 'Stoneware Jugs', in B. W. Cunliffe, *Winchester Excavations, 1949–1960*, i (1964), pp. 140–3; J. G. Hurst, 'Imported Stoneware', in L. Keen, 'Excavations at Old Wardour Castle, Wiltshire', *Wilts. Archaeol. and Nat. Hist. Mag.*, lxii (1967), pp. 73–7; P. J. Davey and J. A. Rutter, 'A Note on Continental Imports in the North-West, 800–1700 A.D.', *Medieval Ceramics*, i (1977), pp. 17–30.

Rather these data should be seen as evidence for a dramatic change in the nature of the market. It appears from imported pottery's new universality that local, regional and international trade were much more integrated than previously.

Such an influx must be related to conditions within Britain rather than at the continental production centres, for drinking jugs had been made at some workshops since the early fourteenth century.[20] The trend in German wares is also matched in the late fifteenth century by other imports, such as Saintonge lobed cups, Netherlands maiolica, and Martincamp flasks from the Beauvaisis.[21] The difference in the distribution of imported pottery coming from the same source, the Saintonge, between the late thirteenth and fifteenth centuries is particularly significant because it demonstrates the change in marketing that had taken place over that time.

This change in the distribution of imports should not be viewed in isolation for it was anticipated by an equally pronounced reorientation of the local pottery industry. In the early fifteenth century the home industry was in the process of reorganization in terms of production techniques, repertoire, and also marketing.[22] Looking first at the products we can see a dissolution of the many

---

[20] For example, B. Beckmann, 'The Main Types of the First Four Production Periods of Siegburg Pottery', in V. I. Evison, H. Hodges and J. G. Hurst (eds.), *Medieval Pottery from Excavations* (London, 1974), pp. 183–220; J. G. Hurst, 'Langerwehe Stoneware of the Fourteenth and Fifteenth Centuries', in M. Apted, R. Gilyard Beer and A. Saunders (eds.), *Ancient Monuments and their Interpretation: Essays Presented to A. J. Taylor* (London, 1977), pp. 219–38. German wares start to be found on rural sites from the later fourteenth century, but the real change occurs from the mid-fifteenth century; see, for example, M. Biddle, 'The Deserted Medieval Village of Seacourt, Berkshire', *Oxoniensia*, xxvi/xxvii (1961/2), pp. 165–6.

[21] It is still difficult to distinguish imports from local copies of lobed cups: J. G. Hurst, 'Sixteenth- and Seventeenth-Century Imported Pottery from the Saintonge', in Evison, Hodges and Hurst (eds.), *Medieval Pottery from Excavations*, pp. 221–55; B. Rackham, *Early Netherlands Maiolica* (London, 1926), pp. 96–106; J. G. Hurst, 'South Netherlands Maiolica', in G. Beresford, 'The Old Manor, Askett', *Records of Bucks.*, xviii (1971), pp. 343–66; J. G. Hurst, 'Imported Flasks', in C. V. Bellamy, *Kirkstall Abbey Excavations, 1960–1964* (Pubns. Thoresby Soc., li, Leeds, 1966), pp. 54–9; J. G. Hurst, 'Martincamp Flasks', in Neal, 'Excavations at the Palace of Kings Langley', pp. 156–7.

[22] For example, J. E. Le Patourel, 'Pottery as Evidence of Social and Economic Change', in P. H. Sawyer (ed.), *English Medieval Settlement* (London, 1979), pp. 86–96; S. Moorhouse, 'Tudor Green: Some Further Thoughts', *Medieval Ceramics*, iii (1979), pp. 57–9.

regional traditions, the completion of the transition to entirely wheel-thrown wares, and the introduction of more standardized forms over much of the county (the 'bifid' rim is the best known illustration of this growing uniformity). Another related development was the expansion of the repertoire. In the fifteenth century the maximum number of vessel types made was *circa* thirty compared with *circa* ten in the late thirteenth century.[23] Many of the new vessel types extended in particular the range of fine table wares; these required a more sophisticated production than the coarse wares, and a different clay. 'Tudor Green' vessels for instance were extremely thin-walled with a thick green glaze and were probably biscuit fired.[24] Similar types of fine ware were also produced alongside coarse wares in other fifteenth-century centres such as Malvern (Worcs.), Cowick and Rawmarsh (Yorks.), Nuneaton (Warwicks.) and Toynton (Lincs.).[25] The introduction of Cistercian ware from the mid-fifteenth century is another aspect of the same development. Here use of two different types of clay and firing in protective saggars again testify to greater technical sophistication. Cistercian-type wares were made throughout the midlands and the north, often at established potteries which continued to produce other types (Malvern, Brill [Bucks.], Nuneaton), although some workshops specialized in fine wares (Sil-

[23] J. G. Hurst, 'White Castle and the Dating of Medieval Pottery', *Medieval Archaeol.*, vi/vii (1962/3), p. 147; J. G. Musty, 'Medieval Pottery Kilns', in Evison, Hodges and Hurst (eds.), *Medieval Pottery from Excavations*, pp. 60–1. This diversification is shown for example in large urban assemblages such as Sidbury, Worcester, and St Peter's Street and Marefair in Northampton: E. Morris, 'Medieval and Post Medieval Pottery in Worcester: A Type Series', in M. O. H. Carver (ed.), *Medieval Worcester: An Archaeological Framework* (Trans. Worcs. Archaeol. Soc., 3rd ser., vii, Worcester, 1980), pp. 226–7; M. McCarthy, 'Pottery Synthesis', in Williams, *St. Peter's Street, Northampton*, pp. 228–9; M. Gryspeerdt, 'The Pottery', in F. Williams, 'Excavations on Marefair, Northampton, 1977', *Northants. Archaeol.*, xiv (1979), pp. 57–67.

[24] F. W. Holling, 'Reflections on Tudor Green', *Post Medieval Archaeol.*, xi (1977), pp. 61–6; Moorhouse, 'Tudor Green'.

[25] A. Vince, 'The Medieval and Post Medieval Ceramic Industry of the Malvern Region', in Peacock (ed.), *Pottery and Early Commerce*, pp. 285–6; D. M. Wilson and D. G. Hurst, 'Medieval Britain [in 1962–3, 1968, 1976]', *Medieval Archaeol.*, viii (1964), p. 297; xiii (1969), p. 287; xxi (1977), p. 259; Moorhouse, 'Tudor Green', pp. 57–8.

coates, Potovens [Yorks.]).[26] Coarse wares such as 'Midlands Purple' were also increasingly harder fired and thinner.

The uniformity of ceramic change during this period argues for a much higher degree of interaction between pottery producing areas than before. Not only were these groups of kilns making similar wares, but the products themselves also had a wider distribution. The Surrey kilns which supplied London and a large area of the south-east from the mid-fourteenth century were perhaps precocious, but a similar pattern can be seen in the extent achieved by, for example, East Midland Reduced Wares in the early fifteenth century.[27] The reorganization of the industries clearly affected the marketing patterns, with dramatic changes in the type of products used on some rural sites. At Wharram Percy (Yorks.) most of the village's pottery came from Staxton, fourteen miles away, but subsequently in the later fourteenth and fifteenth centuries an increasing proportion came from a wider area: York, Scarborough and around the Humber.[28] At Northolt (Middx.) local wares from Pinner were superseded by Surrey products after *circa* 1350 while Midlands Purple apparently dominated the assemblages in the latest phases of Barton Blount (Derbys.).[29] This change can also be charted in small towns such

[26] P. Brears, *The English Country Pottery: Its History and Techniques* (Newton Abbot, 1971), pp. 18–23; P. Mayes, E. Pine and J. Le Patourel, 'A Cistercian Ware Kiln of the Early Sixteenth Century at Potterton, Yorks.', *Antiq. Jl.*, xlvi (1966), pp. 255–76; P. Brears, 'Excavations at Potovens', *Post Medieval Archaeol.*, i (1967), pp. 3–43; K. Bartlett, 'Excavations at Potovens, near Wakefield', *Post Medieval Archaeol.*, v (1971), pp. 1–34.

[27] For example, G. C. Dunning, in J. B. W. Perkins *et al.*, *Medieval Catalogue* (London Museum, London, 1940), p. 211; C. J. Marshall, 'A Medieval Pottery Kiln Discovered at Cheam', *Surrey Archaeol. Colls.*, xxxviii (1924), pp. 79–94; C. Orton. 'Medieval Pottery from a Kiln Site at Cheam. Pt. 1', *London Archaeologist*, iii (1979), pp. 300–4; M. Hinton, 'Medieval Pottery from a Kiln Site at Kingston', *London Archaeologist*, iii (1980), pp. 377–85; L. Webster and J. Cherry, 'Medieval Britain in 1978', *Medieval Archaeol.*, xxiii (1979), p. 277; S. Moorhouse, 'A Distinctive Type of Late Medieval Pottery in the East Midlands', *Proc. Cambridge Antiq. Soc.*, lxv (1973–4), pp. 46–59.

[28] J. G. Hurst (ed.), *Wharram: A Study of Settlement on the Yorkshire Wolds*, vol. i, D. D. Andrews and G. Milne (eds.), *Domestic Settlement, 1: Areas 10 and 6* (Soc. Medieval Archaeol., monograph ser., viii, London, 1979), pp. 74–107, 140–1.

[29] Hurst, 'Kitchen Area of Northolt Manor', pp. 259–76; R. Sheppard, 'A Medieval Pottery Kiln at Pinner, Middlesex', *London Archaeologist*, iii (1977), pp. 31–5; G. Beresford, *The Medieval Clay-Land Village: Excavations at Goltho and Barton Blount* (Soc. Medieval Archaeol., monograph ser., vi, London, 1975), pp. 70–7.

as Newbury (Berks.) where Surrey wares captured the market from the late fourteenth century.[30] The trend is not quite so clear in the larger towns which were frequently supplied by the same nearby kilns throughout the later medieval period (for example, Coventry and Leicester: Nuneaton wares; Oxford: Brill-type wares), although in some towns such as Worcester and Northampton one local ware, respectively Malvern and Potterspury (Northants.), increasingly predominated.[31]

Indeed there is an impression, and it can be no more than this, that by the early fifteenth century pottery production was becoming based in grouped workshops located in the vicinity of towns.[32] The potters there were producing a great range; some of these products required different and more time-consuming methods of manufacture. Indeed such 'sophisticated' wares could only be produced commercially through the economies of scale allowed by reorganization. The larger scale of these workshops probably attracted middlemen to the potteries and ensured a wider distribution of the products, helped by an increased country-wide uniformity which made a particular kiln's pots acceptable over a greater area. Demand must have been sufficiently strong to offset increasing transportation costs, as indeed must have been the case with German imports.

This model of fifteenth-century pottery production and distribution stands in marked contrast to that established by Jope for the thirteenth and early fourteenth centuries. Then the intense regionalism of coarse pottery (and the slightly wider circulation of jugs) reflected the activities of the potter as producer *and* seller. Only part of the potter's year was spent actually making pots; collecting and preparing the raw materials, and transporting, stockpiling and selling his wares at local markets took up the rest of the time. The location of the kilns – sited as they were to take advantage of a

---

[30] A. Vince, *Bartholomew Street, Newbury: A Preliminary Report on the Archaeological Excavations of 1979* (Newbury, 1980), 'Results'.

[31] G. C. Dunning, in K. Kenyon, *Excavations at the Jewry Wall Site, Leicester* (Soc. Antiq. Repts., xv, Oxford, 1948), pp. 236–44; R. Haldon, in Durham, 'Archaeological Investigations in St. Aldates, Oxford', pp. 111–39; Morris, in Carver, *Medieval Worcester*, pp. 226–7; McCarthy, in Williams, *St. Peter's Street, Northampton*, pp. 162, 228–9.

[32] Le Patourel, 'Pottery as Evidence of Social and Economic Change', p. 91.

cluster of nearby markets – reflects this type of organization.[33] In the later medieval period increased production may be reflected in a large increase in clay rents, as for example at Cowick.[34] Increased production/demand caused the potter to leave the sale of his products to the trader who not only extended circulation but in turn influenced the potter's repertoire. The middleman's activities also blurred what difference, if any, may have existed between production for 'urban' as opposed to 'peasant' markets. Possibly the relocation of many potteries was a comment on the sluggish state of local markets, a point which will be discussed later.

The most remarkable feature of the transformation of the ceramics industry is the rapidity with which it occurred, given the accepted view of the potter as innately conservative, and it is worth considering briefly how and why such a shift could take place.[35] The conservatism of the thirteenth- and fourteenth-century potter is well illustrated by the continuity of coarse vessel forms over very long periods. However, there were products, mostly decorated jugs, which did change more rapidly – largely, it is suggested, as a result of fashion.[36] These were precisely the products which were sold over the greatest distances, and which therefore may have been sold by traders rather than by the potters themselves. In the later medieval period more of the potter's repertoire, it is argued, was sold in this way, and thus a greater part of the output was influenced by the entrepreneur, as he presumably interpreted the preferences of the market.

Two main changes in the repertoire can be identified in the later medieval period: the decline of coarse wares, particularly cooking pots; and an increase in table wares, especially those forms associated with drinking.[37] It is commonly argued that the cooking

[33] Jope, 'Regional Character in West Country Medieval Pottery'; Jope, 'Regional Cultures of Medieval Britain'. See also C. V. Bellamy and H. E. J. Le Patourel, 'Four Medieval Pottery Kilns on Woodhouse Farm, Winksley', *Medieval Archaeol.*, xiv (1970), pp. 113–16.

[34] Le Patourel, 'Documentary Evidence and the Medieval Pottery Industry', pp. 107–8, 110.

[35] For example, G. M. Foster, 'The Sociology of Pottery: Questions and Hypotheses Arising from Contemporary Mexican Work', in F. R. Matson (ed.), *Ceramics and Man* (London, 1966), pp. 43–61.

[36] Hinton, ' "Rudely Made Earthen Vessels" of the Twelfth to Fifteenth Centuries', p. 227.

[37] For example, Le Patourel, 'Pottery as Evidence of Social and Economic Change', p. 93; Vince, 'Medieval and Post Medieval Ceramic Industry of the Malvern Region', pp. 284–5; Moorhouse, 'Tudor Green', pp. 57–8.

pot was replaced by bronze vessels because the coarse vessels which were still made were in forms reminiscent of metal cauldrons and skillets.[38] The comparatively few surviving fragments (and complete examples) of metal vessels support this argument: the size of the rims, and therefore the vessels, are similar to the pottery counterparts which they apparently replaced. There seems therefore little possibility that the change in material was associated with a change in culinary practices.[39] Metal vessels are frequently documented from the thirteenth century, but the widespread replacement of pot by metal does not occur until at least a century later. The price (by weight) of bronze vessels, based on Thorold Rogers' admittedly small sample, does not alter significantly between the period 1260–1350 and 1351–1400. Price stability may possibly have enabled more people to buy metal cooking vessels at a time (1350 onwards) when other commodity prices were beginning to rise and there was a general increase in spending power.[40] Large metal containers of three- to four-gallon capacity, however, had always been part of basic household equipment and no doubt continued to be so, despite the trend for

---

[38] For example, Dunning, in Perkins *et al.*, *Medieval Catalogue*, pp. 224–5.

[39] For example, J. D. A. Thompson, *Inventory of British Coin Hoards, A.D. 600–1500* (Roy. Numis. Soc., Special Pubns., i, London, 1956), plates 1–4; K. Marshall, 'Cast Bronze Cauldrons of Mediaeval Type in the Belfast City Museum', *Ulster Jl. Archaeol.*, xiii (1950), pp. 66–75; J. A. Gilks, 'A Fifteenth-Century Bronze Skillet from near Pateley Bridge', *Yorks. Archaeol. Jl.*, li (1979), pp. 147–50; A. Carter, J. P. Roberts and H. Sutermeister, 'Excavations in Norwich, 1973: The Norwich Survey, Third Interim Report', *Norfolk Archaeol.*, xxxvi (1974–7), pp. 43–50, plate 1. Fragments found at Seacourt, Hangleton, Goltho, Southampton, Writtle, East Haddesley, Alsted, Northampton Marefair and St. Peter's: Biddle, 'Deserted Medieval Village of Seacourt', p. 167; J. G. and D. G. Hurst, 'Excavations at the Deserted Medieval Village of Hangleton, Pt. 2', *Sussex Archaeol. Colls.*, cii (1964), pp. 135–6; Beresford, *Medieval Clay-Land Village*, p. 39; Platt and Coleman-Smith, *Excavations in Medieval Southampton*, ii, p. 261; Rahtz, *Excavations at Writtle*, p. 92; Le Patourel, *Moated Sites of Yorkshire*, pp. 90–1; L. L. Ketteringham, *Alsted* (Surrey Archaeol. Soc., research vol. ii, Guildford, 1976), pp. 61–2; Williams, 'Excavations on Marefair', pp. 68–9; Williams, *St. Peter's Street, Northampton*, pp. 258–9. See also P. A. Barker, 'Excavations on the Town Wall, Roushill, Shrewsbury', *Medieval Archaeol.*, v (1961), p. 201; G. Beresford, 'The Medieval Manor of Penhallam, Jacobstow, Cornwall', *Medieval Archaeol.*, xviii (1974), pp. 132–40.

[40] J. E. T. Rogers, *A History of Agriculture and Prices in England*, 8 vols. (Oxford, 1866–1902), i, p. 605, and ii, pp. 482–8.

potters to produce large coarse ware containers during the later fourteenth and fifteenth centuries.[41]

The second main change in the potter's repertoire, the increase in table ware, is shown by the greater number of 'open forms' like jars and bowls, and the more sophisticated lobed cups and drinking mugs. Judging from the late fifteenth-century records of the Inns of Court such pottery vessels replaced those of wood.[42] Greater production of cups could indicate an attempt to compensate for the decline in the popularity of clay cooking wares. It is important to realize that the production of these new forms was well under way by *circa* 1420, predating the influx of German imports.[43] The foreign wares did not apparently then respond more quickly than the local products to a change in demand. The popularity of German jugs was probably due more to their being made of stoneware, a type not manufactured in fifteenth-century England. This high quality pottery must have been more expensive than local wares, because of greater costs in both production and transportation. Could its purchase on such a large scale reflect an increase in standards of living?

Village settlements

The archaeological evidence then for the reorganization of one industry in the course of the fifteenth century is indicative of an expanding market. Can similar trends be seen in other areas of the archaeological record? Is it possible for instance to identify within the medieval village attempts to increase agricultural production for the market?

One way of approaching this problem was suggested as long ago as 1952 by Rodney Hilton in the course of formulating a research programme to examine the transition from feudalism to capitalism. A major obstacle to the accumulation and investment of capital was the small size of the units of production. Hilton

---

[41] Field, 'Worcestershire Peasant Buildings', pp. 137–45; D. A. Hinton, 'A Medieval Cistern from Churchill', *Oxoniensia*, xxxiii (1968), pp. 66–70.

[42] L. Matthews and H. Green, 'Post Medieval Pottery of the Inns of Court', *Post Medieval Archaeol.*, iii (1969), pp. 1–17.

[43] For example, Humber ware drinking pots: Andrews and Milne, *Wharram*, pp. 76, 92; G. Coppack, 'An Excavation at Chapel Garth, Bolton, Fangfoss, Humbershire', *Yorks. Archaeol. Jl.*, l (1978), pp. 119, 130–1. The forms of the German imports were later copied by local potteries; see, for example, Moorhouse, 'A Distinctive Type of Late Medieval Pottery'.

suggested that one aim should be to discover the 'number, size and methods of operation of the larger farms held in the late fourteenth and fifteenth centuries by the thriving elements in the country-side: the big peasants and the smaller gentry'.[44] While it is clearly impossible to investigate complete holdings archaeologically, it could be argued that any substantial change in practices or production on a holding should be reflected in changes at its core, namely the croft and toft. It is precisely these parts of rural settlements which have received the most archaeological attention.

However, only a small number of excavated sites span the fourteenth and fifteenth centuries and so are relevant for this purpose. Yet from this sample a common development has been proposed. Thus the fourteenth century sees the appearance of the 'farm', according to J. G. Hurst's classification. The 'farm' is characterized by the separation of living quarters and the byre – previously under one roof – into discrete buildings. These were often arranged around a central space, which was sometimes cobbled – a 'courtyard'.[45] While there are thirteenth-century examples of this arrangement at Seacourt (Oxon.) and Gomeldon (Wilts.), the majority are dated at least a century later.[46] This replanning has been interpreted as indicating a rise in standards of living and associated with the 'emerging yeomen farmers'. The courtyard arrangement is thought to imitate that of *domestic* buildings in manorial complexes.[47]

The ascription of 'yeoman' status to these farm owners is the result of combining trends discernible in archaeological and documentary material: the increasing polarization of the peasantry from the later fourteenth century; and the fact that many of the excavated examples come from deserted villages where these farms represent the last stages of occupation, and were therefore inhabited by those who remained in the shrunken settlement to

44 R. H. Hilton, 'Capitalism – What's in a Name?', *Past and Present*, no. 1 (Feb. 1952), p. 39.

45 Beresford and Hurst, *Deserted Medieval Villages*, pp. 107–12. Hurst's 'longhouse to farm' scheme was based on a belief that in the early middle ages the longhouse was universal, whereas there is now increasing evidence to suggest the longhouse may never have existed in some parts of the country, for example the south-east.

46 Biddle, 'Deserted Medieval Village of Seacourt', pp. 96–103; D. Wilson and D. G. Hurst, 'Medieval Britain in 1965', *Medieval Archaeol.*, x (1966), pp. 214–16.

47 Beresford and Hurst, *Deserted Medieval Villages*, p. 107.

take advantage of the greater availability of land.[48] While it is clear that such 'to-be-deserted' villages often had a distorted social structure, even 'yeoman farmers' were to a certain extent dependent on the wage labourer.[49] Is it possible therefore that *all* our excavated farms belonged to yeomen? The well-documented late medieval rise in wages, especially from the 1370s, and the remarkably well-equipped tofts recorded for some smallholders require us to use caution in assuming the status of the owners of farms.[50]

Returning to the question of how the toft was used, it is evident that these farms were by no means uniform, and that the process of rearrangement was complex. Two main patterns can be distinguished. First there were those tofts with one house, one byre and a small outbuilding, often interpreted as a bakehouse. Fourteenth-century examples were excavated at Wythemail (Northants.) and also at Upton (Gloucs.) where there were two houses in the same toft, each with an outbuilding. There was a similar fifteenth-century arrangement at Hangleton (Sussex).[51]

The second pattern was characterized by a more thoroughgoing reorganization of the toft. The buildings were still grouped around cobbled areas, but it is the increase in the number and size of the outbuildings (usually interpreted as barns) which is particularly distinctive. At Grenstein (Norfolk) the complete plan of a late fourteenth- or fifteenth-century toft was recovered; it consisted of a small house screened by an earth bank, and occupying the remainder of the ditched toft were six outbuildings (one a byre) grouped round a cobbled yard.[52] Unfortunately the earlier levels

---

[48] *Ibid.*, pp. 104–7.

[49] For example, R. H. Hilton, 'A Study in the Pre-History of English Enclosure in the Fifteenth Century', in his *The English Peasantry in the Later Middle Ages* (Oxford, 1975), pp. 161–73; C. C. Dyer, *Lords and Peasants in a Changing Society: The Estates of the Bishopric of Worcester, 680–1540* (Past and Present Pubns., Cambridge, 1980), pp. 256–63.

[50] For example, *ibid.*, pp. 317–18.

[51] D. G. and J. G. Hurst, 'Excavations at the Medieval Village of Wythemail, Northamptonshire', *Medieval Archaeol.*, xiii (1969), pp. 167–203; R. H. Hilton and P. A. Rahtz, 'Upton, Gloucestershire, 1959–64', *Trans. Bristol and Gloucs. Archaeol. Soc.*, lxxxv (1966), pp. 70–146; P. A. Rahtz, 'Upton, Gloucestershire, 1964–1968', *ibid.*, lxxxviii (1969), pp. 74–126; E. W. Holden, 'Excavations at the Deserted Medieval Village of Hangleton, Pt. 1', *Sussex Archaeol. Colls.*, ci (1963), pp. 54–181; Hurst, 'Excavations at the Deserted Medieval Village of Hangleton, Pt. 2', pp. 94–142.

[52] P. Wade-Martins, 'Village Sites in Launditch Hundred, Norfolk', *East Anglian Archaeol.*, x (1980), pp. 118–24.

could not be excavated extensively so it is impossible to know whether the latest occupation represented a significant reorganization of the toft.

However, this was possible at Caldecote (Herts.) where several crofts were excavated. The 'typical' fourteenth-century croft had a house and barn, and on two crofts (B and E) occupation continued into the fifteenth century. Croft B had a house of a similar size to those in the fourteenth century, but with two large barns and a dovecote. Croft E also had a house and two large barns arranged round a yard. All the fifteenth-century barns had associated corn driers.[53] Crofts at Thuxton (Norfolk) and Faxton (Northants.) also show this pattern of buildings arranged in a square with houses on one side and barns on the other three.[54] At Faxton there was also a corn-drying kiln, and occupation continued into the sixteenth century. Another characteristic of these sites is that neighbouring crofts were frequently annexed, as at Caldecote and Faxton; at Grenstein the neighbouring croft was not used for additional buildings but probably as a paddock.[55]

This increased use of the toft deserves more attention for two main reasons: because of its implications for agricultural practices, and because this intensification was not taking place at the same time as other changes noted in villages. It is clearly not, for instance, contemporary with the archaeological evidence for improvements in standards of living: it comes too late to be connected with the changes in house construction and generally occurs later than the initial rearrangement of the toft into a farm.[56]

The case of Caldecote is particularly instructive, for the fifteenth-century reconstructions involved an increase in the number and size of barns while the domestic house stayed approximately the same size and was of a similar construction to its fourteenth-century predecessors. Only at the very end of the sequence, in the

---

[53] G. Beresford, 'Excavations at the Deserted Medieval Village of Caldecote, Hertfordshire', *Hertfordshire's Past*, iv (1978), pp. 5–10.

[54] D. M. Wilson and D. G. Hurst, 'Medieval Britain [in 1964, 1968]', *Medieval Archaeol.*, ix (1965), p. 214; xiii (1969), p. 279. A similar arrangement appears to have been found at Markshall: G. P. Larwood, 'A Late Medieval Farmstead at Markshall', *Norfolk Archaeol.*, xxx (1952), pp. 358–64; and at Duggleby and Towthorpe: Beresford and Hurst, *Deserted Medieval Villages*, p. 112.

[55] See nn. 51, 52 above.

[56] Beresford and Hurst, *Deserted Medieval Villages*, pp. 93–5, 104–13.

sixteenth century, was the house in Croft B altered.[57] This is not to deny an increasing prosperity to the occupants of Caldecote's crofts, but rather to suggest that this prosperity was diverted not into the improvement of the house but into the expansion of the farm. This expansion cannot be linked to an increase in the size of the household, which would show in the construction – or enlargement – of additional domestic as well as agricultural buildings. It could be argued that the examples given demonstrate an increased investment in the holding, made with a greater involvement in the market in mind. The juxtaposition of corn-drying kilns and barns is important in this respect: grain could be completely dried and then stored in the barns for sale at the best price. Although examples are few at present, archaeological evidence is starting to accumulate for capital investment in agriculture at a village level, associated with attempts to take advantage of the market.

There is slight evidence for a further change in the village during this period in the appearance of specialized buildings, in particular those connected with iron-working. This of course does not preclude the earlier presence of smiths in the village, but it is noticeable that the only smithies recognized are of fifteenth-century date, as for example at Somerby (Lincs.), Braggington (Salop.) and Goltho (Lincs.), where the smith's house and workshop were excavated.[58] It is however possible that it was the very intensity of activity which left sufficient residues for the smithies to be recognized, and this may point to an increasing specialization

---

[57] Beresford, 'Excavations at Caldecote', p. 10. For the changes in housing, see J. T. Smith, 'The Evolution of the English Peasant House in the Late Seventeenth Century', *Jl. Brit. Archaeol. Assoc.*, 3rd ser., xxxiii (1970), pp. 122–47. Discussions about the development of the farm have concentrated on the house with little attention being given to the associated outbuildings: M. W. Barley, *The English Farmhouse and Cottage* (London, 1961); W. G. Hoskins, 'The Leicestershire Farmer in the Sixteenth Century', in his *Essays in Leicestershire History* (Liverpool, 1950), pp. 136–46.

[58] Beresford and Hurst, *Deserted Medieval Villages*, pp. 140–1; D. C. Mynard, 'Excavations at Somerby, Lincs., 1957', *Lincs. Hist. and Archaeol.*, iv (1969), pp. 63–91; P. A. Barker, 'The Deserted Medieval Hamlet of Braggington', *Trans. Shropshire Archaeol. Soc.*, lviii (1968), pp. 122–39; Beresford, *The Medieval Clay-Land Village*, pp. 15, 46. The only earlier smithies (thirteenth and fourteenth centuries) were at Waltham and Alsted, both associated with monastic or aristocratic estate centres: P. J. and R. M. Huggins, 'Excavation of Monastic Forge and Saxo-Norman Enclosure, Waltham Abbey, 1972–3', *Essex Archaeol. and Hist.*, v (1973), pp. 127–84; Ketteringham, *Alsted*, pp. 17–30.

within villages in respect of crafts which were previously part-time activities.

Any alteration in production for the agricultural market should also be visible on the estates of the other 'thriving' element of the later medieval population, the gentry. Evidence is however virtually non-existent. While some moated sites were undoubtedly gentry residences, only a small number of those excavated were occupied in the late fourteenth and fifteenth centuries. Even on sites where this was the case, excavation has yielded results which cannot be used for the present purpose. There are few total plans of moated enclosures and even where recovered, only the domestic ranges were found; the agricultural buildings appear to have been located elsewhere, perhaps in another enclosure. Sampling of such subsidiary areas has failed to locate any structures.[59] The exception is Chalgrove (Oxon.) where the enclosure contained both residential and agricultural buildings. Reorganization in the fifteenth century not only involved the remodelling of hall and service rooms, typical of this time, but also an enlargement of existing outbuildings and the construction of a new barn.[60] While little weight can be placed on a single instance, the case of Chalgrove should alert us to the possibility that changes in gentry residences may mirror developments in the villages.

Towns

Archaeological evidence has rarely been used in the debate about the economic condition of the later medieval town. Although public works such as city walls, gild halls and parish churches have been cited as illustrating an urban vitality, the same evidence could also argue for economic stagnation, much being spent on maintaining the trappings of a top-heavy civic structure.[61]

---

59 H. E. J. Le Patourel, 'The Excavation of Moated Sites', in F. A. Aberg (ed.), *Medieval Moated Sites* (Council for Brit. Archaeol., research rept., xvii, London, 1978), pp. 36–45.

60 Webster and Cherry, 'Medieval Britain in 1978', pp. 270–1.

61 For example, Dobson, 'Urban Decline in Late Medieval England', pp. 8–9; Postan, 'The Fifteenth Century', pp. 160–7; A. R. Bridbury, 'English Provincial Towns in the Later Middle Ages', *Econ. Hist. Rev.*, 2nd ser., xxxiv (1981), pp. 1–24; C. Phythian-Adams, 'Urban Decay in Late Medieval England', in P. Abrams and E. A. Wrigley (eds.), *Towns in Societies: Essays in Economic History and Historical Sociology* (Past and Present Pubns., Cambridge, 1978), pp. 159–85.

Urban excavation however has concentrated on the more typical fabric of a town, namely the tenements, and this material should now be reviewed in the context of the changes which have already been noted.[62] Obviously here too there are clear dangers of claiming that changes noted on a single tenement are indicative of the more general situation within a street or even a town. The worst dangers of such generalization can be avoided thanks to the large scale of some urban excavations: sequences are now available for areas, which sometimes include more than one street. Yet attention must be directed towards change as shown in structures, rather than in the material assemblages, because only interim statements which concentrate on the former, have been published.

Rebuilding in towns during the late fourteenth and early fifteenth centuries is often assumed to reflect economic well-being, particularly at a time when builders' wages were extremely high. Of course such rebuilding need not imply a continuity in the occupations pursued in that area; a change in character is possible involving alteration to accommodate, for example, a new trade. Yet it is more difficult to argue the reverse – that unchanging structures are indicative of stagnation. After all, improved building techniques extended considerably the life of town houses, and reduced the necessity of regular rebuilding or renovation.

Nevertheless most urban excavations have shown that extensive rebuilding took place during this period. At Flaxengate in Lincoln there were thoroughgoing reconstructions in the late fourteenth and again in the early fifteenth centuries; at nearby Danes Terrace in the same city buildings fronting the street were replaced in the late fifteenth century.[63] At Sidbury in Worcester, the frontage of at least three tenements was levelled and lowered twice around 1300 and again in the late fourteenth or early fifteenth century. On

---

[62] It is interesting to note the differing conclusions that can be drawn from the excavations of 'public' and tenement buildings, for example Lower Brook Street, Winchester, where the churches of St Mary and St Pancras show a late medieval expansion when neighbouring tenements were slowly being abandoned. M. Biddle, 'Excavations at Winchester [1962–71]', *Antiq. Jl.*, xliv (1964), p. 119; *ibid.*, xlv (1965), pp. 246–9; *ibid.*, xlvi (1966), pp. 316–18; *ibid.*, xlvii (1967), pp. 262–3; *ibid.*, xlviii (1968), pp. 263–5; *ibid.*, xlix (1969), pp. 305–8; *ibid.*, l (1970), pp. 309–10; *ibid.*, lii (1972), pp. 111–15; *ibid.*, lv (1975), pp. 318–20.

[63] C. Colyer and M. J. Jones (eds.), 'Excavations at Lincoln: Second Interim Report', *Antiq. Jl.*, lix (1979), pp. 50–81.

all three occasions rebuilding followed.[64] At St Peter's Street, Northampton, where both sides of the street have been excavated, the same process can be seen on a grander scale. Houses on the north side had been rebuilt in the fourteenth century and the whole street was redeveloped in the early fifteenth, with renovations and the construction of new houses continuing into the late fifteenth and early sixteenth centuries. The early fifteenth-century reconstruction was widespread, being found also in neighbouring streets.[65]

A similar renovation can be seen in the late fourteenth century on three sites along Much Park Street in Coventry, and again in the late fifteenth and early sixteenth centuries.[66] Fifteenth-century reconstructions have also been found on at least eight sites in Norwich, at St Aldates, Oxford, High Street, Hull, and Bartholomew Street, Newbury.[67] Evidence then is accumulating for considerable vitality in the urban building industry which implies an extensive mobilization of resources. What is more, this activity occurred throughout most of the urban hierarchy, and not just in the larger towns.

The archaeological picture is not however one of continuous and unchecked expansion. The case of Lower Brook Street in Winchester is instructive for the excavation of a series of cloth-working establishments showed a progressive depopulation: the abandonment of one tenement in the early fourteenth century was followed by others in the late fourteenth and fifteenth centuries, while two tenements continued in use until the early sixteenth.[68] The early sixteenth century was also a time when some of the towns which were prospering in the previous century suffered a set-back. In Flaxengate two houses were demolished and not re-

---

[64] Carver, *Medieval Worcester*, pp. 175–9.

[65] Williams, *St. Peter's Street, Northampton*, pp. 137–47 ('Synthesis'), pp. 107–9.

[66] S. M. Wright, *Much Park Street, Coventry: Excavations, 1970–1974* (forthcoming).

[67] A. Carter, J. P. Roberts, H. Sutermeister and M. W. Atkin, 'Excavations in Norwich: [Third, Fourth, Fifth, Sixth, Seventh] Interim Report', *Norfolk Archaeol.*, xxxvi pt 1 (1974), pp. 43–4, 60–3; xxxvi pt 2 (1975), pp. 105–6; xxxvi pt. 3 (1976), pp. 194–200; xxxvi pt 4 (1977), pp. 289–96; xxxvii pt 1 (1978), pp. 19–30. Durham, 'Archaeological Investigations in St. Aldates, Oxford'; J. Bartlett, 'Medieval Hull: Excavations in High Street, 1971', *Kingston on Hull Museum Bull.* (Dec. 1971); Vince, *Bartholomew Street, Newbury*.

[68] Biddle, 'Excavations at Winchester', *Antiq. Jl.*, xliv (1964), p. 119; xlv (1965), pp. 246–9; xlvi (1966), pp. 316–18.

placed, and in St Peter's Street, Northampton, a fire destroyed most of the buildings, perhaps in 1516; only one house was rebuilt.[69]

While archaeology can show a general expansion in many towns during the fifteenth century, and a check in some in the early sixteenth, it is less easy to see any consistent or general change in the arrangement of tenements similar to the alterations seen on rural settlements. The excavation of complete tenements has rarely been achieved, and most work has been concentrated on the frontages. However, it is clear that the amalgamation of two or three tenements into a single unit occurred in some urban areas in the later middle ages. At Sidbury, Worcester, this can be associated with the expansion of a bronze-working industry; there was a similar amalgamation for cloth-working at Lower Brook Street, Winchester, and perhaps for iron smithing at Much Park Street, Coventry.[70] Such events could be interpreted as an increase in the unit of production, although earlier examples of combination and then dissolution of tenements can sometimes be related to their tenurial history. In the case of Lower Brook Street, two plots were first held by the same institution, which subsequently leased out one.

A trend can also be seen towards the creation of residential zones in areas which had previously had a mixture of housing, shops and industrial workshops, as at St Aldates, Oxford, and Much Park Street, Coventry.[71] This could be linked to the building of 'artisan' housing. Such houses, lightly built of cob and uniform in size, were found in early fourteenth-century Winchester, while others were constructed in a more substantial fashion in 'terraces' along St Peter's Street, Northampton, in the fifteenth century, and also perhaps at Carlisle.[72] Similar types of housing, though of a higher status, have been identified in standing buildings at Spon in

---

[69] Colyer and Jones, 'Excavations at Lincoln', pp. 66–7; Williams, *St. Peter's Street, Northampton*, pp. 145–7.

[70] Carver, *Medieval Worcester*, pp. 165–7, 176–9; Biddle, 'Excavations at Winchester', *Antiq. Jl.*, xlv (1965), pp. 246–9; Wright, *Much Park Street, Coventry*.

[71] Durham, 'Archaeological Investigations in St. Aldates, Oxford', pp. 195–200; Wright, *Much Park Street, Coventry*.

[72] Biddle, 'Excavations at Winchester', *Antiq. Jl.*, xlviii (1968), pp. 265–6; Williams, *St. Peter's, Northampton*, pp. 145–6; L. E. Webster and J. Cherry, 'Medieval Britain in 1977', *Medieval Archaeol.*, xxii (1978), p. 173.

Coventry, York, and Tewkesbury.[73] The changing fortunes of particular areas of towns can of course be documented throughout the medieval period, as for example at Southampton.[74] However the most distinctive feature of this late medieval 'zoning' was the 'artisan' housing. Whereas an increase in high-quality housing might suggest a decline in industrial activities in some towns, the construction of poorer housing, with its implication of the continued presence of a (presumably industrial?) workforce, would counter this argument. Much of this new housing can be regarded as speculative building and might confirm that some merchant capital was being invested to obtain increased urban rent in the future. If this were the case, it also illustrates the continued high demand for such housing.[75]

If this hypothetical economic interpretation of the spatial trends in towns is to have any validity, it will need to be supported in the future by evidence which demonstrates a corresponding increase in the concentration of industry, as for example might be the case at Worcester. All of these questions must be asked of the rapidly accumulating material so that the archaeological contribution to the problem of the late medieval town can be more than a mere recitation, as this has been, of particular sites where 'expansion' or 'contraction' is apparent in the structural sequence.

Coinage

Recent research on the money supply has revived 'monetarist' arguments to help explain the economic trends of the medieval period. A new approach has been to look at mint output and coin hoards together to give an indication of the amount of currency actually in circulation.[76] As a correction to the bias towards the high denominations in hoards, Rigold extended this work by analysing coin finds from excavations.[77]

[73] C. Platt, *The English Medieval Town* (London, 1976), pp. 82–7; P. Short, 'The Fourteenth-Century Rows of York', *Archaeol. Jl.*, cxxxvii (1980), pp. 86–137.

[74] Platt and Coleman-Smith, *Excavations in Medieval Southampton*, i, pp. 18–32.

[75] R. H. Hilton, 'Some Problems of Urban Real Property in the Middle Ages', in C. H. Feinstein (ed.), *Socialism, Capitalism and Economic Growth: Essays Presented to Maurice Dobb* (Cambridge, 1969), pp. 326–37.

[76] For example, N. J. Mayhew, 'Numismatic Evidence and Falling Prices in the Fourteenth Century', *Econ. Hist. Rev.*, 2nd ser., xxvii (1974), pp. 1–15.

[77] S. E. Rigold, 'Small Change in the Light of Medieval Site-Finds', in N. J. Mayhew (ed.), *Edwardian Monetary Affairs, 1279–1344* (Brit. Archaeol. Repts., Brit. Ser., xxxvi, Oxford, 1977), pp. 59–80.

Such research is particularly important in the present context because of the link claimed to exist between the money supply and the market. It has been agreed, for example, that by the 1330s the coinage famine, a result of low mint output and a high proportion of coin taken out of circulation through continuous war demands, led to an idle market because of a lack of money in men's pockets.[78] Similar symptoms can be observed in the late fourteenth and fifteenth centuries (at least to 1460); was there a similar effect on the market? The upward movement of prices (and wages) until the 1370s has been seen as a result of an increase in the amount of money per capita, due not only to a reduced population but also to the introduction of a bi-metallic currency in the 1350s. Both Lloyd and Mate have argued that, after an initial distrust of the new gold coins, they were widely accepted from the 1360s and became a suitable medium for hoarding. This had the effect of dishoarding the lower silver denominations and increasing the coinage in circulation.[79] The demonstrable change in the composition of hoards between 1344–60 and 1361–80 supports this; in the earlier period the ratio of gold to silver coins was 1:7, whereas after 1360 this changed to 1:0.84.[80]

After 1380 the drain of silver out of the country, coupled with a general shortage of bullion in Europe, created an acute dearth of coin which was aggravated by a generally low mint output, particularly of low denomination coins.[81] Some numismatists argue for a decrease in the velocity of coin circulation in line with the cumulative reduction in the population. Others would support an increase in coin circulation pointing to an increase per capita of the amount of coin held, and to the greater variety of goods being

---

[78] E. Miller, 'War, Taxation and the English Economy in the Late Thirteenth and Early Fourteenth Centuries', in J. M. Winter (ed.), *War and Economic Development: Essays in Memory of David Joslin* (Cambridge, 1975), pp. 11–31.

[79] T. H. Lloyd, 'Overseas Trade and the English Money Supply in the Fourteenth Century', in Mayhew (ed.), *Edwardian Monetary Affairs*, pp. 111–13; M. Mate, 'The Role of Gold Coinage in the English Economy, 1338–1400', *Numis. Chron.*, cxxxviii (1978), pp. 126–41.

[80] Figures derived from hoards listed in Thompson, *Inventory of British Coin Hoards, A.D. 600–1500*. There is no noticeable increase in the proportion of silver being hoarded during the fifteenth century: the mean is 1 (gold): 3.

[81] For example, Lloyd, 'Overseas Trade'; J. Day, 'The Great Bullion Famine of the Fifteenth Century', *Past and Present*, no. 79 (May 1978), pp. 3–54.

bought when wages after all were still high.[82] So did the shortage of coin help to slow the market?

A sample of coin finds from excavations shows a steady decline in the loss of coin from the early fourteenth century. It is interesting therefore that the period of proposed increased circulation, between *circa* 1360 and 1380, is not reflected in an increased loss. This downward trend was maintained during the fifteenth century when Rigold noted an 'impression' that pennies were rarer than before, and very worn.[83] At first sight then this evidence would support a 'restricted' view of the coinage and therefore of the activity of the market. However, Rigold's analysis does not include all the specie available for exchange purposes at this time. Mayhew has recently reviewed possible means of overcoming this shortage of small change, including the cutting of coin (prohibited in 1280, but still practised in the fifteenth century) and the use of token coins.[84] Token coinage such as foreign base coin, for example Venetian *solidini*, clearly circulated (despite attempts to prevent this) outside London in the early fifteenth century as indeed did the early fourteenth-century crockards, pollards and lushbournes, all tariffed at ½d., in the fifteenth century.[85]

Rigold noted a sharp decline in the rate of coin loss in fifteenth-century towns and proposed, not that this simply indicated economic decline, but that jettons and lead tokens were in use as substitute coin.[86] A recent analysis of coins and jettons from Oxford excavations showed that after the later fourteenth century the number of coins declined but jettons increased.[87] A similar pattern, although based on a smaller sample, can be seen from the

[82] For example, J. L. Bolton, *The Medieval English Economy, 1150–1500* (London, 1980), pp. 77–81.

[83] Rigold, 'Small Change in the Light of Medieval Site-Finds', pp. 60–6.

[84] N. J. Mayhew, 'The Monetary Background to the Yorkist Recoinage of 1464–1471', *Brit. Numis. Jl.*, xli (1974), pp. 62–73.

[85] P. Spufford, 'Continental Coins in Late Medieval England', *Brit. Numis. Jl.*, xxxii (1963), pp. 127–39. Such coins have been found in Sussex and Surrey: K. J. Barton, 'Excavations in the Village of Tarring, West Sussex', *Sussex Archaeol. Colls.*, cii (1964), p. 18; Ketteringham, *Alsted*, p. 63; Mayhew, 'Monetary Background to the Yorkist Recoinage', p. 70.

[86] Rigold, 'Small Change in the Light of Medieval Site-Finds', pp. 68–9.

[87] N. J. Palmer and N. J. Mayhew, 'Medieval Coins and Jettons from Oxford Excavations', in Mayhew (ed.), *Edwardian Monetary Affairs*, pp. 81–95.

excavations at Northampton.[88] Most fifteenth-century jettons found are foreign; the greatest number came from the Low Countries and the Rhineland, with Nuremburg jettons predominating from the early sixteenth century – an interesting parallel to the increase in imported German stonewares. So a shortage of currency in the fifteenth century may have been partly remedied by the use of jettons and lead tokens, some of which appear in contemporary hoards. It is still difficult therefore to argue from the numismatic evidence for a definite contraction of the market during the later medieval period.

Faunal remains

In studying later medieval economic trends historians have noticed that the prices of livestock and dairy produce did not fluctuate so greatly as those of grain during the fifteenth century, and some have interpreted this buoyant demand as indicative of a change in tastes, or the ability of more of the population to afford such items as meat and butter.[89] Can the archaeological evidence support such a view or demonstrate innovations in animal husbandry or meat consumption during this period? To begin with the material is very fragmentary; there are few published large collections of animal bones, and often they have been studied by a variety of methods, so making strict comparison difficult. Moreover there are additional problems for detecting change in this material. The frequent lack of stratification on village sites for instance often means that it is only possible to obtain an undifferentiated assemblage that had accumulated during the total period of occupation. On many urban sites new patterns of rubbish disposal from the fourteenth century result in smaller bone collections.[90]

However variations in demand might be reflected in bone assemblages, for example in the greater occurrence of young cattle which had been reared for the meat market. This in turn would imply a reorganization of animal husbandry, involving an increase in herd size in order to maintain stock for breeding and to satisfy

---

[88] Williams, 'Excavations on Marefair', p. 69; Williams, *St. Peter's Street, Northampton*, pp. 245–6.

[89] For example, M. M. Postan, 'The Trade of Medieval Europe: The North', in his *Medieval Trade and Finance* (Cambridge, 1973).

[90] Cf. M. Maltby, *Faunal Studies on Urban Sites: The Animal Bones from Exeter, 1971–1975* (Exeter Archaeol. Repts., ii, Exeter, 1979), pp. 3–9.

the market. On village sites however there is little evidence of change in terms of age. Most cattle and sheep had reached maturity before being killed and clearly animals retained their importance primarily as suppliers of milk, wool and traction power rather than as a source of meat.[91] This also appears to have been the case on sites where levels of meat consumption would have been higher. At aristocratic hunting lodges and moated sites, although there is evidence of a greater variety of meat (as one would expect), the cattle and sheep bones were from mature animals: the demands then of some aristocratic tables did not significantly affect animal management.[92]

The bias towards mature animals in faunal assemblages is not however so apparent in the large urban collections. The ratio of immature cattle increased at Exeter in the fourteenth century, with a correspondingly high percentage of immature sheep (fifteen to thirty months old).[93] A similar trend was noted on two sites in Bristol and at King's Lynn where an increased proportion of young cattle was found in late fourteenth- and fifteenth-century deposits.[94] It is tempting to use this evidence of an emphasis on younger animals in towns to argue for an increasing market for meat. However this would be premature: there is a lack of good comparative data from nearby urban and rural sites. It should also be said that where this information does exist for towns it demonstrates a gradual development; no dramatic change in the nature of the meat supply occurs until the sixteenth century. Indeed in some towns, such as Northampton, Abingdon, Bedford

---

[91] For example, S. Yealland and E. S. Higgs, 'The Economy', in Hilton and Rahtz, 'Upton, Gloucestershire, 1959–64', pp. 139–43; B. Noddle, 'The Animal Bones', in Rahtz, 'Upton, Gloucestershire, 1964–1968', pp. 124–6; R. A. Harcourt, 'Animal Remains', in D. G. Hurst and J. G. Hurst, 'Excavations at Wythemail', pp. 201–3; M. Jope, 'The Animal Remains', in Biddle, 'Deserted Medieval Village of Seacourt', pp. 197–201; however most sheep were killed when about two years old at Wharram: M. L. Ryder, 'Animal Remains from Wharram Percy', *Yorks. Archaeol. Jl.*, xlvi (1974), pp. 42–52.

[92] For example, R. A. Harcourt, 'Animal Remains', in Rahtz, *Excavations at Writtle*, pp. 113–15.

[93] Maltby, *Faunal Studies on Urban Sites*, pp. 30–54.

[94] B. Noddle, 'A Comparison of the Animal Bones from 8 Medieval Sites in Southern Britain', in A. T. Clason (ed.), *Archaeozoological Studies* (Amsterdam, 1975), pp. 248–60; B. Noddle, 'Mammal Bone' in H. Clarke and A. Carter, *Excavations in King's Lynn, 1963–1970* (Soc. Medieval Archaeol., monograph ser., vii, London, 1977), pp. 378–99.

and Oxford the proportion of mature animals continued at a high level throughout the later medieval period.[95]

Other aspects of faunal assemblages suggest that the demand for meat played a secondary role in stock rearing. This is best shown in the near-universal increase in the proportion of sheep to cattle (even though beef continued to be the meat most commonly eaten) which must reflect a rise in wool production. This is eloquently demonstrated at Exeter, where there was a slight increase in the age of sheep at slaughter – an attempt to obtain more wool from animals before they were sold for meat. This is particularly marked in sixteenth-century Exeter where there was a reorientation of the economy towards wool and cloth production.[96] Similarly clear increases in sheep numbers occur at Northampton, Oxford, Bedford and Abingdon.[97]

The other common feature in late medieval urban assemblages was a decline in the number of pigs. This is surprising if the demand for meat remained buoyant, for the pig had few uses other than as a meat source. In some towns the decline has been related to ever-shrinking woodland, but the pig was the animal most frequently kept in constricted urban yards. Could this decline reflect an increasing pressure on available space in the late medieval town, a counterpart to the archaeologically well-documented cessation of digging rubbish pits in backyards?[98]

A lowering of the age structure of animals at death would seem the only way to substantiate that animal husbandry was increas-

---

[95] M. Harman, 'The Mammalian Bones', in Williams, *St. Peter's Street, Northampton*, pp. 328–32; M. Harman, 'The Mammalian Bones', in Williams, 'Excavations on Marefair', pp. 77–8; R. Wilson, 'The Animal Bones from the Broad Street and Old Goal Sites', in 'Excavations in Abingdon, 1972–4', *Oxoniensia*, xl (1975), pp. 105–21; R. Wilson, 'The Mammal Bones and Other Environmental Records', in M. Parrington, 'Excavations at Stert Street, Abingdon', *Oxoniensia*, xliv (1959), pp. 16–20; A. Grant, 'The Animal Bones from Bedford', in D. Baker et al., 'Excavations in Bedford, 1967–1977', *Beds. Archaeol. Jl.*, xiii (1979), pp. 286–8; B. J. Marples, 'Animal Bones', in Durham, 'Archaeological Investigations in St. Aldates', pp. 166–9.

[96] Maltby, *Faunal Studies on Urban Sites*, pp. 41–54.

[97] Harman, 'Mammalian Bones', in Williams, *St. Peter's Street, Northampton*, pp. 328–32; Marples, 'Animal Bones', pp. 166–9; Grant, 'Animal Bones from Bedford', pp. 286–8; Wilson, 'Animal Bones from Broad Street and Old Goal Sites', pp. 105–21. This increase in sheep numbers at Abingdon is also reflected in the nearby medieval village of Seacourt; see Jope, 'Animal Remains', pp. 197–201.

[98] Harman, 'Mammalian Bones', in Williams, *St. Peter's Street, Northampton*, p. 328.

ingly geared to the market at this time. There is no clear evidence for any improvement in the quality of breeds or stock during the medieval period although the degree to which this can be ascertained from archaeological material is debated. Neither is there any evidence for an increase in animal size: stock seems to have been remarkably uniform in size throughout the medieval period.[99]

*   *   *

This review has demonstrated the fragmentary nature of the archaeological record, but has also tried to illustrate some of the questions future work should try to answer. Nevertheless existing information can contribute to the general debate regarding the economic development of the later middle ages. Emphasis has been given to the market and the influence it might have had on methods of production. However this is not to suggest that the market was a 'prime mover' in determining change in the later medieval economy; rather it is an indication of how far archaeological enquiry has reached. Can this archaeological overview be compared with that derived from the documentation?

The pottery industries demonstrate a widening domestic market in the fifteenth century. This is seen in growing production and an increased input in terms of greater investment to manufacture more sophisticated wares. Associated with this was a different method of distribution where the role of the entrepreneur was crucial, not only in effecting a wider dissemination of wares, but also in influencing the potters' repertoire.

The change in the method of distribution has wider implications. The expansion of those potteries located close to towns (and the withering away of 'country-based' workshops) is remarkable, for it occurred at a time when other, major industries such as that of cloth-making were quitting the large towns for the countryside.[100] The reorientation of the pottery industry may indicate the vitality of some towns in the fifteenth century, a vitality also reflected in the numerous rebuildings of urban tenements.

[99] For example, Maltby, *Faunal Studies on Urban Sites*, pp. 40, 54, 82–94; Noddle, 'Mammal Bone', pp. 384–95; Noddle, 'Animal Bones from 8 Medieval Sites', p. 253.

[100] E. M. Carus-Wilson, 'Evidences of Industrial Growth on Some Fifteenth-Century Manors', *Econ. Hist. Rev.*, 2nd ser., xii (1959–60), pp. 190–205.

Is the shift of the potteries some indication of the declining importance of the smaller markets as centres of trade, and the integration of small units into wider trading areas based on the larger towns? The pottery also illustrates the change to bigger units of production; the rearrangement of some village tofts, where evidence points to an increased expenditure on agricultural buildings, could argue for this trend to larger units becoming widespread. Further confirmation might also be seen in the changing urban bone assemblages, with their implications of larger herds in order to maintain stock and simultaneously satisfy the market.

The coin evidence is ambiguous, but evidence for a token coinage during this period is increasing and this could have offset the stultifying effect of a dearth of coinage on the market.

The archaeological depiction of the fifteenth century as a time of innovation is matched by recent historical research. At a time when it could be argued that seigneurial pressure was relaxed there are signs of greater investment on the peasant holding in the form of improved and more intensive farming techniques which resulted in increased production.[101] This took place at a time of generally low prices and there is some debate about the extent to which such production was market-oriented, considering the high level of wages and evidence for the decline of international and regional trade.[102] Yet the evidence for toft rearrangement and the increasing concentration of some crafts such as brewing and smithing into the hands of a small number of workers would argue for production far beyond the level of self-sufficiency.[103] This trend, however, was associated with a rationalization of markets, where the weakest ones failed, as shown in Staffordshire, Derbyshire and Nottinghamshire, for example.[104] The relocation of the

---

[101] For example, R. H. Hilton, *The English Peasantry in the Later Middle Ages* (Oxford, 1975), pp. 37–54; Dyer, *Lords and Peasants in a Changing Society*, pp. 319–39.

[102] For example, summarized in M. M. Postan, *The Medieval Economy and Society* (London, 1972), pp. 221–32.

[103] Hilton, *English Peasantry in the Later Middle Ages*, pp. 37–53; Dyer, *Lords and Peasants in a Changing Society*, pp. 346–9.

[104] D. M. Palliser and A. C. Pinnock, 'The Markets of Medieval Staffordshire', *N. Staffs. Jl. Field Studies*, ii (1971), pp. 49–63; B. E. Coates, 'Markets and Fairs in Medieval Derbyshire', *Derbys. Archaeol. Jl.*, lxxxv (1965), pp. 92–111; P. T. H. Unwin, 'Rural Marketing in Medieval Nottinghamshire', *Jl. Hist. Geog.*, vii (1981), pp. 231–51.

potteries not only demonstrates this, but also shows that the middleman may have short-circuited the web of small markets and taken over their trade. A similar increase in the importance of the middleman can be seen in the selling of wool and grain during this period.[105]

What role did towns play in this process? The archaeological evidence would support those who see a certain vitality in the late medieval town, but what character did this vitality take? It has already been noted that there is a dearth of archaeological evidence for industrial areas – is this a reflection of the real situation? Is the reorganization of the domestic pottery industry an indication, not of the continuing industrial character of the towns, but rather 'of the once industrialised English provincial towns . . . simply becoming regional markets for agricultural produce and food processing centres'?[106]

At present the archaeological evidence gives a biased picture of increased production in some areas of the economy, and there is little to demonstrate increased demand, or to elucidate its character. This emphasizes the weakness of this review, which cannot provide a social context for economic changes in the village or town. Neither is there sufficient material at present to discern regional differences in later medieval England, nor to define the role of the small town. Clearly these are some of the major problems medieval archaeologists should try to answer in the future.

[105] E. Power, *The Wool Trade in English Medieval History* (Oxford, 1941), pp. 41–62; N. S. B. Gras, *The Evolution of the English Corn Market* (Cambridge, Mass., 1915), pp. 157–82; J. A. Chartres, *Internal Trade in England, 1500–1700* (London, 1977), pp. 47–57.

[106] R. H. Hilton, 'Agrarian Class Structure and Economic Development in Pre-Industrial Europe: A Crisis of Feudalism', *Past and Present*, no. 80 (Aug. 1978), p. 18. It is worth noting that where there is evidence of a decline of residential areas in sixteenth-century towns, for example Lincoln and Northampton, the only subsequent reconstruction in these 'blighted areas' consisted of buildings with malting or drying kilns: Colyer and Jones, 'Excavations at Lincoln', p. 67; Williams, 'Excavations on Marefair', pp. 52–4; Williams, *St. Peter's Street, Northampton*, pp. 96–8.

10. *Serfdom in Later Medieval and Early Modern Germany**

HEIDE WUNDER

I

In German historiography peasant freedom and unfreedom are more than mere terms to describe medieval and early modern agrarian institutions. The inadequacy of bourgeois freedom which had been attained in Prussia and Germany in general in the nineteenth century stimulated the search for the origins of the belated and incomplete emancipation of German society. One explanation put forward was to transpose into the past contemporary political structures: the old German territories (west, north and south Germany) stood for liberal traditions and mild forms of peasant dependency, while east Elbia and especially Prussia represented autocracy, militarism and the extreme exploitation of an unfree peasantry. Despite all scholarly progress since then, this paradigm of agrarian dualism has remained central to the social interpretation of modern German history.[1]

Recently it has been suggested that the personal serfdom (*Leibeigenschaft*) of south-west Germany, which developed from the second half of the fourteenth century onwards, be classified as a 'second serfdom' (*zweite Leibeigenschaft*). Thus a connection is explicitly made with east Elbian hereditary serfdom (*Erbuntertänigkeit*) as though the two were contemporaneous.[2] This proposition, of course, has to be seen against the background of traditional regional historiography which used not to attribute

* I am indebted to Janos Bak and Dieter Wunder for their criticism of an earlier draft of this paper.

1 C. J. Fuchs, 'The Epochs of German Agrarian History and Agrarian Policy', in *Selected Readings in Rural Economics*, ed. T. N. Carver (Boston, Mass., 1906), pp. 223–53; H. Rosenberg, *Bureaucracy, Aristocracy and Autocracy: The Prussian Experience, 1660–1815* (Cambridge, Mass., 1958); F. L. Carsten, *The Origins of Prussia* (Oxford, 1954).

2 P. Blickle, *Die Revolution von 1525* (Munich, 1975), p. 109.

much significance to serfdom as a relevant factor in the peasant's economic and social condition. In contrast, now, serfdom has been shown to be a very effective economic and political instrument in the fourteenth, fifteenth and sixteenth centuries and, to a lesser degree, also in the following centuries.[3] Thus, a new discussion on peasant freedom and unfreedom in south and west Germany has been initiated, which proceeds in part on a comparative basis.[4] Yet, the use of the term 'second serfdom' for south German *Leibeigenschaft* refers not only to a 'first serfdom', which can indeed be identified in the 'first feudal age', but also contains a theoretical notion implicit in the Marxist context from which it is borrowed.[5] The main argument to justify this terminology concerns the renewal and strengthening of personal dependency in the peasant-lord relationship, but no attempt has been made systematically to apply central Marxist categories, such as 'rent' and 'extra-economic' power. Therefore, it seems highly questionable whether it is valid to classify both south German personal serfdom, which appeared from the fourteenth century onwards, and east Elbian 'hereditary serfdom', which developed from the sixteenth century as a 'second serfdom'. The chronological difference could indicate quite different geopolitical and socio-economic contexts and no 'backwardness' in German development. It follows that late medieval peasant freedom and unfreedom in south and west Germany have to be measured by the constituent criteria of early modern hereditary serfdom if they are to achieve at least comparability on a phenomenological level. At the same time, the comparison must be extended to embrace medieval developments in both regions. This proves to be rather difficult because, despite intensive studies on the process of medieval colonization, the notion of 'personal freedom' has re-

---

[3] P. Blickle and R. Blickle (eds.), *Schwaben von 1268 bis 1803* (Dokumente zur Geschichte von Staat und Gesellschaft in Bayern, pt ii, vol. 4, Munich, 1979); C. Ulbrich, *Leibherrschaft am Oberrhein im Spätmittelalter* (Göttingen, 1979); D. W. Sabean, *Landbesitz und Gesellschaft am Vorabend des Bauernkrieges* (Stuttgart, 1972); H.-M. Mauer, 'Die Ausbildung der Territorialgewalt oberschwäbischer Klöster vom 14. bis zum 17. Jahrhundert', *Blätter für deutsche Landesgeschichte*, cix (1973), pp. 465–95.

[4] W. Trossbach, ' "Südwestdeutsche Leibeigenschaft" in der Frühen Neuzeit – eine Bagatelle?', *Geschichte und Gesellschaft*, vii (1981), pp. 69–90.

[5] G. Heitz, 'Zum Charakter der "Zweiten Leibeigenschaft"', *Zeitschrift für Geschichtswissenschaft*, xx (1972), pp. 24–39; C. Goehrke, 'Leibeigenschaft', *Sowjetsystem und demokratische Gesellschaft*, iii (1969), pp. 1399–1410.

mained undisputed.[6] The settlers' medieval 'freedom' and early modern hereditary serfdom still serve as parameters which have not been carefully re-examined. The sequence of medieval freedom and early modern unfreedom will have to wait for a plausible explanation until a comparative and structural analysis of the various east German territories is envisaged.

In these circumstances I want to begin the discussion on late medieval peasant freedom and unfreedom by (1) sketching the recent debate on late medieval personal serfdom in south-west Germany and Bavaria (upper and lower Bavaria, upper Palatinate), and (2) relating the results of this comparison to early modern east Elbian hereditary serfdom as well as to medieval freedom and unfreedom in the east German territories. The decision to compare these particular territories was prompted by the fact that south-west Germany was the centre of the German Peasant War of 1525 which placed the abolition of personal serfdom at the forefront of its demands.[7] On the other hand, Bavarian peasants, though living close to Swabia, did not take part in the Peasant War, neither did peasants in north and west Germany.[8] And while abstention from 'class struggle' has been judged to be causal to the establishment of hereditary serfdom in east Germany,[9] nothing like this has been concluded from the behaviour of Bavarian peasants. This is one of the central arguments used inconsistently to explain the 'division of Germany'. Rather oddly, factors common to all Germany, especially in the twelfth century when German settlers left for the later central and eastern territories, have also been neglected in the argument.

As personal serfdom, constituting a severe burden on peasant freedom, came into existence only during the fourteenth and

---

[6] W. Schlesinger (ed.), *Die deutsche Ostsiedlung des Mittelalters als Problem der europäischen Geschichte* (Vorträge und Forschungen, xviii, Sigmaringen, 1975).

[7] J. Bak (ed.), *The German Peasant War of 1525* (London, 1976); B. Scribner and G. Benecke (eds.), *The German Peasant War, 1525: New Viewpoints* (London, 1979).

[8] G. Franz, *Der deutsche Bauernkrieg*, 10th edn (Darmstadt, 1975); R. Postel, 'Zur Sozialgeschichte Niedersachsens in der Zeit des Bauernkrieges', *Geschichte und Gesellschaft*, Sonderheft 1, 'Der Deutsche Bauernkrieg, 1524–1526' (1975), pp. 79–105.

[9] H. Mottek, *Wirtschaftsgeschichte Deutschlands: Ein Grundriss*, 3 vols. (Berlin, 1957–74), i, p. 339; R. Brenner, 'Agrarian Class Structure and Economic Development in Pre-Industrial Europe', *Past and Present*, no. 70 (Feb. 1976), pp. 59 ff.

fifteenth centuries, the 'crisis of the fourteenth century', also known as the 'crisis of feudalism', so familiar to west European historians, seems to offer itself as an explanatory clue.[10] Yet I do not want to restrict the later middle ages to these two centuries, but prefer to retain the traditional periodization of German history, and include the period from the late twelfth century to the beginning of the sixteenth century which saw, at its beginning, the culmination of medieval peasant freedom and at its end the emergence of personal serfdom.

To begin with, some problems of terminology stemming from the long German discussion on peasant freedom and unfreedom have to be explained.[11] The origins of historical research on the subject can be dated to the eighteenth century when an enlightened society became engaged in a fervent debate on hereditary serfdom and the lord's right to such dominion, which was an inconvenient phenomenon in moral philosophy and economic theory. Kant and Kraus, the famous professors at the University of Königsberg, were among the combatants. To the peasant serf, so vividly described by the Silesian Christian Garve,[12] was juxtaposed the 'free' Westphalian peasant, who was presented as the model for a modern peasantry. Within the context of the emancipation of the peasantry (*Bauernbefreiung*), this debate was continued in the historical schools of jurisprudence, political science (*Staatswissenschaften*) and economics. Georg Friedrich Knapp is its best known representative.[13] The still nascent branch of historical science was more interested in peasant freedom and

---

[10] P. Kriedte, 'Spätmittelalterliche Agrarkrise oder Krise des Feudalismus?', *Geschichte und Gesellschaft*, vii (1981), pp. 42–67.

[11] J. Schlumbohm, *Freiheitsbegriff und Emanzipationsprozess* (Göttingen, 1973); C. Dipper, H. Gunther, D. Klippel and W. Conze, 'Freiheit', *Geschichtliche Grundbegriffe*, ii (Stuttgart, 1978), pp. 425–538; W. von Hippel, *Die Bauernbefreiung im Königreich Württemberg*, 2 vols. (Boppard, 1977), i. As the term 'Leibeigenschaft' is so ambiguous, I have decided to use 'unfreedom' as the general term. L. Kuchenbuch and B. Michael, 'Zur Struktur und Dynamik der "feudalen" Produktionsweise im vorindustriellen Europa', in L. Kuchenbuch and B. Michael (eds.), *Feudalismus – Materialien zur Theorie und Geschichte* (Frankfurt, Berlin and Vienna, 1977), pp. 694–761, at p. 733, have proposed the term 'Servilität', but this does not seem adequate, because this term already has a definite meaning in the German language: 'servility'.

[12] C. Garve, *Über den Charakter der Bauern und ihr Verhältnis gegen die Gutsherren* (Breslau, 1786).

[13] G. F. Knapp, *Die Bauern-Befreiung und der Ursprung der Landarbeiter in den älteren Theilen Preussens* (Leipzig, 1887).

its continuity from the early middle ages.[14] When once the theory concerning the existence of Germanic freemen (*Gemeinfreie*) was questioned around 1900 new forms of high medieval peasant freedom, originating in service to the king and in the work of clearing woodlands or draining marshes, were detected (*Königs- und Rodungsfreie*). Under the influence of Gierke's community theory (*Genossenschaftstheorie*) individual peasant freedom was correlated with free peasant communities. Nowadays, however, even these free peasantries have not stood the test of historical research: their reduced obligations made them more 'free' and 'less dependent' than other peasant groups, but they remained dependent peasants and could not change their social status. Thus, their 'liberties' were always in danger.

The notions of freedom and unfreedom, thus derived by different disciplines with diverging interests and modes of systematization, vary because no common frame of reference has been developed. It is a noticeable tendency in traditional German historical research to build theories which contain the notion of peasant freedom/unfreedom – such as the concept of the manorial system (*Grundherrschaft*) – but these concepts have been taken as a 'true' description of reality, and not as a model which needs to be constantly verified or disproved. The majority of German historians, however, have always questioned theories ranging far over time and space – feudalism is an example –[15] because they could not capture historical complexity in all its detail. The other German tradition, the larger universal tradition from Hegel, Marx to Max Weber, was only taken up by outsiders such as Lamprecht and Hintze. Now the prolonged process of confronting history and theory has resulted in a new approach to history: history is taken as a result of social interaction: economic pressures are taken as relevant historical facts; and peasant resistance for the first time has been accepted as a historical force.

The fundamental shortcomings in the debate on peasant freedom/unfreedom in German history can be summarized under two propositions: (1) that no satisfactory correlation between the

---

14 G. Franz (ed.), *Deutsches Bauerntum im Mittelalter* (Darmstadt, 1976); H. K. Schulze, 'Rodungsfreiheit und Königsfreiheit: Zu Genesis und Kritik neuerer verfassungsgeschichtlicher Theorien', *Historische Zeitschrift*, ccxix (1974), pp. 528–50.

15 H. Wunder (ed.), *Feudalismus* (Munich, 1974); Kuchenbuch and Michael (eds.), *Feudalismus – Materialien zur Theorie und Geschichte*.

dominant lord-peasant relationship and the diversity of phenomena has been achieved, and (2) that the diversity of phenomena has not been explained as an expression of historical development. By definition serfdom is the characteristic relationship between peasant and lord up to the age of reform in the nineteenth century, no matter which theoretical approach is taken – whether the traditional model of the manorial system (*Grundherrschaft*)[16] or feudal relations of production.[17] Though logically and historically peasant serfdom stands in the middle between Germanic freedom and bourgeois freedom, historians irrespective of their theoretical orientation speak of peasant freedom. By freedom they mean: enough land, secure rights of possession, free movement, small or no labour services, fixed obligations in kind or money. The individual peasant's freedom is complemented by the free peasant community, its 'autonomy' being the more effective the more 'liberties' it is able to achieve.[18] When peasants are not successful in acquiring (how many?) liberties, they appear as being subjected and unfree. These inconsistencies follow from a confusion in the use of theoretical terms, which contrast freedom and serfdom as two sharply differentiated conditions, while the documented legal terms actually show them standing in close relation to one another as 'liberties'. They are also the outcome of the wish to define serfdom as the unifying criterion of the feudal period, on the one hand, and, on the other, to explain the emergence of bourgeois freedom not only in the cities and under the impact of the modern state, but from within feudal peasant society.

II

1. South-west Germany[19]

South-west Germany did not form a political unit during the late

---

16 H. K. Schulze, 'Grundherrschaft', *Handwörterbuch zur deutschen Rechtsgeschichte*, i (1971), pp. 1824–42; Konstanzer Arbeitskreis für mittelalterliche Geschichte, *Protokolle*, 224 (1978), 229 (1979), 231 (1979), on late medieval 'Grundherrschaft'.

17 J. Bak, 'Serfs and Serfdom: Words and Things', *Review*, iv (1980), pp. 3–18; Kuchenbuch and Michael, 'Zur Struktur und Dynamik der "feudalen" Produktionsweise im vorindustriellen Europa'; W. Rösener, 'Bauer, Bauerntum', *Lexikon des Mittelalters*, i (Munich, 1977), pp. 1563 ff.; O. Brunner, 'Europäisches Bauerntum', in *Neue Wege der Verfassungs- und Sozialgeschichte*, 2nd edn (Göttingen, 1968), pp. 199–212.

18 T. Mayer (ed.), *Die Anfänge der Landgemeinde und ihr Wesen*, 2 vols. (Vorträge und Forschungen, vii, viii, Konstanz and Stuttgart, 1964).

19 See nn. 3, 11 above. A. Strobel, *Agrarverfassung im Übergang* (Freiburg and

middle ages. Apart from some larger territories, such as the *Markgrafschaft* of Baden and the earldom (later dukedom) of Württemberg, the political structure was distinguished by a large number of lay and ecclesiastical lordships with no definite topographical boundaries. Especially on ecclesiastical estates, parcels of land and rights over men were dispersed over large areas which meant that hardly any village or peasant had only one lord. The second significant feature of this region was a dense network of towns and cities which, like the nobility and ecclesiastical lords, developed their own landed interest. Though the empire was the overall political framework, it did not provide effective political organization; instead, this task was taken up by confederation of towns (for example the Swabian towns in 1376) and the nobility (for example St Jörgenschild, about 1408), and later by the Swabian Confederation (Schwäbischer Bund, 1488–1534).

The debate concerning late medieval peasant freedom or unfreedom starts from the dissolution of the old pattern of the manorial system (*ältere Grundherrschaft*) which from the twelfth century changed conditions for all groups of manorialized peasants, but had a deep impact on *homines proprii* (*Eigenleute*), both as peasants and day workers. The dissolution of the old manorial system meant, first of all, the disappearance of large-scale demesne farming, making obsolete the labour services to be rendered by *homines proprii*, which were instead converted into a modest money payment (*Leibzins*). Those *homines proprii* who took over part of the divided demesne, and thus became economically independent peasants, did not, however, secure hereditary rights of possession and in case of death the family had to surrender part of the moveable possessions to the lord (*Leibherr*). *Homines proprii* who were not able to make a living on the manor of their lord were allowed to take over holdings in other manors, or could move into the numerous nearby towns, but they remained subject to the lord of the manor as long as they had not bought their freedom or had obtained it by the principle that 'Stadtluft

Munich, 1972); O. Herding, 'Leibbuch, Leibrecht, Leibeigenschaft im Herzogtum Wirtemberg', *Zeitschrift für Württembergische Landesgeschichte*, xi (1952), pp. 157–88; H. Rabe, *Das Problem Leibeigenschaft* (Wiesbaden, 1977); W. Rösener, 'Die spätmittelalterliche Grundherrschaft im südwestdeutschen Raum als Problem der Sozialgeschichte', *Zeitschrift für die Geschichte des Oberrheins*, cxxvii (1979), pp. 17–69; see also Konstanzer Arbeitskreis für mittelalterliche Geschichte, *Protokolle*.

macht frei' (Town air makes a man free), that a man became free having stayed in town for a year and a day. This was the pre-condition for rights of citizenship (*Bürgerrecht*) in towns. The dissolution of demesne farming allowed *homines proprii* more freedom, that is, economic independence and freedom of movement. But lords took great pains to ensure that their number was not reduced when those belonging to different lords married or when they married free peasants. In some cases the children's legal status was fixed by customary law (for example they followed their mother's status), but when this was not the case, constant conflicts arose between lords and between lords and peasants, which finally were settled by contracts stipulating the mode of sharing the children (*Teilungsverträge*). In individual cases when the ties between lord and *homines proprii* were severed by distance a new legal device for the legitimate transfer of rent was needed, which was found in the system of personal dominion (*Leibherrschaft*). It also meant that wide discrepancies between a peasant's legal status and his economic position could arise. The situation became even more complicated when rights of jurisdiction were dissociated from manorial lordship, and/or appropriated from kings and territorial lords, because they were then treated as a source of income which could be bought and sold. Thus a lord might have peasants who held his land, were his 'men', and stood under his jurisdiction, but as well he might have others who were subjected to him only in one or two of these aspects and there might be yet others who were free peasants, and could do what they wished with their land, but had given themselves into his lordly protection (*Vogtei*) only.[20] Even among his own peasants there might be wide differences in legal and economic status, bearing witness to the complex and prolonged process of manorialization. Yet, the classification of peasants by legal status and manorial organization did not necessarily influence relations between them, as is demonstrated by the numerous inter-marriages.

There is no doubt that these changes in the lord-peasant relationship were prompted to some extent by demographic growth up to the thirteenth century, and by the competition for

---

[20] H. Ebner, *Das frie Eigen: Ein Beitrag zur Verfassungsgeschichte des Mittelalters* (Klagenfurt, 1969); G. Droege, *Landrecht und Lehnrecht im hohen Mittelalter* (Bonn, 1969).

men stirred up by towns and colonizing landlords. But this development was halted by bad harvests and the Black Death in the middle of the fourteenth century, when the peasant population was dramatically reduced. And, because of perennial plagues, it remained at a low level. Though all landlords were afflicted, the great number of ecclesiastical estates were hit harder because their dispersed possessions and men made it difficult for them to control their losses and to undertake effective counter-measures. As they were better administrators and record keepers, we know best what happened on their estates as a reaction to the crisis.

To equate their losses in income, lords followed three strategies: (1) They tried to keep and attract peasants by improving their rights of tenure and by reducing rent. I shall come back later to the consequences of the peasants' improved bargaining position. (2) They called back their *homines proprii* who held tenures outside the manor, tried to bind them to their holdings by various means, and tried to enlarge their number by forbidding marriages outside the *familia*. Those departing without the lord's permission had to face high fines or the loss of the holding. The same measures were taken to prevent marriages outside the *familia*. Oaths of allegiance and firm sureties from families and communities were enforced to ensure 'good behaviour'. Ecclesiastical lords even had recourse to ecclesiastical punishments. On top of this, peasant families suffering the recurrent epidemics were subject to strict demands for heriots. Lastly, children born into 'mixed' families now generally inherited the inferior status (*ärgere Hand*), and thus the personal unfreedom (*Eigenschaft*) of peasants increased with every new generation. This type of marriage could not be avoided in consequence of the dispersed condition of estates. (3) Not only did lords exchange land as they had done before to consolidate their estates but they also exchanged their *homines proprii*. This did not mean that individual peasants were displaced, only that they exchanged personal lords.

These strategies resulted in a tendency for landlords to re-assert rights of dominion over people and land. Finally, only peasants who were willing to accept personal dependence were granted a holding. Thus, the former principle of lordship based on rights over people was replaced by territorial lordship, having a new political impact that coincided with the emergence of the modern state. The instrument used to achieve this in a region characterized by dispersed rights in land and men, and in a period that was subject to frequent epidemics, was personal dominion. It helped to overcome economic losses by appropriating more of the peasants' means, who only then became personally unfree (*Leibeigene*). It helped as well to establish a firm territorial base and a legally and socially homogeneous subject population as a pre-condition for the development of modern political power. In the larger territorial states – such as Württemberg and Baden – universal personal unfreedom became the precursor of general citizenship and therefore did not carry with it social discrimination. Its economic value so dwindled in importance that territorial lords abolished it altogether in the seventeenth century.

The establishment of personal serfdom as the general peasant status and its economic and constitutional consequences were somewhat different on many ecclesiastical estates, of which those of the abbey of Kempten is the most prominent example. Against the abbot's violent and illegal actions the peasants organized strong resistance, but it was only successful after the process of territorial consolidation, described above, had been completed during the second half of the fifteenth century. Then the peasantry secured contracts which defined their legal status and alleviated their economic situation by reducing their obligations; for example *mainmorte* was reduced to the best beast and the best gown. Similar contracts are known from many other monastic estates. Another remarkable feature has to be mentioned: these contracts were not only effected through peasant protest and action, but also by virtue of the constitutional situation in south-west Germany which enabled arbitrary jurisdiction – often exercised by extra-territorial authorities – to play an important role in securing legal support for the peasantry. This description of personal serfdom in south-west Germany would be misleading if, apart from intensified economic exploitation, another aspect were not underlined: it was just these 'personally enserfed' peasants on many of the small ecclesiastical estates who attained rights of corporate representation in the sixteenth century, and who were thus able to participate to some degree in the modest exercise of political power which their territorial lords commanded.[21]

---

[21] P. Blickle, *Landschaften im Alten Reich: Die staatliche Funktion des gemeinen Mannes in Oberdeutschland* (Munich, 1973).

The form taken by personal serfdom among peasants in late medieval south-west Germany does not seem in itself wholly to justify their plea for its abolition in the Peasant War (1525). Setting aside the ideological use of the term 'personal serfdom' from the fifteenth century onward,[22] which was further generalized by the Reformation, there was another feature in lords' behaviour which had great impact on peasant consciousness. Lords had not only tried to exercise their legal rights inherent in the concept of personal dominion, but they had also forced free peasants who were only under their protection (*Vogtei*) to enter their *familia*, that is to submit to personal serfdom also. Thus the number of free peasants – irrespective of origin – and the amount of non-customary land (*freies Eigen*) were drastically reduced. Furthermore, lords illegally extended their claims under *mainmorte* to the free land, which free peasants and *homines proprii* might possess. Both actions meant economic deprivation and social degradation for the peasants concerned and extended the area of customary land. These illegal proceedings, which were accompanied by brutal violence, were deeply resented by the peasantry and aroused general peasant resistance against personal serfdom.[23] This resistance becomes the more understandable when we consider that the change from the status of *homines proprii (Eigenschaft)* to personal serfdom (*Leibeigenschaft*) was paralleled by the emergence of a new understanding of the meaning of property (*Eigentum*) which the peasants had been watching since the fourteenth century.[24] Lords tried to appropriate all the perquisites which they had to share with the peasants (*gewere*). It can be argued that to the peasants personal serfdom must have appeared analogous to the lords' usurpation of private property. Therefore, the argument put forward against personal serfdom in the Twelve Articles, though very close to the condemnation of serfdom (*Eigenschaft*) in the *Sachsenspiegel* (1220–30),[25]

---

22 W. Müller, 'Wurzeln und Bedeutung des grundsätzlichen Widerstandes gegen die Leibeigenschaft im Bauernkrieg, 1525', *Schriften des Vereins für Geschichte des Bodensees und seiner Umgebung*, xciii (1975), pp. 1–41.

23 'Der Kemptener Leibeigenschaftsrodel', ed. P. Blickle, *Zeitschrift für bayerische Landesgeschichte*, xlii (1979), pp. 567–629.

24 D. Schwab, 'Eigentum', *Geschichtliche Grundbegriffe*, ii (Stuttgart, 1978), pp. 65–115; H.-R. Hagemann, 'Eigentum', *Handwörterbuch zur deutschen Rechtsgeschichte*, i (1971), pp. 882–96.

25 *Sachsenspiegel: Landrecht*, ed. C. Frhr. von Schwerin (Stuttgart, 1953), pp. 114–16.

is much more rooted in peasant experience and of more bearing on peasant society as a whole.

In my argument I have put more stress on the interrelationship of economics and politics, because I think it more characteristic of the peasant-lord relationship in Germany, than dwelling on economic development as a prime mover in the context of the 'crisis of the fourteenth century'. The consolidation of territorial and hence of political power by 'feudal' instruments, such as personal dominion and serfdom, can of course be termed 'manorialization' (*Vergrundherrschaftung*), but I am hesitant to parallel this process with the 'feudalization' of the early middle ages by using the term 'refeudalization' since, in the fifteenth century, manorialization did not return to a system of personal dominion but was used to establish modern abstract forms of domination by the state.

Finally, I want to indicate very briefly how intricately economics and politics were also interwoven in respect of the peasants' freedom and unfreedom. The 'crisis of the fourteenth century' not only inflicted on many of them personal serfdom, it also enabled many of them to change the terms of rent payments in their own favour by fixing its amount and by securing hereditary rights of tenure which really amounted to 'more freedom', and which was so perceived by the peasantry. As effective as economic pressure was the peasants' control over customary law when set down in custumals (*Weistümer*) and *Öffnungen* (the Swiss term for the same); these were a basic requisite of legitimate domination, especially during the Black Death which hit lords and peasants alike and made traditions uncertain.

The general insecurity could not be handled by lords who, instead, contributed much to create it (*Fehde*), and thereby enhanced cohesion in local peasant communities. The same effect was produced by the lords' 'struggle for rent', especially in those regions with divided lordships as in south-west Germany.[26] Peasant communities functioned both as a system of domination and as an organ of local 'self-government', providing peasants with 'extra-economic power', not as individuals but as a corporation of equals who shared pleasure and pain (*Freud und Leid*). Lords depended on the community and thus strengthened peasant self-consciousness. These communities were not only apt instruments

[26] K. Arnold, 'Dorfweistümer in Franken', *Zeitschrift für bayerische Landesgeschichte*, xxxviii (1975), pp. 819–76.

to organize peasant resistance – this could also be achieved by manorial organization, as is proved by the Kempten peasants – but they were able to extend their territory and accumulate rights of local domination (*Zwing und Bann*) in consequence of the numerous deserted fields and villages and the weakness of many petty lords.[27]

Faced with the strength of peasant communities and their communal politics, the conclusion must be drawn that they, as well as their lords, contributed to the stabilization of 'feudal' relations of production in the fifteenth century. The peasant community not only took action to reduce manorial 'transaction costs', collect rent, organize services and control communal life – even if, by so doing, it acquired some elements of 'extra-economic power' – but it also mediated between the diverging interests of different peasant groups and hindered the private appropriation of common land and communal rights.[28]

2. *Bavaria*[29]

By the thirteenth century Bavaria – in contrast to south-west Germany – was on the way to establishing itself as a consolidated territorial state. The Wittelsbach dynasty was favoured because several noble families, which held large estates and important rights of overlordship (*Herrschaftsrechte*), died out, and their fiefs reverted to the territorial lords. Besides, many ecclesiastical lords, in conflict with the lay nobility, ceased to submit to their protection (*Vogtei*) and sought instead that of the territorial lords to

---

[27] K. S. Bader, *Studien zur Rechtsgeschichte des mittelalterlichen Dorfes*, 3 vols. (Weimar, 1957–73), ii, *Dorfgenossenschaft und Dorfgemeinde*; H. Jänichen, 'Markung und Allmende und die mittelalterlichen Wüstungsvorgänge im nördlichen Schwaben', in Mayer (ed.), *Die Anfänge der Landgemeinde und ihr Wesen*, i, pp. 163–222.

[28] Sabean, *Landbesitz und Gesellschaft am Vorabend des Bauernkrieges*.

[29] M. Spindler (ed.), *Handbuch der bayerischen Geschichte*, ii (Munich, 1966); K. Bosl (ed.), *Zur Geschichte der Bayern* (Darmstadt, 1965); A. Sandberger, 'Entwicklungsstufen der Leibeigenschaft in Altbayern', *Zeitschrift für bayerische Landesgeschichte*, xxv (1962), pp. 71–92; G. Kirchner, 'Probleme der spätmittelalterlichen Klostergrundherrschaft in Bayern', *Zeitschrift für bayerische Landesgeschichte*, xix (1956), pp. 1–94; I. Bog, 'Geistliche Herrschaft über Bauern in Bayern und die spätmittelalterliche Agrarkrise', *Vierteljahresschrift für Sozial- und Wirtschaftsgeschichte*, xlv (1958), pp. 62–75; H. Rubner, 'Die Landwirtschaft der Münchener Ebene und ihre Notlage im 14. Jahrhundert', *Vierteljahresschrift für Sozial- und Wirtschaftsgeschichte*, li (1964), pp. 434–53; E. Schremmer, *Die Wirtschaft Bayerns* (Munich, 1970).

avoid being exploited in the interest of the lay nobility. As the amount of land held by ecclesiastical lords was rather large – it has been estimated at about half of Bavaria – the monasteries' subordination was a remarkable extension of the power of lesser lay lords and of their legitimate right to ask the population for taxes and services – claims which were connected with *Vogtei*. The comparative strength of territorial lords was a barrier to the full development of the authority of the nobility and the imperial monasteries (*Reichsklöster*). Yet, up to the fifteenth century the dukes had to care for the monastic lordships, which formed part of their territorial base, and these were not to be weakened by the competition over *homines proprii* between lords and towns. The Wittelbach's double interests in land and people, as territorial lords and as manorial lords, account for their 'double strategy'.

With the disintegration of the old system of demesne farming territorial lords were able to influence the reorganization of the peasant-lord relationship. On their own estates the peasants were organized in administrative districts (*Ämter*), and the danger of their estrangement was less imminent than on the smaller ecclesiastical and noble estates. Personal dominion was of little significance to them and the problems of 'mixed' marriages were settled early by agreements to divide the offspring (*Teilungsverträge*) and by allowing the intermarriage of all peasants on ducal estates. This reduced the rate and the necessity of mixed marriages. As the dukes were also the main founders of towns and markets they prohibited the migration of their peasants to the towns, but not the migration of other *homines proprii* such as craftsmen. This policy is one reason why the monasteries complained about their peasants migrating to the towns and tried to get them set on an equal footing with the peasants on ducal estates. Indeed, the towns were a real economic danger to the monasteries which were not at the same time urban lords (*Stadtherren*) as were the dukes. Their *homines proprii* who moved to towns could change their personal status, becoming 'free' burghers with no further obligations to their former personal lord. They could even become burghers while staying on in the country (*Ausbürger, Pfahlbürger*) and try to get their holdings treated as 'free' according to their personal status, which meant that the monasteries lost the holdings as a source of rent.

These potential conflicts between lords, towns and peasants

flared up after the bad harvests in the first half of the fourteenth century and the Black Death when an acute shortage of people was experienced. It seems significant that these conflicts were settled by territorial legislation (*Landfrieden, Landrecht*) favouring the lords, and obliging *homines proprii* to return to their lords' estates to cultivate their holdings. Helped by territorial legislation, jurisdiction and executive power, the monasteries tried to recall their *homines proprii* and to engage them by oaths of allegiance. They also tried – as in Swabia – to grant holdings only to those willing to submit to personal serfdom at the same time. But again, as in Swabia, no attempts were made to re-establish extensive demesne farming to overcome the economic crisis, rents in money and kind remaining the typical form of exactions. In contrast to the peasants on ducal estates who were able to buy hereditary rights of possession at the beginning of the fifteenth century, peasants on ecclesiastical estates could not use their good bargaining position to attain more security, but kept their holdings by rights of *Freistift* which obliged them to appear in court every year to prove their dependency even though, in fact, they had permanent tenure.

The crucial point which made personal dominion and personal serfdom so different in Bavaria and south-west Germany was that it was used only to overcome temporary economic crisis and could not be made an instrument for developing political power. By the fourteenth century, territorial lordship was so well established that personal dominion was unnecessary and, because of their subordination, ecclesiastical and lay lords were not able to draw on personal dominion to extend and intensify lordship. Bavarian peasants did not attain corporate representation, but they were protected by ducal jurisdiction from private appropriation. This comparative security is one explanation why Bavarian peasants did not take part in the German Peasant War.

Despite the differences, there are common features in south-east and south-west German personal serfdom. The term personal serfdom, which is first documented as *proprius de corpore* in the thirteenth century and in 1388 as a German legal term, is not only a new word[30] but also a new 'thing', a special kind of unfreedom

---

[30] D. Schwab, 'Eigen', *Handwörterbuch zur deutschen Rechtsgeschichte*, i (1971), pp. 877–9; F.-W. Henning, 'Leibeigenschaft', *Handwörterbuch zur deutschen Rechtsgeschichte*, ii (1978), pp. 1761–72.

and not serfdom in general. The dissolution of demesne farming, combined with the division of rights of lordship, allowed the economic, legal and local emancipation of *homines proprii*: thus, they became an important group in the settling of newly founded towns and villages. Their new personal status, though called *Eigenschaft*, was free compared to their former, totally dependent status, because they had attained more or less free movement and economic independence. Yet, the main principle of feudal domination remained untouched: if an *homo proprius* bought his freedom, he lost at one and the same time his lord's protection and, even more important, the right to be granted a peasant holding on his lord's estate. Personal freedom in these circumstances could only constitute a transitional status, for the free man then had to submit to new dependencies or to change his status altogether by acquiring citizenship and corporate protection. Nevertheless, it is essential to remember that the disintegration of the manorial system brought more freedom to all peasants, especially to the large group of *homines proprii*. It was only under the impact of the economic and demographic crisis that lordly dominion was transformed into personal serfdom for *homines proprii* and those 'free peasants' who were forced to submit to it. The comparison of Bavaria and south-west Germany has also demonstrated that personal serfdom cannot be analysed as an isolated legal institution. To find out the real significance of the relationship between lords and peasants, its political and economic connotations have to be kept in mind. Bavarian personal serfdom was only used for a comparatively short period to stabilize the lords' economic situation, and, during the fifteenth century, exactions connected with it were reduced. In contrast, south-west German personal serfdom was an effective instrument for establishing political units for about two hundred years. It was very important economically to the numerous smaller lords who had no resources other than their agrarian income.[31] Last, but not least, it contributed to reduce the complexity of the peasantry's legal status. Both regions were similar in that lords did not revive demesne farming and labour services, which have always been regarded as the most burdensome form of rent. Only those lords

---

[31] W. Rösener, 'Adelige Grundherrschaften im Südwesten im Spätmittelalter', in Konstanzer Arbeitskreis für mittelalterliche Geschichte, *Protokolle*, 224 (1978), pp. 69–71.

who had kept their demesnes, for example the Teutonic Kinghts at Beuggen, tried to enforce more labour services.

3. *East Germany*

Finally, peasant freedom and unfreedom in the east German territories have to be outlined in order to test them as preconditions for early modern hereditary serfdom. The situation in these regions differed widely when confronted with German expansion after the high middle ages.[32] Some estates were already consolidated territorial units – comparable to Bavaria – others were more or less in their tribal phase. Their economic structures and political organization varied enormously, as is shown by comparing the small west Slavonic lordships with Silesia which, by 1000, was already Christianized and politically unified.

During the first seigneurial phase of German expansion, Slavonic peasants were made dependent. German landlords transformed their economies and their settlements to increase agrarian production and rent which, to the Slavonic peasants, meant manorialization and the intensification of dominion, as, for example, in Wendland.[33] During the second phase, German lords combined with German and Dutch peasants to settle in the more or less thinly populated Slavonic regions. The freedom of the settlers has to be defined on two levels: first, they were made free

---

[32] H. Grundmann, 'Die deutsche Ostbewegung im Spätmittelalter, der Ordensstaat und die Hanse', in *Handbuch der deutschen Geschichte*, i, 9th edn (Stuttgart, 1970), pp. 579–606; W. Schlesinger, 'Der Osten', in *Handbuch der deutschen Geschichte*, ii (Stuttgart, 1970), pp. 667–764; H. K. Schulze, 'Die Besiedlung der Mark Brandenburg im hohen und späten Mittelalter', *Jahrbuch für die Geschichte Mittel- und Ostdeutschlands*, xxviii (1979), pp. 42–178; M. Hamann, *Mecklenburgische Geschichte* (Cologne and Graz, 1968); F. Mager, *Geschichte des Bauerntums und der Bodenkultur im Lande Mecklenburg* (Berlin, 1955); W. A. Boelcke, *Verfassungswandel und Wirtschaftsstruktur: Die mittelalterliche und neuzeitliche Territorialgeschichte ostmitteldeutscher Adelsherrschaften als Beispiel* (Würzburg, 1969); J. J. Menzel, *Die schlesischen Lokationsurkunden des 13. Jahrhunderts* (Würzburg, 1978); K. Kasiske, *Die Siedlungstätigkeit des Deutschen Orderns im östlichen Preussen bis zum Jahre 1410* (Königsberg, 1934); H. Wunder, *Siedlungs- und Bevölkerungsgeschichte der Komturei Christburg, 13. – 16. Jhdt.* (Wiesbaden, 1968); H. Harnisch, *Die Herrschaft Boitzenburg: Untersuchungen zur Entwicklung der sozialökonomischen Struktur ländlicher Gebiete in der Mark Brandenburg vom 14. bis zum 19. Juhrhunderi* (Weimar, 1968).

[33] H. K. Schulze, *Adelsherrschaft und Landesherrschaft: Studien zur Verfassungs- und Besitzgeschichte der Altmark, des ostsächsischen Raumes und des hannoverschen Wendlandes im hohen Mittelalter* (Cologne and Graz, 1963).

from all exactions and services which the Slavonic peasants had to render; secondly, they were granted legal and economic 'liberties' which they had already enjoyed in their home countries, and they could enlarge their rights: for example they enjoyed fixed rent and hereditary tenure, daughters were accepted as heiresses, and local communities had local jurisdiction. The tendency to change all obligations into a fixed sum of money only became general after the German expansion was no longer merely an affair of lords and peasants, and was given a new impetus by the movement to found towns, thereby influencing the character of agricultural production and creating strong market links.

The towns also transformed the Slavonic peasants' conditions. It is fundamental to the understanding of peasant freedom and unfreedom in these territories that German peasant freedom was based on Slavonic peasant unfreedom, because Slavonic peasants had to perform all the services from which the Germans had been freed.[34] Though they were soon integrated into the movement of settlement, the process of assimilation was greatly advanced by market-integration. There remained some Slavonic settlements of the older type which were not measured and therefore could not be taxed by rational (impersonal) rent, and there were also some cases where assimilation remained incomplete. There can be no doubt that by the beginning of the fourteenth century peasant conditions varied greatly but, on the whole, the development was directed at assimilating all to the legal and economic standards of the German settlers – as long as the interests of both peasants and lords coincided. So the thesis that east Elbian hereditary serfdom was rooted in Slavonic unfreedom is not proven. The same is true for the thesis that the stage was set for large-scale farming by the large demesnes originating in the period of colonization.

To explain the emergence of east Elbian hereditary serfdom, some reflections on personal freedom, which is supposed to be at at the heart of peasant freedom in east Germany, might be helpful. It is held that personal freedom consisted in free movement and in the fact that obligations were due from the land and not from the person. The settlers had indeed bought their freedom before departing from home, if they were *homines proprii*,

---

[34] *Urkunden und erzählende Quellen zur deutschen Ostsiedlung im Mittelalter*, ed. H. Helbig and L. Weinrich, 2 vols. (Darmstadt, 1968–70), i, pp. 68–205.

or just went off secretly. Yet, in their new homes, they also had to look for a protector which, in many cases, was the territorial lord himself. From this, it follows that it was the territorial lords who in the fifteenth century contracted with neighbours to return fugitive peasants. Free movement was necessary to ensure quick expansion; nevertheless, it might become a problem to landlords who had to fear the competition for men from towns, and other lords offering better conditions. This explains why restrictions on free movement are recorded as early as the thirteenth century in Silesia: a peasant was only allowed to leave his village after he had paid all his obligations, procured another peasant for his holding and secured the lord's consent.[35] These same provisions are known from Prussian territorial legislation at the beginning of the fifteenth century.[36] But these regulations were not a general rule: in the midst of the 'crisis of the fourteenth century', the Uckermark peasants, for example, definitely had the right of free movement.[37]

What seems important to the argument on peasant freedom and unfreedom is that personal freedom was no safeguard against enserfment, and personal serfdom (*Eigenschaft*) was not necessarily identical with restrictions on free movement and economic prosperity. Restrictions upon freedom could also arise from obligations which were based on the use of land, for relations between lords and peasants were never purely economic or purely 'protective': they were mutual obligations. Peasants' tenurial agreements conferred the 'right' to till the lord's land and at the same time the obligation to till it.

Exemption from labour services is usually counted as the second criterion of German peasant freedom. Labour services could not amount to a severe burden until the lords took to large-scale demesne farming, which only occurred in the second half of the fifteenth century. Though German peasants were obliged to serve for some days a year, this was not looked upon as reducing their freedom. So we have to be careful not to isolate one criterion as essential while neglecting others. It was rather a range of criteria

---

[35] *Ibid.*, no. 3, p. 77.
[36] *Acten der Ständetage Preussens unter der Herrschaft des Deutschen Ordens*, ed. M. Toeppen, 5 vols. (Leipzig, 1874–86), i, p. 199 (1412), and ii, p. 364 (1441).
[37] W. Lippert, *Geschichte der 110 Bauerndörfer in der nördlichen Uckermark* (Cologne and Vienna, 1968), p. 70.

and their interaction with economic, social and political forces which produced real peasant freedom and unfreedom.

During the German expansion, peasants had acquired a good bargaining position, had experienced more freedom and developed more self-reliance. This changed after the work of colonization had been finished and the 'normal' peasant-lord relationship was established, which was no longer favourable to the preservation of peasant freedom. This process of consolidation overlapped with economic, demographic and political crises in the fourteenth century. Although the concept of a 'crisis' in eastern Germany is much debated, there can be no doubt that restrictions on peasants' free movement, already mentioned, were a result of crisis.[38] But these measures did not imply a radical change in the structure of rent which was to become typical of early modern hereditary serfdom. Lords did not enlarge their demesnes by taking in abandoned land, instead they tried to get their villages settled again by peasants, enticing them with favourable rents and concessions such as freedom from exactions during the period of resettlement. So the peasants' situation in general was not yet altered for the worse. In some regions offering good marketing opportunities peasants also prospered by using deserted fields for enlarging market production.[39] The decisive stimulus to large-scale demesne farming was not the direct consequence of the desertion of villages, but a reaction to a new market situation which arose in Scandinavia and the Netherlands from the second half of the fifteenth century. The ensuing enforcement of peasant labour services was no necessary pre-condition for an economy of great estates (*Gutswirtschaft*). The hereditary subjection of peasants could only be enforced because territorial princes had given up much of their power to the landed nobility, which established lordship on great estates (*Gutsherrschaft*), and thus the former had lost control of the countryside.[40]

---

[38] E. Engel and B. Zientara, *Feudalstruktur, Lehnbürgertum und Fernhandel im spätmittelalterlichen Brandenburg* (Weimar, 1967).

[39] Hamann, *Mecklenburgische Geschichte*, p. 280.

[40] J. J. Menzel, *Jura Ducalia: Die mittelalterlichen Grundlagen der Dominialverfassung in Schlesien* (Würzburg, 1974).

III

Having compared late medieval freedom and unfreedom in west and east Elbia, we need to recall the essentials of early modern hereditary serfdom.[41] Peasants were not allowed to leave their holdings without the lord's permission, they themselves and their children were forced to work on the demesne fields and often had to care for the lord's cattle as well; the children were not allowed to be trained in an urban craft or profession. Labour services gradually became the most profitable part of rent which diverted a considerable amount of labour from the peasants' own holdings, and so, in extreme cases, these only yielded subsistence and the cattle necessary to work the lord's fields. Rights of tenure varied from traditional hereditary tenure to non-hereditary short-term leasehold. Lords were able to enforce labour services because they also exercised jurisdiction, and as magistrates handled the policing (*gute Polizey*) of their tenantry. It was very difficult for peasants to appeal to territorial courts and they had no possibility at all of appealing to imperial courts. Lords' estates established themselves as 'intermediary lordships' separating their peasants from the territorial lord and from the towns by reducing drastically the amount of their marketable products. All these measures were justified by a shortage of people, and in this respect a great difference emerges between east Elbia and south-west Germany. The connection between a scarce labour force and pressure upon the peasantry is proved to some extent by developments in the eighteenth century, when population growth caused lords to work their estates with free labourers.[42]

East Elbian hereditary serfdom differed widely from late medieval personal serfdom in south Germany, both in its functional as well as in its phenomenological aspects. It served neither to

---

41 An excellent presentation is given in Boelcke, *Verfassungswandel und Wirtschaftsstruktur*, pp. 387–407; see also F.-W. Henning, *Herrschaft und Bauernuntertänigkeit: Beiträge zur Geschichte der Herrschaftsverhältnisse in den ländlichen Bereichen Ostpreussens und des Fürstentums Paderborn vor 1800* (Würzburg, 1964).

42 H. Plehn, 'Zur Geschichte der Agrarverfassung von Ost- und Westpreussen', *Forschungen zur brandenburgisch-preussischen Geschichte*, xvii (1904), pp. 383–466; xviii (1905), pp. 61–122.

overcome short-term economic crisis nor to form political units. Hereditary serfdom was the means to achieve private appropriation of the peasantry, and not just the appropriation of part of their produce. This was the real scandal of east Elbian hereditary serfdom. The theory put forward that the state in east German territories was too weak to restrain the nobility's local power[43] deserves serious consideration especially when the example of Bavaria is recalled. The Bavarian dukes were able to influence what happened to the peasants by the treatment of their own large peasantry (*Urbarsbauern*) and by controlling the nobility, while in east Germany territorial lords had to follow standards set by the nobility, notwithstanding that peasants on the estates of territorial lords with demesnes (*Domänenbauern*) were in general better off than private peasants. But even in this respect much more information is needed. Until recently, it was assumed that the status of peasants in east Prussia improved, when their labour services were changed into money rent (*Hochzinser*). Now, a detailed analysis of the Prussian duke's demesne economy has shown that these changes took place when prices for cereals were low, and payers of rent were made to do labour services (to become *Scharwerksbauern*) when prices once rose again.[43] This means that in times of good prices peasants were forced to work the demesne instead of their own fields, and in times of low prices they had to bear the risks of the market. In any case, they were not able to exploit profitable situations. More than anything else, the Prussian duke's rational administration demonstrates that money rent is by no means an unequivocal sign of peasant freedom; in the Prussian case fundamental peasant unfreedom is evident, which subordinated the peasant to the changing interests of lords.

This comparison leads on to a further observation. It does not seem helpful to term both late medieval personal serfdom and early modern hereditary serfdom as 'second serfdom', as has been suggested, for neither of them corresponded to the system of peasant dependence on high medieval manorial estates. This was characterized by independent peasant economies at the periphery and the personal dependence of *homines proprii* at the centre. With east Elbian large-scale farming, just the opposite is true: the

---

[43] I. Wallerstein, *The Modern World-System: Capitalist Agriculture and the Origins of the European World-Economy in the Sixteenth Century* (New York and London, 1974), pp. 310–12.

personal dependence of the peasants was much more oppressive than the dependence of the day labourer, for it endangered their economic independence by diverting their labour from their holdings. In contrast, an independent peasant economy was typical of south-west Germany's ossified system of manorial estates, whose owners contented themselves with part of the peasants' yields as rent in kind and money.

The differences in a chronological context between late medieval personal serfdom and early modern hereditary serfdom, cannot be assimilated into one illustration of German backwardness (*Verspätungen*): they point to different functions. In the imperial context, new forms of peasant unfreedom, which developed to overcome the 'crisis of the fourteenth century', contributed to the emergence of political power in territorial states. East Elbian hereditary serfdom was not caused by economic and demographic crisis, but rather by new economic opportunities arising out of a new international division of labour originating in fifteenth-century western Europe, but immensely strengthened by the European expansion of the sixteenth century.[44] The same process which robbed upper Germany of its prominent role in European industry and trade promoted the emergence of unfree agricultural labour in the Baltic countries. North-west European capitalist labour relations did not immediately alter 'feudal' labour relations in these countries. At first, landlords developed an interest in trade, and only tried to enlarge their amount of marketable grain by obliging their peasants to sell their harvests to them, rather than to the towns – often for a lower price. The second step was to extend the demesnes and fully appropriate the peasants' labour in the seventeenth century: the peasants' services were calculated and became part of the estate's value. Where peasant services could not be calculated, because they were arbitrary, everything above that necessary for the peasant family's subsistence and the keeping of its holding, was counted as the lord's income.[45]

---

[44] M. North, *Die Amtswirtschaften von Osterode und Soldau: Vergleichende Untersuchungen zur Wirtschaft des frühmodernen Staates am Beispiel des Herzogtums Preussen in der zweiten Hälfte des 16. und der ersten Hälfte des 17. Jahrhunderts* (forthcoming).

[45] For a good example, see W. Abel, *Geschichte der deutschen Landwirtschaft* (Stuttgart, 1962), pp. 192 ff. The rather similar evaluation of land and of negro slaves in the American South comes to mind.

Having surveyed the conditions of east Elbian hereditary serfdom, doubts may arise whether these 'relations of production' can justly be termed 'feudal'. Under the rule of hereditary serfdom the peasant was no longer an independent producer: he provided only for his own subsistence and therefore could not get more out of his work than a wage labourer. Thus, he was subordinated to his lord's capitalist interests by 'extra-economic coercion' – but the notion of 'unfreedom' alone cannot define 'feudal relations of production'.

11. *Time, Space and Use in Early Russia*

R. E. F. SMITH

One consequence of the outbreak of the Great War was that Jane Harrison, a Cambridge classicist, started to learn Russian. Within a few weeks she drafted the outline of a paper subsequently delivered at the Heretics Club.[1] She argued that a 'people's philosophy of life is, if you will hunt for it, always to be found in its language, and found most surely because expressed unconsciously'.[2] Her brief acquaintance with Russian had convinced her of the central difference between tense and verbal aspect:

Tense gives the order of time, aspect gives quality of action . . . The singular, the characteristic trait of the Russian language is, not that it has a perfective – we all have that – but that it clings to the imperfective, at all costs, even at the cost of having laboriously to create a new form . . . Reason has little use for the imperfective, but emotion, sympathy hungers after it.[3]

This romantic, but stimulating interpretation of Russian, however, was pursued still further. Russian was weak in tenses 'because the time-interest is not in the first plane. Russia lives *sub specie aeternitatis*', she wrote almost on the eve of the cataclysm of 1917.[4] Jane Harrison's argument may be challenged by modern linguists; the tenses in Russian are perhaps less well represented morphologically than in some other languages, but time can be expressed by means other than verb-forms.[5] Linguistic arguments apart, is there any evidence that Russia lived *sub specie aeternitatis*? What time-concepts existed there, if any?

Let us first look at the terms used for various units of time. This

---

[1] Jane E. Harrison, *Russia and the Russian Verb* (Cambridge, 1915).
[2] *Ibid.*, p. 5.   [3] *Ibid.*, pp. 7, 9.   [4] *Ibid.*, p. 11.
[5] For a recent discussion, see F. F. Avdeev, 'O vtorichnykh funktsiyakh yazykovykh znakov v svyazi s voprosom o funktsionirovanii glagol'nykh kategorii vida i vremeni' [On Secondary Functions of Language Signs in Relation to the Functioning of the Verbal Categories of Aspect and Time], *Acta et commentationes Universitatis Tartuensis*, fasc. 439 (Tartu, 1978), pp. 10–23.

may help to make the idea of 'eternal Russia' at least somewhat more precise by indicating areas where eternity or timelessness did not apply. Perhaps we can then go a little further by examining terms for another basic element of social activities, space. The terms for these and some other measurements (money, for example) may illuminate the Russian 'philosophy of life', in the broad sense. The material is certainly 'expressed unconsciously'; it is therefore likely to be reliable and, moreover, to help overcome the often profound disjunction between the literate and the mass, the document and the deed, which continually faces us in studying early Russia.

Karamzin noted that 'the Slavs, without being literate, had some acquaintance with arithmetic and chronology. Housekeeping, war and trade led them to complex calculation . . .'.[6] The term 'time' (*veremya, vremya*), as might be expected, covered hour (*chas*), day (*d'n'*, later *den'*), month (*mesyats*) and year (*leto*) according to an eleventh-century source.[7] But by the twelfth century 'time' also indicated especially the right time, the season: 'in spring is not the time to fight'.[8]

'Year' was represented by two words. *Leto* meant time in general (it was used to translate Greek *chronos*), but it also commonly meant 'summer' as a state or period. *God*, on the other hand, sometimes also meant an indefinite time, a period or a term, as well as 'age' (and sometimes translated Greek *hora* and *kairos*).[9] In the Novgorod letters on birch bark *god* (and the related *godina*) seem to mean 'time', 'period'.[10] *God* also meant 'measure', 'limit' in some contexts. 'Do not drink without limit

6 N. Karamzin, *Istoriya Gosudarstva rossiiskago* [A History of the Russian State], 3rd edn, 12 vols. (St Petersburg, 1830–1), i, p. 81.

7 *Izbornik 1073 g.* [The 1073 Miscellany] (St Petersburg, 1880), p. 232; D. Prozorovskii, 'O Slavyano-Russkom do khristianskom schislenii vremeni' [On Pre-Christian Slavonic-Russian Calculation of Time], in *Trudy VIII arkheologicheskago s"ezda* [Proceedings of the Eighth Archaeological Congress], 4 vols. (St Petersburg, 1892–7), iii, p. 200, listed 'centuries' and 'weeks' as well for pre-Christian times.

8 *Polnoe sobranie russkikh letopisei* [Complete Collection of Russian Chronicles], ii (1103). Cf. the aphorism 'Time beautifies, lack of time ages': M. I. Mikhel'son, *Russkaya mysl' i rech'* [Russian Thought and Speech], fasc. i (St Petersburg, 1902), p. 126.

9 M. Vasmer, *Etimologicheskii slovar' russkogo yazyka* [Russian Etymological Dictionary], 3 vols. (Moscow, 1964), i, p. 426.

10 A. V. Artsikhovskii, *Novgorodskie gramoty na bereste* [Novgorod Birch-Bark Charters] (Moscow, 1954), nos. 68 (thirteenth century), 19 (fifteenth century).

(*bez goda*) but enough and not to drunkenness' urged an early churchman.[11] In some translations of the Greek testaments, however, both *godina* (and, sometimes, *god*) and *chas* were used to translate Greek *hora*.[12] But while the former had the sense of both 'hour' and a particular 'time', the latter meant 'moment', 'instant'.[13]

Semantically, therefore, 'time', at least in the sense of right time, had some analogies with 'year'. Both were rewarding. The root appears in the modern Russian for 'weather' (*pogoda*) and 'benefit', 'advantage' (*vygoda*).[14] It is also the root of the word for 'appurtenance' (*ugod'e*), meaning any area, other than the standard elements of the farm unit, giving income, usually in kind; it covered sites for the extraction of sand or clay, fisheries or hunting areas and even mills.[15] *God*, therefore, probably indicated the time measured from harvest to harvest. The church year, however, started from March.[16] The Byzantine year had commenced with September. This meant that the year starting in March would have six months either before (March to August) or after (September to February) the Byzantine year; the former is referred to as the older or ultra-March year, the latter as the younger, or simply the March year.[17] Both forms of dating are found in the Russian chronicles. The ultra-March year was used from early in the twelfth century and disappeared from almost all chronicles in the

11 'Pouchenie Arkhiepiskopa Luki k bratii' [Instruction of Archbishop Luke to the Brethren], in *Russkiya dostopamyatnosti* [Russian Memorials], 4 vols. (Moscow, 1877–83), i, p. 10.

12 A. S. L'vov, *Ocherki po leksike pamyatnikov staroslavyanskoi pis'mennosti* [Essays on the Vocabulary of Old Slavonic Documentary Materials] (Moscow, 1966), pp. 259–61, 266.

13 *Ibid.*, p. 262. Cf. modern Russian *totchas, seichas* 'this instant', 'right away', and (from *god*) *togda* 'then', *kogda* 'when', etc.

14 Vasmer, *Etimologicheskii slovar' russkogo yazyka*, i, p. 426.

15 I. I. Sreznevskii, *Materialy dlya slovarya drevne-russkago yazyka* [Materials for an Old Russian Dictionary], 3 vols. (St Petersburg, 1893–1903), i, col. 1135. See also pp. 285–6, nn. 66, 72 below on *mesto*.

16 N. G. Berezhkov, *Khronologiya russkogo letopisaniya* [The Chronology of Russian Chronical-Writing] (Moscow, 1963), p. 36; S. I. Seleshnikov, *Istoriya kalendarya i khronologiya* [A History of the Calendar and Chronology], 2nd edn (Moscow, 1972), pp. 154, 156.

17 N. V. Stepanov, 'Kalendarno-khronologicheskii spravochnik' [A Calendrical and Chronological Guide], in *Chteniya v Moskovskom obshchestve istorii i drevnostei rossiiskikh* [Readings at the Moscow Society of History and Russian Antiquities] (Moscow, 1917), bk 1.

early fourteenth century.[18] Apparently it is not known whether the ultra-March year was used other than in chronicles.[19] The year starting with September in Russia dates from 1492 and lasted until Peter I introduced the Julian calendar on 1 January 1700.[20]

The year was divided into months; the month (*mesyats*, 'moon') was the lunar month among all Slavs. The Ostromir Gospel of 1144 gives Old Russian, not borrowed, names for two, but other sources supply terms for twelve or, possibly, thirteen months.[21] There was at least one other Old Russian name (*veres*, 'heather') in addition to the twelve or thirteen referred to.[22] Perhaps it is wrong to believe that the pre-Christian Slav year had twelve months; it seems more reasonable to assume that it had thirteen.[23] The meanings of the old names are varied and obscure, but most appear to refer to vegetation (*berezozol*, birch; *travnyi*, grass; *revun*, rowan) or natural conditions (*sukhii*, dry; *studenyi*, cold); one is the name of an insect (*izok*, cricket). After the official conversion to Christianity in 988, the Graeco-Latin names of the twelve months were introduced at least in formal documents. It is noteworthy that there is some lack of equivalence between the two sets of terms: *listopad* meant either October or November; *prosinets* either December or January (between these was a month called *gruden*, a term which probably indicated the first thin snow covering of the winter road).[24] The old name for February, *sechen'* (cf. *sech'*, to chop, cut), probably referred to the ringing of trees to

---

[18] Berezhkov, *Khronologiya russkogo letopisaniya*, pp. 16–18.

[19] E. I. Kamentseva, *Khronologiya* [Chronology] (Moscow, 1967), p. 56.

[20] Seleshnikov, *Istoriya kalendarya i khronologiya*, p. 157; *Polnoe sobranie zakonov* [Complete Collection of Laws], 45 vols. in 48 (St Petersburg, 1830), iii, no, 1736.

[21] *Ostromirovo evangelie, 1056–1057* [The Ostromir Gospels, 1056–1057] (St Petersburg, 1843), gives *prosinets* and *zarev*. Karamzin, *Istoriya Gosudarstva rossiiskago*, i, p. 81; Prozorovskii, 'O Slavyano-Russkom do khristianskom schislenii vremeni', p. 206.

[22] F. von Miklosich, 'Die slavischen Monatsnamen', *Denkschriften der kaiserlichen Akademie der Wissenschaften. Philosophisch-historische Classe*, xvii (1868), pp. 1–32, lists the names in various Slavonic and a number of other languages. See also M. P. Nilsson, *Primitive Time-Reckoning* (Skrifter utgivna av humanistiska vetenskapssamfundet i Lund, 1920), pp. 284–8.

[23] Prozorovskii, 'O Slavyano-Ruskom do khristianskom schislenii vremeni', p. 206. Seleshnikov, *Istoriya kalendarya i khronologiya*, pp. 153–4, gives nine additional names, but these do not appear to be documented for Old Russian. There were some additional regional Russian names recorded in the nineteenth century.

[24] Karamzin, *Istoriya Gosudarstva rossiiskago*, i, n. 159.

be burnt in the slash and burn system. *Berezozol'* (cf. *bereza*, birch; *zola*, ashes – an alternative but improbable derivation suggests *ol''*, ale, i.e. birch-sap), April, may have indicated when the burning took place. When slash and burn was practised in the nineteenth and twentieth centuries, however, trees were cut in May or June and the trees left at least till early spring. This change occurred because slash and burn then had to be accommodated in the gaps in the calendar of work of the field system.

The week (*nedelya*) was a post-conversion phenomenon.[25] The term means rest-day or Sabbath; in a number of Slav languages other than Russian it signifies Sunday, but in Russian *voskresen'e*, 'resurrection', came to have that meaning only some time after the conversion to Christianity.[26] *Nedelya* long continued to be used in the sense of 'Sunday', as at least one text of an eleventh-century source makes clear: 'For *nedelya* is not called *nedelya*, as you say, but the first day of the whole week is [so] called: for Christ our Lord arose from the dead on that day and it is called Sunday (*voskresnyi den'*, lit. Resurrection day), the second day is called Monday . . .'.[27] Possibly the term *sedmitsa* (from *sedm'*, seven) may have been a pre-Christian word. The conversion of Slavs certainly brought changes in both the calendar and the related terminology, but the statement by Herbordus that Otto of Bamberg taught the Slav tribes he had converted in Pomerania in 1124 the church festivals and also 'the distribution of the months and the organization of the whole year according to the Christians' was probably an overstatement.[28]

The days of the week in Russian have names mostly indicating

[25] F. von Miklosich, 'Die christliche Terminologie der Slaven', *Denkschriften der kaiserlichen Akademie der Wissenschaften. Philosophisch-historische Classe.*, xxiv (1876).

[26] A. P. Pronshtein and V. Ya. Kiyashko, *Khronologiya* [Chronology] (Moscow, 1981), p. 86, state that *voskresen'e* 'began to be used to signify the rest day only in the sixteenth century'; they adduce no evidence. This view appears mistaken.

[27] Feodosii Pecherskii (d. 1074), text given in I. P. Eremin, 'Literaturnoe nasledie Feodosiya Pecherskogo' [The Literary Heritage of Feodosii Pecherskii], in *Trudy Otdela drevne-russkoi literatury* [Proceedings of the Old Russian Literature Section] (Leningrad, 1947), v, pp. 159–84, at p. 168.

[28] *Herbordi dialogus de vita Ottonis episcopi Babenbergensis*, ii. 17 (ed. R. Köpke, Monumenta Germaniae Historica, Scriptores Rerum Germanicarum in usum scholarum, xxxiii, Hanover, 1868, p. 67).

their order: 'after Sunday' (*ponedel'nik*, Monday), 'second day' (*vtornik*, Tuesday), 'middle day' (*sreda*, Wednesday), 'fourth day' (*chetverg*, Thursday), 'fifth one' (*pyatnitsa*, Friday), Sabbath (*subbota*, Saturday). This appears to be a learned invention, but, of course, one not from the Latin-based terms used in West European languages.[29] Some believe this peculiar system denies any borrowing.[30] Earlier, there may have been a link between the names of the seven main gods (Svarog, Dazhd'bog, Perun, Kh"rs, Stribog, Simar'gl, Mokosh') and a seven-day period.[31]

The period of twenty-four hours came to be called *sutki* (lit. 'contact', 'touching', 'junction' of night and day; from *tykati*, 'to push'), but probably not earlier than the seventeenth century.[32] It is significant that a term probably confused with this, though from a different root (*tok*, 'flow'), had previously been used in the spatial sense. In 1499, for example, a monk claimed he had established a peasant 'in the forest at the site on the junction (*v sutokekh*) between the rivers Vorya and Talitsa'.[33]

It appears, therefore, that the pre-Christian East Slavs had a calendar which was not highly formalized. The year and especially the months were indicated by terms directly related to the environment of nature and work; since the environment changed with location and over time, the month names were also sometimes adjusted. Designations were approximate, not at all absolute. The subdivisions of months were days and nights, but probably not weeks.

Christianity, however, stressed the eternal verities and was concerned with both worldly and other-worldly time. The church in this world needed to regulate the hours of the day, and night, to ensure that its offices were performed; and it had to establish the

---

[29] P. Skok, 'La semaine slave', *Revue des études slaves*, v (1925), pp. 14–23, and the note by N. Durnovo, in *Revue des études slaves*, vi (1926), pp. 107–8.

[30] Prozorovskii, 'O Slavyano-Russkom do khristianskom schislenii vremeni', pp. 200, 216.

[31] *Ibid.*, p. 216.

[32] Prozorovskii, 'O starinnom russkom schislenii chasov' ['On the Old Russian Calculation of the Hours'], in *Trudy II arkheologicheskago s"ezda* [Proceedings of the Second Archaeological Congress], 2 vols. (St Petersburg, 1876–81), fasc. ii, section iv, pp. 161–2; R. M. Tseitlin, in *Uchenye zapiski Instituta slavyanovedeniya*, xvii (1959), pp. 234–5.

[33] *Akty sotsial'no-ekonomicheskoi istorii severovostochnoi Rusi* [Documents on the Social and Economic History of North-East Rus'], ed. B. D. Grekov and L. V. Cherepnin, 3 vols. (Moscow, 1952–64), i, no. 623.

annual dates of the church festivals. It also had duties involving writing chronicles and other official records for the princes; these demanded more precise, and also longer, versions of time. In 1136 a deacon in a Novgorod monastery, Kirik, wrote an 'Instruction by Which a Man May Know the Numbers of All Years'.[34]

As regards the smaller division of time, however, there was no uniform system of hours in early Russia. Church calendars had two variants. The first had the length of the day and night (twelve 'hours' each) determined for a whole month with a difference of one hour from the preceding month to allow for the changing length of daylight; this was taken from a church regulation (*typikon*) of the Jerusalem monastery of St Savva the Blessed, and so retained the Jerusalem time with daylight varying from fifteen to nine clock-hours.[35] This was only subsequently adjusted to Russian conditions with maxima of seventeen and seven hours.[36] The second variant was arranged by half-months, but with the same difference of one hour between one another. There were local variations in the hours established by the church; the Novgorod half-monthly variant started a day earlier than that used in Moscow where, in the seventeenth century, the civil hours were the same as those of the church.[37] In the fifteenth century, however, 'the Moscow count of hours of the day differed from that of the sixteenth and seventeenth centuries; while in the sixteenth century the Novgorod hours of the night did not coincide with those in Moscow'.[38] The 'day' was divided into four periods each of three hours: morning, the first half of the day, the second half and evening; when the 'day' started, however, is sometimes unclear. Matins for the following day was sometimes celebrated during, or even at the start of, the night.

Such variations and obscurities were not restricted to church hours. Days starting from daylight are sometimes found in the

[34] On Kirik, see *Trudy i letopisi Obshchestva istorii i drevnostei rossiiskikh* [*Proceedings and Annals of the Society of History and Russian Antiquities*], pt iv (1828), bk 1, pp. 122–9. Text in *Istoriko-matematicheski issledovaniya* [Research on the History of Mathematics], fasc. vi (Moscow, 1953), pp. 171–91.

[35] Prozorovskii, 'O starinnom russkom schislenii chasov', p. 106.

[36] A detailed tabulation of this variant, with nineteenth-century clock hour equivalents, is given in Kamentseva, *Khronologiya*, pp. 106–9.

[37] Prozorovskii, 'O starinnom russkom schislenii chasov', pp. 107–8, 162.

[38] *Ibid.*, p. 162.

chronicles.[39] On other occasions the day seems to have started at night.[40] Prozorovskii concluded that the twenty-four hours started during the night:

> the second part of which was also the time for matins. Some-times the hours of the first part of the night were counted with the following day of twenty-four hours, because the event continued in the second part, or because it reached the end of the first part and almost coincided with the second.[41]

The hour (*chas*) was divided, at least in the seventeenth century, into six sub-units (called, in the singular, *chasovets*) of ten minutes or seventy-two points (*tochki*). Such sub-units were apparently equated with money units for calculations. There were 432 points in an hour, just as there were 432 dengas in a sixteenth-century Novgorod ruble. This was probably not chance; bead-boards adapted for calculating money (and land areas) could then be used for calculating time.[42] It may, therefore, be significant that the sixfold division of the hour is found in a trade manual (*torgovaya kniga*) of the sixteenth century.[43] There can have been few cases where production or commerce demanded accuracy to within an hour, however. Perhaps the earliest occurrence was when, in the mid-seventeenth century, the church came so to dominate society for a brief period that it extended its time-keeping outside the church. The reforming zeal of some church leaders led to attempts to ensure attendance at church and to control the consumption of drink in Russia. The Patriarch urged that:

> on Saturday evening they are to cease from any work . . . three hours before night and to stop trading, close the market rows and the baths where they pay . . . and people of all ranks are not to go to the baths; and in the morning, on Sunday, the rows are not to be opened before five o'clock in the day and nothing is to be dealt in; when four hours of the day are past, at the start

[39] *Ibid.*, p. 165 (18 Apr. 1299, 19 May 1389, 5 Apr. 1472, 3 Dec. 1533).

[40] *Ibid.*, p. 165 (24 Feb. 1095, 5 Sept. 1484, 7 Mar. 1490, 8 Nov. 1491, 11 Oct. 1554).

[41] *Ibid.*

[42] On such boards, see I. G. Spasskii, 'Proiskhozhdenie i istoriya russkikh schetov', *Istoriko-matematicheskie issledovaniya* [Origin and History of Russian Counting Frames, Research on the History of Mathematics], (Moscow, 1952), fasc. v, pp. 269–420.

[43] 'Torgovaya kniga 1575 i 1610 g. po sp. XVII v.' [The 1575 and 1610 Trade Book in a Seventeenth-century Version], *Zapiski Otdeleniya russkoi i slavyanskoi arkheologii Arkhoeologicheskago obshchestva*, i, pt 3 (1851), pp. 106–39.

of the fifth they are to open the rows and to trade in all sorts of goods and foodstuffs . . . And in winter-time, when there are seven hours in the day, on Sunday they are to trade at the start of the fourth hour of the day; and on Saturday evening to cease from any work an hour before night.[44]

Sales at drink-shops were restricted to certain days and hours. How could the market-traders, the drinkers, or even the drink-shop officials have known when it was opening time?

Clocks had been known in Russia from early in the fifteenth century. In 1404 Lazar' the Serbian, a monk from Mount Athos, had constructed a clock in the Moscow Kremlin, for which the Grand Prince paid him an enormous sum, more than 150 rubles.[45] 'This hour-marker (*chasnik*) is called an hour-measure (*chasomer'e*); each hour a hammer strikes the bell, measuring and counting the hours of the night and of the day', wrote a chronicler.[46] 'No man strikes it, but it is somehow wondrous strangely fashioned to look like a man and sound and move of itself, by man's cunning, with great invention and cleverness'. In a sixteenth-century illuminated manuscript this clock is shown with a large central weight and two smaller ones on either side. The dial of the clock in the illustration evidently rotated; it has no hand, but twelve numerals (indicated by letters), and is surmounted by a large hammer; the bell is apparently inaccessible in a separate bell-tower.[47] The original, about a century and a half before this fanciful illustration, probably had no dial, but simply struck the hours. In 1436, Evfimii, archbishop of Novgorod, built a striking clock over his palace.[48] In 1477 another archbishop of Novgorod, Feofil, sent a striking clock to Pskov and subsequently had it erected there.[49] Such fifteenth-century clocks were exceptional

---

[44] *Akty Arkheograficheskoi ekspeditsii* [Documents of the Archaeographic Expedition], 4 vols. (St Petersburg, 1836), iv, no. 324 (14 July 1647).

[45] About this date a village with several hamlets and clearances might cost as much as 20 rubles: *Akty sotsial'no-ekonomicheskoi istorii severovostochnoi Rusi*, i, nos. 19, 25.

[46] *Polnoe sobranie russkikh letopisei*, xviii, p. 281.

[47] The illustration has often been reproduced; see *Istoriya Moskvy* [A History of Moscow], ed. S. V. Bakhrushin *et al.*, 2 vols. (Moscow, 1952–3), i, p. 69; *Ocherki russkoi kul'tury, XIII–XV vekov* [Outlines of Russian Culture, Thirteenth to Fifteenth Centuries], 2 pts (Moscow, 1969–70), pt 1, p. 229.

[48] *Polnoe sobranie russkikh letopisei*, iii, p. 112.

[49] *Pskovskie letopisi* [Pskov Chronicles], (Moscow, 1941–55), fasc. i; *Polnoe sobranie russkikh letopisei*, iv, p. 254.

innovations which demonstrated wealth and prestige. They were probably restricted to locations such as Moscow and Novgorod where wealth and foreign influence were concentrated, but they also enabled native clock-makers to be trained. Names of some Russian clock-makers are known from the sixteenth and seventeenth centuries and there was even a Russian responsible for a clock in Isfahan in 1623.[50]

Watches were even rarer than clocks. In the 1580s Ivan IV had a brass watch 'like a book'.[51] Neither watches nor clocks (both are designated by the same term in Russian) could be widespread in Russia at this time because of the variations in the length of hours; 'they would have been suited to the Novgorod system, but this had ceased before the hour-measurers began to be disseminated'.[52]

Precise measurement of time within the day, then, was limited to the church until the seventeenth century and even then was not greatly needed by the general populace. Clocks were an ostentatious luxury. A wider section of the populace would hear the church bell, not see a dial, even when there was one.

The only hint of attempts to measure time within daylight which might possibly have been at all common seems to be the existence of simple portable sundials. A point of light from the sun passed through a small hole and was aligned with a set mark; a suspended thread, held taut by a small weight, then indicated the hour on a scale. Two types of such dials were common, one, designed to measure a seventeen-hour day, was in cast copper; central European Russia has, approximately, a seventeen-hour day in June.[53] This type was still used by shepherds in the Vladimir area in the late nineteenth century, but may have been in use as early as the late seventeenth century. It has been suggested that it is a crude version of a remote, possibly Arab, original.[54] The other type, a wooden triangle with large central hole, measured a nineteen-hour day at the maximum. Only ethnographic examples of this type are known and these are from the nineteenth century.

[50] *Khozhenie kuptsa Fedota Kotiva v Persiyu* [The Journey of the Merchant Fedot Kotov to Persia] (Moscow, 1958), p. 78.

[51] Prozorovskii, 'O starinnom russkom schislenii chasov', p. 169.

[52] *Ibid.*

[53] V. N. Shchepkin, 'Russkie solnechnye chasy XVII veka' [Seventeenth-Century Russian Sun Clocks], *Drevnosti: Trudy Imp. Moskovskago arkheologicheskago obshchestva*, xviii (1901), pp. 43–8.

[54] *Ibid.*, p. 48.

It seems unlikely that either type was ever very common. It has been suggested that the first type was somewhat widespread, since a mould implies several copies.[55] On the other hand, the simpler second type, made of readily available wood, might be expected to be commoner. The difficulty is to envisage circumstances in early Russia in which, say, shepherds might need to know the time so accurately.

Calendars, however, were useful, if not essential, to a wider section of the population. Peasants dispersed in tiny hamlets may have had a few occasions for communal or social activities, but the latter were thereby all the more important. Traditional dates, at least for certain farm work, for local feasts and for the commemoration of parents, had to be observed.

Russian wooden calendars have survived. They are usually fairly solid sticks one or two feet long, multi-sided, with notches along the edges to indicate the days; significant days are marked by letters or signs on the flat sides. Usually on such tally-sticks the year started with March or September.[56] The Finns of European Russia used such tallies before the mid-fourteenth century when Stefan of Perm' converted the local Finns to Christianity and introduced the calendar starting with March.[57] The saints' days marked are overwhelmingly pre-eighteenth century; and the signs used coincide with those on lead seals dated from the tenth to the fourteenth centuries and suggest that the calendars were elaborated before the Mongol invasions.[58] Probably the spread of printed calendars in the eighteenth century resulted in the tallies not developing, but continuing to show the earlier stage of the calendar.

Characteristically, the greatest number of festivals marked on the tallies fall in the winter and the fewest in the spring and summer: 'This proves the peasant nature of the calendars, since

[55] *Ibid.*, p. 45.

[56] N. A. Konstantinov, 'Narodnye reznye kalendari' [Folk Calendar-Tallies], *Sbornik Muzeya antropologii i etnografii*, xx (1961), pp. 84–113. One 'calendar' on a pot has also survived: B. A. Rybakov, 'Kalendar' IV v. iz zemli polyan' [A Fourth-Century Calendar from the Area of the Polyane], *Sovetskaya arkheologiya* (1962), no. 4, pp. 66–89.

[57] P. I. Savvaitov, 'O zyryanskikh derevyannykh kalendaryakh' [Zyryan Wooden Calendars], in *Trudy I arkheologicheskago s"ezda* [Proceedings of the First Archaeological Congress], 2 vols. (St Petersburg, 1871), ii, p. 411.

[58] Konstantinov, 'Narodnye reznye kalendari', pp. 88–90.

fewer festivals are indicated for the period of most intense agricultural work (April, June, July) and most in the winter which is not filled with intensive agricultural labour (November, December).'[59] It also raises the question of how far the Christian calendar was continuing pre-Christian Slav festivals, the majority of which occur in the winter cycle of rituals.[60] The marks used were either Cyrillic, or derived from a Cypriot syllabary, or pictograms; almost half of the latter were connected with agricultural work.[61] Much remains obscure about these objects; their earliest versions omit the dates of some saints popular in Russia: Boris, Gleb, the spring Nicholas and Paraskeva, for example.[62] The majority of feasts marked are from the fourth century and almost all are pre-thirteenth century. By that time local variants had been elaborated; but who carried out such work? If, as seems likely, monks or priests were responsible, why were agricultural elements included and, indeed, indicated by pictograms, not Cyrillic letters? We have here, it seems, an amalgam of clerical and popular cultural elements and this raises questions, especially about the latter, in early Russia.

Terms indicating aspects of time, as well as the artefacts relating to time, thus suggest that the church was mainly concerned in this aspect of culture. No regulation of time appears in Ivan IV's reforms of the mid-sixteenth century. Only in the late sixteenth to seventeenth centuries are there indications that some more precise measurement of time (hours and their subdivisions) was applied in trade and consumption. The calendar was adjusted under Peter the Great who introduced the Julian Calendar from 1 January 1700. The tally-calendars imply, as one would expect, that peasants were more concerned with the days of the year than with smaller units of time.

Such evidence suggests that in early Russia the needs arising from practical concerns in the household, the market or the centralizing administration were the main constraints which largely determined what was measured and how. That world had

[59] *Ibid.*, p. 91.

[60] See V. I. Chicherov, *Zimnii period russkogo narodnogo zemledel'cheskogo kalendarya XVI–XIX vekov* [The Agricultural Winter Folk Calendar in Sixteenth- to Nineteenth-Century Russia] (Moscow, 1957); V. Ya. Propp, *Russkie agrarnye prazdniki* [Russian Agrarian Festivals] (Leningrad, 1963).

[61] Konstantinov, 'Narodnye reznye kalendari', pp. 107–13.

[62] *Ibid.*, p. 87.

little use for the abstract concepts of time and space which we require; but even so, some small element of abstraction was present. Pipes has pointed out that the peasant 'had great difficulty understanding "distance", unless it was translated into so many units of *versta*, the Russian counterpart of a kilometre, the length of which he could visualize'.[63] But to visualize is a limited form of abstract thought; and did the peasant visualize a *versta* as distance or as time? Were the two concepts then differentiated?

In modern Russian there is a term which means 'while' or 'until'. It is now somewhat old-fashioned or used only in popular speech. In Old Russian this term retained its literal meaning, 'to those places', (*pokamest*, from *mesto* 'place'), at least in some contexts: 'I have given the establishment of the Holy Saviour . . . my heritable waste, the Spaskoe ['Saviour'] site . . . with everything, wherever (*pokamest*) the plough has gone and the scythe, as well as the wild bee area'.[64] In general, however, the temporal rather than the spatial meaning of this term is attested earlier. 'I have given those villages and the property to St Basil, to the abbot and the brethren, for his soul and for as long as (*pokamest*) that holy cloister shall stand'.[65] Clearly, here the term *mesto* lacks its spatial meaning; perhaps the nearest parallel in English would be 'point' (we can have both 'to the point where' and 'to the point when'). In Russian of the thirteenth to late seventeenth centuries there were a number of other compound adverbial or prepositional expressions which involved *mesto*, and many examples have temporal, not spatial, meaning.[66]

As a noun *mesto* had and has a variety of spatial meanings: 'an (open) space', 'locality', 'region'; 'place' in order of rank etc.; 'spot' as both place and mark; 'seat' and, in dialect, 'bed',

[63] R. Pipes, *Russia under the Old Regime* (London, 1974), p. 157.

[64] Sreznevskii, *Materialy dlya slovarya drevne-russkago yazyka*, ii, col. 1102 (*circa* 1400). *Akty yuridicheskie* [Juridical Documents] (St Petersburg, 1838), p. 147 (1563), has a similar phrase.

[65] Sreznevskii, *Materialy dlya slovarya drevne-russkago yazyka*, ii, cols. 1252–3.

[66] See *ibid.*, col. 247; A. Dyuvernua, *Materialy dlya slovarya drevne-russkago yazyka* [Materials for a Dictionary of Old Russian] (Moscow, 1894), pp. 100–1. Similar usage of compound phrases with *mesto* having no semantic value have survived to the present day: L. A. Ivashko, 'O znacheniyakh slova *mesto* v severno-russkikh govorakh' [The Meanings of *mesto* in North Russian Dialects], in *Iz istorii slov i slovarei* [On the history of Words and Dictionaries], ed. B. A. Larin (Leningrad, 1963), p. 52.

'bedclothes'.[67] Of particular interest are contexts where it indicates an area of economic value. A chronicle entry for 947 noted that Ol'ga went to Novgorod establishing rents and tributes 'and her hunting grounds are throughout the whole land, her signs and places and halts'.[68] Such 'places' were evidently particular localities or, more likely, areas used for specific purposes, especially gathering or hunting. In the late 1350s or 1360s, for example, a prince donated to bishop Basil 'a place on the river Kishnya, a purchase and private wild bee land of the first bishops; in his village are sixty rezankas and income from justice and beavers'.[69] The document later adds that 'in the river Kishnya are beavers', as if to stress the importance of this valuable animal. That 'places' were of value is shown by efforts in the early fourteenth century to prohibit outsiders entering them.[70] Late in the same century princely wills refer to 'remote places' (*ot"ezdnye mesta*) which again suggests gathering.[71] In the fifteenth to seventeenth centuries, however, the term is more frequently specified by an adjective indicating the type of place (forest, hay, salt, fish, mill; sometimes, too, in the sense of the site of a building: tenement, house, barn etc.).[72] Here, too, the stress seems to be on extractive activity, or on location in a more neutral sense.

Place, then, was, at least in some meanings, an area of a particular form of activity which was often extractive and thus reminds us of *ugod'e*[73] and the year (*god*). The term which came to

---

[67] Sreznevskii, *Materialy dlya slovarya drevne-russkago yazyka*, ii, cols. 245–7; Ivashko, 'O znacheniyakh slova *mesto*,' pp. 47–50.

[68] *Povest' vremennykh let*, ed. Adrianova-Peretts, i, p. 43.

[69] *Akty sotsial'no-ekonomicheskoi istorii severovostochnoi Rusi*, iii, no. 315; *ibid.*, no. 316 (1356–72) notes 'a place on the Don with income from justice and the beaver runs' also given to the bishop.

[70] Sreznevskii, *Materialy dlya slovarya drevne-russkago yazyka*, ii, col. 246.

[71] *Dukhovnye i dogovornye gramoty velikikh i udel'nykh knyazei XIV–XVIvv.* [Wills and Contracts of the Grand and Appanage Princes. Fourteenth to Sixteenth Centuries], ed. S. V. Bakhrushin (Moscow and Leningrad, 1950), no. 11 (1389), no. 12 (1389); the latter specified that the Mozhaisk area produced 167 rubles of income and the remote places there 68 rubles.

[72] G. E. Kochin, *Materialy dlya terminologicheskogo slovarya drevnei Rossii* [Materials for a Terminological Dictionary of Ancient Russia] (Leningrad, 1937), pp. 89–90. In a document of 1619 there is even the expression 'places of land' (*mesta zemli*), that is places of arable: N. P. Voskoboinikova, 'Rodovoi arkhiv krest'yanskoi sem'i Artem'evykh-Khlyzovykh' [The Archive of he Artem'ev-Khlyzov Peasant Family], *Arkheograficheskii ezhegodnik za 1966g.* [Archaeographic Annual for 1966] (Moscow, 1967), p. 390.

[73] See p. 275 and n. 15 above.

mean 'space' as an abstract concept in modern Russian (*prostran'stvo*) existed in early Russia, but had not then acquired its present meaning.[74] The root of the term (*storona*) meant simply 'side', 'part', 'land'.

Area was often indicated by reference to use (as in the spatial example with *pokamest* above); implements or their parts also provided terms indicating area (*sokha*; *luk*, 'bow', either for hunting or for the horse-harness; *obzha*, 'shaft' of a *sokha*). These terms do not seem always to have indicated a precise size. Sown areas were estimated in terms of the volume of seed required. Forest was either counted in terms of the areal *desyatina* (a 'tenth') or of the *versta*; in the latter case the unit of length was used alone, and no indication was given of the depth of such forest. Space (*prostran'stvo*) was here measured in terms of the primary meaning of its root (*storona*). Indeed, it seems that in so far as space was actually measured, rather than estimated, units of length were more frequent than those of area.

Measures of length were, in the main, of two types, but neither was standardized. The first was a vague indication such as a stone's throw, a bow-shot; the latter was at first indicated by the term 'shot' (*perestrel*) alone; later it was modified by the addition of 'bow' (*luchnyi*).[75] Rather unexpectedly, in one instance a stone's throw was one and a half bow-shots.[76] Terms such as *pop'rishche* (a 'run') were used to indicate what might be thought to be precise distances, but there are clearly considerable differences in different sources; this term was equated both with two-thirds of a versta and with one and a half verstas.[77] It was sometimes used to translate Greek *milion*, and sometimes taken as a versta.[78] *Versta* itself derives from a root signifying 'turn' and seems to have meant a furlong in the sense of a length worked when tilling; when it became established as a standard measure of distance, however, it amounted to two-thirds of a mile. These terms all represent bodily actions.

The second type was used for shorter lengths and consisted of

[74] Sreznevskii, *Materialy dlya slovarya drevne-russkago yazyka*, ii, cols. 1579–80.
[75] Dyuvernua, *Materialy dlya slovarya drevne-russkago yazyka*, p. 134.
[76] *Polnoe sobranie russkikh letopisei*, ii (1234).
[77] Sreznevskii, *Materialy dlya slovarya drevne-russkago yazyka*, ii, cols. 1203–4.
[78] E. I. Kamentseva and N. V. Ustyugov, *Russkaya metrologiya* [Russian Metrology] (Moscow, 1965), pp. 24–5.

terms derived from parts of the body. The fathom or *sazhen'* (from *syagati*) was the length measured by the outstretched arms, but there was also a diagonal version measured from the toes of one foot to the outstretched fingers of the opposite hand.[79] The ell (*lokot'*), measured from the elbow to the fist, was a quarter of the fathom and was standardized as early as 1135 in Novgorod, no doubt because of the importance of trade, including imported textiles, there.[80] In the late fifteenth century, that is after Moscow's conquest of Novgorod, references to Moscow and Lübeck fathoms appear.[81] A sixteenth-century trade manual noted that the western merchants measured the ell 'along the back, but our custom is to measure by the selvedge'.[82] Trade with the east was more important than the western trade, however, for this terminology. In the late fifteenth century a new term for the ell came into Russian; this was *arshin*. It is Turkic in origin and at first related to cloth and silks from Kafa (Theodosia); within a century, however, it had largely displaced *lokot'* and became an established term in the mid-sixteenth-century reforms; it survived into modern times.[83]

There is a certain amount of evidence that even in the sixteenth century the *arshin* was used as a measure of length not only for textiles; but it seems to have become established as a general measure only in the following century and last of all in wholesale trade. Even then an important difference was that the old term for the ell (*lokot'*) continued to be used for locally produced textiles. This distinction between the use of *lokot'* for local and *arshin* for

---

[79] B. A. Rybakov, 'Russkie sistemy mer dliny XI–XVvv.' [Russian Systems of Measuring Length in the Eleventh to Fifteenth Centuries], *Sovetskaya etnografiya* (1949), no. 1, pp. 67–91. The *sazhen'* was standardized in modern times as 7 feet.

[80] M. P. Bulgakov, *Istoriya russkoi tserkvi* [History of the Russian Church], 12 vols. (St Petersburg, 1866–83), ii, p. 381. See also A. A. Tits, *Zagadki drevnerusskogo chertezha* [Enigmas in Old Russian Drawings] (Moscow, 1978), pp. 18–19, on the different lengths of the old fathom.

[81] G. Ya. Romanova, 'Iz istorii russkoi metrologicheskoi leksiki' [On the Vocabulary of Russian Metrology], in R. I. Avanesov *et al.* (eds.), *Voprosy slovoobrazovaniya i leksikologii drevnerusskogo yazyka* [Problems of Word-Formation and Lexicology in Old Russian] (Moscow, 1974), p. 236.

[82] Cited in *ibid.*

[83] I. N. Shmeleva, 'Leksika torgovoi knigi XVI veka' [The Vocabulary of a Sixteenth-Century Trade Book], *Uchenye zapiski Leningradskogo universiteta, seriya filologichenskikh nauk*, cclxvii (1960).

imported textiles has been noted from the mid-sixteenth century.[84] It is assumed that locally produced cloth was actually measured from elbow to fist and that the ell therefore survived because it continued to have practical use.

A smaller measure of length was the span (*pyad'*), measured between thumb and index finger. Two spans made an ell. There were, however, different spans in different areas and, in any event, this unit did not effectively survive the seventeenth century, at least as an official measure.

Space and distance, then, as reflected in the terms used, were either linked with parts of the body or with bodily activities, or, especially for larger units still, were expressed in imprecise units of time. The use of 'place' (*mesto*) in expressing time had a parallel but opposite usage in the miniatures which illustrated chronicles: the same illustration might depict incidents which occurred at different times. As with a modern strip cartoon (though without the separation into discrete spaces), time here has to be apprehended spatially.[85] In certain linguistic and visual contexts, therefore, the distinction between time and space was not made as sharply as might seem usual to us nowadays. This is no evidence, however, let alone proof, that the concepts of time and space were continually blurred. In most situations there was no need to demarcate time and space sharply; in practical terms it was likely to be a disadvantage, because of its unnecessary complexity. Even today, for most the wrist-watch chronometer with split-second timing is a status symbol rather than a practical instrument of daily life.

The terms for measurements of time and space before the sixteenth century varied from area to area, as did their objective meanings. On the basis of the measurements of surviving buildings it has been claimed that there existed two systems for measures of length: one in the Pskov-Novgorod area, the other in the Moscow-Vladimir-Chernigov area.[86] These ultimately derived from the size of the standard local brick. We have already seen that there were

---

[84] Romanova, 'Iz istorii russkoi metrologicheskoi leksiki', pp. 242–3.

[85] D. S. Likhachev, *Poetika Drevnerusskoi literatury* [The Poetics of Old Russian Literature] 3rd edn (Moscow, 1979), p. 38. Many examples are shown and discussed in O. I. Podobedova, *Miniatyury russkikh istoricheskikh rukopisei* [Russian Historical Manuscript Miniatures] (Moscow, 1965).

[86] Rybakov, 'Russkie sistemy mer dliny XI–XVvv.' pp. 73–4.

differences between the time systems of Novgorod and of Moscow. While the country had not been brought under a single rule and trade was weak, such regional variations are not likely to have proved a major difficulty. Once Moscow had established its dominance, however, regularization began; but this was a long drawn out process with implications for measurements not only of time and space, but of another aspect of trade – money.

The first reforms, in Moscow's attempt to regularize measures in the late fifteenth century, dealt with money. At this time, however, two regional systems remained: in Novgorod and Pskov the denga coin weighed twice as much as in Moscow and Tver'.[87] More extensive reforms and the first steps towards uniformity throughout the Moscow state were attempted in the mid-sixteenth century. In 1550, for example, Ivan IV sent a standard copper measure of capacity to the officials on the northern Dvina and stated that 'I have sent such measures to all towns alike'.[88] Standard measures of length were also probably sent out in the second half of the sixteenth century, since references occur then to such measures bearing the royal eagle. It was at this time, too, that the *arshin*, as has been mentioned, was being accepted as a general measure of length and was no longer used only for eastern textiles. This process appears to have been completed in the code of laws of 1649 where the fathom (*sazhen'*) 'with which land or anything else is measured' was to be three arshins, 'neither more nor less'.[89] In this definition two major factors which contributed to the attempts to standardize measures are brought together: land allocations to servitors and the growth of trade.

The system of allocations to servitors was developed particularly in the century from 1550. Standard allotments for servitors of different ranks were laid down in 1550 and in 1587 in the Moscow area.[90] The disorders of the early seventeenth century known as the Time of Troubles resulted in the need to carry out surveys which were undertaken particularly from 1620 on. The officials

[87] Kamentseva and Ustyugov, *Russkaya metrologiya*, p. 64.

[88] *Dopolneniya k aktam istoricheskim* [Supplements to Historical Documents] 12 vols. (St Petersburg, 1846–72), i, no. 45.

[89] In *Pamyatniki russkogo prava* [Memorials of Russian Law], ed. S. V. Yushkov et al., 8 vols. (Moscow, 1952–61), vi, ch. 16, p. 212, para. 46.

[90] A. A. Zimin, *Tysyachnaya kniga 1550 g.* [The 1550 Book of the Thousand] (Moscow and Leningrad, 1950), pp. 53–5; *Pamyatniki russkogo prava*, v, pp. 434–5.

were then issued with standard measuring ropes from the Moscow department responsible, and procedures were laid down in a fair amount of detail.[91]

Similarly, major changes took place in the regulation of trade though these had started somewhat earlier. In 1497 a regulation on tolls was sent to Beloozero and a few such individual documents for areas are known from the following half century.[92] At this stage tolls were not imposed uniformly. Apart from variations in rates between different areas, there were also certain exempt or privileged categories within areas. A privilege of 1510 to the St Joseph of Volokolamsk monastery illustrates the point:

> But if the monastery's peasants in the monastic villages and hamlets begin to trade in any goods on festivals, then I . . . have ordered no trade or transit tax to be had from their goods. But if townspeople . . . and *stan* and *volost'* people and people of other towns begin to trade in any goods in the villages and hamlets on festivals, then my customs men are to take for me, from those people who have come, trade and transit tax and the branding due and every sort of customs due . . . And if the monastery's peasants start to trade in any goods on festivals in Ruza town or travelling through the volosts, then my customs men are to have a trade tax for me from all goods.[93]

Thus, local trade was accepted as not liable to impositions, but inter-district trade was regarded as so liable. It is as if local deals within the village or estate scarcely counted as trade, perhaps because they formed an integral part of the peasant economy. Trade between estates or settlements in different districts, sometimes via the town, however, was evidently felt to be something different, outside the range of normal activities of the peasant household unit.

91 V. Sedashev, *Ocherki i materialy po istorii zemlevladeniya Moskovskoi Rusi v XVIIv.* (Essays and Materials on Seventeenth-Century Landholding History in Moscow Rus'] (Moscow, 1912). See also *Akty pistsovago dela* [Documents on Inquisitions], ed. S. Veselovskii, 2 vols. (Moscow, 1913).

92 A. T. Nikolaeva, 'Otrazhenie v ustavnykh tamozhenykh gramotakh Moskovskogo gosudarstva XVI–XVIIvv. protsessa obrazovaniya vserossiiskogo rynka' [The Formation of the All-Russia Market as Reflected in Sixteenth- to Seventeenth-Century Toll Regulations of the Moscow State], *Istoricheskie zapiski*, xxxi (1950), pp. 245–66. Her list of such documents (pp. 264–6) has been amended by Tikhonov; see n. 95 below.

93 TsGADA, GKE, no. 10240, cited in *Pamyatniki russkogo prava*, iii, p. 131. *Stan* and *volost'* were terms indicating district areas.

Even when, from the mid-sixteenth century, such regulations had become general, treatment for certain categories continued to be differentiated. In a charter of 1560 farming out the tolls on the Dvina, purchases and sales of small quantities of weighed goods ('any grain' and turnips – essential foodstuffs – were specifically mentioned) were exempt from imposts.[94] Also a generally higher rate of tax was charged for those from other areas and sometimes an additionally increased amount for foreigners.[95] Thus, even in the second half of the sixteenth century when privileged corporations of great merchants were formed, local and small-scale trade continued to have some features more characteristic of exchanges within a household than in trade.[96] It was not until 1653 that a single tolls regulation was established which applied to all goods (including grain, it noted) in both Moscow and other areas, whether from local people or those from elsewhere.[97] In 1667, in order to meet the demands of the great merchants for protection against foreign traders, a new trading regulation was issued.[98]

Yet, despite the growth of the state, its concern for income and the consequent reforms relating to many aspects of land allocations, trade and finance, uniformity of measurement was not achieved. Even late in the seventeenth century different terms were used for the same measures, and identical terms indicated different quantities in different regions (quite apart from government adjustments). Local units of measure continued to survive to such an extent that 'it is not possible to give an exhaustive list of all local measures. This material has not yet been collected'.[99]

The state had modified the terms used in some sectors of activity, but the life of the estates and local trades remained

---

[94] Published by N. S. Chaev in *Letopis' zanyatii postoyannoi istoriko-arkheograficheskoi komissi* [Chronicle of Work of the Permanent Historical Archaeographical Commission], i (xxxiv) (Leningrad, 1928?), pp. 199–203.

[95] Yu. A. Tikhonov, 'Tamozhennaya politika Russkogo gosudarstva s serediny XVIv. do 60-kh godov XVIIv.' [Customs Policy of the Russian State from the Mid-Sixteenth Century to the 1660s], *Istoricheskie zapiski*, liii (1955), pp. 258–90, esp. Tables, pp. 264, 281.

[96] On the great merchants, see S. H. Baron, 'Who Were the *Gosti*?', *California Slavic Studies*, vii (1973), pp. 1–40. See also P. Bushkovitch, *The Merchants of Moscow, 1580–1650* (Cambridge, 1980), pp. 16 ff.

[97] *Sobranie gosudarstvennykh gramot i dogovorov* [Collection of State Charters and Contracts] 5 vols. (Moscow, 1813–97), iii, pp. 490–3.

[98] *Pamyatniki russkogo prava*, vii, pp. 303–28.

[99] Kamentseva and Ustyugov, *Russkaya metrologiya*, p. 100.

remarkably resistant to its encroachments. The system of measuring time and space in Russia which lasted into the twentieth century was only finally established early in the eighteenth century, because, despite all the developments, the largely self-sufficient household unit remained the basis of society. Local units of measurement survived because of their practical use and because their disadvantages were not great enough to cause their abandonment. Early Russia lived as much in terms of the local and immediate as in terms of the eternal. However well developed the market and exchange was in the seventeenth century, for the majority concepts relating to measurement remained rooted in use-values. Even money was not so much a universal medium of exchange as a special crop: rye had to be produced to sustain the family, but oats for the horse and money for the lord.

12. *Plough and Pen: Agricultural Writers in the Seventeenth Century*

JOAN THIRSK

The seventeenth century was the golden age for English books of husbandry. During this hundred years, they advanced beyond the early pioneering efforts of Fitzherbert and Tusser, gained confidence in their powers to influence farming practice, struck out on new lines of farming endeavour, and conveyed a message that successfully reached a wider circle of readers. But books were not yet so abundant as to be commonplace: they were treasured, lent to close friends, copied out, discussed in correspondence – in short, handled with respect.

If we, in turn, are to understand the role of books of husbandry in advancing agricultural improvement, we too must handle them with respect. There are signs that this is at last happening, not in England only, but in western Europe generally. German scholars have recently reprinted some of their earliest texts. The first German author, Konrad Heresbach, who published in 1570 in Latin, was translated for the first time ever into German in 1970–7.[1] An illuminating essay on him as humanist, educationalist and government servant, a man for whom Erasmus had the deepest regard, has recently been published by Madame Corinne Beutler and Dr Franz Irsigler.[2] Two slightly later sixteenth-century German treatises, one by Martin Grosser, a parson from Lower Silesia, written *circa* 1585 and published in 1590, the second by Abraham von Thumbshirn, a gentleman landowner from Saxony, published in 1616, though written some twenty or thirty

---

[1] Konrad Heresbach, *Vier Bücher über Landwirtschaft*, vol. 1, *Vom Landbau*, ed. Wilhelm Abel and H. Dreitzel (Meisenheim, 1970); *Handbüchlein der Thereutik, das heisst über Jagd, Vogelfang und Fischerei*, ed. Jürgen Blusch (Boppard, 1977).

[2] C. Beutler and F. Irsigler, 'Konrad Heresbach, 1496–1576', *Rheinische Lebensbilder*, viii (1980), pp. 81–104.

years earlier, were reprinted in 1965.[3] Their editor was Gertrud Schrodër-Lembke who, in 1978, published more essays on German agricultural writers, linking their books with their farming practice.[4] The French historian, Madame Corinne Beutler, is now surveying all the European literature, its content, and transmission across countries through translation and revised editions. She published a preview of her final assessment in *Annales, E.S.C.* in 1973.[5] Meanwhile the older literature coming from Italy is being surveyed by Professor Mauro Ambrosoli of Turin, in order to uncover the economic and social circumstances which inspired it, and also to assess its influence in other European countries, especially England.[6]

The seventeenth-century English writers took up their pens at a time when this literary genre was well launched in Europe. For a long period of some hundred and fifty years, or five generations, foreign literature on husbandry had trickled through to a select group of English readers. Such books were, of course, only a handful among foreign scholarly works on many different subjects. Nevertheless, now and then this particular category would engage the special interest of a landowner, a scholar, or a parson – or, more effectively, one individual who was all of these things at the same time – and persuade him to extend his interest beyond bookish reading to practical experiments on farming and its improvement.

These keen readers with practical purposes in mind were but a small group of men in the beginning, widely scattered, but they were brought into contact and correspondence with each other by their common interests, and their enthusiasm slowly but surely infected their kinsmen and friends. Gradually their influence spread until it seeped into every county in the kingdom. Such men

---

[3] Martin Grosser, *Anleitung zu der Landwirtschaft* [and] Abraham von Thumbshirn, *Oeconomia*, repr. in *Zwei frühe deutsche Landwirtschaftsschriften*, ed. Gertrud Schröder-Lembke (Stuttgart, 1965).

[4] Gertrud Schröder-Lembke, *Studien zur Agrargeschichte* (Stuttgart, 1978).

[5] Corinne Beutler, 'Un chapitre de la sensibilité collective: la littérature agricole en Europe continentale au XVIe siècle', *Annales. E.S.C.*, xxviii (1973), pp. 1280–1301.

[6] Mauro Ambrosoli, 'Agricultural Knowledge and the Diffusion of Fodder Crops: English Agriculture in a European Perspective, 1450–1870' (forthcoming). For a discussion of the role of books in the wider field of learning and technical progress, see Elizabeth Eisenstein, *The Printing Press as an Agent of Change*, 2 vols. (Cambridge, 1979), i, pp. 107–13, and ii, pp. 554 ff.

always had a multiplicity of interests, were frequently employed in government or served as local J.P.s, as well as owning and farming land. They were avid readers, and sometimes translators or creative writers on matters far removed from farming, on witchcraft, Spanish literature, or English history. But amid all this, land improvement became a particular concern, and in the end some were prompted to write books of their own which improved in some way on those they had read.[7]

Entering upon the scene comparatively late, English writers enjoyed many advantages from that very fact. They absorbed a long tradition of such books in print. The logical arrangement for a work of husbandry was all set in a pattern which they could follow. But far more important was the philosophical justification for such writing which had been laid down for them by others, and which they were happy to accept. The argument was the more powerful, because it combined several different propositions, all of which were gaining currency in the sixteenth century. Principally it rested on the claim that the cultivation of land was the most honourable of labours, virtually the only one in which innocence still prevailed, where most contentment could be found, and the irksome vexations of a more sophisticated world forgotten. This point of view was eloquently put by Heresbach in his introduction to his work, entitled *Four Books of Husbandry*. It was set in the form of a dialogue between himself, he being a landowner and government official at the court of the duke of Cleves, who had just returned home to enjoy some peace and quiet on his estate, and a messenger who arrived within two days to summon him back to his duties at court. 'I am glad I have found you in the midst of your country joys and pleasures', the messenger declares. 'Surely you are a happy man that, shifting from the troubles and turmoils of the court, can pick out so quiet a life, giving over all, can secretly lie hid in the pleasant country, suffering us in the meantime to be tossed and torn with the cares and business of the

---

[7] Examples of such men include John Smith of Nibley, Glos., whose *Lives of the Berkeleys*, 3 vols. (Gloucester, 1883) shows his interest in agricultural improvement and his careful reading of books, for example, by Gervase Markham (*ibid.*, iii, p. 43); Barnaby Googe, who was a government servant, Lincolnshire landowner, and translator of several foreign works, including *The Proverbes of Sir J. Lopes de Mendoza* (London, 1579, S.T.C. 16809) as well as the work of Konrad Heresbach; and Reynold Scott, a Kentish landowner, who wrote about hop-growing (1574) and about witchcraft (1584).

common weal'. The messenger is only half serious, for he is also taunting Heresbach. Deep down he believes that the country existence is coarse and crude, a life with beasts, louts of the country, and trees. The serious purpose of life is to serve 'our country, our common weal, and State, whereto we are called'. Heresbach puts him firmly in his place. The common people out of ignorance envy court life, but they do not realize 'what heaps of sorrows lies hid under that grave and glittering misery'. Heresbach believes his life on his estate to be much richer in every sort of satisfaction, whether in contemplation of the wonderful work of God, which he beholds in trees, plants and beasts, in the time he has for reading, in the contentment of knowing that his meal is something produced from his own land, or in seeing his estate and farm efficiently managed. And in order to ensure efficient management he, the master, takes a close interest in the day-to-day routine, whenever he is at home. He is one of the first in his household to rise in the morning, and normally it is he who allots the tasks of the day. He inspects his fields, meadows, pastures and livestock once a day, or at least every second day. No tour of his estate passes without his returning to give fresh orders. And he never forgets the axiom of Aristotle and Xenophon: 'The best dung for the field is the master's foot, and the best provender for the horse the master's eye'. This, of course, became an axiom among English gentlemen in the sixteenth and seventeenth centuries.[8]

Heresbach's book gained a large following in England, being translated into English seven years after publication by an English landowner and government official, Barnaby Googe, whose political career and intellectual and farming interests were remarkably similar to those of Heresbach.[9] It passed through several editions in the sixteenth century, and was reissued yet again (with some alterations) by Gervase Markham in the early seventeenth cen-

---

[8] Heresbach, *Vier Bücher über Landwirtschaft*, ed. Abel and Dreitzel, i, pp. 16 ff. For the English translation by Barnaby Googe, see *Foure Bookes of Husbandry* (London, 1577, S.T.C. 13196). The proverb cited here derives from Aristotle, *Oeconomica*, i.vi. 3–6 (in the Loeb edition), claiming to cite a Persian, who, being asked what kept a horse in best condition, replied 'his master's eye', and a Libyan who, when asked what kind of manure was best, answered 'the master's footprints'. Xenophon also cited the Persian: *Oeconomica*, 12. 20.

[9] See *Dictionary of National Biography, sub nomine.*

tury. In the 1670s it was still read and respected: 'noble Heresba-chius' one writer called its author.[10]

In the title of this essay the plough is placed alongside the pen, for, in fact, most writers handled the tools of both trades. In the case of Heresbach, we can only guess, but as he started life as the youngest of seven children of a modest but comfortably endowed landowner, it is reasonable to think that the routine of farming was as familiar to him as eating and sleeping. In the case of other writers, we have more precise knowledge of their practical exper-ience, and can see it reflected in their writing. We betray the world we live in when we put the doers and the writers at opposite poles. We inhabit a world of specialists who look sceptically upon those who do not single-mindedly pursue one activity. But western man's dedication to the division of labour is a matter of conve-nience and circumstance, not a permanent principle of human life. In the middle ages it was exalted as a means of ensuring a living for all, in a world where resources and opportunities were limited. Craftsmen were not expected to be husbandmen, nor husbandmen craftsmen. It was an offence against one's fellow men to gather 'divers men's livings in one man's hand'.[11] But in the course of two centuries between about 1500 and 1700, economic life encou-raged, or compelled, men to turn increasingly to supplementary activities, though, cautiously and wisely, they maintained a link with their old occupations as well. They began to thrive by combining several occupations, supplementing one source of livelihood with another. And as the pace of change quickened, men's versatility proved remarkable. Clothiers who were also country gentlemen provoked the surprise of one observer at the beginning of the sixteenth century; rural husbandmen who were also weavers provoked the wrath of government, which accused them of causing the decay of towns.[12] Historians are now uncov-ering examples of multiple occupations, and of rapid chopping and changing of occupations on a far bolder scale than anything that the disapproving edicts of government envisaged. It was not a sign

---

[10] Review of J. B. Gent, *pseud.*, *The Epitome of the Whole Art of Husbandry* (London, 1675), in *Phil. Trans. Roy. Soc.*, x (24 May 1675), p. 321.

[11] For Heresbach's obvious practical knowledge of some aspects of farming, see Beutler and Irsigler, 'Konrad Heresbach, 1496–1576', p. 92; *Tudor Economic Documents*, ed. R. H. Tawney and Eileen Power, 3 vols. (London, 1924), i, p. 353.

[12] *Tudor Economic Documents*, ed. Tawney and Power, iii, p. 5, and i, pp. 173–5.

of human fecklessness. Rather this was a dynamic period of exploration in new directions, of resourceful expedients which laid the foundations of a new future. After 1700, however, when the new forms of enterprise were more securely established, a fresh wave of arguments appeared in support of the division of labour. The highest productivity in carpentry, in watchmaking, and in pin-making, it was argued, was achieved where labour was most divided. The circumstances had sufficiently changed for a fresh enunciation of the virtues of labour specialization.[13]

It was in the period between 1500 and 1700, then, when the principle that one man must confine his activities to one job was gradually relaxed, and almost abandoned, that substantial advances were made in new directions. For a time circumstances favoured those who were jacks of all trades, ready to turn their hands to anything. And in that world, men who were both farmers and writers were less suspect. So in order to understand and appreciate them as their fellow readers appreciated them, we have to shed the prejudices with which we as specialist historians are saddled. They were not hacks and plagiarists; their books combined the wisdom of their practical experience and their reading of others. The urge to write sprang from sound agricultural knowledge, coupled with a philosophical conviction that was idyllic in expression, but was as much political as religious in inspiration. Humanism and the ideals of the commonweal blended in support of a political objective: writers believed that their fellow men would get a better living from the land if new ways of farming and new crops from abroad were better publicized. Both economic and political purposes were entwined in their sense of moral duty to exploit more efficiently the riches of the natural world.[14]

The seventeenth-century writers are numerous, and only three are selected for consideration here, but those three, Gervase

---

[13] Anon. [Lawrence Braddon], *To Pay Old Debts without New Taxes* (London, 1723), pp. 115–18. I wish to thank Mr Stephen Macfarlane for drawing my attention to this pamphlet. See also Adam Smith, *The Wealth of Nations*, bk 1, chs. 1–3, on the division of labour.

[14] See, for example, the treatise by John Stratford of Winchcombe, Glos. (1627) on the benefits of growing hemp and flax in England (Public Record Office, London [hereafter P.R.O.], S.P. 16/57, no. 28), and on his own practical efforts to do so (P.R.O., S.P. 16/57, no. 14). For more experiments with tobacco and coleseed, and their social purpose, see P.R.O., S.P. 14/180/79.

Markham, Walter Blith and John Worlidge, are outstanding figures, each of whom personifies certain distinctive characteristics of his generation. Markham belongs to the early seventeenth century, Blith to the period of the Interregnum, and Worlidge to the period after the Restoration. All three were gentlemen, or became gentlemen, all possessed a sound practical knowledge of farming, all had a serious sense of purpose in writing, and all hoped to promote agricultural improvement among their contemporaries.

How successful were they? Throughout the century the strongest stimulus to experiment came from gentlemen farmers such as these. They led the way, and they made the bulk of the readers of books. But the writers hoped to interest yeomen and gardeners, even husbandmen, and they styled their writing consciously to win that larger audience. They had no great success in this endeavour, but their attention to practicalities did win them a much larger readership among gentlemen. The gentry then spread the message by example, by demonstrations in their fields, which yeomen and husbandmen could observe and readily understand. It was these demonstrations before their very eyes which persuaded peasant farmers to follow suit. In this way the literature had a decisive influence in spreading improvements and became increasingly effective.[15]

For many gentlemen an interest in farming improvements was first awakened by their enthusiasm for breeding and training fine horses.[16] The quality of their horses, which were publicly displayed in ceremonies and in war, depended in the last resort on the way they were bred, fed and managed on the gentry's home farms. Gervase Markham's career is one of the best illustrations of this sequence of developing interests. Markham was the son of a Nottinghamshire gentleman, not richly endowed, whose family had a long tradition of service to the crown dating back to the twelfth century. He was well educated at school and university, but he was a younger son; he had to be resourceful if he was to

---

15 The evidence is set out at length in *The Agrarian History of England and Wales*, v, *1640–1750*, ed. Joan Thirsk (forthcoming).

16 It is noticeable that some gentlemen's interests in new crops are only, or most clearly, shown in measures taken to grow the new grasses, such as sainfoin, to feed horses. See Joan Thirsk, 'Agricultural Innovations and their Diffusion', in *Agrarian History of England and Wales*, v.

survive in the class into which he had been born.[17] The surname Markham almost certainly stood for horse-fancying and fine horse-breeding in the sixteenth century. In an influential text on the *Art of Riding, circa* 1560, Thomas Blundeville wrote of Master Thomas Markham of Ollerton in Nottinghamshire, on the fringe of Sherwood Forest, owner of a well-trained horse that passed to the earl of Leicester. John Markham, probably his son, later acted as agent for Lord Arundel, buying in 1616 an Arab horse which was sold to James I. Gervase's own father also took great pleasure in his skill in horsemanship. This we learn from his son's dedication to him of his *Discourse of Horsemanship* (1593).[18] As for Gervase himself, on his own admission, he spent his youth among horses. Then, in his teens, he served in the household of the duke of Rutland at Belvoir Castle, and there extended his knowledge of horses and country sports. He also took a course of instruction at Master Thomas Story's riding school at Greenwich, where he was introduced to the circle of Italian riding instructors and stable men attending the horses of the great lords of the realm. At about the age of twenty-one years (that is to say, from 1589 onwards) he developed close literary and social connections with the Sidneys of Penshurst in Kent.[19] Sir Henry Sidney was a special commissioner under Elizabeth, appointed in 1580, to execute her national policy to increase and improve the breed of English horses. This commission revived the policy, that had been inaugurated by Henry VIII, of improving the quality and the number of English horses; they had proved so weak and inadequate in the French and Scottish wars in the 1540s.[20] Sir Henry Sidney, with other commissioners of the queen, set a personal example. He took great pride in his stables and bought horses far and wide; and in 1589 he bought a horse from Gervase's father.[21]

Horsemanship, and then in the 1590s, soldiering in the Low

[17] F.N.L. Poynter, *A Bibliography of Gervase Markham, 1568?–1637* (Oxford Bibliog. Soc., new ser., xi, Oxford, 1962), pp. 4–9.

[18] Joan Thirsk, *Horses in Early Modern England: for Service, for Pleasure, for Power* (Reading, 1978), p. 16, n. 76; Poynter, *Bibliography of Gervase Markham*, pp. 84–5.

[19] Poynter, *Bibliography of Gervase Markham*, pp. 9–12, 14, 84–6, 90–4.

[20] Thirsk, *Horses in Early Modern England*, pp. 12–16.

[21] Kent Archives Office, Sidney papers, *passim*, but see, for example, U1475/021/2, 'A Note of the Names and Number of All Horses as My Lord Hath in Ireland, November 1577', and U1475/A55, Stable Account, 1571–2; Poynter, *Bibliography of Gervase Markham*, p. 10.

Countries, in Spain and Ireland, again calling for horsemanship, launched Gervase into adult life. But when he married in 1601, he had to find a more secure livelihood. His father's estate was not destined for him, and so he turned to farming. 'Although a piece of my life was scholar, a piece soldier, and all horseman, yet did I for nine years apply myself to the plough', he wrote later in an unusual piece of autobiographical detail. And evidently they were satisfying years. 'For divers years', he wrote in 1613, 'wherein I lived most happily, I lived a husbandman amongst husbandmen of most excellent knowledge'. Some of the time was spent on the estates of his godfather's family at Leighton Bromswold in Huntingdonshire, some as a tenant farmer on the land of his cousin, Sir John Harington, near Bath. At the end he counted himself 'worthy to be a graduate in the vocation'. 'I both observed well those which were esteemed famous in the profession, and preserved . . . those rules which I found infallible by experience'.[22]

So, having written books on horsemanship in the 1590s and early 1600s, Gervase moved on to writing general books of husbandry. They surveyed every branch of the subject, the management of arable, meadow and pasture, kitchen and pleasure gardens, orchards and woodlands. Over and over again he reiterated his belief in reason (what we would call 'common sense') and experience, and, as Mr F. N. L. Poynter, his bibliographer, has expressed it, he gave particularly 'close attention to method and detail' whenever he was describing matters of which he had personal experience.[23]

A work which admirably exemplifies this high regard for precise detail – the more exact the better – is a slim work entitled *The Inrichment of the Weald of Kent*. Markham did not claim to be the author. The manuscript had come his way, and he thought it deserved publication.[24] Markham knew the writer, though he tantalizes us by not giving his name. He describes him as 'a man of great eminence and worth', who, when new editions were issued, helped Markham to revise, enlarge and correct them. Markham dedicated the book to Sir George Rivers of Chafford, an influential Kentish gentleman and justice of the peace, living in the parish

---

[22] Poynter, *Bibliography of Gervase Markham*, pp. 10, 13–14, 18.

[23] *Ibid.*, pp. 94, 82.

[24] *Ibid.*, p. 150. The first edition of *The Inrichment of the Weald of Kent* was published in London in 1625 (S.T.C. no. 17363).

of Ashurst, in the Kentish Weald. Since the Sidneys lived at Penshurst in the next-door parish, it was possibly through Markham's connection with them that he came to know the Rivers family of Chafford. Perhaps, indeed, a Rivers was the author of the manuscript.[25] This part of the Weald was full of parks where lived families who, in Henry VIII's day, were prominent in their efforts to keep horse studs and improve the breed, and who vied for grants or keeperships of parks where their horses might roam freely.[26] Traditions like this were very persistent in families, and so it is this friendship among enthusiastic horse fanciers which seems to lead into the next phase of Markham's interest, in ways of improving agriculturally some of the rough pastures and scrub in that extensive area of wood and heathland stretching through Kent and Sussex.

The text of *The Inrichment of the Weald of Kent* is a careful description of different types of Wealden soils and of ways of improving each with different kinds of marl. It is quite obviously a work of precise observation and ripe experience. The author not only knows the area in close, intimate detail, he can also view it in long historical perspective. He remarks, for example, that the Weald does not contain as many manors or courts in proportion to its size as do other regions of Kent, that the dens – the first clearings in that great forest – were once larger units that have gradually been broken down by gavelkind inheritance. He has observed the land slowly being brought under the plough. The difficulty lies in the fact that the land quickly reverts to frith and wood if not continually manured and cultivated. So the writer faces the day-to-day problems of farming the land, field by field, in a way that will maintain the advance of cultivation, without set-backs. Some land has been made productive for a while, but then the treatment has failed and the land now lies exhausted, 'incapable of amendment'. In other places, however, farmers have achieved lasting success. They have found a routine that keeps the land continuously in heart: they take five to six years of crops in succession, followed by three to four years of rest, followed by another five to six years of crops. Different results derive from the fact that the exact art of applying marl is not fully understood. So

[25] Poynter, *Bibliography of Gervase Markham*, p. 150.
[26] Thirsk, *Horses in Early Modern England*, pp. 14–15.

the author offers four different recipes. His advice is detailed, taking the reader through every season of the year on each type of soil.[27]

Markham's textbook was popular, and with good reason; it was so firmly anchored in firsthand knowledge. First published in 1625, it was reissued in 1631, 1636 and 1649, twice in the 1650s (1653, 1656), three times in the 1660s (1660, 1664, 1668), once in the 1670s (1675), once in the 1680s (1683), and once in the 1690s (1695).[28] Rarely is it possible to demonstrate how bookish precepts were put into practice, but we come reasonably close in this case. A first edition of Markham's book was carefully bound by an unknown owner, probably around 1642, into a volume in which he also incorporated a miscellany of hand-written notes, culled from five other books, all dealing with the uses of marl.[29] Someone was collecting advice from several different sources on the way to use marl. Surely it was for a practical purpose?

As for men's efforts at improving land in the Weald of Kent, a descendant of Sir George Rivers of Chafford, to whom *The Inrichment of the Weald* had been dedicated, was the owner of land and tithes in Hadlow parish in the Weald in the 1670s. This younger George Rivers claimed tithe of grain in 1673 from husbandmen who were engaged in the very same task of wresting crops from small acreages of 'very barren, poor heathy ground', two or three acres here, nine or ten acres there. In one tithe dispute, they described the hard labour involved. You could offer the land at a groat an acre to anyone who would convert it to tillage, and find no one to take up the challenge. But one or two stalwarts in Hadlow were persisting with efforts at improving and manuring. Five crops (just as the book laid down) had been taken from one piece of ten acres. Other parcels had yielded two, three,

---

27 Gervase Markham, *The Inrichment of the Weald of Kent* (London, 1642 edn), pp. 2, 4–5, 10 ff.

28 Poynter, *Bibliography of Gervase Markham*, pp. 150–1, 163, 165, 167, 169, 171, 172, 174, 176–8.

29 British Library, London, Sloane MS. 1607. The notes in this MS. were copied from William Folkingham, *Feudigraphia* (London, 1610, S.T.C. 11123), Hugh Plat, *The Jewell House of Art and Nature* (London, 1594, S.T.C. 19991), Gervase Markham, *Farewell to Husbandry* (London, 1625 edn, S.T.C. 17373), Francis Bacon, *Sylva sylvarum* (London, 1626, S.T.C. 1168), and the French writer, Bernard Palissy. A copy of the same edition in the Bodleian Library, Oxford, has marginal notes, including oral advice given to the owner of the book, supplementing the printed word.

five and even seven crops. It was a tough battle and the farmers begrudged the payment of tithe when their harvest did not repay their outlay. But hopes of ultimate success spurred them on.[30]

Markham's books on husbandry suited the mood and encouraged the aspirations of contemporaries, and his work was widely acclaimed. He plainly respected the husbandmen whose labours he had shared and observed. He was always inquisitive to have things explained, so that he could pass on better advice. 'I could not indure to have anything hid till I did by proof find that action and discourse went even hand in hand together'. This was the recipe for successful writing and successful farming. Even the first settlers in Virginia placed their trust in Markham. The ship *Supply* taking victuals and equipment across the Atlantic in September 1620 took Markham's works on 'all kinds of English husbandry and huswifry', as well as Barnaby Googe's translation of Heresbach. Their recipient in Virginia was advised to guard the books under his own hands, 'otherwise you will be defrauded of them'.[31]

A celebrated author under the Commonwealth, Walter Blith, writing in the years 1649 to 1653, moved in another social circle, more characteristic of a republic than a monarchy. He had little to do with noblemen and courtiers, though he had easy converse with gentlemen. He was more familiar with yeomen and husbandmen, having been born and brought up in the same circle. He was the son of a small farmer of Allesley in Warwickshire in the Forest of Arden. His father, John, lived by dairying and grain growing, and left at his death in April 1626 a dairy herd of 13 cows, heifers and weanlings, one little pig, 4 mares and 8 sheep. His sown grain implies some 30 acres of land under crop, or arable of 40–50 acres altogether, if one counts in the fallow. The farmhouse comprised hall, parlour and little chamber on the ground floor, while the upper floor was divided into five rooms, and included a cheese chamber and 'a man's chamber' for the servants. Lean-to's and outbuildings afforded kitchen, dairy, buttery and nether house. John Blith left bequests totalling £230 to four of his children,

---

[30] P.R.O., E.134, 25 Charles II, Mich. 12, of which part was reprinted in *Seventeenth-Century Economic Documents*, ed. J. Thirsk and J. P. Cooper (Oxford, 1972), pp. 164–5.

[31] Poynter, *Bibliography of Gervase Markham*, p. 12; *The Records of the Virginia Company of London: The Court Book*, ed. S. M. Kingsbury, 4 vols. (Washington, 1906–35), iii, *1607–22*, p. 400.

though his goods were valued at only £133. 6s. 7d. Living in the Forest of Arden, he probably called himself a yeoman, though in a richer part of the country, with that size of farm, he would have been deemed a husbandman.[32]

In writing the best and most comprehensive textbook on husbandry of the middle seventeenth century, Walter Blith faithfully represented a new generation. He served as a captain in the Parliamentary army, probably most of the time in the midlands; quite by chance we find two men and three horses of Captain Blith camped for one night in April 1644 in Wroxall in Warwickshire.[33] In 1643 he was solicitor and agent for sequestering royalist land in Warwickshire and Coventry, and also collector of rent from lands of the bishop, and dean and chapter of Worcester. In 1649 and 1650 he was a surveyor of crown lands, and drew up twenty-seven surveys of estates in Bedfordshire, Cambridgeshire, Huntingdonshire and Norfolk. He also became a soldier purchaser of a royal estate in Potterspury, Northamptonshire.[34] From these facts we may infer that experience in campaigning across England and in surveying forfeited lands gave Blith many insights into the agricultural condition of central England.

In 1649, following the execution of Charles I, great hopes of an economic transformation were entertained by the Parliamentary party. New and radical policies of many kinds were under discussion. These obviously inspired Blith's first book, published in 1649, entitled *The English Improver: or, A New Survey of Husbandry*. It began with an address to both houses of parliament, setting out the major obstacles to agricultural improvements, as Blith saw them. They were essentially practical matters, such as any landowner-farmer would encounter: the absence of any system of compensation to tenants for improvements, for example; the conflict between millers and farmers, both wanting to divert watercourses for different purposes. Indeed, Blith confessed to his own share of such trouble when he diverted a little brook to water

---

[32] Joint Record Office, Lichfield, Wills 1626B. John Blith was assessed to the subsidy in 1624 at £3 in goods: P.R.O., E.179/193/298.

[33] *Dictionary of National Biography, sub nomine*; P.R.O., S.P. 16/510, no. 28.

[34] *Calendar of State Papers, Domestic, Addenda, 1625–49*, p. 648; *Calendar of State Papers, Domestic, 1641–3*, pp. 510–11; *Calendar of the Committee for compounding*, i, pp. 108, 189; iii, p. 2029, 149; S. J. Madge, *The Domesday of Crown Lands* (London, 1938), p. 345; I. Gentles, 'The Purchasers of Northamptonshire Crown Lands, 1649–1660', *Midland Hist.*, iii (1976), p. 219.

a meadow; he greatly increased his hay harvest, but encountered objections from a neighbouring miller. Blith also broached larger issues: the overstocking of commons, obstacles in the way of enclosure, and the need to compel men always to plant trees when others were cut down.[35]

Having addressed the policy-makers, Blith's main purpose was to offer six ways of improving land to the ordinary farmer. Hence he promised to write in country language, using homespun terms. The improvements he recommended were concerned with standard procedures for cultivating or maintaining different qualities of arable, meadow, pasture, commons and woodlands, using generally recognized fertilizers like sand, chalk, marl and lime. But three years later, in 1652, Blith published a new edition, which was virtually a rewritten book, and with a fresh title, *The English Improver Improved*. It now included six newer pieces of improvement, in addition to the six that had been offered in the first edition. He now wrote of clover, sainfoin, and lucerne, woad, weld and madder, hops, saffron and liquorice, rape, coleseed, hemp and flax, and the planting of orchard and garden fruits. Plainly Blith had learned a lot more about innovations in husbandry than he knew in 1649. In fact, he made a slightly peevish comment by way of apology for the inadequacy of his earlier work. He had failed to write about weld, a useful dye-crop on chalky soil; 'It is my desire to make public whatever comes under my experience', he wrote, 'Yet this hath been used this [sic] many years by many private gentlemen in divers parts, but not discovered for public practice . . . I fear men's spirits are strangely private, that have made excellent experiments, and yet will not communicate'. Blith's book had evidently been read and criticized, and this was the result – a greatly extended list of new ways in agriculture.[36]

The introductory epistles, and an entirely new appendix to the 1652 edition, show how Blith's thinking on agriculture had clarified between 1649 and 1652. Men had passed through a fearful experience between 1646 and 1651 when disastrous weather conditions had ruined harvests and spread sickness among lives-

---

[35] Walter Blith, *The English Improver: or, A New Survey of Husbandry* (London, 1649).

[36] *Ibid.*, pp. 2–4, and *passim*; Walter Blith, *The English Improver Improved* (London, 1652), title page, and pp. 224–5.

tock. Conditions had improved by 1652, but the years of food shortages and high prices had taught harsh lessons concerning the urgent need to use land more productively. Neglected forests, wastes and commons must be improved; through enclosure, employment must be increased.[37]

Lively discussions on agricultural improvement were taking place within the parliamentary circle at this time, much stimulated by Samuel Hartlib, who encouraged meetings between agricultural improvers, urged them to write books, and published them. Walter Blith was plainly involved in these debates. But that is only a general explanation for the development of his ideas between 1649 and 1652. More personal influences were at work. The first is seen in his remarks on the draining of fen lands. In 1649 he had some sour comments to make about drainers 'who under pretence of drawing water, floating land, and doing wonders' persuaded many gentlemen to pay well for their skill, but then 'at last when all hath failed, a fair pair of heels hath been the greatest advantage'. As for the processes of drainage, he had little to say beyond criticizing past failures, and giving simple instructions concerning the straightening of rivers and the checking of levels.[38] Nevertheless, he evidently felt inadequate in writing of something about which he lacked personal experience. So he added a sentence praising the efficient drainers, 'whose works and experiments I must admire and honour, *to whom I desire to be a pupil*'.[39] Thus he humbly expressed a willingness to learn more. It is almost certain that the drainers took Blith at his word. A fresh Act for draining the Great Level of the fens (the earl of Bedford's scheme) was passed in May 1649, and in January 1650 Vermuyden was appointed director of the works. This great scheme for fen drainage around the Wash, which had fallen into abeyance because of the Civil War, was now fanned into life again. And in the

---

[37] Blith, *English Improver Improved*, pp. d3–f1.

[38] Blith, *English Improver*, Epistle to the Ingenuous Reader, pp. 37–44.

[39] *Ibid.*, p. 45. See also p. 43 for another enigmatic remark on similar lines: 'hereafter (if God please to give another opportunity) I shall more largely discourse of further experiences herein, as I have both seen and heard, and am now endeavouring more certain trials of them'. It is worth noticing that Sir William Dugdale, who later wrote *The History of Imbanking and Draining*, lived at Blythe Hall in Shustoke parish, next door to Blith's native parish of Allesley. But he did not embark on this work until after Blith's death, seemingly in 1657: *The Life, Diary and Correspondence of Sir William Dugdale, Knight*, ed. W. Hamper (London, 1827), pp. 101, 104.

revised edition of his book in 1652, Blith's remarks on fen drainage and marsh embankments were altogether different. He devoted a whole chapter to them, and was hot in their defence: 'let not curs snarl nor dogs bark' at 'the unparalleled advantages of the world'. He himself had once held false notions about the fens, he confessed, 'before I knew them in some measure'.[40] Carefully chosen sentences make it fairly clear that Blith had been a witness of the quarrels between drainers and commoners. Wrangles about the costs of the operation led to endless, damaging delays, further compounded by self-interest and piecemeal tinkering with drainage. But Blith could now offer more mature reflections on the practicalities, not only on technical matters, but more particularly on labour management. The key to success, he now concluded, was a good overseer. 'I have seen some bailiffs . . . stand telling a story, while all his workmen have stood looking him in the face, admiring him for his rhetoric, and this hath pleased him as well as their working'. In short, the man with the gift for organizing, who could extract efficient work and loyalty from his men, would succeed when all others failed. Blith all but said that he had supervised embanking work in the marshes or fens but had failed miserably to wear that air of authority that inspired confidence and loyalty from his workmen. 'A good method or platform to advance each man's labour to the best furtherance of a work is difficult, requires great ingenuity, and laborious study. I find it most difficult, though I have had as large experience of it as most Englishmen, yet cannot accomplish it, but many times ran into confusion, through men's rudeness, and my want of each particular experience in each work, the which I instance as a rock for others, to beware and prize and value a good overseer, whose countenance and observation is such with workmen as will not only awe and force them, but his wise and loving demeanour will compel them to their utmost faithfulness. A work in its gears will thrive exceedingly'.[41]

Some possibly supporting evidence for Blith's experience in the fens comes from his will. Proved in the early weeks of 1654, the following words were subscribed by the clerk in the probate court: '*Memorandum*, that whereas the deceased wrote himself of

[40] Blith, *English Improver Improved*, ch. 9, pp. 45, 48.
[41] *Ibid.*, pp. 51–3, 62–4; H. C. Darby, *The Draining of the Fens* (Cambridge, 1968), pp. 66–70.

Leicestershire, yet for four years before his death, he with all his family have lived in Lincolnshire, where all his estate is'. Did he end his days in the Lincolnshire fens? Many of his dreams of agricultural improvement were being realized there as new farms for husbandmen were created from the once-drowned commons, and 'the Excellency of Tillage', propounded in chapter 13 of his book, was being demonstrated on the ground. Blith was convinced that 'tillage yieldeth the greatest profit to landlord or occupier', and that all Scripture exhorted men to till for corn, though in the next generation, men would think otherwise.[42]

Yet more revealing autobiographical detail is embedded in Blith's will, drawn up in 1649, shedding light on the course of contemporary debates on enclosure. Blith then described himself as a gentleman of Cotesbach in Leicestershire.[43] Much is known of the history of Cotesbach in the early seventeenth century. It had been enclosed amid angry turmoil and unrest, following two changes of lordship in quick succession. The enclosure was bitterly fought by the tenants, and in consequence Cotesbach was one of the centres of the Midland Revolt against enclosure in 1607. Subsequently the manor experienced four more changes of ownership (in 1607, 1608, 1609 and 1626), coming finally to rest in 1626 in the possession of a London salter, in whose family it remained for a century. It was described in 1622 as a 'very fine lordship and exceeding good ground, now (for the most part) converted into sheep pasturage'.[44]

Here Blith found himself, in 1649, when Cotesbach had been enclosed for some forty years. More significant still, he was the neighbour of Joseph Lee, who had been inducted as rector in 1645. Five years later, in 1654, Lee published a celebrated pamphlet entitled *Considerations Concerning Common Fields and Inclosures, Dialoguewise*, strongly supporting their enclosure. In it

---

42 P.R.O., P.C.C. Wills, PROB. 11/235, fo. 142; Blith, *English Improver*, p. 72; Blith, *English Improver Improved*, p. 83. In his text (1653 edn, p. 44) Blith mentioned that he lived in a country of windmills, not water-mills, which also implies fenland. Dr Robert Child, in a letter to Hartlib in 1652, hoped that Blith would write more concerning draining, so that the English, who were draining bogs in Ireland, would be helped: Sheffield Univ. Lib., Hartlib MS. 15/5/12. I wish to thank Lord Delamere for permission to consult these MSS.

43 P.R.O., P.C.C. Wills, PROB. 11/235, fo. 142.

44 L. A. Parker, 'The Agrarian Revolution at Cotesbach, 1501–1612', in W. G. Hoskins (ed.), *Studies in Leicestershire Agrarian History* (Leicester, 1949), pp. 41, 52, 56, 66, 68, 74–5.

he voiced the fiercest disapproval of abuses in the common fields, not merely in general terms, but in lively detail, describing the practical problems of herding stock in common pastures, the quarrels about quillets of land, and the injustice involved in assessing taxation by the yardland, without regard for exact acreages or for the fertility of the soil.[45]

Blith and Lee together were well placed to observe the effects of enclosure in this Leicestershire parish. We can almost see these two walking the lanes, debating and modifying each other's views. Both men were strongly in favour of enclosure, yet the procedures for enclosure which they preferred were different. Blith wanted to resolve disagreements by allowing the encloser to have his way, but obliging him to pay for the damage inflicted on his unwilling neighbours. Lee held another view, clearly expressed in his second pamphlet, published after Blith's death; he wanted enclosure by agreements that were enrolled in Chancery, and made due provision for the poor; and in the case of insoluble disagreement, he believed that the decision of a majority of landowners should prevail over a reluctant minority.[46]

There was plainly room for many different opinions on the best procedure. The controversy flared in 1655 in the political arena (after Blith's death) when petitions against enclosure in Leicestershire and Warwickshire prompted Major-General Whalley to lay a

---

[45] Lee's pamphlet was reprinted in John Nichols, *The History and Antiquities of the County of Leicester*, 4 vols. (London, 1795–1815), iv, pt 1, pp. 85 ff. Lee's essay was an answer to John Moore, another Leicestershire parson, at Knaptoft, who in 1653 published a tract inveighing against the hardships of the poor caused by enclosure, *The Crying Sin of England, of Not Caring for the Poor*.

[46] Blith, *English Improver*, Prefatory Epistle to Parliament. Blith here suggested compensation adjudged 'by indifferent men'. In the *English Improver Improved* (1652 edn), Prefatory Epistle to Cromwell, he suggested compensation judged reasonable 'by indifferent men or competent judges'. Blith also contemplated an agreement, or possibly even an act, ensuring that at each enclosure certain proportions of land be kept in tillage, meadow and pasture: *ibid.*, p. 79. Direct personal experience of enclosure may have come Blith's way during the enclosure of Allesley, his native parish, in 1650. It was carried out by agreement, and a Chancery decree was enrolled in 1653: P.R.O., C.54/299/583/1. I owe this information to the kindness of Mrs Joy Woodall of Solihull, who sent me information on Blith from the Warwickshire Record Office, much of which had been collected by Mr Philpotts. To his work, in transcribing Allesley material, I am much indebted. For Lee's views on enclosure agreements, see Pseudomisus [Joseph Lee], *Considerations Concerning Common Fields and Inclosures, Dialoguewise* (London, 1654), p. 28.

bill on enclosure before parliament. Whalley favoured yet another solution – a commission of three justices of the peace, acting with a jury at every enclosure to adjudicate between opposing interests, but paying special attention to the protection of the poor.[47] His bill before parliament in 1656 was thrown out after the first reading. But it is one piece in the larger jigsaw puzzle, namely the long debate between politicians at Westminister, county administrators like Whalley, parsons protecting their flocks and their tithes, like Lee, and agricultural improvers, like Blith. They now mostly agreed on the benefits of enclosure, but they were still seeking the fairest means to make that change – and the alternatives were many.

Blith, then, was one of the notable writers of the Commonwealth period, who had served his turn as surveyor, farmer, and improver of his own land. He stood on the margin of politics, but he was certainly not a detached observer, closeted in a book-lined study. Indeed, he may have been more deeply involved than we know in policy debates. His older brother, Francis, was married to Sir Arthur Hazelrigg's sister, Mary. Samuel Hartlib, who published so many books on agricultural improvement, introduced interested improvers to one another, and certainly had the ear of government, described him as his 'very loving and experienced friend'. It is even possible that Walter's son, Samuel, was named after Samuel Hartlib; the Christian name was certainly not traditional in the Blith family.[48]

The story of Blith's heir in the next generation ends appropriately. Samuel inherited his Uncle Francis's estate, for Francis's marriage to Mary Hazelrigg produced no children.[49] So Walter Blith's eldest son moved as an equal in a circle of enterprising, energetic, landowning, farming gentry, still living in the Warwickshire Arden, but in a countryside well on the way to being

---

[47] G. Jagger, 'The Fortunes of the Whalley Family of Screveton, Notts.' (Southampton Univ. M. Phil. thesis, 1973), pp. 187–91. I wish to thank Mr Jagger for permission to quote from his thesis. See also *Diary of Thomas Burton*, ed. J. Towill Rutt, 4 vols. (London, 1828), i, pp. 175–6. This episode is discussed at greater length in Joan Thirsk, 'Agricultural Policy', in *The Agrarian History of England and Wales*, v.

[48] I owe my information on the Hazelrigg connection to Mrs Joy Woodall; [Sir Richard Weston], *A Discourse of Husbandrie used in Brabant and Flanders*, [ed. Samuel Hartlib] 2nd edn (London, 1652), To the Reader.

[49] P.R.O., P.C.C. Wills, PROB. 11/364, fo. 160.

improved agriculturally from pastoral forest to arable felden.[50] Socially it had become a most congenial place for gentlemen to inhabit.

In the last third of the seventeenth century the initiative in agricultural improvement remained with the gentry. The third author in this study, John Worlidge, belonged in this social milieu, but had the slightly more aloof bearing that one expects of a gentleman after the Restoration, concerned with agricultural improvement but also concerned with maintaining the honour and prestige of his class. He came from Hampshire, from the little market town of Petersfield, which throbbed with vitality after 1660 because of the growth of the military and naval town of Portsmouth. Petersfield, lying on the main road from London, saw all sorts passing through, soldiers, sailors, ambassadors, colourful government servants like Samuel Pepys, and kings – Charles II, James II, even Peter the Great from Russia in 1698. This traffic kept Petersfield inhabitants in touch with current developments of all kinds, and the Worlidges were at the centre of the web, respected members of the gentry and urban professional class since the early seventeenth century. John, the author, accumulated a landed estate in Petersfield in the 1660s, and was a sufficiently public figure to serve as mayor in 1673. He was also deputy steward of Chalton Manor from at least 1689, and, possibly, as one contemporary describes him, wood steward at one time (*circa* 1665) to the earl of Pembroke.[51] Certainly he was responsible in 1665 for erecting the first Persian wheel for watering land in the grounds or fields of Wilton House, and in his will he mentioned a property, bestowed on his daughter by the earl of Pembroke.[52]

Worlidge lived in a different economic climate from Blith, and his books reflect this fact. His first publication in 1669 appeared in the midst of a great depression, when the House of Lords was

---

[50] For Samuel Blith's will (he died in 1685), mentioning his watch, rings, jewels, silver tobacco box and silver-hilted sword, see P.R.O., P.C.C. Wills, PROB. 11/380, fo. 67.

[51] J. H. Thomas, *Petersfield under the Later Stuarts: An Economic and Social Study* (Petersfield Papers, no. 6, Petersfield Area Hist, Soc., Petersfield, 1980), *passim*, but esp. pp. 5, 12–13, 39–40; J. S., *The Present State of England* (London, 1683), p. 101.

[52] John Worlidge, *Systema agriculturae*, 3rd edn (London, 1681), p. 21; P.R.O., P.C.C. Wills, PROB. 11/415, fo. 133.

investigating the decay of rents and trade. Food was now being produced in such abundance that the price of grain, wool and cattle had slumped, and the rents of land similarly. All classes of men were turning to alternative specialities in farming and horticulture which paid better. Walter Blith had taken account of many of these enterprises in his six new pieces of improvement. Now they were sufficiently well established to deserve fuller treatment, and the list required to be extended. Worlidge came from a part of southern England where alternative enterprises were legion: the soils of Hampshire varied from chalk to clay to sand, and supported woodlands, orchards, hop gardens, vegetable gardens, rabbit warrens, duck decoys and fish ponds. Worlidge could write from direct observation of them all. Hence his books included not only a straightforward survey of conventional agriculture, *Systema agriculturae* (1669), but a whole *Survey of Horticulture* (1677), a whole *Treatise on Cider and Orchards*, and another on *Bee-Keeping* (1676). Many further editions of these works appeared, followed by compendia that incorporated all these separate publications in one volume, supplemented by a dictionary of agricultural terms.[53]

Worlidge's books were so comprehensive that they displaced earlier works, particularly Walter Blith's. Blith's republican sympathies did not ingratiate him with the ruling gentry of post-Restoration England, and his books were not reprinted after his death. But Worlidge was in many respects the direct heir of the men who had argued so strongly for agricultural improvements in the 1650s, echoing some of their very words, or developing their ideas one stage further. Like Blith, he relied on his readers and friends to improve each new edition of his books. He too favoured enclosure by legislation, that would compel the will of the majority to prevail.[54] Like Blith he urged men to labour diligently, praised

---

53 *Seventeenth-Century Economic Documents*, ed. Thirsk and Cooper, pp. 68–78. For examples of Welshmen's use of Worlidge's textbooks, see Frank Emery on Wales, ch. 12 of *The Agrarian History of England and Wales*, v: the steward of the Gwydir estate wrote his notes on the cultivation of rye grass and clover as addenda to his copy of Worlidge's *Systema agriculturae*; and Watkin Owen had forty blank pages for his own notes bound into his copy of the reissue of the fourth edition (1698).

54 John Worlidge, *Systema agriculturae*, 4th edn (London, 1687), Dedication, pp. 10–12; *ibid.* (1681 edn), p. 13.

adventurous experiments, and condemned the slothful husband-man. But he saw more clearly than Blith perhaps the economic and social advantages of labour-intensive vegetable gardening and horticulture, the benefits of the spade above the plough, in increasing the yield of land and employing more people.[55] And he was obviously deeply interested and personally experienced in hop-growing, bee-keeping, and the watering of meadows.

Worlidge moved beyond Blith to accommodate the idea of more formal societies for spreading information on agricultural im-provements; he applauded the work of the Royal Society, and even envisaged the idea of provincial societies that would collect information on experiments and communicate them to the grander society.[56] The phraseology which he used to declare his goal was slightly different from Blith, but perhaps in a subtle way it reflected changing social relations after the Restoration. Blith had aspired 'to make the poor rich and the rich richer'. Worlidge aspired 'to make the poor rich and the rich honourable'.[57]

Worlidge's writing conveys the impression of a modest, rather than a flamboyant, personality. He did not readily disclose details of his personal life. He allowed only one prejudice to slip from his pen: dried cured tobacco was very good as manure, he remarked, 'which use is better than that to which it is now usually put unto'.[58] But generally he preferred personal privacy. Yet he plainly meditated upon the difficulties of those who tried to handle the plough and spade, and yet write judiciously and well. One of his manuscripts he described as an undigested piece, that had failed to reach the height of perfection he aspired to. He was more than ready to commit it to the flames, to give way to a better book written by someone else.[59] Worlidge was moving with his contem-poraries into a world that favoured greater specialization, that would separate the writer from the gentleman farmer.

The three writers on husbandry described here illuminate three different periods and societies in the seventeenth century. Gervase Markham's world was centred on gentry who were also courtiers,

[55] John Worlidge, *Systema horti-culturae* (London, 1677), pp. 173–7; John Wor-lidge, *Vinetum Britannicum; or, A Treatise of Cider* (London, 1676), Preface.

[56] Worlidge, *Systema agriculturae* (1687 edn), pp. 6, 16–17.

[57] Blith, *English Improver Improved* (1652 edn), Epistle to the Industrious Reader, p. C3; Worlidge, *Systema agriculturae* (1687 edn), p. 17.

[58] Worlidge, *Systema horti-culturae*, p. 252.

[59] Worlidge, *Systema agriculturae* (1687 edn), p. 18.

horsemen and gentlemen farmers. He traversed the highly cultivated countryside of south-eastern England, where most agricultural improvements started in the sixteenth century, and the east
midlands, where enclosure was so forceful a movement and so
controversial. Walter Blith leads us into the west midlands, where
remarkable progress was made in his lifetime to turn woodland
into dairy pastures and ploughland, in order to support a growing
industrial population around Birmingham. He was a Parliamenta-
rian, imbued with the ideals of the Commonwealth. Agricultural
improvers of his generation were so successful in producing an
abundance of foodstuffs that the government was forced into
adopting a new policy after 1656 of encouraging food exports, in
order to maintain prices that would adequately reward the farmer.[60] Worlidge after 1660 reflected the compelling interest of all
classes in producing special crops and less common kinds of meat
and drink that yielded much more profit. These included vegetables, fruits, flowers, shrubs and trees, honey, cider and other fruit
drinks. Worlidge wrote about them all. Appropriately he lived in a
busy expanding market town where professional and other mid-
dle-class purchasers were developing a taste for more varied food
in their diet, and sought to beautify their houses and gardens with
flowers, shrubs and trees. These same interests also gave new
opportunities to husbandmen and labourers to make a living by
meeting this demand with the help of the spade, growing as much
food on one acre as formerly grew on four.

Like Markham and Blith, Worlidge hoped his books of advice
would reach humbler men. He too produced works that were
small in bulk and price, and were written, so he hoped, in plain
style, suited to the vulgar.[61] They were, certainly, clear and
straightforward, though they did contain rather a lot of flowery,
classical quotations as well, and the Latin titles of the books did
not suggest popular literature for the common man. In the event,
peasants were more impressed by practical examples than by
books, and in the later eighteenth century Arthur Young still
placed his highest hopes of innovation on gentry, through whom
the peasantry might be persuaded.[62]

---

[60] Thirsk, 'Agricultural Policy'.   [61] Worlidge, *Systema horti-culturae*, p. A4.

[62] Arthur Young, *A Six Weeks' Tour through the Southern Counties of England and Wales*, 3rd edn (London, 1772), p. viii, I wish to thank Dr Roger Richardson for this reference.

Seventeenth-century circumstances encouraged gentlemen farmers to be writers to good effect. But the eighteenth century
parted them again when the division of labour was again exalted as
the path to progress. One of the earliest dissertations in favour of
the division of labour was written in 1723, some decades before
Adam Smith's famous eulogy appeared in *The Wealth of Nations*.
Its author was anonymous, but significantly he was much
concerned with promoting employment both on the land and in
industry by fostering labour-intensive occupations. In both fields
of endeavour he recommended labour specialization, both to
produce more and better foodstuffs and goods as well as to employ
more people.[63] In 1731, when Jethro Tull published his work on
horse-hoeing husbandry, he too firmly distinguished between
those who wielded the plough, and those who wielded a pen.
'Writing and ploughing are two different talents', he wrote, 'and
he that writes well must have spent in his study that time which is
necessary to be spent in the fields by him who would be master of
the art of cultivating them'. In other words, no man could master
the two skills. Tull evidently regarded himself as an exception, for
he was a master of husbandry, and yet he was now intending to
embark on a work of authorship. Yet he could not refrain from
voicing deep prejudices against other authors. He knew 'a late
great man', who read all the learned works on husbandry, but,
'notwithstanding their eloquence', he ordered them 'to be carried
upon a hand-barrow out of his study, and thrown into the fire, lest
others should lose their time in reading them, as he had done'.[64]
Something of that same attitude to writers of farming books has
long prevailed among historians. But in the late twentieth century,
when we are forced to see some of the drawbacks in an excessive
specialization of labour, we are put in a better frame of mind to
appreciate farmers who were writers and many other things as
well. We occupy a better vantage point now than for a long time
past – to understand the economic and social circumstances that
shaped the agricultural literature, and to concede its substantial
practical achievements.

[63] Anon., *To Pay Old Debts without New Taxes*, *passim*, but esp. pp. 101–5,
115–18.
[64] Jethro Tull, *A Supplement to the Essay on Horsehoing Husbandry* (London,
1736), p. 253.

Bibliography of R. H. Hilton's works to January 1982*

Compiled by JEAN BIRRELL

BOOKS

The Economic Development of Some Leicestershire Estates in the Four-teenth and Fifteenth Centuries (Oxford, 1947).
With H. Fagan. *The English Rising of 1381* (London, 1950).
  Translated into Japanese as *Igirisu Nōmin Sensō – 1381 nen no Nōmin Ikki* (Tokyo, 1961).
A Medieval Society: The West Midlands at the End of the Thirteenth Century (London, 1966; New York, 1967).
The Decline of Serfdom in Medieval England (Studies in Economic History series, London, 1969).
Bond Men Made Free: Medieval Peasant Movements and the English Rising of 1381 (London, 1973; New York, 1973).
  Ch. 1 reprinted in L. Kuchenbuch and B. Michael (eds.), *Feudalis-mus – Materialen zur Theorie und Geschichte* (Frankfurt, Berlin and Vienna, 1977), pp. 481–522.
  Translated into French as *Les mouvements paysans au moyen âge* (Paris, 1979).
  Translated into Spanish as *Siervos liberados* (Madrid, 1978).
The English Peasantry in the Later Middle Ages: The Ford Lectures for 1973 and Related Studies (Oxford, 1975).
  Ch. 1 translated into Spanish as 'El campesindo como clase'.

EDITIONS

a)
Ministers' Accounts of the Warwickshire Estates of the Duke of Clarence, 1479–80 (Dugdale Society, xxi, Warwick, 1952).
The Stoneleigh Leger Book (Dugdale Society, xxiv, Warwick, 1962).
'Swanimote Rolls of Feckenham Forest', in *Miscellany I* (Worcestershire Historical Society, Worcester, 1960).

---

* This Bibliography omits reviews, short notices and the like. While every effort has been made to include all foreign translations, some may inevitably have escaped notice.

b)

E. A. Kosminsky, *Studies in the Agrarian History of England in the Thirteenth Century*, trans. Ruth Kisch (Oxford, 1956).
Peasants, Knights and Heretics: Studies in Medieval English Social History (Past and Present Publications, Cambridge, 1976).

ARTICLES

'A Thirteenth-Century Poem on Disputed Villein Services', *English Historical Review*, lvi (1941), pp. 90–7.

Winchcombe Abbey and the Manor of Sherbourne', *University of Birmingham Historical Journal*, ii (1949), pp. 31–52. Reprinted in H. P. R. Finberg (ed.), *Gloucestershire Studies* (Leicester, 1957), pp. 89–113.

'Kibworth Harcourt: A Merton College Manor in the Thirteenth and Fourteenth Centuries', in W. G. Hoskins (ed.), *Studies in Leicestershire Agrarian History* (Leicester, 1949), pp. 17–40.

'Peasant Movements in England before 1381', *Economic History Review*, 2nd ser., ii (1949), pp. 117–36. Reprinted in *The Middle Ages* (Institute of History of the Academy of Sciences of the U.S.S.R., Moscow, 1956–7) and in E. M. Carus-Wilson (ed.), *Essays in Economic History*, 3 vols. (London, 1954–62), ii, pp. 73–90. Translated into Japanese in *Hōkensei no Kiki* [*The Crisis of Feudalism*] (Seminar Series of Social Sciences, no. 8, Tokyo, 1956).

Social Structure of Rural Warwickshire in the Middle Ages (Dugdale Society, Occasional Paper, no. 9, Warwick, 1950). Reprinted in *The English Peasantry in the Later Middle Ages*.

With H. A. Cronne. 'The Beauchamp Household Book: A Journey from London to Warwick in 1431', *University of Birmingham Historical Journal*, ii (1950), pp. 208–18.

'Y eut-il une crise générale de la féodalité?', *Annales. E.S.C.*, vi (1951), pp. 23–30. Translated into Japanese in *Hōkensei no Kiki* (Seminar Series of Social Sciences, no. 8, Tokyo, 1956).

'Capitalism – What's in a Name?', *Past and Present*, no. 1 (1952), pp. 32–43. Reprinted in *The Transition from Feudalism to Capitalism* (London, 1976), pp. 145–58. Translated into Japanese in *Hōkensei no Kiki* (Seminar Series of Social Sciences, no. 8, Tokyo, 1956).

'Life in the Medieval Manor (With a Short Glossary of Manorial Terms)', *Amateur Historian*, i (1953), pp. 82–9.

'A Comment', *Science and Society* (Fall 1953). Reprinted in *The Transition from Feudalism to Capitalism: A Symposium* (London, 1954), pp. 65–72, and in *The Transition from Feudalism to Capitalism* (London, 1976), pp. 109–17, and in L. Kuchenbuch and B. Michael (eds.), *Feudalismus – Materialen zur Theorie und Geschichte* (Frankfurt, Berlin and Vienna, 1977), and translated into Spanish in *La transición del feudalismo al capitalismo* (Barcelona, 1977).

'Gloucester Abbey Leases of the Late Thirteenth Century', *University of Birmingham Historical Journal*, iv (1953), pp. 1–17. Reprinted in *The English Peasantry in the Later Middle Ages*.

'Medieval Agrarian History', in *Victoria County History of Leicestershire*, ii (London, 1954), pp. 145–98.

'The Content and Sources of English Agrarian History before 1500', *Agricultural History Review*, iii (1955), pp. 3–19. Also in *Journal of Czechoslovak Academy of Agricultural Sciences*, ii (1956).

'A Study in the Pre-history of English Enclosure in the Fifteenth Century', in *Studi in onore di Armando Sapori*, 2 vols (Milan, 1957), i, pp. 674–85. Reprinted in *The English Peasantry in the Later Middle Ages*.

'Dzieje spoteczno-gospodarcze Anglii w XIV : XVw', *Przeglad History-czny*, xlviii (Warsaw, 1957).

'L'Angleterre économique et sociale des XIVᵉ et XVᵉ siècles', *Annales. E.S.C.*, iii (1958), pp. 541–63.

'The Origins of Robin Hood', *Past and Present*, no. 14 (1958), pp. 30–44. Reprinted in *Peasants, Knights and Heretics*.

'Old Enclosures in the West Midlands: A Hypothesis about their Late Medieval Development', *Annales de l'Est*, mémoire no. xxi (Nancy, 1959), pp. 272–83.

With P. H. Sawyer. 'Technical Determinism: The Stirrup and the Plough', *Past and Present*, no. 24 (1963), pp. 90–100.

'Medieval London', *Past and Present*, no. 26 (1963), pp. 98–101.

'Freedom and Villeinage in England', *Past and Present*, no. 31 (1965), pp. 3–19. Reprinted in *Peasants, Knights and Heretics*.

'Rent and Capital Formation in Feudal Society', in *Second International Conference of Economic History: Aix-en-Provence, 1962*, 2 vols. (Paris, 1965), ii, pp. 33–68. Reprinted in *The English Peasantry in the Later Middle Ages*.

'Building Accounts of Elmley Castle, Worcestershire, 1345–6', *University of Birmingham Historical Journal*, x (1965), pp. 78–87.

'The Manor', 'Serfdom & Villeinage', 'Robin Hood' and 'Yeoman', in *Encyclopaedia Britannica* (1965).

With P. A. Rahtz. 'Upton, Gloucestershire, 1959–64', *Transactions of the Bristol and Gloucestershire Archaeological Society*, lxxxv (1966), pp. 70–146.

'Some Problems of Urban Real Property in the Middle Ages', in C. H. Feinstein (ed.), *Socialism, Capitalism and Economic Growth: Essays Presented to Maurice Dobb* (Cambridge, 1967), pp. 326–37.

'Villages désertés et histoire économique: recherches françaises et anglaises', *Études rurales*, xxxii (1968), pp. 104–9.

'A Rare Evesham Abbey Estate Document', *Vale of Evesham Research Papers*, ii (1969), pp. 5–10.

'Lord and Peasant in Staffordshire in the Middle Ages', *North Stafford-shire Journal of Field Studies*, x (1970), pp. 1–20. Reprinted in *The English Peasantry in the Later Middle Ages*.

'A Crisis in England, 1376–1399'. *Mediaevalia Bohemica*, iii (1972), pp. 149–61.

'Further Dimensions for Local Historians?', *Local Historian*, x (1973), pp. 390–4.

'Some Social and Economic Evidence in Late Medieval English Tax Returns', in S. Herost (ed.), *Spoleczenstwo gospodarka kultura: Essays Presented to Marion Malowist* (Warsaw, 1974), pp. 111–28.

'Medieval Peasants: Any Lessons?', *Journal of Peasant Studies*, i (1974), pp. 207–19.

'Peasant Society, Peasant Movements and Feudalism in Medieval Europe', in H. A. Landsberger (ed.), *Rural Protest: Peasant Movements and Social Change* (London, 1974), pp. 67–94.

'Warriors and Peasants', *New Left Review*, lxxxiii (1974), pp. 83–94.

'Soziale Programme im englischen Aufstand von 1381', in P. Blickle (ed.), *Revolte und Revolution in Europa* (*Historische Zeitschrift*, Beiheft iv, Munich, 1975), pp. 31–46.

'Feudalism and the Origins of Capitalism', *History Workshop*, i (1976), pp. 9–25. Also appears as *Introduction to The Transition from Feudalism to Capitalism* (London, 1976), translated into Spanish as *La transición del feudalismo al capitalismo* (Barcelona, 1977). The German edition of *Transition* contains a *Postscript* (1978).

'Reasons for Inequality among Medieval Peasants', *Journal of Peasant Studies*, v (1978), pp. 271–84.

'Idéologie et ordre social', *L'Arc*, lxxii (1978), pp. 32–7.

'A Crisis of Feudalism', *Past and Present*, no. 80 (1978), pp. 3–19.

'Féodalité et seigneurie', in D. Johnson, F. Bederida and F. Crouzet (eds.), *De Guillaume le Conquérant au Marché Commun: dix siècles d'histoire franco-brittanique* (Paris, 1979), pp. 43–56; published in Britain as *Britain and France: Ten Centuries* (Folkestone, 1980), pp. 39–50.

'Siervos liberados', in *Siglo veintiunt de espana* (Madrid, 1979).

'Towns in English Feudal Society', *Review* (*Journal of the Fernand Braudel Centre for the Study of Economies, Historical Systems, and Civilizations*), iii (1979), pp. 3–20.

'Individualism and the English Peasantry', *New Left Review*, cxx (1980), pp. 109–11.

'Robin des Bois', *L'histoire*, xxi (1980), pp. 39–47.

'Popular Movements in England at the End of the Fourteenth Century', in *Il tumulto dei ciompi: un momento di storia fiorentina ed europea* (Florence, 1981), pp. 223–40.

Index

323